THE JOURNAL OF SŌCHŌ

The
Journal of Sōchō

Translated and Annotated by

H. MACK HORTON

Stanford
University
Press
Stanford,
California

Stanford University Press
Stanford, California
© 2002 by the Board of Trustees of the
Leland Stanford Junior University

The Journal of Sōchō was published with the
assistance of the Center for Japanese Studies,
University of California, Berkeley.

Printed in the United States of America on acid-free,
archival-quality paper.

Cover: Portrait of Sōchō
Collection of Saiokuji temple, site of Sōchō's Brushwood
Cottage. The work is signed Kanō Ryūsetsu, a name used
by several different members of the Kanō School, the
earliest of whom was Kanō Hidenobu 狩野秀信
(c. 1647–1712) (*Dai Nihon shoga meika taikan*).

Library of Congress Cataloging-in-Publication Data
Sōchō, 1448–1532.
  [Socho shuki. English]
  The journal of Sōchō / translated and annotated by
H. Mack Horton.
    p. cm.
  ISBN 0-8047-3283-8 (cloth : alk. paper)
  ISBN 0-8047-3506-9 (paper : alk. paper)
    1. Sōchō, 1448–1532—Diaries. 2. Poets, Japanese—
1185–1600—Diaries. I. Horton, H. Mack. II. Title.
PL792.S58 Z47813 2000
895.6'82403—dc21
[B]   99-086374

Original printing 2002

Last figure below indicates year of this printing:
11 10 09 08 07 06 05 04 03 02

Designed by Eleanor Mennick
Typeset by Tseng Information Systems, Inc. in
Bembo type

To Professors
William H. McCullough
Helen Craig McCullough
and Kaneko Kinjirō
in affectionate memory

migaku to mo
hitori wa kokoro
nani naramu

Contents

List of Abbreviations	ix
Eras and Reigns During Sōchō's Lifetime (1448–1532)	xi
A Note to the Translation	xiii

Book One

Second Year of Daiei (1522)	7
Third Year of Daiei (1523)	25
Fourth Year of Daiei (1524)	41
Fifth Year of Daiei (1525)	61
Sixth Year of Daiei (1526)	89

Book Two

Sixth Year of Daiei (1526)	95
Seventh Year of Daiei (1527)	135

Appendixes

A: The Imagawa House	173
B: The Historical Context of the "Asahina Battle Chronicle"	177
C: Chronology of *The Journal of Sōchō*	181
Notes	191
Bibliography	317
Index of First Lines	335
General Index	343

Abbreviations

The following abbreviations have been used in the text and footnotes of the text. Full publication information is given in the Bibliography, under author or editor where indicated.

GSRJ	*Gunsho ruijū*
JS	*Journal of Sōchō* (English translation)
KB	*Koten bunko*
KNS	*Katsuranomiyabon sōsho*
KSSMR	*Kokusho sōmokuroku*
KT	*Kokka taikan*
NKBT	*Nihon koten bungaku taikei*
NKBZ	*Nihon koten bungaku zenshū*
NKT	*Nihon kagaku taikei*
NKZ	*Nihon koten zensho*
RJGPS	*Renju gappekishū* (under Ichijō Kaneyoshi)
RSR	*Rengashi ronkō* (under Kidō Saizō)
SI	*Suruga no Imagawashi*
SKGSRJ	*Shinkō gunsho ruijū*
SN	*Sōchō nikki* (under Sōchō)
SNKBT	*Shin Nihon koten bungaku taikei*
SNKS	*Shinchō Nihon koten shūsei*
ST	*Shikashū taisei*
ZGSRJ	*Zoku gunsho ruijū*
ZZGSRJ	*Zoku zoku gunsho ruijū*

Eras and Reigns During Sōchō's Lifetime (1448-1532)

Era	Emperor	Shogun
Bun'an 文安 1444	Gohanazono 後花園 1419–71 (r. 1428–64)	
Hōtoku 宝徳 1449		Ashikaga Yoshimasa 足利義政 1436–90 (r. 1449–74)
Kyōtoku 享徳 1452		
Kōshō 康正 1455		
Chōroku 長録 1457		
Kanshō 寛正 1461	Gotsuchimikado 後土御門 1442–1500 (r. 1464–1500)	
Bunshō 文正 1466		
Ōnin 応仁 1467		
Bunmei 文明 1469		Ashikaga Yoshihisa 足利義尚 1465–89 (r. 1474–89)
Chōkyō 長享 1487		Ashikaga Yoshitane 足利義植 1466–1523 (r. 1490–1501?)
Entoku 延徳 1489		
Meiō 明応 1492		Ashikaga Yoshizumi 足利義澄 1481–1511 (r. 1494–1511)
Bunki 文亀 1501	Gokashiwabara 後柏原 1464–1526 (r. 1500–26)	
Eishō 永正 1504		Ashikaga Yoshitane 義植 (r. 1508–21)
Daiei 大永 1521		Ashikaga Yoshiharu 足利義晴 1511–50 (r. 1522–1547)
Kyōroku 享録 1528	Gonara 後奈良 1497–1557 (r. 1526–57)	
Tenbun 天文 1532		

Sources: *Dokushi biyō*, Kuwata 1980, Inagaki 1985

A Note to the Translation

  The Journal of Sōchō (*Sōchō shuki*) was compiled from 1522 to 1527 by Saioku-ken Sōchō (1448–1532), the preeminent linked-verse (*renga*) poet in Japan at the time. It depicts four major journeys between the Kyoto area and Suruga, where Sōchō served as the poet laureate of the Imagawa daimyo house, as well as several shorter excursions and long periods of stasis at various hermitages. Much of Sōchō's time in and around the capital was spent at Daitokuji or other temples related to his spiritual master, the Zen prelate Ikkyū; in the east, he generally divided his time between lodgings in the Suruga capital and in his Brushwood Cottage (Saioku), in Mariko not far away.

  The historical and literary context of the work is introduced in the companion volume to the translation, entitled *Song in an Age of Discord*: The Journal of Sōchō *and Poetic Life in Late Medieval Japan*. As described in that study, Sōchō's journal was written during the Age of the Country at War (Sengoku jidai), a century of unprecedented collision between social groups and artistic genres. It was perhaps for that reason that linked verse was the most popular and widely practiced literary form during that era, for its practitioners linked not only verses but cultures as well. Renga masters traveled between the capital, still Japan's cultural center, and the periphery, facilitating interaction and cultural borrowing as they linked verses into long renga sequences.

  Sōchō's journal reflects the interaction of the period and the diverse upbringing of its author, a companion of daimyo and warlords, a disciple of Sōgi, the renga master who sought to preserve orthodox poetic neoclassicism, and a devotee of Ikkyū, the iconoclastic Zen priest. It provides one of the most personal literary self-portraits in the medieval literary corpus. The work is notable for its breadth and freshness of observation, not only of the activities of linked-verse poets and the affairs of great courtiers and daimyo, but also of the lives of local warriors and commoners. This richness of cultural detail is matched by the variety of genres included in the journal; the diarist was a master not only of formal "high" (*ushin*) renga but also of the unorthodox or comic (*haikai*) verse that was becoming increasingly important at the time. Sōchō was rare among diarists of the period in the degree of attention he paid to both strains of contemporary poetry. His journal is an introduction in microcosm to many of the important types of contemporary literary composition; while it begins as travel diary, it also includes eremitic passages, historical chronicles, conversations, letters, and more than six hundred poems of nearly every type: renga, waka, haikai, chōka, and linked poetry in Japanese and Chinese. Such variety makes *The Journal of Sōchō* particularly evocative of the literary and cultural character of Japan during the century of transition from the medieval to the early modern era. But it also results in a work that is at times ill-organized and unbalanced. Modern readers may be inclined to skip, for example, the "Asahina Battle Chronicle," a lengthy account of now-forgotten provincial warfare that Sōchō inserts immediately after he begins his narrative. The author's warrior patrons, however, were doubtless particularly engaged by such passages. (For the background to the "Asahina Battle Chronicle," see Appendixes A and B, and for a summary of the contents of the journal, see Appendix C.)

The translation of *The Journal of Sōchō* is based on the Shōkōkan manuscript, reproduced in Shimazu Tadao, ed., *Sōchō nikki* (Iwanami Shoten, 1975), 7–143. In preparing the translation and annotation, I collated Shimazu's recension with the Saiokuji manuscript, which I photographed at Saiokuji temple (site of Sōchō's Brushwood Cottage), and four alternative texts:

Sōchō michi no ki (an abridged version of *Sōchō shuki*). Yūtoku Inari Jinja ms. In Shigematsu 1983: 201–73.

Sōchō shuki. In *GSRJ* 18: 256–327.

Sōchō shuki. In *SKGSRJ* 14: 645–701 (the *GSRJ* ms. collated with the Naikaku Bunko ms.).

Sōchō Suruga nikki (Naikaku Bunko ms.). Ed. Uzawa Satoru. Vol. 344 of *KB*.

Page numbers in the translation are referred to as "*JS*"; poems are referred to as "*JS* no." The numbers of those poems not by Sōchō have been italicized for the sake of clarity. Poems in the original manuscripts are not numbered or indented, and subtitles do not subsect those manuscripts as they do here (those subtitles are taken by and large from the Shimazu edition).

The two maps were prepared with the assistance of cartographer Jennifer

A Note to the Translation

Freeman on the basis of Shimazu 1975: 168–71, Takahashi 1983: between 372 and 373, and Sawa et al. 1984: 142. In the translation, toponyms are occasionally abbreviated for euphony in poetic contexts.

This translation is indebted to the generous help of the many individuals and organizations named in the preface to the companion volume. But responsibility for the errors that remain is my own.

THE JOURNAL OF SŌCHŌ

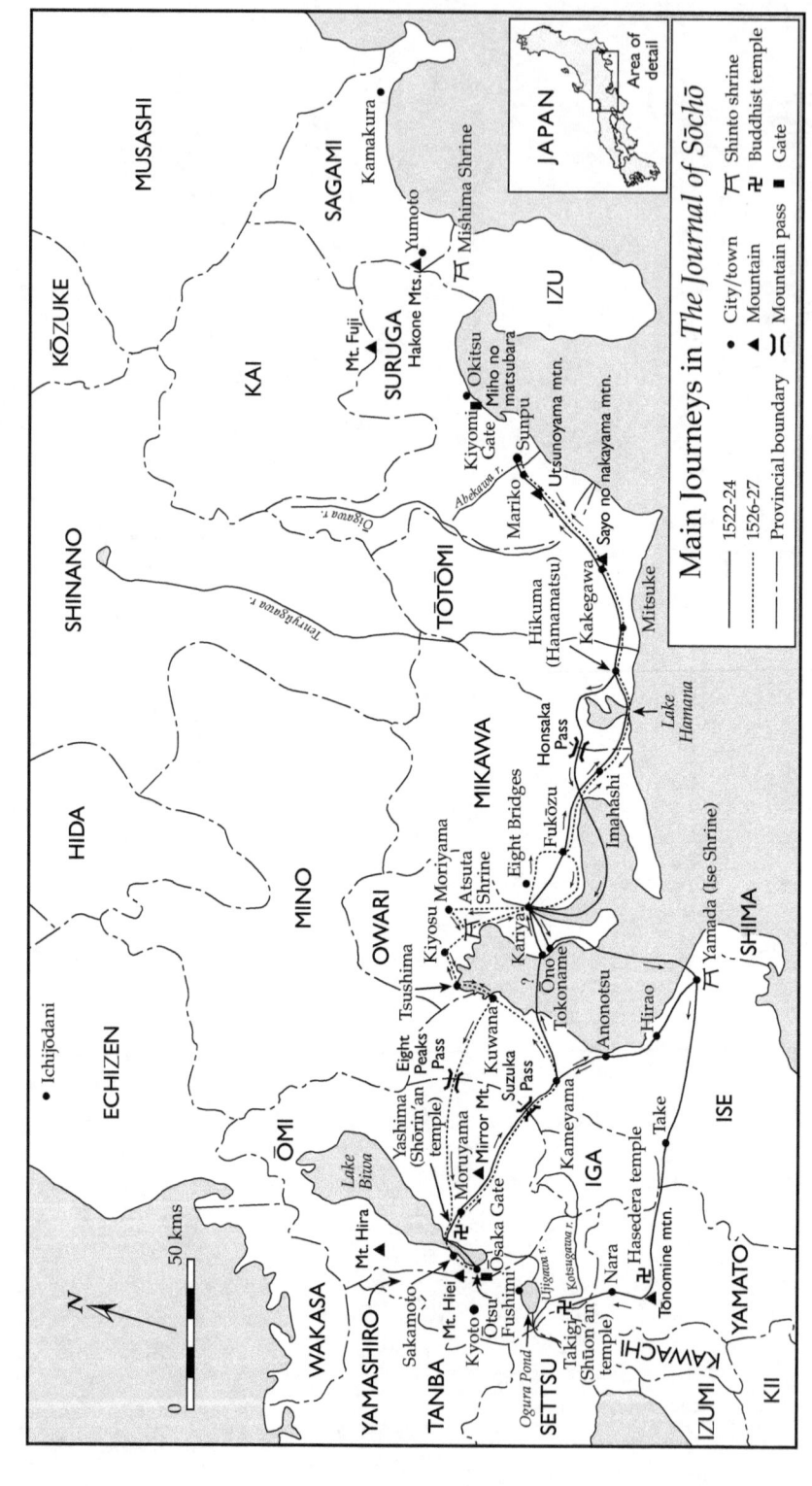

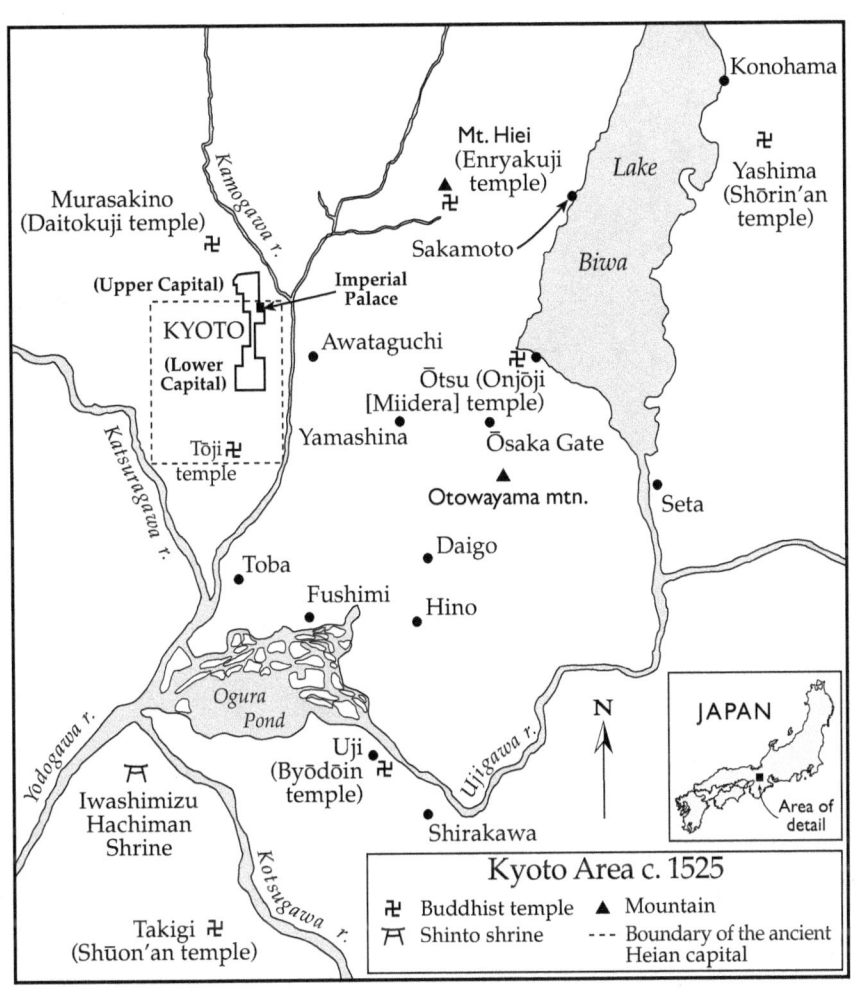

Book One

Second Year of Daiei

1522

Departure

In the fifth month of the second year of Daiei, I set out on a journey to the northland with an acquaintance from Echizen.[1] Though Kaeruyama, the Mountain of Returning, reminded me I could not expect to return home again, I pressed onward past Utsunoyama mountain, and when I reached Sayo no nakayama, I composed this:

1	kono tabi wa mata koyubeshi to omou to mo oi no saka nari sayo no nakayama	Even though I hope I will pass this way again on my journey home, this is the hill of old age. Sayo no nakayama.[2]

Kakegawa

Kakegawa.[3] Stayed at the residence of Yasuyoshi. A construction project is currently under way. The outer castle is about thirteen or fourteen hundred yards in circumference.[4] Around it they have dug a moat and built earthworks, after the manner of the main compound.[5] The ground here is hard as rock; they might as well have built of iron. There is also a moat between the main and outer compounds. The ramparts are so steep it is frightening to look over.

I composed this hokku at the castle:

2	samidare wa	Summer rain—
	kumoi no kishi no	on cloud-covered cliffs,
	yanagi kana	willow trees![6]

There is a lake to the south. With its tall cliffs and expanse of water, it is like the sea itself. One might call it "Dragon Pond."[7] Another hokku here:

3	ike no omo ya	The surface of the pond—
	kishi wa suminoe	clear cliffs like Suminoe
	haru no umi	by the springtime sea.[8]

The History of Kakegawa Castle

The following occurred four or five years ago.[9] There is a well in the main castle's compound. When the late Asahina Yasuhiro had just received his commission in this province, Tōtōmi, he chose this mountain on which to build his castle, but he could not locate a water source.[10] His men dug with picks, pikes, spades, hoes, and many other implements of every description for two or three hundred days, but still did not strike water. Just when they were about to abandon the effort, they discovered a small black frog and a small snake in a basket used to draw up excavated earth. All took heart, thinking water could not be far off, and in the end they reached it. They had dug down to the river at the foot of the mountain. The draw rope was more than one thousand feet long![11] What can the Undiggable Well of Musashi have been like?[12] They probably named the castle Kakegawa because of the river that flows below it.[13] The fortress is on the highroad running east and west between the capital and the provinces.[14]

The 'Asahina Battle Chronicle' 1

The following is a chronicle of Asahina Bitchūnokami Yasuhiro's loyal service in battle in this province.[15] Lord Saemonnosuke had been headquartered in a castle on Yashiroyama mountain.[16] When he was exiled, he withdrew to Futamata Castle, where freebooters from this province and Owari flew to his cause, bringing the uprising into the open. All the lands to the borders of Shinano and

Mikawa fell to him, including the castle held for years by Horie Shimotsukenokami west of Tenryūgawa river at Murakushi.[17] Called Kuroyama, it has a main fortress and an outer fortress and is bounded by Lake Hamana to the north and south. Sōun and Yasuhiro laid their plans then assaulted it with forces raised in this province.[18] In two or three days the castle fell.[19]

Then Ōkōchi Bitchūnokami, commissioner of the Hamamatsu Estate (fief of Lord Kira), joined with Horie Shimotsukenokami and absconded.[20] Iio Zenshiro Katatsura was accordingly ordered down from Kira to serve as temporary commissioner in Ōkōchi's stead.[21] The appointment was in recognition of the extraordinary military service of his father Zenzaemonnojō Nagatsura, who had been commissioner of that estate when Yoshitada entered the province years earlier.[22] When Yoshitada met with calamity while returning to his home province, Nagatsura too was struck down and killed, after loosing all his arrows at the enemy in the glorious defense of his lord.[23] His son Zenzaemon Katatsura, Katatsura's son Zenshirō Noritsura, and Noritsura's uncle Zenrokurō Tamekiyo ever honor his exploits.[24]

The 'Asahina Battle Chronicle' 2

At the beginning of the ninth month of the first year of Eishō [1504], war broke out between the Yamanouchi and the Ōgigayatsu houses (known together as the "Two Uesugi," the Yamanouchi being the deputies in Kamakura).[25] The Ōgigayatsu were allied with Sōun and held Kawagoe and Edo.[26] The Yamanouchi held Uwado and Hachigata. The conflict became general and overran the borders of Musashi Plain. For three Kantō leagues the foe would not fall back, nor could our allies advance.[27] When the deadlock had continued more than ten days, the Ōgigayatsu requested support from Imagawa Ujichika, who immediately set out at the head of an army.[28] On the thirteenth, Asahina Yasuhiro and Fukushima Saemonnojō followed with their forces from Tōtōmi and Suruga.[29] On the twentieth, twenty-first, and twenty-second of the same month, Sōun made camp at Masukata.[30] The enemy appeared to have pulled back. Our allies pursued them, making camp one night in the open. The next day, at about nine o'clock in the morning, our allies and the foe caught sight of one another through the mist of Musashi Plain, both armies thick as a mountain forest. They met with a crash like thunder.[31] At about noon the cavalry charged and the battle raged for several hours thereafter. The foe was defeated and their main force retreated to their stronghold at Tachikawa.³² Contact was lost with them in the night. Two thousand and more were missing, killed, cut down and left for dead, or made prisoner, and horses and armor were taken in abundance.

After a day and a night, Imagawa Ujichika withdrew, making camp in Kamakura on the fourth of the tenth month. He stayed two days, then took the waters in Atami for seven. He then rested from the rigors of battle for two or three days at Nirayama, after which he returned to Suruga.³³ It was at that time that he petitioned the god of Mishima Shrine.³⁴ I thereupon spent three days composing a thousand-verse sequence at that shrine, beginning on the tenth.³⁵ The ten hokku followed the order of the four seasons.³⁶ The first and second were as follows:

4	tanabiku ya chisato mo koko no harugasumi	It trails afar— over a thousand leagues, this springtime haze.³⁷
		Ujichika
5	aoyagi ya kakesou mishima yūkazura	The light-green willows— a divine addition to Mishima's garlands.³⁸

The 'Asahina Battle Chronicle' 3

Eight or nine more years passed, and Ōkōchi Bitchūnokami staged another audacious uprising.³⁹ He invaded the Hamamatsu Estate and secured himself in Hikuma Castle with freebooters and farmers of the province. Thereupon Yasuhiro set out and burned every temple and house. Ōkōchi was about to be killed, but Lord Kira pleaded on his behalf, and he was pardoned. All returned to their camps.

That winter Yasuhiro unexpectedly died of illness. As his son Yasuyoshi was not yet old enough to rule, Yasuyoshi's uncle Yasumochi was made temporary regent.⁴⁰

The 'Asahina Battle Chronicle' 4

Then Ōkōchi Bitchūnokami raised troops in Shinano, Mikawa, and Owari and fomented a great uprising.⁴¹ Ujichika now set out in person to quell it. He drew up his horse at Ryōgonji temple in the Kasai Estate, and his forces made

Second Year of Daiei (1522)

camp at Daibosatsu Mountain across Tenryūgawa river.[42] At Mitake Mountain to the north, Ii Jirō staunchly served the Martial Defender and also gathered freebooters and others of lower station.[43] Their watchfires at night were many as the stars in the sky before dawn. Yasumochi easily defeated them, and the Martial Defender flew to Okunoyama and thence to Owari.[44] This was the castle that several thousand troops under Kai Minonokami had earlier assailed for three years without success.[45] Because of Yasumochi's military prowess, the province remained secure.

The 'Asahina Battle Chronicle' 5

Thereafter Ujichika dispatched troops in support of a campaign launched by Takeda Jirō in Kai.[46] Seeing their opportunity, Ōkōchi and freebooters in this province of Tōtōmi summoned local warriors from Shinano and requested aid from the Martial Defender.[47] They then began seizing lands here and there on both sides of Tenryūgawa river.

That winter, the Asahina built the Hachiman Shrine at Kakegawa Castle.[48] My celebratory hokku:

6   kore ya yo ni   It flows in all seasons
    kōranu nagare   without freezing,
    iwashimizu   this rock-pent spring.[49]

Yasuyoshi's uncle Tokishige steadfastly defended Hachiman Shrine and both Tōtōmi and Suruga in Ujichika's absence.[50]

The next summer, in the latter part of the fifth month, Ujichika set out for that castle.[51] There was a flood at the time and Tenryūgawa river was like a great sea. Ujichika built a pontoon bridge with three hundred and more boats lashed together with ten or twenty huge bamboo ropes. It was solid as the ground itself. I made a thousand verses in prayer for a safe crossing. The hokku:

7   minazuki wa   The Waterless Month—
    kachibito naranu   no victor who does not cross on foot,
    seze mo nashi   as there are no waves.[52]

It now occurs to me I ought to have said, "a crossing made by victors, / all of them on foot."[53]

The enemy came out on the far side of the river, and their arrows fell like rain. Tens of thousands of Imagawa troops crossed easily, and the foe pulled back. Ujichika encircled their castle six or seven fold, covering an area about fifty chō around.[54] There, from the sixth through the eighth month, he harassed them.[55] The soldiers inside the stronghold resisted for several days, then capitulated on the nineteenth of the eighth month. Ujichika used men from the Abeyama gold mines to undermine the well in the castle, and there was not a drop of water to be had inside.[56] The Ōkōchi—brothers, fathers, and sons—the Ōmi, the Takahashi, and the others in the castle with them, were either killed, cut down and left for dead, or taken prisoner.[57] The fleeing men and women were a pitiful sight.[58] Because of certain circumstances the Martial Defender was allowed to leave the castle, and he took holy orders at a nearby Zen temple called Fusaiji.[59] All those in his service took orders as well and were sent to Owari. The castles at Yashiroyama, Futamata, and Okunoyama of the Ii house rose in this manner three or four times. How is one to account for it? Ōkōchi Bitchūnokami fought the Imagawa in Tōtōmi three or four times as well.

The 'Asahina Battle Chronicle' 6

This province of Tōtōmi and half of Owari are Imagawa lands. Some time ago they were made the domain of the Martial Defender for a time (the reason for that decision is unknown).[60] Norikuni (Lord Jōkōji) was born in the fifth year of Einin (Hinoto tori) [1297], Noriuji was born in the fifth year of Shōwa (Hinoe tatsu) [1316], Yasunori was born in the first year of Kenmu (Kinoe inu) [1334], Norimasa was born in the third year of Jōji (Kinoe tatsu) [1364], Noritada was born in the fifteenth year of Ōei (Tsuchinoe ne) [1408], Yoshitada was born in the eighth year of Eikyō (Hinoe tatsu) [1436].[61] Was it in the time of Yasunori that the Imagawa house lost its rights in the province? The facts of the matter are unclear. Eighty-five years later, Yoshitada entered Tōtōmi and occupied the Fukōin estates of Kawawa and Kakegawa.[62] The estates had been transferred to him, and he possessed documents for both in proof.[63]

At that time, Ōmi Shinzaemonnojō, a vassal of Lord Kira, administered those estates and was residing on them.[64] He built a strong castle and together with Kanō Kunainoshō, then vice constable of Tōtōmi, he opposed Imagawa entry.[65] Thereupon Yoshitada set out in person to deal with them. From the eighth through the eleventh month he kept the Kanō castle in the Tōtōmi provincial capital under attack, and on the twentieth of the eleventh month Kanō took his own life.[66]

Second Year of Daiei (1522)

This Kunainoshō was of the same family as Kanō Suke of Izu.[67] He lent support to Kanō Kaganokami, a district constable in Tōtōmi Province and a subordinate of the Martial Defender, as they bore the same name.[68] But Kunainoshō later caused Kaganokami's son Jirō to be killed, took over the succession, and ran the province according to his whim.[69] His defeat was brought about by the Asahina.

Then Kanō Suke of Abe rose in rebellion against the Imagawa.[70] The mountains in that region run into Kai province, and it was difficult to attack him. Three years passed. Kunainoshō led several thousand Tōtōmi troops into those mountains to aid Kanō Suke. The Asahina, using guides, went in and destroyed all of them. Peace was immediately restored. This was an act of uncommon merit on the part of the Asahina.

The recent Imagawa entry into Tōtōmi began when Shogun Ashikaga Yoshimasa sent an order by Isenokami during the Ōnin era instructing Yoshitada to reinforce allied troops, including those of Hosokawa Sanukinokami, who was then at war with Tōjō Ōminokami Kuniuji, vice constable of Mikawa.[71] In return for that meritorious service, Yoshitada was to be granted rights to the province. That was the reason for the eradication of Kunainoshō and the Ōmi. Then he sent two forces, about one thousand troops, to Hikuma Castle near the border of Mikawa, and returned to his home province in the twelfth month.[72] The next year freebooters rose up, and Horikoshi Mutsunokami was unexpectedly struck down along with some of his men at Sayo no nakayamaguchi.[73] Our allies nevertheless met with good fortune in various other battles. But the remainder of the defeated forces would not desist, and Yoshitada was again forced to mobilize. His generals were not in accord, however, and they rejoiced when an ally met misfortune. In the end they fell to killing one another. And in three years Yabe Saemonnojō, Higonokami Yasumori, and Okabe Saemonnojō all died of illness.[74] There was something unnatural at work. After meeting with setbacks in several battles, Yoshitada returned home.[75]

The 'Asahina Battle Chronicle' 7

It was over twenty years after Yoshitada's untimely death that Ujichika entered Tōtōmi Province.[76] Though it was peaceful there, insurgents in surrounding provinces rose continually. Tahara Danjōnochū and Suwa Shinanonokami incited mercenary bands and captured a castle belonging to forces allied with the Imagawa on Funakata Mountain at the border of Mikawa.[77] The lord of the castle, Tame Matazaburō, was killed, and the enemy took residence.[78] Asahina Yasumochi wasted no time in crossing Lake Hamana.[79] He recovered the castle, killing or capturing many, then dispatched over half his forces to the interior and returned to his castle at Kakegawa.[80] Yasumochi served for ten years as advisor to Yasuyoshi then relinquished his position and asked leave to go down to Suruga, where he lives quietly near the provincial capital. But even so, one hears he cannot avoid the call of duty.[81]

Hamamatsu

Spent two days with the commissioner of the Hamamatsu Estate, now Iio Zenshirō Noritsura.[82] Then went by boat from Yamazaki in that estate past Inasa Inlet to the manor of Hamana Bitchūnokami, where we had a day's renga:[83]

8	mizu harete	Clear now over the water—
	sora ya satsuki no	the sky has dressed
	amatsutsumi	for the fifth-month rain.[84]

Kachiyama

We crossed Honsaka and were guided to lodgings with the Saigō, then spent a day at Kachiyama, castle of Kumagai Echigonokami.[85] We composed renga:

9	ōchi saku	Bead trees blossom
	kumoi o chiri no	in the clouds, though dust
	fumoto kana	covers the slope below![86]

Lodgings with the Makino

Near Yawata, at lodgings at the residence of Makino Shirōzaemonnojō, in a field called Honnogahara, we had a day of renga:[87]

10	yuku sode o	Grasses tall enough
	kusaba no take no	to touch a traveler's sleeve—
	natsuno kana	a summer field![88]

Second Year of Daiei (1522)

Kariya

Fighting has been breaking out from time to time with no warning in this province, so we could not cross Yahagigawa river and the Eight Bridges.[89] We went by boat to the castle of Mizuno Izuminokami in this province and lodged in Kariya one night.[90]

Tokoname

Stayed a day at Mizuno Kisaburō's in Tokoname in Chita District, Owari Province.[91] Yoshitomo's tomb is located at a place called Noma.[92]

Ise Senku at Yamada in Ise Province

We crossed to Ōminato harbor in Ise and proceeded to Yamada, where we visited Ise Shrine.[93] The matter had been raised earlier of a thousand-verse sequence to be presented to the shrine, and I had invited the priest Sōseki down for that purpose.[94] He arrived near the end of the seventh month, and we began composing the sequence soon thereafter, on the fourth of the eighth month. Two hundred verses a day for five days. The work was commissioned as a votive sequence by the present shogunal deputy, Hosokawa Takakuni, when he returned to the capital from Ōmi.[95] Daitokuji temple in Murasakino received his patronage when I was staying there at Shinjuan, and I composed it in gratitude for that as well.[96] His hokku for the first hundred verses was sent from Kyoto:

11	asahikage yomo ni nioeru kasumi kana	Everywhere aglow in the morning sunlight— the haze![97]
		Takakuni
12	ume sakite arashi mo nabiku yanagi kana	Plum trees blossom, willows bend, and even the wind abates![98]
		Sōchō

Such hospitality in Yamada—I could not believe my eyes.[99]

Sōseki then left for Owari. Knowing it was likely to snow before long, I decided to set out for the north on the sixteenth.[100] There has been fighting in this province beyond Kumozugawa river and Anonotsu, making it difficult to get from place to place.[101] Beyond where they are fighting lives Seki Minbuno-taifu, who is now retired and goes by the name Kajisai.[102] It was arranged that Miyahara Shichirōbyōenojō Moritaka from Take would provide us with escorts as far as Yawata in Anonotsu, and he personally accompanied us from Yamada to Hirao, where we spent the night.[103]

We left Hirao when it was still dark. It began to rain in earnest about nine o'clock in the morning. The tide was high at Three Crossings, and with that and the wind Kumozugawa river again overflowed.[104] We were accompanied to the town by many people and palanquins from Moritaka. Anonotsu has been desolate for more than ten years, and nothing but ruins remains of its four or five thousand houses and temples.[105] Stands of reeds and mugwort, no chickens or dogs, rare even to hear the cawing of a crow. The wind and rain at the time were terrifying.

Our escorts all returned home and no others arrived to meet us. We lost our way, and after wandering in the wrong direction we hired a local foot soldier on the advice of an acquaintance. The soldier took us two leagues to a place called Kubota.[106] That night the party sent by Kajisai, equipped with palanquins and such, found us. I am amazed we saw the day through safely.

Stayed there one night and had a bath. On waking in the night:

13	omoitatsu	How bitter
	oi koso urami	to set out at my age across
	suzukayama	the Suzuka Mountains—
	yuku sue ika ni	what is to become of me
	naran to suran	as I travel on my way?[107]

Kameyama

As I feared, the road to Ōmi has been impassable since yesterday. Kajisai's castle at Kameyama is three leagues into the mountains.[108] We stayed at the Jōjuin subtemple of the *ritsuin* Shinpukuji, three chō away.[109] I was surprised by how clean and neat it was. Rested there more than ten days. Each day's pleasant company moved me deeply. There was a renga session:

14	yaso no se no	High, the headwaters
	minakami takashi	of the eighty rapids.
	aki no koe	The sound of autumn.[110]

Second Year of Daiei (1522)

This simply refers to the lines "the eighty rapids / of Suzuka River."[111]

15	nagare mo kiri no	The current in the deep mists
	oku fukaki yama	of the mountain recesses.

Kajisai[112]

At the session were Kajisai's three fine sons, aged seventeen, thirteen, and eleven, resplendent as flowers in autumn fields.

Fighting near here as well. No time for anything but preparations for war. The castle of the Gamō in Ōmi was reduced by the constable, and for days freebooters have been banding together.[113] One hears of rear-guard skirmishes from time to time.

After leaving Kameyama, we were guided through the dangerous places along the route, but the road was fit only for travel on foot.[114] Since it was impossible to arrange for palanquins, I considered returning to Yamada, but the rain and wind were incessant, so I stayed near Kajisai's residence:

16	azusayumi	Today too spring rain,
	oshite harusame	recalling catalpa bows
	kyō mo furu	that one bends to string.
	asu mo furu to te	No doubt rain tomorrow too—
	yado ya sadamen	shall I take up lodgings here?[115]

By this I meant that if it were going to continue raining, I would stay on in luxury. I wrote that poem and others in a haikai vein, littering them about my inkstone. Someone must have shown them to Kajisai, for he sent this:

17	ika de kimi	Would you have chosen,
	yadori sadamen	good sir, to take up lodgings here
	azusayumi	if not for the rain,
	oshite kyō furu	recalling bent catalpa bows,
	ame nakariseba	that falls upon us today?

An elegant reply.

Composed on request for a hokku of mine from Rokudaiin in Kubota:[116]

18	suzukayama	The Suzuka Mountains—
	iroiro ni naru	their essence multi-hued
	kokoro kana	and all-encompassing.[117]

This refers to the nature of the central image of that temple, Kannon.

To dispatch someone to Echizen, one sends an escort who knows the way from here to Sakamoto.[118]

Anonotsu

We were taken from Kajisai's to a thatched dwelling like a salting hut in a village outside Anonotsu. Stayed there the next day waiting for our escort from Miyahara Moritaka. At the urging of some people from Anonotsu, we composed some linked verse:

19	kaeru yo o	When will they return?
	matsu ya shiranami	The pines know not, nor the white waves
	aki no umi	of the autumn sea.[119]

These villagers are no doubt waiting for the time they can move back to Anonotsu.

I went out to the beach when evening fell. I could see into the far distance, and "the shore at the border of Ise and Owari" stood out bright and clear.[120] As I tarried there, some young men gathered, bringing things on hand nearby to eat and drink, as well as flutes and drums, and we made merry.[121] I recalled the poem: "neither cherry blossoms / nor colored foliage" and composed this in response to it:

20	kono yūbe	Here this evening
	hana mo momiji mo	cherry blossoms and colored foliage
	aru mono o	abound
	ura no tomaya no	in the heart of one
	hito no kokoro ni	by the thatched-roof huts beside the bay![122]

Later that night they left. There I was, feeling "pillowed on the waves," when one of the youths returned from somewhere to ease my travel loneliness.[123] After he left the next morning, I sent this poem:

21	omowazu no	Of that unexpected
	ashi no karine no	brief rest upon the reeds,
	seze no nami	touched then abandoned
	shikisuterareshi	by the ceaseless waves,
	nagori nashi ya wa	can no trace still linger?[124]

Second Year of Daiei (1522)

Kumozugawa

On the first of the ninth month we left and went back to Anonotsu harbor, taking sake back with us. Later we departed with regret and reached Kumozugawa river, where we were met by a mountain ascetic sent by Asakura Tarōzaemon Norikage. I read the letters he brought, and we then accompanied him to lodgings in Hirao. The next morning I wrote a reply:

22	koshiji ni zo	What is the point
	nani zo wa ari to	of its being in Koshi,
	uramitsuru	one wonders, vexed.
	na wa kyō kaeru	Today the name Returning Mountain
	suzukayama kana	means those of Suzuka instead![125]

Moritaka too got word of our stopping here, and he once more sent the day's escorts. On the second of the month we reached Yamada, and I recorded my old and bent wanderings of the last few days.

Saigyō Valley

After the twentieth of the same month, I visited Kenkokuji temple of the Inner Shrine at Ise.[126] There it was decided that we should all go to Saigyō Valley, site of that great priest's ancient dwelling.[127] We crossed Isuzu Mimosusogawa river downstream and walked along the narrow paths between the rice paddies of Yamada, pressing through the bush clover and pampas grass withered under a thin frost.[128]

When we reached the grounds all was quite desolate. Mountain water brought in by a bamboo pipe, pine posts from the days of old, a fence of woven bamboo, a dozen or so nuns in tumbledown quarters, paper coverlets, stitched hempen garments, the smell of anise incense—I felt the past before my eyes and put into verse what arose in my breast:

23	kikishi yori	More poignant the sight
	miru wa aware ni	than anything I had heard—
	yo o itou	how moving, this dwelling,
	mukashi oboyuru	so redolent of the past,
	sumai kanashi mo	in which he renounced the world!

BOOK ONE

I wrote it on a pine fence post and went back to Kenkokuji. Those who had invited me requested that I compose a hokku for a sequence:

| 24 | aki fukashi
kamiji no oku no
tani no koe | Autumn deepens.
In Mount Kamiji's reaches,
the sound of the valley. |

| 25 | tsuki wa yūbe no
mine no matsukaze | The moon—evening wind
in the pines on the peak. |

Kenkokuji

Both poems recall the old verse by that great priest.[129]

Take

In the tenth month we left Yamada and stayed two or three days at Take.[130] There was a renga session:

| 26 | kaminazuki
momiji o fukeru
nokiba kana | The tenth month—
roof eaves thatched
with colored foliage! |

Hasedera

I made a pilgrimage to Hatsuse and stayed a day or two.[131] An old acquaintance came to visit from the capital, and we spent the day chatting. After he left, I sent this after him:

| 27 | hatsuseyama
iriai no kane o
kiku made ni
mukashi o ima no
kyō mo wasureji | At Mount Hatsuse
we talked until we heard
the temple's vesper bell,
bringing the past to life
on a day never to be forgotten.[132] |

Tōnomine

I had an invitation from Tōnomine to observe a festival and so climbed the mountain.[133] It was even more impressive than I had heard. Stayed at An'yōin.[134] We composed renga. The hokku:

Second Year of Daiei (1522)

28 shimo o aya / kozue o tatamu / nishiki kana

A frost of damask, / with leaves at branch tips woven / into rich brocade!

Konparu Shichirō came late at night, and we invited temple boys and drank sake.[135] Continued until dawn.

Nara and Takigi

The next day I visited Tachibanadera temple and lodged a night in Yagi, capital of Yamato Province.[136] Stayed the next day at the residence of Hōgen Chōei in Shiratsuchi.[137] Then, the next day, at Senjuin in the Southern Capital.[138] Accompanied by Chōei. My hokku for a renga sequence:

29 fuyu ya itsu / wakakusayama no / haruhi kana

When is winter? / At Wakakusa Mountain, / springtime sun![139]

A day there, then to Jison'in.[140] Lodged there more than ten days. This renga hokku:

30 kesa chiru ya / arashi no hana no / yuki no niwa

They fall this morning— / a garden of snow-blossoms / blown by the brisk wind.[141]

At Rengein:

31 majire chire / arashi no yuki no / hana momiji

Mingle and scatter! / tempest-tossed snow-blossoms / and colored foliage.[142]

A pilgrimage to the Great Buddha, then up to Takigi in Yamashiro.[143] A number of people went ahead and waited at Hannyaji Hill to see us off.[144] Countless boxes of food. We warmed sake by burning fallen needles beneath the pines on the slope and entertained ourselves.[145] A few cups of sake at a temple building at Hannyaji before setting out. On the slope I went to get out of my palanquin and landed flat on my backside. Whereupon:

32 tanomikoshi / tsue tsukiorite

Breaking the cane / on which he so long relied,

	rōdō wa	the old warrior
	tsuzukanu oi no	with no lookout to the rear
	musa to korobinu	carelessly took a tumble.[146]

We finally made our way to Shūon'an in Takigi.[147]

The Death of Jōsū

Jōsū, a monk and shakuhachi musician, was originally a member of the Higashiyama Ryōzen Ji sect.[148] He spent four or five years at Jōfukuji temple at Gojō Higashinotōin and at Daitokuji's Daisen'in, and until recently he maintained a cottage in Sakai in Izumi Province.[149] He made his living from shakuhachi students and patrons. I happened to be staying in Yamada when he arrived at Ise Shrine on a pilgrimage; he called on me and stayed more than ten days, until I had to leave for Takigi in Yamashiro. They tell me he was fêted thereafter in Yamada morning and evening. Then came the news he had thrown himself into Futami Bay—what could have happened to make him do such a thing? I composed this on learning of it:[150]

33	mujōshin	That one melody
	okosu ikkyoku	"Perceiving the Law of Change"—
	ika ni shite	how could he play it
	fukishizumiken	then sink into the sea?
	ana umi no yo ya	How awfully sad, this world![151]

I must have been in the Southern Capital when I received the news. I sent the verse to Yamada.

His sister, a nun of the Ji sect, told them several times she would like to have his shakuhachi flute returned to her so that she might sell it to pay for services in his memory. But they never sent it back. No, they never sent back the shakuhachi to exchange for money, recalling the changing shallows of Tomorrow River.[152]

An Exchange of Poems with Sanjōnishi Sanetaka

Hearing I was at Shūon'an, Lord Sanetaka sent this:[153]

34	ori ni au	Though you have firewood
	takigi wa ari tomo	for this season in Takigi,

Second Year of Daiei (1522)

haru chikaki	give some thought as well
miyako no hana no	to the flowery name of the capital
na o mo toe kashi	now that spring is near!¹⁵⁴

Though I could not manage a suitable reply, I sent him this about winter in my mountain hut:

35 tsurezure to   I dwell in tedium
    kurasu takigi no   with nothing to rely on
        yamazato no   save "firewood,"
    na o nomi tanomu   name of this mountain hamlet,
    yuki no uchi kana   in my hut beneath the snow!

A Letter to Sōseki

Sōseki went to the province of Tsu and back without sending me word. I recalled that old poem of Seiin Sōzu on the first wind in Ikuta and sent to Sōseki the following:[155]

36 kimi sumaba   Were you here, good sir,
    towamashi mono o   then I would call upon you.
        yamashiro no   In the Wood
    iwata no mori no   of Iwata in Yamashiro,
    yuki no shitakaze   snowy wind beneath the trees.[156]

Year's End

I hope to end my days at Shūon'an. Even so, I composed the following in private celebration at the end of another year:

37 negawaku wa   This is my request—
    kotoshi no kure no   that I might vanish before
        takigi kiru   the snow on the peaks
    mine no yuki yori   where they cut firewood
    saki ni kienan   in the last days of the year.[157]

Third Year of Daiei 1523

An Exchange of Poems with Sanjōnishi Sanetaka

In the first month of the New Year, Sanetaka was good enough to send five poems to me at Shūon'an:[1]

38   nodoka ni te　　　　　　Your years will surely
      sara ni yowai mo　　　　continue to increase,
      nobinubeshi　　　　　　　　as you greet
      chiri no hoka naru　　　the spring in tranquillity
      haru o mukaete　　　　　out beyond the mundane dust.[2]

39   ito haya mo　　　　　　　Make haste and come forth
      tani no to ide yo　　　from your valley door!
      matsu sato no　　　　　　　The pine hamlet
      hitokata naranu　　　　awaits you with rare anticipation,
      haru no uguisu　　　　　peerless springtime warbler![3]

40   fuji no yuki　　　　　　　I am enticed
      kiyomi ga tsuki o　　　by spring in the hills where you live,
      kokoro ni te　　　　　　　your heart pure and bright
      sumuran yama no　　　　as the snow on Mount Fuji
      haru zo yukashiki　　　or the moon at Kiyomi.[4]

BOOK ONE

41 yamabito no   Would that I could go
   oeru na ni aru   and call on you beneath
    takigi o ba   the blossoms' shade
   hana no kage ni mo at Takigi, known for the wood
   yukite towabaya   the mountain dweller carries.[5]

42 ware mo ima   Because I too
   sumi yori samuki   have a heart now grown more chill
    kokoro ni te   than burnt charcoal,
   nori no takigi mo   I lack the strength to gather
   hiroiwabinuru   the firewood of the Good Law.[6]

I present these crude and hastily expressed thoughts to the old man of Brushwood Cottage, who is now on a journey of Zen meditation.[7] Third year of Daiei [1523], first month, twenty-second day.[8] Sanetaka.

I sent these poems in return:[9]

43 onozukara   How my thoughts turn
   omou haru kana   of their own accord to peaceful spring,
    nodoka ni te   though I know naught
   chiri no hoka to wa of living in tranquillity
   waku mi naranedo out beyond the mundane dust.[10]

44 odorokasu   Had it not received word
   miyako no haru no awakening it to springtime
    tsute nakuba   in the capital,
   isa shirayuki no   it would be unaware, the warbler
   tani no uguisu   in the valley of white snow.[11]

45 izuko o ka   Where else
   omoiyaramashi   could I let my thoughts stray
    me no mae no   when here before my eyes
   haru no ōhie   this spring are Mount Hiei
   uji no watari ni   and the crossing at Uji?[12]

46 yasumu beki   I will first
   kage o zo kanete   search out a shady spot
    mitsutsu semu   where we can take our rest
   takigi no mine mo once the blossoms have appeared
   hana shi sakaba   on Takigi's hills as well.[13]

47 asayū no   Morning and evening
   minori no takigi   yet for many, many years

Third Year of Daiei (1523)

iku tose mo	you, my lord,
yowai to tomo ni	will still be gathering
kimi zo hirowan	the firewood of the Good Law.

An Exchange of Poetry with Others in the Capital

In answer to a letter from the capital, on my complaints about old age:

48
oitsutsu mo	As I grow in years,
omou koto to wa	I anticipate the hour
kyō asu no	of my death
ima wa no hoka no	today or tomorrow—
nagusame zo naki	I have no other consolation.

In the first month of the same year, I sent this in acknowledgment of some wheat crackers and mirror rice cakes:[14]

49
waga yowai	I hate to look
tori mo mimauki	at myself in my declining years
asana asana	morning after morning,
kono kagami ni wa	but with these mirrors before me
uchi zo emaruru	I can bring myself to smile![15]

Composed in response to a request for a hokku from Kozu:[16]

50
yama kasumu	Is it melted snow
yukige no mizu ka	from the haze-covered mountains?
izumigawa	Izumi River.[17]

Composed in response to requests from the Southern Capital:

51
somekakuru	For how many days
saokaze ikuka	has springtime been tinted
haru no iro	by the wind of Sao?[18]

52
uguisu no	Its branches woven
ito ni yoraruru	into strings by bush warblers—
yanagi kana	a weeping willow![19]

An old friend of mine named Rikijū lives at Gokokuji temple at Higuchi Aburanokōji.[20] He called on me at my place of retirement, and for more than ten nights we slept side by side. He is an extraordinary lie-abed—a Time sect monk who cannot tell the time!

53 kazoureba   Counting up the hours,
   nanatsu mo mutsu mo it is past four, now past six—
    itsu to te ka   when does he think it is,
   toki shiranu jishu   that Time sect monk fast asleep,
   yama wa fuji no ne   as dead to time as Fuji's peak.[21]

An Exchange of Poems with Tsujinobō at Shirakawa in Uji

From Tsujinobō at Shirakawa in Uji came a New Year's greeting with a load of "Willow" sake, two kegs of pickled plums, a keg of pickled green plums, and other things, together with this poem:[22]

54 harusame no   In view of your
   tsuyu mo wasurenu   unforgettable kindness,
    kokorozashi   dew of spring rain,
   ito hosonade no   how slender must seem
   yanagi to ya mimu   these strings of willow branches![23]

I sent this with a fan and other things:

55 asamidori   These two barrels
   yanagi ni mume no   containing plums as well as willows
    futaoke wa   of the lightest green—
   futa akeaezu   before even opening their lids,
   motehayasu kana   I treasure them![24]

Memories at Shinden'an

At Shinden'an in Takigi, I came across a letter case containing correspondence sent now and again about an offer to raise my son, the novice Jōha, about whom the writer had so often heard.[25] On the back of one letter was a copy of the *Diamond Sutra* I had had young Jōha make at thirteen years of age. Shinden'an was built by the Zen nun Jikō, widow of Nose Inabanokami Yorinori.[26] I perused the sutra and at the end, to the side, I wrote:

56 tsuyukesa wa   These dew-like tears
   tada fuku kaze ni   are all that now remain

Third Year of Daiei (1523)

yashinai no	after the wending wind,
hahaso no iro no	a nurturing mother,
asakaranu ato	brought deep color to the oak leaves.²⁷

Inabanokami Yorinori did me great favors in the past, and I have been told that he said until the day he died that he regretted not seeing more of me. Because of his uncommon taste for renga, I inaugurated a memorial thousand-verse sequence at An'yōji temple in Higashiyama for the repose of his spirit.²⁸ I discussed the matter with Lord Sanetaka, and for the occasion the Zen priest Shōhaku, Sōseki, Teramachi, Hahakabe, Kawarabayashi Tsushimanokami, and others came up to the capital.²⁹ It was quite a special event. I composed the tenth hokku of the thousand verses:

57
tsuki ni awaba	In the moon's clear light
aramashikaba mo	all mundane desires
yumeji kana	are but a path of dreams.³⁰

The Zen nun Jikō was grateful for the memorial, and she may have conceived the idea of adopting Jōha in consequence.³¹

Shirakawa

On my way from Takigi to the capital in the third month, I composed this at the Tsujinobō retreat in Shirakawa in Uji:

58
haru ya hana	Spring! and the blossom
tsune o wasurenu	that continues to remember—
hatsuzakura	the first cherry.

This is related to the "Sawarabi" chapter of *Genji monogatari*, in which "the temple across the way" appears.³²

To the Capital

At lodgings in the capital:

59
utsusemi no	Fleeting as the cicada,
usuhanazakura	pale cherry blossoms
saku yo kana	are now in bloom!³³

Composed on request from Yamashina:[34]

60 iku iwane   Through the serried cliffs
    otowa no takitsu   of Otowa Falls sound the surging
    haru no mizu   springtime waters.[35]

Composed on request from Tango:[36]

61 matsu tateru   In the haze that spreads
    kasumi ni nami ya   round the stand of pines come waves—
    yosa no umi   the Sea of Yosa.[37]

In the intercalary third month:

62 ai ni ainu   One upon the next—
    urū no yayoi   in the extra third month,
    hana no haru   blossoming spring.[38]

For the anniversary of someone's death:

63 hana ni chō   Butterfly amid blossoms—
    furinishi tama ka   an old, gem-like spirit alighting?
    haru no kaze   The spring wind.[39]

Composed on request from Miidera:[40]

64 koe zo seki   Its voice, a barrier—
    tare sugimura no   who can pass these cedars
    hototogisu   when the cuckoo calls?[41]

Rebuilding the Sanmon Gate at Daitokuji

Some years ago, the Zen priest Soshin of Daitokuji, who resided in his last years at Shingakuji temple at Ichijōdani in Echizen, wrote at the end of his life asking me to come down and discuss the rebuilding of the Sanmon gate at Daitokuji in Murasakino. He sent a palanquin to Kyoto for me.[42] I agreed to go and arrived on the fifteenth of the third month, [1519]. Asakura Tarōzaemon Norikage had promised to contribute to the building project, and I was asked to convey this information to Daitokuji. Soon after that Soshin passed away, and I returned to the capital.[43] I subsequently went down to Suruga and the next year

Third Year of Daiei (1523)

returned to the capital again, where the building project at Daitokuji was not proceeding as planned. I then received a letter from the abbot of Shinjuan saying it was to be held in abeyance.[44] I too had made arrangements for a donation, so I instead gave fifty *kanmon* toward the repair of the main gate at Myōshōji at Takigi.[45] The matter of the Daitokuji Sanmon gate remained undecided.

Journey to Echizen

The abbot of Shinjuan then did me the honor of calling on me at my travel lodging and told me that the temple wished me to go to Echizen again and revive the matter of a donation.[46] I demurred, wondering how I could do so since Norikage had already been told that Daitokuji was postponing the project. But it was difficult to decline their request, and I finally agreed to go. When I arrived, I was informed that Norikage had prepared fifty thousand hiki and that others with connections to Daitokuji had pledged over twenty thousand hiki more. I hear, however, that the funds have yet to reach the capital. Now all seems indeed to have borne out the judgment of the abbot of Shinjuan.[47] I have donated about thirty thousand hiki myself to date through the sale of this and that.

A man named Teraki Shirōzaemon, who was recently in the capital but is now back in his home province, promised to supplement my donations in view of our particularly deep friendship.[48] As of the fourth month of last summer, he too had pledged thirty thousand hiki to the temple. He wrote to me saying that depending on the results, he would donate more.

Hokku I composed while in Echizen:

65	yuku to ku to kozue ya ōchi mine no kumo	Coming and going, they meet in bead-tree branches— the clouds on the peak.[49]
66	ame kaoru hanatachibana no satsuki kana	The rain is redolent of orange blossoms in the fifth month![50]

At Sakuuken, the garden of which boasts unparalleled rocks and trees:

67	yūdachi ya makaseshi mizu no iwakosuge	An evening shower— rivulets of rain run off onto rock-pent sedge.[51]

68　　　　omokage wa 　　　　　　In my imagination
　　　　fumiwakegataki　　　　　they lie too deep to walk through—
　　　　　hitoha kana　　　　　　　a single leaf![52]

For the anniversary of Sōgi's death:

69　　　　matsumushi ya　　　　　Pine crickets—
　　　　yomogi ga moto no　　　 deep within the mugwort,
　　　　　aki no koe　　　　　　　voices of autumn.[53]

70　　　　hagi susuki　　　　　　The bush clover
　　　　fukanu nowaki no　　　　and pampas grass in the still morning
　　　　　ashita kana　　　　　　 after the tempest.[54]

On the fourteenth of the eighth month:

71　　　　tsuki yo ika ni　　　　　The moon—how clearly
　　　　teran asu no yo　　　　　it will shine tomorrow night,
　　　　　kuma mo nashi　　　　　without a trace of shadow![55]

Composed on request from Heisenji temple:[56]

72　　　　yuki okite　　　　　　　Even without snow
　　　　shirayama no na ya　　　it is worthy of the name White Mountain,
　　　　　tsuki no aki　　　　　　under autumn's moon.[57]

Return to the Capital

Composed at Kannonji in Ōmi Province, on my way up to the capital from Echizen:[58]

73　　　　asagiri no　　　　　　　The nearby mountains
　　　　toyama wa yae no　　　　make multi-layered clearings
　　　　　harema kana　　　　　　in the morning mist![59]

74　　　　mishi ya mina　　　　　I have beheld them—
　　　　kozue utsurou　　　　　　every branch changing color
　　　　　asato kana　　　　　　　outside the door at morning![60]

75　　　　shika no ne ya　　　　　Calls of a deer
　　　　onoe no arashi　　　　　 and gusts of wind on hilltops—
　　　　　yūzukuyo　　　　　　　 a moonlit evening.[61]

Third Year of Daiei (1523)

At Shiga:[62]

76 aki no umi
    hana saku nami no
    chigusa kana

The autumn sea—
on its billows blossom
a thousand flowers![63]

Composed for a linked-verse session in the capital with a merchant from Bōnotsu in Satsuma:[64]

77 iso no ue no
    chishio mo aki no
    yūbe kana

A rocky strand
tinted and retinted by the myriad waves
on an autumn evening!

At Shijō, Bōmonchō:[65]

78 yoru wa shigure
    asato wa shimo no
    itaya kana

Chilling rain at night,
then frost outside the door at morning—
a plank-roofed cottage![66]

Arima

While taking the waters in Arima, at Koyadera temple, I composed this:[67]

79 shinagadori
    inano o yuki no
    ashita kana

Off to Inano,
a name recalling grebes side by side,
in the morning snow![68]

80 ariake ya
    sora ni shimogare no
    hanasusuki

The moon before dawn—
frost-withered against the sky,
ears of pampas grass.[69]

For a thousand-verse sequence at Nose Gengorō's, at Shiroyama:[70]

81 kurete nao
    nodokeki toshi no
    hikari kana

Sunset, and yet
gentle still—the light
of the passing year.[71]

Haikai at Year's End at Takigi

Saw out the old year in an abandoned dormitory beside Shūon'an in Takigi. Six or seven of us gathered around the hearth and after tofu with miso, we composed a number of haikai verses:[72]

82	asu no shiru tama kagiri naru arame kana	Broth for the morning, with just a glint of *arame* sea plant.[73]
83	kao wa shiwasu no haru no hatsuyome	Her face lined in the twelfth month, the new bride greets the spring.[74]

❁

84	fujiwara uji ka mon wa fujinami	Is he a Fujiwara? his crest is wisteria.[75]
85	umakura wa kinpukurin no genkurō	His horse's saddle is the gold-inlaid one of Genkurō.[76]

❁

86	hikitsuretsutsu mo nebari koso sure	Bring one along with you and it will stick to you like glue.[77]
87	tsu no kuni no yunoyamamono o makura ni te	A hot potato from Yunoyama in Tsu beside one's pillow.[78]

❁

88	kōya hijiri no yado o kau koe.	The voice of a beggar monk from Kōya craving lodging.[79]
89	natsu no yo no yabure kayado tachiidete	On a summer night, leaving his thatched hut and its torn mosquito net.[80]

❁

90	hannyajizaka no ōkojikidomo	Brawny beggars around Hannyaji Hill.[81]
91	kokoro mina sechibenbō ya monjuin	Are all the monks at Monjuin temple miserly at heart?[82]

Third Year of Daiei (1523)

❀

92　　　fuzei mo tsukite   Out of elegant topics,
　　　　hiki ya irenan   are they going to retire?

93　　　　　hito ni tsuki   The moon, for them both
　　　　omoshirogarare   the center of attention,
　　　　　　fukinikeri   has sunk out of sight.[83]

❀

94　　　chigo ka onna ka   Is it a boy or a girl
　　　　nete no akatsuki   fast asleep before dawn?

95　　　　　mae ushiro   Feeling fore and aft,
　　　　saguru ni tsuki no   there beneath
　　　　　　ariake ni   the late-rising moon.[84]

❀

96　　　aruji mo zusa mo   Both master and retainer
　　　　tsue o koso tsuke   bolstered by their walking sticks.

97　　　　　morotomo ni   Together making verses
　　　　koshiore uta o   as bent as their backs
　　　　　　yomitsurete   while they walk along.[85]

❀

98　　　nanbō gozareta   How stale it has grown
　　　　hana ni tawabure   as they frolicked beneath the blossoms.[86]

99　　　　　ocha no mizu   The water they brought
　　　　umekae koso ni   and poured into the kettle
　　　　　　kumiyosete   to freshen the tea.[87]

❀

100　　koshōdō mina   Novices all in a group
　　　　hanami o zo suru   out enjoying the blossoms.

101　　　　chigo kosode   The lads' short-sleeved robes—
　　　　yanagi sakura o   willows and cherry trees
　　　　　　kokimazete   blending in profusion.[88]

❀

102　　nyake no atari wa   Nothing but asters,
　　　　tada kiku no hana   where the temple boys are.[89]

103   akikaze no
          fukiage niou
              tobosogami

           The autumn wind
           wafts a fragrance
              from the doorway.⁹⁰

104   torinukashitaru
          subariwakazō

           The young temple boy with
           the tight ass passed wind.⁹¹

105   motenashi no
          hara no oto koso
              kikoekere

           And for an extra treat
           you could also hear
              his belly rumble!

106   ichijō nijō
          harima suihara

           One or two quires of paper
           from Harima Suihara.⁹²

107   hikidemono
          ōgi no kaze ni
              nabikasete

           The prizes he won
           flutter in the breeze
              from his folding fan.⁹³

108   kasumi no koromo
          suso wa nurekeri

           The robe of haze
           is soaked at the hem.

109   nawashiro o
          oitaterarete
              kaeru kari

           Shooed away
           from the seed beds where the young rice grows,
              geese flying homeward.⁹⁴

110   gojō atari ni
          tateru amagoze

           In the Fifth Ward
           stands someone in a nun's habit.

111   taga goke no
          ukarekimi to wa
              narinuran

           Whose wife
           did that lady of the night
              used to be?⁹⁵

112   onaji toshi koso
          sannin wa are

           In the same year—
           all three people!

113   maotoko
          futakata shimuru
              hara no uchi

           The womb of a wife
           who embraced two
              illicit lovers.⁹⁶

Third Year of Daiei (1523)

114	omoshiroge ni mo akikaze zo fuku	The autumn wind blows with it a feeling of excitement.[97]
115	tatenarabe tanabata oreru ashihyōshi	The rhythm of feet weaving on a row of looms at Tanabata.[98]

❀

116	omoki kata ni wa motare koso sene	One ought never find oneself leaning toward the heavy side.[99]
117	somo koi yo chin ni te mo tare yatowarenu	In love as well, who would undertake to sin even for money?[100]

❀

118	hito no nasake ya ana ni aruran	All her emotions in the word "respectfully."[101]
119	onna fumi kashiko kashiko to kakisutete	A woman's letter signed with a careless flourish, "Most sincerely yours."[102]

❀

120	tanomu wakazō amari tsurena ya	The boy I propositioned was so terribly unkind!
121	hikkunde sashi mo ireba ya chigaeba ya	Would we could grapple, with me stabbing into him, then dying from his thrust![103]

❀

122	ware yori mo seitaka wakashu machiwabite	How he waits and waits for the lad Seitaka, taller than himself.
123	fudō mo koi ni kogarakasu mi ka	Even Fudō burns with unrequited love?[104]

❀

124	kami no yo yori no sugi no zungiri	Cut clean through—a cedar there since the age of the gods.[105]
125	chihayaburu miwayamamoto no chayabōzu	At the foot of Mount Miwa, name of divine might, a tea-selling bonze.[106]

❧

126　　fushitsu korobitsu　　　　He throws himself on the ground,
　　　　mukashi kourashi　　　　longing for the days gone by.

127　　　　toyakaku to　　　　　　　Try as he might,
　　　　suredomo oenu　　　　he has the will for love
　　　　　　monoomoi　　　　　　but not the way.¹⁰⁷

❧

128　　kasumi komaka ni　　　　They have been drawn
　　　　hikimawashikeri　　　　delicately as the haze itself.¹⁰⁸

129　　　　utsukushi na　　　　　　How beautiful!
　　　　tada marugao no　　　　A round face with the eyebrows
　　　　　hōzukimayu　　　　　　　brushed on with cherry paint.¹⁰⁹

❧

130　　uma ni noritaru　　　　　Look at Hitomaro
　　　　hitomaro o miyo　　　　as he sits astride his horse!

131　　　shimo ni tatsu　　　　　　Standing beneath,
　　　　chūgen otoko　　　　　　there is but a single man
　　　　　hitori nite　　　　　　　　in his service.¹¹⁰

❧

132　　　　oitsukan　　　　　　　"I'll catch up with him,
　　　　oitsukan to ya　　　　　I'll catch up"—is that
　　　　　hashiruran　　　　　　what he thinks, running?

133　　kōya hijiri no　　　　　　Behind a Kōya monk,
　　　　ato no yarimochi　　　　a lancer.¹¹¹
　　　　　　　　　　　　　　　　　　Sōkan

[132　　　　oitsukan　　　　　　　"He'll catch up with me,
　　　　oitsukan to ya　　　　　he'll catch up"—is that
　　　　　hashiruran　　　　　　what she thinks, running?]¹¹²

134　　kōya hijiri no　　　　　　Ahead of a Kōya monk
　　　　saki no himegoze　　　　a young girl.¹¹³

My verse is better linked to the sense of "catch up" (*oitsukan*).

❧

135　　goban no ue ni　　　　　Atop the *go* board
　　　　haru wa kinikeri　　　　spring has arrived.

Third Year of Daiei (1523)

136   uguisu no
      sugomori to iu
        tsukurimono

A centerpiece made
to look like "a bushwarbler
sitting on its nest."[114]

        Sōkan

[135   goban no ue ni
      haru wa kinikeri

Atop the *go* board
spring has arrived.]

137   asagasumi
      sumizumi made wa
        tachiirade

The morning haze
has yet to reach
the corners.[115]

        Sōchō

Here too, my verse is the better linked.

Fourth Year of Daiei   1524

First Calligraphy of the New Year

First day of the first month, fourth year of Daiei. At Shūon'an, Takigi. Early in the morning I heard someone outside the gate announce that he had left the world and craved admission:

138
    aratama no   He has shorn his hair
      hatsumotoi kiri   that he dressed for the new season—
        hitotose ni   though he is the same,
    kozo to ya iwan   should we call him last year's scamp,
   koshami to ya iwan   or should we call him this year's novice?[1]

"Testing the brush" at Shūon'an with felicitations to the abbot:[2]

139
     nanasoji ni   Today as I add
  nanatose no kyō o   another year, the seventh,
      kuwōreba   to my seventy,
  kimi ga chitose no   I am still far, far behind
   haru haruka nari   the thousand springs that will be yours.[3]

A poem "testing the brush" at the start of the year, presented in return to the old man of Brushwood Cottage:[4]

140 yukusue mo   On this springtime day,
   nao harubaru no   yet a long, long while before
    haru no hi ni   we reach journey's end,
   kimi ga yowai o   may your years be a mirror
   kagami ni mo miyo in which to see my own.[5]

After the tenth of the same month, I dreamt during the night that my spirit had left my body.[6] I woke from my dream, wondering if the spirit had, in fact, been mine:

141 mikagirite   It abandoned me
   waga mi ideyuku and left my body;
    mukuinan   now I would be repaid.
   zeni no ontama   Make my errant spirit
   irikawaritame   into copper change![7]

This is a poem praying that my spirit be replaced with coins forthwith!

An Exchange of Poems with Nakamikado Nobutane

From Lord Nakamikado:[8]

142 samukaranu   Come up to the warmth
   miyako no haru ni of spring in the capital,
    takigi o ba   and leave the Takigi
   hiroisute koyo   firewood that you gathered,
   yamazato no tomo friend of the mountain village.[9]

He wrote the following on the wrapping paper:

>My sentiments are difficult to express. Through this one poem I hope to convey a myriad of words. I am over eighty and cannot do justice with my poor brush to my desire to see you again in my old age.

I sent this reply:

143 nodoka naru   For the road leading
   miyako no michi ni to the balmy capital,
    takigi o ba   he would abandon
   hiroi zo suten   his Takigi firewood,
   haru no yamabito this springtime mountain dweller.

Fourth Year of Daiei (1524)

In the same month:

| 144 | toshidoshi no
haru ya tachikaeru
asagasumi | Each and every year
it returns with the spring—
the morning haze.[10] |

A poem composed on request from the Southern Capital:

| 145 | izuku yori
wakakusayama no
haruhi kana | Whence does it spring?
At Wakakusa Mountain,
springtime sun![11] |

Yawata

For a single sheet of verses at Umenobō in Yawata:[12]

| 146 | ume no hana
utsurishi sode ka
asagasumi | Sleeves perfumed
by the scent of plum blossoms?
The morning haze.[13] |

When night fell, there was food and drink with a number of boys in service at the temple. I left early, pleading old age. They sent me several invitations, but I was lying down and unpresentable. Still I did not wish to be unsociable and so sent this, attached to a small branch of plum:

| 147 | omoiyare
yanagi no ito no
midaregoe
mukashi wa yoso ni
kikishi haru ka wa | Please understand,
you whose voices are tangled
as willow branches—
in springtimes past would I
have simply listened from afar?[14] |

Presently I heard a voice reading it aloud at the party.

In the Capital

| 148 | azusayumi
oshinabete haru no
hikari kana | Like a catalpa bow,
it bends and overspreads all—
spring's shining light![15] |

Shōzōbō of Miidera came to the capital, and we had a linked verse session:

        [itsu idete   When did it take leave
  kasumu yama no ha   of the hazy mountain ridge?
      yūzukuyo.]   The evening moon.][16]

This would be a reference to the poem made at that temple, "Now I find how hard it is / to forsake the mountain crest."[17]

For the "Shogunal Deputy's Thousand Verses in One Day:"[18]

149   nabiku yo wa   All bow to it—
       ame nodoka naru   blades of grass beneath
         kusaba kana   a gentle rain![19]

Iba senku

A three-poet thousand-verse sequence. Lord Sanetaka, Sōseki, and myself. Tanemura Nakatsukasanojō sponsored it at Sōseki's Gessonsai residence:[20]

150   uguisu ya   The bush warbler,
       ono ga nū hana   resting beneath the hat
         kasa yadori   it sewed of blossoms.[21]

An Exchange of Poems with Toyohara Muneaki

Toyohara Muneaki wrote this on the wrapping paper of some medicine he sent me:[22]

151   kimi mo ware mo   Through the use
       oizu shinazu no   of this tincture of eternal youth,
         kusuri ni te   I sincerely hope
       mata ai min mo   that you and I will meet
       kokoro narikeri   one another yet again.

My reply:

152   kore ya kono   Is it the one
       tōku motomeshi   once sent for from afar,
         ikugusuri   this tincture of eternal youth
       ima mo oisenu   that you, sir, young as ever,
       kimi tsutaeken   have passed along to me?[23]

I was out of the capital at the time.

Fourth Year of Daiei (1524)

An Exchange of Poems with Nakamikado Nobutane

From Lord Nakamikado:

153	oi no tomo	If you are aware
	matsu zo to shiraba	that your old friend awaits you,
	kaerikoyo	then make your way back,
	tago no uranami	even if Tago's billows
	tachi wa yuku tomo	rise up only to depart.[24]

My reply:

154	kimi ni yori	There is not a day
	tago no urawa ni	when the aged billows
	oi no nami	of the Bay of Tago
	omoi shi tatanu	do not rise up in longing
	hi mo zo nakaran	to go coursing back to you.

A Poem on Asakura Norikage's Hawks

In the garden of his residence, Asakura Tarōzaemon Norikage had for four or five years set up nests for hawks. Last year for the first time two, one large and one small, hatched chicks. It was a very rare event. The retired abbot of Ikkeken at Kenninji temple wrote of the chicks in his *Yōyōki*, and various poems in Chinese and Japanese were written about them as well.[25]

I therefore composed this:

155	mata kikazu	Unheard of before:
	togaeru yama no	bringing chicks up from nestlings
	mine narade	not in the mountains
	sudatasesomuru	where they go to molt,
	niwa no matsu ga e	but in the boughs of a garden pine!

Leaving the Capital

I had received invitations now and again to stay for a time with an acquaintance in Owari, and I accordingly left the capital on the eleventh of the fourth month on a journey to the east.[26] I went south first to Shūon'an in Takigi near Yawata, where the reverend monk Ikkyū passed away, to light incense and announce my departure. Some of my friends accompanied me to the Lower Capital, and others saw me south as far as Hōshōji and Fukakusa.[27] As I took my leave, regretting our parting, I composed this:

156	nagaraeba	Should I live so long,
	mata mo noboran	people of the capital,
	miyakobito	I will come again—
	motonaku negau	there is no need to make
	koto shi aru rō	a special request of this old one!

See appended note.[28] A comic last line—a haikai in jest. "People of the capital" are the ones who had come to see me off.

Fushimi

On the way I called on the Tsuda Bizen Lay Priest in Fushimi about a promise he had made earlier to arrange for carters to carry from this port to Daitokuji a donation of lumber from the mountains around Takigi.[29] The sun was still high thereafter, and I decided to hurry and go up Ujigawa river by boat.

Composed on request for a hokku:

157	kuretake no	Beneath the bamboo
	natsu fuyu izure	in both summer and winter,
	yoyo no kage	shade for all the ages.[30]

This was in celebration of the locale.

The Water Wheels of Ujigawa River

As we went upriver from Fushimi toward Uji Bridge, we could see Mizu no mimaki pasture and Yawata Mountain.[31] Kotsugawa and Ujigawa rivers flow together there to form an expanse as broad as a lake.[32] The people we invited from Kyoto enjoyed themselves, "beating in time on the boat sides," playing shakuhachi and pipes, and singing popular songs like "Water wheels revolving in Uji's rapids—are they turning over thoughts of this woeful world?"[33] The deutzia on the banks and the irises at the water's edge looked lovely, blooming together. There were innumerable stretches of rapids, and the boatman sang old songs like "struggling against the current at a tow rope's end."[34] We finally put into shore and alighted, sorry the trip was over.

Fourth Year of Daiei (1524)

Shirakawa in Uji

Spent the night at Tsujinobō at Shirakawa. Before dawn I heard the cry of a waterrail:

| 158 | tani fukami
kuina no meguru
toyama kana | So deep the valley,
the waterrail flies round and round
in the nearby hills. |

This is a haikai verse.[35]

Saw Tōunken at the constabulary of this province.[36] Had sake with him while waiting for our escort arrangments to be made to Takigi. He wanted to compose a single sheet of verses, but we were pressed for time, so I only composed a hokku:

| 159 | hototogisu
tsuki ya ariake no
asahiyama | A cuckoo!
The late moon in the dawn sky
over Sunrise Mountain.[37] |

I was sorry to leave.

From Takigi to Ōtsu

One night at Shūon'an. I arranged for the lumber to be transported and on the thirteenth burned incense before Ikkyū's image. The same day the young monk from Miidera named Shōzōbō who had joined me in a linked-verse session in Kyoto this spring came to escort me to a lodging at the beach at Ōtsu. That evening to Jōkōin.[38] The Bettō of Hakone in Sagami lived there for two or three years when he was still in youth's attire.[39] He took his vows this spring. Hyōbukyō had the sake cups brought out, and we stayed until late at night.[40] The next day the master held a session to compose a single sheet of verses. I could not avoid composing the hokku:[41]

| 160 | hototogisu
yama no i no akanu
hatsune kana | As at a mountain well,
one still thirsts for more—
the cuckoo's first call![42] |

This simply makes an association with the locale through the verse, "As one thirsts for more / at a mountain well too soon / muddied by the drops."

| 161 | iwao mo shiroshi | The cliffs too are white! |
| | sakeru unohana | Blossoming deutzia. |

Hyōbukyō[43]

This too was based on a foundation poem, "blooming / even on the rocky cliffs."[44]

I heard that Sōseki and two companions had arrived in Sakamoto the previous day to attend a festival, so I sent a messenger to them before dawn.[45] They paid me a visit later in the morning; it was most enjoyable. After we finished a single sheet of verses, sake was brought out, and Tōenbō, an old monk near to receiving his Eighty-Year Staff, played shakuhachi.[46] At night Hyōbukyō took up his shakuhachi as well and performed a few pieces in the *hyō* mode.[47] It brought to mind Shunzei's poem on the sound of pine crickets in the mugwort that he composed for a hundred-waka sequence well after reaching his eightieth year.[48] Near daybreak I returned to my lodgings in Ōtsu.

Ōmi

On the fifteenth, the master of this house, Sōkei, urged us to hold a linked-verse session.[49] Unable to refuse, I began it with this:

162	yoru nami ya	Breaking billows!
	hana no yamagoe	blossoms on a mountain pass—
	natsu no umi	the summer sea.

This simply means that the waves at the foot of the hills looked just like blossoms.

Halfway through the session a boat came for me from the residence of Motosu Yamatonokami in Konohama.[50] In a complete flurry while being rowed out, I recalled the hokku I made this spring in the capital at Shōzōbō's linked-verse session:

163	itsu idete	When did it take leave
	kasumu yama no ha	of the hazy mountain crest,
	yūzukuyo	the evening moon?

The following verse was composed at this temple:

| 164 | tsuki o nado | I never understood |
| | matare nomi su to | why the moon always |

Fourth Year of Daiei (1524)

omoiken	kept us waiting.
ge ni yama no ha wa	Now I find how hard it is
ideukarikeri	to leave the mountain crest!

Is it from *Senzaishū*?[51] I felt just the same as my boat departed.

When night fell a wind blew up from the south, and we raced across the lake in a moment.[52] It was the night of the fifteenth, and the full moon rose in unclouded brilliance from behind Mirror Mountain, looking itself very like a mirror hanging in the sky.[53]

Linked verse again two days later:

165
kuina naku	The waterrail calls
muranae hakobu	and villagers carry rice shoots
asato kana	outside the door at morning![54]

Then a palanquin came for me from Kawai Suruganokami.[55] To Moruyama, past Mirror Mountain.[56] Linked verse the day after:

166
unohana ya	The deutzia—
miru miru fureru	falling even as I watch,
kigi no yuki	snowflakes from treetops.[57]

Tanemura Nakatsukasanojō and others came down from Kannonji.[58] Suruganokami's son, who is called Gorō, surnamed Kawaii like his father, took part in the linked-verse session, appearing in youth's attire.[59] It was so pleasant I forgot my old age.

Across the Suzuka Mountains

On the twenty-second we departed, after having been several times detained. A palanquin to Sakanoshita in the Suzuka Mountains.[60] Horses for the rest of the company. Sake and food had been left ahead of time for us along the way at Inohana, Tsuchiyama, Uchi no Shirakawa, and Soto no Shirakawa.[61] Our trip through the mountains was unforgettably pleasant. From place to place people came out to guide us, and at the barriers no one challenged us. We arrived at Sakanoshita, where I received another palanquin from Kameyama and rested my aged self from the rigors of the day. That night, an inn at Sakanoshita. I was reminded of the "reed hut" of the vestal's temporary palace in these mountains on her trip east to Ise.[62]

I woke in the night to the cuckoo, calling insistently:

167 suzukayama   A cuckoo
   shino ni nakikeru   singing over and over
    hototogisu   in the Suzuka Mountains—
   miyako ni ika ni   in the capital,
   kikan to suran   how one would listen![63]

"Singing over and over" is a phrase associated with the Suzuka Mountains.[64] Also, when that great priest crossed these mountains, he composed this:

168 suzukayama   In the Suzuka Mountains,
   ukiyo o yoso ni   I cast aside
    furisutete   this world of sorrow—
   ika ni nariyuku   what will come to pass
   waga mi naruran   in this life of mine henceforth?[65]

Full of envy, I wrote:

169 suzukayama   In the Suzuka Mountains,
   furisutenu mi no   what is sad about
    kanashiki wa   *not* casting off the world
   oikagamareru   is having my old, bent back
   koshi o kakarete   carried in a palanquin![66]

Haikai, in jest. Again, on being told we were to cross Suzuka River:

170 kyō wataru   Shameful, my reflection
   kage hazukashiki   as today we cross
    suzukagawa   Suzuka River,
   yasose no nami o   my wrinkles of age
   oi no shiwa nite   many as its eighty rapids' waves.[67]

Kameyama

That day at noon we arrived at Kameyama.[68] Lodged at Nomura Ōinosuke's residence.[69] Immediately had a bath.

Kajisai had been at his mountain lodge at Shōhōji at Washiyama since the previous day.[70] The temple is affiliated with Daitokuji and is about fifty chō away from here. I was told he had gone there to attend a memorial service.

On the twenty-third he sent a palanquin for me early in the morning.[71] The

Fourth Year of Daiei (1524)

temple was not so very far into the mountains.[72] As we drew nearer, storm clouds began to appear in the sky, with "four or five mountain peaks painted in rainy colors."[73] Soaring cliffs, thick moss, and countless stands of pine and cedar. It was very much like Jingoji at Mount Takao.[74]

The first temple one reaches is Dairyōji.[75] A brook meanders through the valley, spanned by a bridge. One is reminded of Toganoo.[76] It resembles a hermit's dwelling; the handle of one's axe might truly rot away there.[77] Had an interview with the abbot of Shōhōji. Took sake with the noon meal and thereafter with Kajisai. Became quite intoxicated. Hurried to return to Kameyama before it started to rain.

The next day, the first of the sixth month, the sun shone bright and clear. I received an invitation from Kajisai. Took my morning and evening meals at his residence, after which I returned. We composed linked verse. When I visited here the autumn before last on my way to the capital, I made this hokku for a single sheet of verses:

171	yaso no se no minakami takashi aki no koe	High, the headwaters of the eighty rapids. The sound of autumn.[78]

I therefore felt that it would not be right for me to compose the hokku this time and demurred several times.[79] Whereupon Kajisai offered this:

172	toru tabi ni mototsuha takashi yaesakaki	The more boughs one breaks off, the higher the old leaves remain— *sakaki* trees.[80] <div align="right">Ikkan [81]</div>
173	yū kakete nake yamahototogisu	Call throughout the evening, mountain cuckoo! [82] <div align="right">Sōchō</div>

Skipped the next day, then composed another single sheet of verses:

174	uete konata iku kotoshi oi sono no take	Since they were planted, how many years have they grown, the garden bamboo?

Sightseeing at Washinosuyama

Two or three days later, we breakfasted at Shōhōji temple. Slept there the night before. A bath was provided for all in my company.

The next day we decided to see Washinosuyama mountain by palanquin.[83] Kajisai's invitation. The narrow, mossy path was slippery, and the water cascaded down through the valley like the sea itself. The bearers reached out for what holds they could on the rock wall but could not stop their legs.

They say there was a mountain temple here in the past. Might the site be used in battle? A natural shield of cliffs. Pillars of rock to support a gatehouse. It appears to cover fifty square chō around the valley. Here one could confront tens of thousands of soldiers with impunity.

That day we visited Shōhōji and also Kōzenji, a branch temple of Tōfukuji.[84] The abbot arranged a session of linked Japanese and Chinese verse:

175	washi no sumu yama to ya tōki hototogisu	Is it because this is the mountain where eagles dwell that the cuckoo is so distant?[85]
176	hito gogatsu no ryō no gotoshi	In the fifth month one feels cool.[86]

When we reached the back of the single sheet, sake was brought out, and we shared several cups with the acolytes.[87] Did not leave till evening.

Again on the twenty-fifth of this month, for a monthly dedicatory linked-verse session of a temple called Jionji:[88]

177	samidare ni masuge no mizu no sueba kana	In the summer rains, water builds on the outer leaves of the sedge grass![89]

And again on the twenty-ninth, at Shinpukuji:

178	kaoru ka wa hanatachibana no satsuki kana	A fragrance rises from the orange blossoms— the fifth month![90]

This was a proxy poem for Shirō Tanemori.[91]

Sixth month, second day. At Kajisai's residence, a one-round waka sequence on fifteen topics.[92] His son Jirō Moriyoshi chose the topics from *Meidaishū*, and

Fourth Year of Daiei (1524)

all composed impromptu.⁹³ Again the sake cups were brought out, and we stayed late drinking. I gave someone a fan, and he asked me to write something on it:

179	tare o ka mo	Is there no one left
	tomo to wa iwan	that I may call a friend?
	nagaraeba	If we live longer,
	kimi to ware to shi	it will be you and me
	takasago no matsu	and the pine of Takasago.⁹⁴

There was a picture of a pine on the fan. He, seventy-eight; I, seventy-seven.

At my lodging in Kameyama, Nomura Ōinosuke's residence, they had been keeping a goose in a cage since spring. Feeling sorry for it, I filled a cask from the garden with water, fed the bird some parsley, and otherwise did what I could for it. On the morning I was to leave, I affixed this poem to a post:

180	kari ni shi mo	Do not neglect
	tsuyu kakesutsu na	this goose even for a moment,
	sasoikon	until it can join
	aki o tanomu no	its friends who will come calling
	tomo ni au made	with the advent of autumn.⁹⁵

Kajisai's son Jirō Masayoshi called at my lodging unexpectedly one night. The next morning I sent him this:

181	hito yori mo	I know not of yours,
	oi no omowan	but the feelings this morning
	koto o shi zo	of this old one
	kesa wa midarete	are all in confusion—
	kokoro to mo naki	I am completely at a loss.

His reply:

182	kokoro ni mo	The words that
	arade midarete	you wrote about feeling
	omou chō	all in confusion
	hito no koto no ha	and completely at a loss
	kuma ya nakaran	are nothing less than eloquent.⁹⁶

Masayoshi

At Kajisai's I took great comfort from all the kind people who came to visit during the disagreeable summer rains. One of the most pleasant times was when, during the course of a conversation, Kanbe Ukyōnoshin Morinaga showed me a Mon'ami shakuhachi.[97] I praised its beauty, so he said I must have it and brooked no refusal. I sent him a note expressing my joy:

183	akatsuki no	I have just found
	tomo o zo etaru	a friend for the dawn,
	isonokami	though there is no point
	furinishi oi no	for one old as Isonokami
	kai wa nakeredo	to go on living longer.[98]

On being sent some rice cakes and two kinds of rice crackers:[99]

184	kokorozashi	I see your kindness
	miyama no shigeki	in rice cakes abundant
	sasachimaki	as mountain bamboo
	kazu wa senshū	and rice crackers enough
	senbei ni shite	to last me a thousand autumns![100]

At Kameyama, I was shown a worm-eaten scroll of a hundred-waka sequence by Sugihara Sōi, the Iga Lay Priest, written in his own hand.[101] I asked to copy it. The original had been sent by the present Iganokami Takamori.[102] My usual poor attempt:

185	ima mo yo wa	It is true today
	sa mo koso arame	just as in the past!
	isonokami	These words ancient
	furu koto no ha	as Isonokami Shrine
	tagui nakaran	can nowhere find their equal.

There are four *ritsuin* temples in Kameyama: Jionji, Shinpukuji, Amidaji, and Chōfukuji, each with the requisite seven buildings.[103] Aside from those, there are inns here and there, as well as east and west markets.

When I had already decided to leave for Owari, I twice received messengers bearing letters telling me to arrange to go to Suruga with the physician Sei Kunaikyō Hōin.[104] It was unavoidable, so I sent various people to the capital, and Kajisai ordered fifty or sixty horses with their grooms to be posted from the Minakuchi station to Sakanoshita in the Suzuka Mountains to escort him here. The doctor arrived in Kameyama on the fifth of the sixth month. I cannot say enough about Kajisai's hospitality and generosity.[105]

Fourth Year of Daiei (1524)

From Kameyama to Sunpu

One day of rest. On the seventh, Mori Hayatonosuke said he would see us off.[106] On the ferry "at the border of Ise and Owari," I had the boat pause and sent this back to the others who had come with us from Kajisai's:[107]

186	shizuka naru	Looking back and looking back
	nami no awai no	toward the border
	umizura o	and the billows
	kaeri miru miru	that break gently on its coast,
	yuku sora zo naki	I give no thought to the way ahead.[108]

My stay at Kameyama lasted fifty days. I cannot thank Kajisai enough for his unfailing consideration.

Sixth month, seventh day. Stayed at Ōno in Owari, Chita District.[109] On the eighth, a night at Kariya in Mikawa, the residence of Mizuno Izuminokami.[110] Then a day at Dora Ikkōdō in the same province.[111] On the tenth, stayed at Makino Denzō's residence in Imahashi.[112] The eleventh, Kibi in Tōtōmi.[113] The twelfth, stayed at Iio Zenshirō's residence in Hikuma.[114] The thirteenth, lodged at Kakegawa, and remained a day.[115] The fifteenth, Kiganji temple in Fujieda, Suruga Province.[116] The sixteenth, Fuchū.[117]

An evening shower was falling when we arrived, and we took shelter at Utsunoyama.[118] The teahouse has long been famous for its "ten dumplings."[119] The girls scooped up exactly ten with each dip of the ladle, much to our amusement. Arrived in the provincial capital that night.

Sunpu

Two days' rest. Audience with Lord Ryūōmaro.[120] Celebratory sake. The matter of Lord Ujichika's eye medicine. He improves daily.

Okitsu

I had planned to visit the site of Kiyomi Gate and offered to serve as a guide for the visitors from the capital. We arrived at the residence of Okitsu Tōbyōenojō Masanobu, and on the twenty-seventh of the seventh month decided to go out to the beach after nightfall:[121]

187	nami no oto	The sound of breakers
	yūyami fukete	deepens with evening's darkness,
	iwazutau	and fishing torches
	isoma no michi o	illumine the seaside path
	terasu isaribi	that winds around the cliffs.

On the twenty-eighth at the seaside we held a one-round waka sequence on thirty topics for the visitors from the capital. We composed on topics set by the Former Palace Minister, Ōgimachisanjō Sanemochi, who currently resides in the province.[122] His poem led the sequence. This was sent from Kiyomi Strand by Ohara Chikataka:[123]

188	matsuran to	Thinking they awaited me,
	koma no ashinami	I set out, pony prancing,
	yoru idete	to where waves rush in
	kiyomigaseki ni	at Kiyomi Gate,
	hirune o zo suru	but now I nod here napping![124]

My reply:

189	chigirishi mo	The aged waves
	wasurenikeri na	forgot what they had promised
	oi no nami	until the tide
	asa mitsu shio no	that rises in the morning ebbed,
	hirune suru made	and you took your noontime nap![125]

On the twenty-ninth, I recalled the journey that the late Sōgi made to this province years ago, and since it was the anniversary of his death, I made a single sheet of verses to forget the years:[126]

190	omoiizuru	My sleeve remembers—
	sode ya sekimoru	like the gate it holds
	tsuki to nami	the moon and waves of teardrops.[127]

The poem is based on a hokku Sōgi composed for a single sheet of verses at the gate when I invited him years ago to this temple, Seikenji:

191	tsuki zo yuku	The moon is departing.
	sode ni sekimore	At least hold it on my sleeve,
	kiyomigata	Strand of Kiyomi![128]

Fourth Year of Daiei (1524)

Thus my verse, "My sleeve remembers." In *Shinkokinshū* this appears:

192	mishi hito no	Hold the image
	omokage tome yo	of my dear one, Kiyomi Strand,
	kiyomigata	in the channel
	sode ni sekimoru	of the waves of tears that slip past
	nami no kayoiji	the gate and course down my sleeves.[129]

Might that have been the poem on which Sōgi based his?

This year marks the fifty-eighth since Sōgi spent the night at this temple. After the single sheet of verses, I made a poor waka on the topic "recalling the past beneath the moon":

193	tsuki wa shiru ya	Is the moon aware
	kono iso narete	I have known this rocky strand
	nanasoji ni	for seventy years
	mitsu yotsu made no	and seven with their salty
	aki no shiokaze	autumn breezes off the sea?

Zuiun'an subtemple is higher than the pagoda of Seikenji temple proper.[130] Leaning on my staff, I climbed up and, filled with enthusiasm from the day's events, I composed this haikai waka:

194	mite mo mite mo	Though I look and look
	nao mata mite mo	and then look once more,
	nami no ue no	it sleeps alone
	kumo o katashiku	on clouds spread upon the waves—
	akatsuki no tera	the temple before dawn.[131]

A man from Kyoto named Unpa built a hut near Shōkaian subtemple here after having made a vow in the capital to do so, and he lived in it for ten years and more.[132] He has long since passed away, and the hut has fallen to ruin:

195	musubi oku	The cottage of grass
	kiyomigaiso no	that he fashioned for himself
	kusa no io	at Kiyomi Strand
	arasu ya nami o	has gone to ruin—
	katami naruran	will these billows be his keepsake?

Shōkō too came down to Suruga years ago.[133] I invited him to Kiyomi Strand as well and had a boat row us about Mihogasaki.[134] On the return he composed this:

196	tsuki nagara	Under the moonlight
	iku yo no nami o	for how many ages
	kiyomigata	have the waves rolled in
	yosete zo arasu	on Kiyomi Strand
	seki no aragaki	and ravaged the fence at the gate?

He wrote it on a fence post of the old Kiyomi Gate. Now even that has completely rotted away.

197	kakitsukeshi	Even the post
	hashira dani koso	of the rude fence at the gate
	aragaki no	on which he wrote them
	kuchite nokoranu	has rotted away,
	nami no koto no ha	and the wave-like words remain no more.

After this temple was burned all that was left was Lord Tōjiin's image hall. Shōkō prayed before the statue of Kankoku that stood in a dusty corner and, weeping bitter tears, composed this:[135]

198	kiyomigata	Would that the rude fence
	seki no aragaki	of the gate at Kiyomi
	yoru nami o	might send back to the past
	mukashi ni kaese	the waves that come rolling in
	kuni zo sakaen	and see the nation prosper.[136]

He then returned. Shōkō thereafter desired to have a part of the fence made into a box for poem strips, and soon Lord Yoshitada ordered it done and sent off. Shōkō also asked him to include one of his own compositions:

199	tazunetsu to	Tell all in the capital
	miyako ni katare	that you were here—
	kiyomigata	this piece from the rude fence
	kore zo shirushi no	at Kiyomi Strand
	seki no aragaki	will bear witness.

Shōkō had the poem lacquered in *makie* on the lid and treasured it. The constable of Noto now has it, I am told.[137]

Fourth Year of Daiei (1524)

Fujimasu

Fujimasu, a lad of thirteen or fourteen, writes with a truly accomplished hand.[138] At his father's Ichikawa residence, the day after the beginning of the eighth month, we composed a single sheet of verses.[139] Fujimasu as scribe:

200	hayashisomete	Praise the bush clover
	iku soma no hana	growing up like mountain timber,
	hagi no tsuyu	dew on its blossoms.

This was meant as praise of the lad's accomplished hand and correct demeanor, using the poem (from *Man'yōshū*?) that goes "made from bush clover / growing straight as timber / and just beginning to flourish." I believe that verse uses *somakata* to mean bush clover growing widely dispersed and therefore straight and tall.[140]

Sunpu

We returned to Sunpu. A linked-verse session for the visitors from the capital:

201	sasowareba	Were it invited,
	miyako no fuji no	Fuji would bring autumn snow
	aki no yuki	to the capital.

What this means is that if Mount Fuji here could be invited to the capital, there would be snow in the capital in autumn.[141]

Through the middle of the eighth month, the cuckoo sang both night and day, making my mealtimes unbearable:

202	kiku tabi ni	Each time I hear you
	mune warokereba	I feel queasy,
	hototogisu	cuckoo bird,
	hetotogisu to koso	so one really ought to call you
	iu bekarikere	"puke-oo bird" instead.[142]

In the beginning of the ninth month, I rode about four or five chō from here and on the way home fell from my horse. My upper body aches and my right hand is useless:

203	ika ni sen	What am I to do
	mono kakisusamu	without the hand I write with
	te wa okite	to console myself?
	hashi toru koto to	How will I hold my chopsticks and
	shiri nogō koto	how will I wipe my behind?

In a message entrusted to the monks from Shūon'an in Takigi, who were returning with others from the capital:

204	aware naru	How melancholy,
	waga kotozute ya	the message I send to you,
	yamashiro no	that I must cut wood
	takigi korubeki	in Takigi, Yamashiro,
	nanasochi no hate	at my eighth decade's end.[143]

This is to inform them that I expect to die at Shūon'an.

Okitsu

At the end of the tenth month, after a restorative hot brine bath in Okitsu, on request for a hokku on the landscaping of the castle garden, I composed this:

205	miru tabi ni	Each time I see it,
	mekarenu niwa no	I cannot take my eyes
	kikusa kana	from the garden's unwithered flora![144]

Various things happened before the end of the year, but I have omitted them.

Fifth Year of Daiei

1525

A Solo Linked-Verse Sequence

The fifth year of Daiei [1525], beginning of the first month, a solo linked-verse sequence with the first verse by Lord Ryūōmaro:

206   yuki no uchi no   Through the garden
      ume saku niwa no   where plums bloom in lingering snow,
      arashi kana   a gusting wind![1]

207   hatsune no hi to ya   As if to match First Rat Day,
      matsu no uguisu   a warbler's first song in the pines.[2]

                Sōchō

208   aratama no   The New Year has come
      toshi no iku haru   as it will for springs hereafter
      kasumuran   amid the haze.[3]

Composed on request from Anonotsu in Ise:

209   ama obune   Fishing boats in spring,
      haru ya akogi no   rowing out beyond the pines
      ura no matsu   of Akogi Bay.[4]

BOOK ONE

Composed on request from a person in Kai Province:

210 kasumikeri   The surrounding haze—
  haru ya asa mitsu recalling morning's high tide,
  shionoyama   spring at Mount Shio.[5]

At my lodging by the river:[6]

211 sue ya mina   Its current downstream
  kawakami sumeru is clear as its upper reaches—
  haru no mizu   the springtime water.[7]

See note.[8]

Okitsu

At Yokoyama Castle in Okitsu, near Kiyomi Gate:[9]

212 haru no kumo no Spring clouds
  yokoyama shirushi mark the long line of mountains
  nami no ue   above the waves.

At the monthly poetry session of Lord Ōgimachisanjō and his son, Kin'e:[10]

213 hototogisu   The cuckoo!
  makoto o kyō wa In truth it is on this day instead
  hatsune kana   that we hear the "first song."[11]

At my residence by the river:

214 yūsuzumi   In the cool of evening
  mi mo hi mo samushi the water, the day, and I are chilled.
  kawarakaze   River wind.[12]

Long Poem (chōka)

A poem I composed in my leisure and sent to an acquaintance in the capital:

215 minazuki no   The rainfall today
  atsusa o arau that washed away the heat
  kyō no ame   of the Waterless Month[13]

Fifth Year of Daiei (1525)

niwa no ikemizu	filled the pond in my garden,
hachisuba no	and dew now lies
tsuyu wa shiratama	on the lotus leaves like white jewels—
kazukazu no	all the different kinds
utsushi ueoku	of trees and verdant grasses
ki mo kusa mo	I transplanted here
magaki no take mo	and the bamboo by the fence
wakaetsutsu	begin to revive,
kokoroyoge naru	the gladdening leaves
sueha ni mo	at the tips of their branches
oi o nobaete	easing the burdens of age—
toridori ni	but though my cottage
miru wa kotonaru	offers me so rich a choice
yado nagara	of changing vistas,
omou koto to wa	the thoughts that come to mind the most
meshi oashi	are of food, and funds,
nigori kukon mo	and cloudy cups of sake
maremare ni	I sip so seldom—
sasuga ni hito no	to be sure, I have people
ideiri wa	coming and going
tayuru hi mo naku	day after day without fail
miekuredo	to pay me visits
nani motekoneba	but they bring nothing with them,
motenasazu	naught have I to give,
mune nomi sumite	so sated just in spirit
tsurezure wa	I can only ask
oncha o dani to	"Will you take at least some tea?"
iu bakari	meager as that is—
mukashigatari no	trading tales about the past
oi no tomo	with a friend of years,
kataneburi shite	I feel myself start to nod
hatehate wa	and then in the end
tachisaru o sae	I am not even aware
shirazariki	he has departed—
koko ni shimeoku	the thatched-roof cottage
waga io wa	that I am keeping here
suruga no kō no	stands by the capital
katawara ni	of Suruga Province—
takeami kakuru	outside the window that is
madogoshi no	latticed with bamboo,
fuji no keburi wa	smoke from the smudge fires rises
kayaribi no	with Mount Fuji's
yūgao shiroki	over fences blooming white

kakitsuzuki	with "evening faces"—
koiegachi naru	and throughout the neighborhood
atari ni te	chock-a-block with huts,[14]
ichime akibito	the merchants and market maids
sariaezu	raise their voices:
na sōrō imo sōrō	"Greens and potatoes for sale!
nasubi sōrō	I've eggplants for sale!
shirofuri sōrō to	Melons for sale! White melons!"
koegoe ni	one after the next
kado wa tōredo	passing in front of my gate,
itsu to naku	but since my fortunes
waga kyō asu no	(shifting as the shallows
asukagawa	of Tomorrow River
kawarubeki se mo	that vary from day to day)
taenureba	have forborne to flow,
mimi ni nomi fure	I can but sit and listen
sugosu natsu kana	and let summer pass me by.[15]

I am sure you have a good idea of my country cottage from what I have written. How are things in the capital? Here in the country this summer, heavy rain has been pouring down from morning till night. I have not been able to poke my head outside, and there has been no way even to reach my neighbors:[16]

216
izuku mo ka	Is it so elsewhere?
koshiba sumi tae	kindling and charcoal used up,
cha sake tae	tea, sake used up,
miso shio shiranu	miso and salt unseen,
ame no tsurezure	time hanging heavy in the rain.[17]

The cuckoo has been singing constantly through the seventh month until nearly the Festival of the Dead.[18] On the thirteenth:

217
asu wa komu	Leave me and go
kako shōryō ni	instead to guide the souls
tachikaware	that come on the morrow,
matsuran shide no	cuckoo waiting
yamahototogisu	on the Mountain of the Dead![19]

The Anniversary of Sōgi's Death

Seventh month, twenty-ninth day. A sequence for the anniversary of Sōgi's death. The hokku:

Fifth Year of Daiei (1525)

218	nokoshitsuru yo ya wa wasururu aki no tsuki	Could we ever forget the night he left us behind? The autumn moon.[20]
	Jōki[21]	
219	asagao ni sake inishie no yume	May you flower with the morning glories, Oh dream of days now fled![22]
	Sōchō	

In addition:

220	hitori shite omou kai naki itonami ni kimi o zo kyō wa koikurashinuru	The rituals were so lacking when performed alone, and I spent the day wishing you could have been here with me.

I appended this to the linked-verse sheets and sent them to Sōseki.[23]

The First Anniversary of the Death of Toyohara Muneaki

For the first anniversary of the death of Toyohara Utanokami Muneaki:[24]

221	kozo no kyō tsukihi kakitsuru hitofude no kore o kagiri to omoikeru kana	I know that the letter last year bearing today's date would be his last.[25]
222	itsu ka mimu miyako no kaze no tsute goto ni koishi yukashi no utsunoyama fumi	Will I ever see another of those wind-borne letters from the capital, each expressing longing for Utsunoyama mountain?
223	tamayura mo kakaru to ya iwan sue no tsuyu hakana no hagi no moto no shizuku ya	Do they linger like this for even a brief moment, dew on leaf tips and evanescent drops on stems of bush clover?[26]
224	koishisa mo kagiri arikeri	There is no one I long for more than him,

	narenarete	of all of those
	naki ga ōku no	to whom I was once close
	aru ga naka ni	and who are now gone from me.[27]

225	omoi dani	How I wish for even
	tayuru ma mo ga na	a brief respite from my longing!
	aki no tsuyu	Ever since I heard
	kieshi to kikite	that he vanished like autumn dew,
	hiru yo nakereba	my tears have never dried.[28]

226	au tabi ni	Every visitor
	sayo no nakayama	to Sayo no nakayama
	nakadachi mo	carried back to him
	tada aramashi no	my invitation,
	fuji no shirayuki	but Fuji's snow he never saw.[29]

227	karisome mo	Our painful parting,
	oshimishi hina no	which I took to be but brief
	nagori koso	when I left for home,
	katami ni nagaki	has proven now to be
	wakare narikere	an eternal separation.[30]

228	morotomo ni	The words he spoke
	oizu shinazu no	about eternal youth
	koto no ha wa	for the both of us
	tsune naranu yo no	were naught but consolation
	susabi to zo omou	in an evanescent world.[31]

229	kazoureba	Reckoning it up,
	hitotsu otori mo	I find that though a year behind me,
	sakidachite	he passed on before,
	kono kami ni sae	and now he is ahead
	naru yo narikeri	in the world to come.[32]

230	hakanashi ya	How fleeting it was,
	shirabe no michi no	the greatness of his fame
	tagui naku	in the way of music,
	kikoe agekemu	which had risen to such heights
	na koso takakere	that no one could approach it.

Toyohara Muneaki and I exchanged letters until we were both nearly eighty, and whether I was in the provinces or the capital, there was never a day that I did not think of him. Last autumn I sent a letter to the capital and on this day one year ago, the nineteenth of the eighth month, he answered from his deathbed,

Fifth Year of Daiei (1525)

speaking of how remarkably fortunate it was that the letter reached him before he died. The amanuensis wrote that he passed away the next day, the twentieth.

Muneaki was a giant in his field; he was tutor to the emperor, and his music echoed in the empyrean. He also presented a sequence of a thousand Japanese poems for imperial delectation.[33] The waka he composed at various sessions earned him a reputation for elegant poetry. He was a man of deep feeling and showed no little consideration even toward me. Were I now in Kyoto, I would have solicited poems of mourning from his friends and presented them in his memory today. There must be many others who feel the same. Lord Sanetaka too is no doubt holding a single-round poetry sequence today. I can only imagine it. I composed the above ten waka on rising before dawn simply to express my feeling for Muneaki. Lord Ōgimachisanjō Sanemochi is in residence in this province, and so I asked him for ten poems as well, which I append here:

Ōgimachisanjō Sanemochi's Memorial Poems for Toyohara Muneaki

> I read the ten poems Sōchō composed on the first anniversary of the death of Muneaki for the repose of his spirit, and I too felt deep sorrow. Sōchō honored me with a request for poems as well, and I therefore made these poor attempts:

231 oguruma no
    meguru ya hayaki
       kozo no aki no
    kyō no wakare o
    omoiizuru ni

How quickly the year
seems to have gone round,
    like a little wheel,
when I realize he passed away
upon this day last autumn.[34]

232 ima wa tada
    miyako no kaze no
       tsute to te mo
    nao naozari ni
    kiki ya nasuran

Now that he is gone,
when other letters come wind-borne
    from the capital,
one is apt to give them
only scant regard.[35]

233 saku hagi no
    moto no shizuku ya
       sue no tsuyu to
    kieshi nagori mo
    nokoru koto no ha

Water drops on stems
of blossoming bush clover
    or dew on leaf-tips—
like those, the leaf-like words
left behind by one departed.[36]

234 oriori wa
    ware mo narekite

Through the passing years
we grow accustomed to each other,

      karakoromo
    haru iku aki no
      aware souran

      as to a robe of Chinese cut—
for how many springs and autumns
will my feelings further deepen?[37]

235   omokage wa
    mazu tachikiete
      fuetake no
    ne nomi kumoi ni
    nao nokoruran

    Though he has departed,
leaving not a trace behind,
    the music
of his bamboo flute continues
to resound above the clouds.[38]

236   tsuyu fukami
    kusa no kage ni mo
      ukehiku ya
    koto no ha goto no
    kyō no tamuke ni

    So deep is the dew
of my tears, he may not hear
    in the grassy shade
each of the leaf-like words
of my parting prayer today.[39]

237   yoshi ya ima
    yume to narite mo
      utsunoyama
    utsutsu ni nokoru
    omokage mo ga na

    Well then, so be it—
if he must now become a dream,
    would that his image
might here remain as real for us
as Reality Mountain![40]

238   aki no yo no
    nagaki yamiji mo
      mayowaji na
    kotoba no tama no
    kazu no hikari ni

    Do not lose your way
on the dark and distant road
    in the long autumn night—
be guided by the light
of your many jewel-like verses!

239   yume narade
    ima wa ika de ka
      mizukuki no
    ato ya mi ni sou
    katami naramashi

    If not in a dream
there is no way to see him,
    but the traces
of his brush
will linger and remind.[41]

240   nochiseyama
    shiite nochi tou
      koto no ha no
    iro ni ya fukaki
    nasake miyuramu

    In the deep color
of your leaf-like words
    hoping against hope to meet again
like the mountain of that name,
one sees your deep feelings for him.[42]

241   hito no ue ni
    ii wa kawasedo
      tare mo mata
    asu o tanomanu
    ukiyo kanashi mo

    Though you and I exchange
these poems about another's death,
    how sad that none of us
may count upon tomorrow
in this melancholy world![43]

Fifth Year of Daiei (1525)

Toyohara Muneaki's Posthumous Letter

Your letter of the third of the last month arrived today, the nineteenth.[44] It was my cherished desire that I might hear from you again.

I am gratified to know that you had no trouble en route and arrived in Suruga safely.[45] I rejoice to hear that Lord Ujichika's condition is improving.

I received the goose-skin paper you promised.[46] This is another example of your great consideration, and I cannot find words to do it justice. I am deeply obliged.

On the fifteenth of last month I chanced to be stricken with the flux, and I believe this day will be my last. That your letter arrived in time was the result of our remarkable bond over these many years. It is a marvel beyond comprehension. How I wish I could live long enough to see you again! As I am completely bedridden, I have been forced against my will to ask someone to write this for me.

My sincerest regards,
Muneaki [seal]

Eighth month, nineteenth day
With respect, to the Master of Brushwood Cottage

That was his answer. He passed away the following day.

Sanjōnishi Sanetaka's Memorial Poems for Toyohara Muneaki

Ten poems by Lord Sanetaka arrived on the twelfth of the eleventh month for the first anniversary of the death of Muneaki. I include them here as well:[47]

Ten poems in mourning for Lord Muneaki (each beginning with a syllable of the title of the *Lotus Sutra*).[48]

242	me no mae ni
	kienu omokage
	  mono iwaba
	taezu mukashi no
	koto ya kawasan
		If his image
		that remains before my eyes
		  had the power of speech,
		we would both talk on and on,
		trading memories of the past!

243	utsusemi no
	yo no uki fushi ya
	  itotake no
	koe o shiru chō
	hito mo taeyuku
		How sad a time
		in a world empty
		  as a cicada's shell,
		now that he who knew the music
		of the pipes and strings is gone.[49]

BOOK ONE

244 hokekyō ni
chigiri musuberu
　　kai arite
kanarazu nagaki
yami o izuran

It was well
he placed his trust
　　in the *Lotus Sutra*,
for he is certain to emerge
from the long darkness.[50]

245 uchinasu ni
hana o moyōsu
　　shirabe o ba
te ni makaseteshi
tsuzumi to zo shiru

Here is the drum
on which he performed
　　so skillfully the song
that when played before the flower buds
is said to make them blossom.[51]

246 reijin no
naka ni idetatsu
　　oriori mo
mono ni magirenu
sugata narishi o

Even at the times
when he appeared with the rest
　　of the musicians,
he could never be confused
with any of the others.

247 mutsumaji to
hedatenu mono ni
　　mizukaki no
hisashiku nareshi
nagori o zo omou

Our friendship
was ever close and cordial,
　　and his absence now,
long as the shrine's sacred fence,
gives rise to sad reflections.[52]

248 kyō wakare
asu wa to tanomu
　　kono yo dani
nagori wa hito ni
kanashikarazu ya

Even in this life,
when those who part one day
　　may meet again the next,
is it not sorrowful
to take leave of another?

249 kimi ni tsutae
hito ni oshiete
　　fuetake no
michi no kiwame wa
tada hitori nomi

Tell it to our lord
and teach it to the others—
　　there was only one
who reached perfection
in the way of the bamboo flute.

250 yayoya mate
to bakari dani mo
　　kikaseba ya
oi wa okururu
hodo araji mi ni

Wait a moment!
I wish he would heed
　　that plea at least,
for I am far too old
to have another die before me.

251 utsutsu aru
mono to wa nani o
　　omoigawa

Is there anything
that has true reality?
　　Look upon

Fifth Year of Daiei (1525)

    miyo ya kieyuku   the River of Longing,
    mizu no utakata   and watch the bubbles disappear.[53]

Lord Sanetaka kindly sent the above verses for the first anniversary of Muneaki's death together with the "Since I" hymn written in his own hand.[54] His postscript reads:

> This hymn of praise is the essence of the sutra from which it comes, and it expresses the profound wish of all Buddhas who manifest themselves in this world. Today on the first anniversary of the death of the late Lord Muneaki, I wiped away my tears of old age and inked my unskilled brush. I hope for the attainment of Buddhahood by the spirit of the deceased and for commensurate benefit for all throughout the universe.
>
>   Fifth year of Daiei [1525],
>   eighth month, twentieth day.
>   Priest Gyōkū[55]

252   shitau zo yo   How I yearn for it,
       tsuki wa hatsuka no   the faint twentieth-day moon
          kumogakure   now hidden in the clouds,
       tsune ni aru sora to   although one thinks of it
       omou mono kara   as always in the sky.[56]

Verses Composed in Sunpu

In the autumn, on having planted bush clover and reeds beneath the eaves of my travel lodging:

253   kokoro kara   This is an evening
       kurabe kurushiki   when it is hard to choose
          yūbe kana   in my heart between them!
       hagi ogi uete   Wind and dew in the bush clover
       kaze to tsuyu to ni   and in the reeds I planted.[57]

I broke off a branch of bush clover and sent it to someone with this:

254   teru tsuki mo   The shining moon
       yoru no nishiki no   wove a long brocade by night
          hagi ga hana   of bush clover blossoms—
       orihae kyō ya   I broke off a branch, and today you too
       tsuyu mo miyuran   may see it cloaked with dew.

On hearing the chirping in the garden of bell crickets, perhaps those I caught and then released here last year:

255
    aware koso   How moving the thought—
    tazune hanachishi   could they be the ones that I caught
    sore ka aranu   and then released?
    susuki ga moto no   In the pampas grass
    suzumushi no koe   the chirping of bell crickets.[58]

They chirped for five or six nights, then disappeared. Thereafter the pine crickets started in:

256
    tachikawari   In the others' place
    otoranu mono ya   does it move one any less?
    kore naranu   Once the singing
    suzumushi no ne ni   of the bell crickets; now the chirping
    matsumushi no koe   of the pine crickets instead.

Osada Chikashige

Osada Shirōtarō Chikashige had been ill for years and become unsound of mind, making service as a samurai impossible. After being deprived of his stipend, he recovered his health but was too mortified to show himself in public. As the months went by with no one to speak a word in his behalf he grew desperate. He sold everything, even his long and short swords, to pay priests for purification rites or to buy food for the next meal. His dwelling might have been named "Hunger and Cold." Finally he sent his wife and children away and spent his days alone. He could not pay back old debts and was constantly pressed by his creditors but could do nothing. How miserable he must have been!

On the evening of the seventeenth of this month, he went to the nearby Kannon temple, then returned and drank water to purify himself. He must not have owned even a spare piece of rope, for they say he put his neck into the hearth-hook cord, made it fast to a roof beam, then let go. At about ten the next morning a maid found his body and told the neighbors. He must have been suffering terribly to do such a thing. He had eaten nothing morning or evening for five days—how sad to think that he must have been preparing to die.

Everyone knows it is natural for samurai to run one another through in a sudden argument or be cut down on the field of battle. "The tiger dies and leaves its pelt; a man dies and leaves his name."[59] His was a most unnatural death.

Fifth Year of Daiei (1525)

To console his spirit I made six poems, beginning each with a character from the Holy Name and ending each with all six. There was nothing else I could do to express my sympathy.[60]

257	nagori naku tsuyu no inochi no kakedokoro wakaruru hate wa namu amida butsu	His dew-like life passed, leaving not a trace behind when he hanged himself— now parted, we have but faith in Amida.
258	mube mo koso omoiirikeme tomokakumo kanawanu hate no namu amida butsu	How right he was to have made that choice when everything was lost, and there was nothing left but faith in Amida.
259	asagao no tsuyu no inochi no aki o hete kaze o mo matazu namu amida butsu	Not even waiting for the wind at autumn's end he gave up his life, dew on a morning glory, his faith in Amida.
260	mitsusegawa wataru mizao ni kake yukan minaregoromo mo namu amida butsu	He hangs his well-worn robe on the pole that propels his boat across Mitsuse River, all his faith in Amida.[61]
261	tarachine no kokoro ya mata mo tachikaeri aware kakubeki namu amida butsu	How his loving parent must be filled with grief at this reversal of fate— one must feel for him, putting faith in Amida.[62]
262	fureba kaku uki koto o shi mo mitsu kikitsu inochi nagasa no namu amida butsu	The older one grows, the more melancholy things one sees and hears— the longer one lives, the more faith in Amida.

His father, Saitō Kaganokami Yasumoto, is an old friend of mine, and I owe him a great debt.[63] In my deep regret at having lived to see this, I composed the following:

263 tare to naki   If the like
   ochikatabito no   were to happen
    ue ni te mo   even to a stranger
   kakaru o kikeba   in a distant place,
   nagekazarameya   how could one not but lament?

Also, among my poor verses from the last eight or nine years:

264 kaku omou to wa   No one else knows that
   hito wa shiraji na   I feel the way I do.

265   taga uki mo   I would exchange it
   mi zo kau bakari   for anyone else's,
    kanashiki ni   so great is my sadness.[64]

On the fourth of the ninth month a terrible typhoon blew up, and I spent all night frightened out of my aged wits. I composed this about the dew in the garden the next morning:

266   hagi ga hana   The bush clover lies
   to fushi kaku fushi   bent over this way and that
    oi ga mi no   like my old body—
   nowaki seshi yo no   after a storm in the night,
   hana no asatsuyu   morning dew on the blossoms.

Selling 'Genji monogatari'

To contribute to the reconstruction of the Sanmon gate of Daitokuji, I sold this and that, though nothing special, and finally decided to part with the copy of *Genji monogatari* I had used over the years:[65]

267   kyō yori wa   What further changes
   nani ni kawaramu   will occur from this day forth?
    asukagawa   White waves of old age
   kono se o hate no   at the end of the shallows
   oi no shiranami   of Tomorrow River.[66]

To the person to whom I let the book go:

268   miru tabi no   Every time
   tsuyu okisoe yo   you take it up let teardrops fall
    tsurezure no   on its leaf-like words,

Fifth Year of Daiei (1525)

nagusamegusa no	grasses that beguiled me
koto no ha goto ni	when time hung heavy on my hands.

A poem someone sent me about my request to break off a branch of bush clover:

269
    aki kaze no   Would I begrudge you
    fukimidasuran   one insensible bough
      itohagi no   of slender bush clover
    kokoro naki eda mo   that will be blown into disorder
    oshimi ya wa suru   by the autumn wind?

My reply:

270
    aki kaze wa   Though the autumn wind
    fukimidasu to mo   may blow the clover branches,
      itohagi o   it is perhaps he who asked
    orite to iu ya   that one be broken off
    kokoro nakaramu   who is the more insensitive.[67]

Travel Lodgings in Sunpu

I had a *maki* evergreen of about ten feet in height dug up and brought from about five leagues away for my garden. I composed this for a dedicatory sequence:

271
    maki no ha wa   Evergreen needles
    miyama no kiri no   in the mist deep in the mountains
      asato kana   outside the door at morning![68]

Those at the session each brought a dish of food and a flask of sake, and we made merry.

Okitsu Hikokurō sent me this poem he composed while at Kiyomi Gate:[69]

272
    kiyomigata   At Kiyomi Strand,
    akemaku oshiki   where one regrets the end of night,
      nami no ue ni   keep the moon
    tsuki no sekimore   from slipping away over the waves,
    sue no shirakumo   white clouds in the distance![70]

Though it was no reply, I sent him this:

273	kiyomigata	Your words of hope
	sekimoru tsuki no	that the moon be kept from passing
	koto no ha no	over Kiyomi Strand
	nagame o yosuru	were carried to me here
	ochi no shiranami	on white waves from far away.

Longevity Celebration

On the last day of the ninth month this autumn, deploring my longevity, I made a poem on the topic of being seventy-eight at the end of the ninth month:[71]

274	kyōgoto no	Once again today
	nagatsuki o shi mo	the ninth month passes
	sakidatsuru	while this old one remains—
	oi ni ika naru	how many more years will roll round,
	shizu no odamaki	like a spool of flaxen thread?[72]

Matching that were poems by Ōgimachisanjō Sanemochi, his son Kin'e, Imagawa Ujichika, Sekiguchi Ujikane, Ohara Chikataka, Yui Hōgo, and Shueki:[73]

275	kurikaeshi	Around and around,
	shizu no odamaki	like a spool of flaxen thread,
	nagatsuki ya	will roll the ninth month!
	iku tabi kyō ni	Surely you will greet this day
	awan to suran	on many more occasions!
	Sanemochi	

276	oiraku no	At the dwelling
	kaku chō yado wa	where you have reached venerable age,
	nagatsuki ya	the ninth month passes!
	kyō iku kaeri	Many more such days will roll round,
	shizu no odamaki	like a spool of flaxen thread.
	Kin'e	

277	chitose hemu	Today ends autumn,
	yasoji wa koen	and soon you will pass eighty
	kyō no aki	on your way to a thousand,
	kurikaeshi kurikaeshi	this day rolling round and round,
	shizu no odamaki	like a spool of flaxen thread.
	Ujichika	

Fifth Year of Daiei (1525)

278   sara ni hen
       oi ga chitose no
          nagatsuki no
       kyō no kururu wa
       oshimazarikeri

You will see many more
during your thousand-year life,
and so we do not
begrudge the passing
of this last day of the ninth month.

            Ujikane

279   iku tose no
       nagatsuki no kyō o
          sakidatete
       oi senu yado no
       shiragiku no hana

White asters
beside a dwelling that never ages,
however many times
it sees this day go by
at the end of the ninth month.[74]

            Chikataka

280   morotomo ni
       oi o zo chigiru
          kyōgoto no
       nagatsuki mo nao
       yukusue no aki

I make a vow
that we shall grow old together,
each year on this day
in the ninth month finding us
still far from our final autumn.

            Hōgo

281   oiraku no
       nao yukusue mo
          nagatsuki no
       kyō ni kurete mo
       shizu no odamaki

It is yet far off,
the end of your long journey,
and though the ninth month
ends today, more will roll around,
like a spool of flaxen thread.

            Shueki

Okitsu Hikokurō requested the poem strips. I sent them, thinking they would make good models for poetic composition. They were so elegant I was moved to compose another:

282   kyō ni kurete
       iku aki oi no
          nagatsuki ya
       yukusue mo nao
       shizu no odamaki

Today autumn passes—
how many more ninth months
remain for this old one?
Before the end more will roll around,
like a spool of flaxen thread.

At the beginning of winter, Hikokurō sent me a goose. I included this in my reply to his appended letter:

283	oto ni nomi	Though I only heard
	hatsukarigane no	the calls of the first goose
	akikaze no	upon the first autumn wind,
	tsubasa o kawasu	I behold one now with both wings bound
	kaminazuki kana	in the tenth month![75]

Ujichika was good enough to send a sprig of blossoming white gentians, with this poem attached:

284	aru ga naka ni	Unlike all the rest,
	kono hitoeda no	how does it happen
	ika ni shite	that this solitary bough
	yuki matsu hana no	blossoms with flowers tinted
	iro ni sakuramu	as if waiting for the snow?

My humble reply:

285	kazukazu ni	How could my eye stray
	me ya wa utsuramu	to any of the others?
	aru ga naka ni	Unlike all the rest,
	mare naru hana wa	this sprig is seen as seldom
	udonge ni shite	as the *udonge* blossom.[76]

A Visit from Nasu Suketarō

Nasu Suketarō of Shimotsuke Province, now a lay monk, stopped by to see the garden of my cottage.[77] He told me about his plans for a pilgrimage to Mount Kōya and asked me for a poem to take with him.[78] A monk in his company told me that Suketarō was mourning the death in battle of a youth to whom he had been strongly attached, and in his unabated grief he wished to console the young man's spirit.[79] I was moved to compose this:

286	akatsuki o	You journey there
	ika ni chigirite	hoping for enlightenment
	tazunuran	before the dawn
	takano no oku ni	under the late-night moon
	ariake no tsuki	in the depths of Mount Kōya.[80]

They immediately said they must write the poem on the grave marker.

Fifth Year of Daiei (1525)

A Verse in Memory of Miura Yatarō

In the tenth month, Miura Yatarō, a man of excellent conduct, fell ill with the flux and died after some days.[81] He had been attached to young Saitō Shirō, and I sent this along with a sprig of asters, just then in bloom, to assuage Shirō's grief:[82]

287	yoso ni dani	Even when another
	kiku no ue no tsuyu	hears the news, dew falls
	ika bakari	upon the asters,
	kakaran kimi ga	and so I can imagine
	sode o shi zo omou	how much lies on your sleeves.

Miscellaneous Verses

Awake in the night, I heard geese calling as they flew overhead. I composed this, thinking of the old poem "A single cry / of the cuckoo / in the dawn twilight / as it passes . . . / through this melancholy world":[83]

288	akatsuki no	In the dawn twilight
	arashi ni musebu	the birds fly by with choked cries
	tobutori no	in the gusting wind,
	koe shidoro nari	their voices in disorder.
	izuchi otsuran	Wither will they come to earth?

Yui Mimasakanokami (whose religious name is Hōgo) sent me a bundle of Fuji silk floss as wadding for a paper robe. I sent this off in thanks:[84]

289	naninani ni	Fuji always wears
	tokaku suruga no	a silken cap in Suruga,
	fuji wata no	where one lacks nothing,
	taenu susono ni	but even so I had no cap myself
	yuki wa furitsutsu	for snow falling on foothill fields.[85]

Hōgo's reply:

290	yuki wa tada	The silken cap
	kesa furu fuji no	that Fuji wears is only snow
	watabōshi	that fell this morning—
	taenu susono mo	soon you too will wear one
	shibashi matanan	down in those foothill fields.[86]

The Anniversary of the Death of Sōchō's Father

On the anniversary of my father's death, I held no formal observance:[87]

291 toshidoshi ni Year after year
  kyō no namida no only the gem-like teardrops
   tama nomi wa I shed on this day
  nani no hikari mo have served as my offering,
  naki tamuke kana without a spark of luster.[88]

Having suffered recently from the flux, I wrote this for amusement:

292 omowazu mo Before I knew it,
  hitatare o koso I "donned a warrior's robe"
   kitarikere and have the runs.
  na o ba kusoichi Would the name "Kusoichi"
  komeru to iwanu put an end to laying waste?[89]

In my leisure I spent a whole day chatting with Shiki Suruganokami Yasumune, head priest of the main shrine here.[90] He spoke to me of the building projects and votive prayers through which generations of constables have shown their reverence for the shrine. I sent this poem in a letter to him afterward, as he seemed to have a poetic bent:

293 ato tareshi I was awed to hear
  shizuhatayama no your words illuminate
   sono kami no the history of the god
  michi no kumanaku of Shizuhatayama
  kiku mo kashikoshi who manifests the One Law.[91]

Ujiteru's Coming of Age Ceremony

On the twelfth of the eleventh month, Lord Ryūōmaro's coming-of-age ceremony was held. He took the name Gorō Ujiteru.[92] The observations were of surpassing grandeur. On the twenty-fifth, a votive linked-verse session was held in celebration:

294 shimo tōshi Long yet till frost
  hatsumotoyui no lies on the hair newly tied
   wakamidori with a cord of fresh young green.[93]

Fifth Year of Daiei (1525)

I sent Ujiteru five books of lecture notes and eight sheets of esoteric oral teachings on *Kokinshū*. I could not but feel embarrassed by their unreliability, and when Ujiteru has passed his twentieth year and become deeply versed in the way of poetry he may see for himself that my notes have no value and discard them. If that occurs, I think he ought to consign them to the flames.

295	asakeredo	Though it be but slight,
	kikishi bakari o	what I received I bequeath
	kimi wa kore	to you, my lord,
	waga ie no michi ni	that it may be handed down
	tsutaesoenan	and further enrich your house.

The late Sōgi pursued the way of poetry with great application and served as tutor to various aristocratic houses. In particular he is said to have conferred the secret traditions individually on their excellencies the Konoe and on Lord Sanetaka.[94] I lived with him, but for years showed no perseverance and understood not a single page. Finally I acquired a little familiarity with the *Kokinshū* anthology, but only in the most general way, hearing Sōgi lecture on it in the company of Jibukyō Hōgan Taijin of Shōren'in.[95]

I had been at odds with someone, but as time passed we were reconciled. On the tenth of the twelfth month, we took part in a renga session together. My hokku:

296	kaze ya haru	Springtime in the wind—
	furutoshi ni tokuru	ice that melts away
	kōri kana	with the old year![96]

This was based on the verse "the water / I once cupped in my hands / wetting both my sleeves."[97]

At Hasedō, a branch temple for the worship of Hasedera Kannon, someone's carelessness with a hearth fire nearly caused a conflagration, but the flames were extinguished in time.[98] In their gratitude for their good fortune, they held a votive linked-verse session and asked me for the hokku:

297	uzumibi no	The water freezes
	ikemizu kōru	in a pond of smoldering embers
	ashita kana	in the morning![99]

This was based on the line "The pit of fire would turn into a pool."[100]

The former abbot of Kenchōji is in Sunpu to see out the year. Perhaps to take advantage of this good fortune, Asahina Tokishige held a session of linked Japanese and Chinese verse:[101]

298 katae sakite   One branch blooms
     katae haru made   while another waits for spring—
     ume no hana   the plum blossoms.

299 yuki kiete   The snow melts
     nao rōten   but still a wintery sky.
                            Abbot of Chōrakuji, affilitated with Kenchōji[102]

300 ōji wazuka ni   A young bush warbler
     kataru o manabu   tries a tentative note.
                            Abbot of Yōtokuji, affilitated with Tenryūji[103]

I composed the hokku in lieu of Gorō Ujiteru.

The priest Sōseki (Gessonsai) sent me a letter that included a waka. One of its seven-syllable lines was missing two syllables. I sent him this:

301 miyako ni wa   In the capital
     misomoji amari   it seems that there are poems
     hitomoji no   where the usual
     futamoji taranu   thirty syllables plus one
     uta mo arikeri   are seen as two too many!

The paperer Saburōgorō lives near the intersection of Ayanokōji and Muromachi Streets, on the north side.[104] I sent him inquiries from time to time concerning an order of mine, but he would not return the finished work. When I returned to Suruga, he wrote that he had not contacted me because of the outstanding balance. I sent him the remainder with:

302 atsurae no   Herewith is the rest
     kagiri nobosetsu   of the money for the work;
     kudasaren   will you send it down?
     saburōgorō   Saburōgorō, the keeper
     tema no sekimori   of payments at Hindrance Gate.[105]

Fifth Year of Daiei (1525)

The Death of Nakamikado Nobutane

Nobutane, of the First Rank at court, died on the seventeenth of the eleventh month. I learned of it from a messenger to Suruga. I was indebted to him day and night while in Kyoto. For seven days I offered tea, hot water, and incense.

On the seventeenth of the intercalary eleventh month, the first monthly anniversary of his death, I was shown his death poem:

303	higashi naru	I expect to meet
	hito o mo nishi ni	again in the Western Paradise
	aimin to	with the one in the east,
	saran wakare mo	and so despite this fated parting
	sue wa tanomoshi	I place my faith in the future.[106]

I composed this verse and sent it:

304	omoiaezu	With no warning,
	aware uchimiru	I beheld with deep sadness
	uchitsuke no	the marks of his brush,
	sode ni nagaruru	and suddenly teardrops
	mizukuki no ato	began coursing down my sleeves.

A wet nurse affixed this to the head of my letter and sent it back in lieu of a reply:[107]

305	mireba nao	When I beheld
	namida ochisou	the marks of your esteemed brush,
	sode no ue	my tears, like yours, fell again
	okidokoro naki	until there was no room
	mizukuki no ato	for more upon my sleeves.

I initiated a one-round waka sequence for the monthly anniversary, each verse to begin with one of the syllables from his death poem. I asked Lord Ōgimachisanjō Sanemochi to select the topics for the thirty-one verses. Two of mine were included, one on "the first dew of autumn" and one on "opening a book and encountering the past":

306	aki no kaze	Like the upper leaves
	ogi no uwaba mo	of the reeds in autumn's wind,
	tabi ni shite	will these sleeves of mine

	sode ni ya tsuyu no	become accustomed to the dew
	naren to suran	as I journey on my way?
307	nochi mo oshi	They will be treasured
	aru ka naki ka no	hereafter as well,
	isonokami	these faint traces of the brush
	yoyo hete kienu	that will not vanish for ages
	fude no omokage	long as Isonokami Shrine's.

The wet nurse saw the verses from the session and in a letter included this:[108]

308	mite nageki	Lamenting when I see them,
	kikite toburau	and mourning when I hear them,
	minahito no	I am moved
	koto no ha shigeki	by the burgeoning leaf-like words
	koto o shi zo omou	you have composed.

A Conversation with Asahina Tokishige

Asahina Shimotsukenokami Tokishige came to visit. We had a pleasant conversation by the hearth about frustrations at year's end, the repayment of loans, the allotment of rice stipends, and the lack of enough of anything, during the course of which I rambled on in my dotage as follows:[109]

Item. Those who borrow money or rice with no prospect of paying it back will be shamed and censured, and even men of substance will soon lose their principles and change completely.

Item. In short, there is nothing like going into business for profit. People who do so never speak of gods or Buddhas, give no thought to the world's prosperity or decline, know nothing of the elegant pursuits of snow, moon, and blossoms, grow distant from friends, reject appeals from their near and dear, and spend every waking moment thinking of making money.[110] But that is how to get on in the world. Note, though, that those with even nominal lands, and monks with temple properties, should not take an interest in business.[111] But note too that sake dealers in the capital, Sakai, the Southern Capital, Sakamoto, and also in this part of the country do very well.[112]

Item. Giving alms to pilgrims each time they come round is benevolent indeed, but in China pilgrims are referred to as "occupationless people" and are not afforded charity. One ought to provide alms for holy services or other pious works, but not incessantly.

Fifth Year of Daiei (1525)

Item. Consider the low-ranking samurai, starving and with no land to call his own. There is no help for him. He obviously cannot part from his wife and children. Their food runs out, and the woman must draw water and the man must gather brushwood.[113] Their children are taken away before their eyes to slave for others. Their bowing and scraping is pitiful. Driven to that pass, those with self-respect may even do away with themselves.[114] Someone said that to such unfortunates one should give a little something. That is the essence of charity. Of course one must give as well to those who beg by the roadside and wait by houses and gates.[115] As the monk Jichin wrote:

309	tare zo kono	Who can he be,
	me o oshinogoi	that hapless one wiping tears
	tateru hito	from his eyes as he stands
	kono yo o wataru	off to the side of the road
	michi no hotori ni	down which others pass through life?[116]

The crux of the verse is the phrase "down which others pass through life."[117] There is also this, from *Kokinshū* I believe:

310	wabibito no	Beneath the tree
	wakite tachiyoru	toward which the forlorn one
	ko no moto wa	made his way
	tanomu kage naku	there can be no shelter,
	momiji chirikeri	for the autumn leaves are fallen.[118]

To none is fate more cruel.

Item. Lion dancers, monkey trainers, bell ringers, bowl beaters and the like have something they can do to make a living.[119] People somehow provide for them, though their need is no greater than that of those I have just mentioned. It is the latter, for whom there is no help at all, who are the world's true unfortunates, even more than lepers and beggars. They are truly wretched.

Item. People who pursue the study of Zen are embarked on a difficult and estimable course. But those who are perfunctory in their Zen practice, even highly placed samurai in the capital and provinces, easily fall into error.

Item. Where today can one find an inspirational teacher of the doctrines of "separate transmission outside the teachings" and "nonverbalization"?[120] Some call today's Zen practitioners a pack of devils, of the lowest guttersnipe sort. Abbots, monks, and novices these days consort with the high and mighty, curry donations from provincial gentry, pursue their austerities only when it suits them, run hither and yon all day, and dally with other practitioners. But who are the masters they practice with themselves? Some say it is far better to repeat the Holy Name. I am more attracted to those who follow a simple and ignorant practice, as I do.[121]

Item. With regard to observances for ancestors and monthly memorial offerings for deceased parents, I do not hold with calling in a head monk and many assistants (with the exception of the Festival of the Dead and the equinoxes).[122] The number each month should be kept small. If there are several memorial days each month, the cost of rice gruel and such for those who attend can lead one into debt before one realizes it.

Item. Acquiring bows, horses, and armor and maintaining good retainers—that is the way of the samurai. But there is no need to run out and buy things for which one has no specific purpose. Constant spending and extravagance must be avoided, I am told.[123]

Return to Brushwood Cottage

I have maintained a place of retirement by Utsunoyama mountain for some time, and I decided to take up residence there on the twenty-sixth of the twelfth month, after having been away five or six years in the capital:[124]

311	toshi no kure no takigi korubeki kadode nomi utsutsu no yama no yado motomu nari	Though I only just left for Takigi, where I planned to cut firewood at year's end, I have taken shelter instead by Reality Mountain.[125]

By "though I only just left," I meant that I had set out for Takigi in Yamashiro only a short time ago.

312	ima yori wa chiyo no takigi mo korinubeshi utsutsu no yama no matsu ni makaseba	From this day onward I must cut my firewood for the ages here, placing my trust in the pines of Reality Mountain.[126]

I repaired the thatched fence, coarse rush blinds, and bamboo flooring of this mountain dwelling and straightaway took up residence. Then on the morning of the twenty-seventh a heavy snow fell, and everything took on a new, fresh look:

Fifth Year of Daiei (1525)

313 waga io wa
    kayaya komogaki
        ashisudare
    suzuro ni yuki o
    motehayasu kana

Here at my cottage
the thatched roof and rice-straw fence
    and blinds made of reeds
all seem somehow to set off
the snow to its advantage!

At this time I wrote ten poems on snow:

314 haruka ni te
    tachikaeri sumu
        kesa shi mo are
    furusatobito wa
    niwa no shirayuki

This morning
I have returned from far away
    to take up residence,
but no village folk have come by
to see the white snow in my garden.[127]

315 tateueshi
    niwa no iwaki ni
        hana sakite
    izuko aru to mo
    mienu yuki kana

It brings blossoms
to the trees and the rocks
    that I put into my garden
and hides the ruder parts
from view—the snow![128]

316 yamazato no
    mitsu no tomo to ya
        kesa no yuki
    kakine no shitodo
    mado no kuretake

These are my three friends
here in this mountain village:
    the snow this morning,
the bunting on the fence,
and the bamboo by my window.[129]

317 yuki fureba
    kakine mo tawa ni
        fuminarashi
    sokohaka to naku
    kayou yamazato

Hidden by snow,
the fence seems to have been
    trampled underfoot—
a mountain village where people
make their way uncertainly.

318 tsuta kaede
    hi no me mo itsu ka
        miyamaji mo
    amari arawa ni
    yuki wa furitsutsu

This mountain path
where the ivy and maples
    blocked even the sun
now seems altogether stark
beneath snow that falls and falls.[130]

319 yo o fukaku
    michi madourashi
        furu yuki ni
    tego no yobisaka
    hito toyomu nari

He seems to have lost
his way in the dead of night.
    In the falling snow
out on Maiden-Calling Slope,
the shouts of someone echo.[131]

BOOK ONE

320	morotomo ni	Together,
	kokorobosoku mo	forlornly,
	kiyuru nari	they disappear—
	kakehi no take no	the snow in the bamboo trough
	yuki no akatsuki	and the dawn light upon it.

321	kasumi tachi	He has set his mind,
	kiyubeki mine no	this aged one, on waiting
	haru o nomi	for the springtime,
	matsu koto ni suru	when the winter snow on the peak
	oi no shirayuki	will disappear in rising haze.

322	yasoji made	This cottage,
	idein koto o	in which I lament having lived
	ureesumu	nearly eighty years,
	yado mo yuki o zo	must likewise be embarrassed
	hazubekarikeru	by the snow that lies upon it.[132]

323	yuki no uchi	Now beneath the snow,
	tsumioku to iu mo	I understand his advice
	ima zo shiru	about stacking it up.
	hitotsukane ni mo	I do not have brushwood left
	taraji tsumagi o	to make a single bundle.

I was recalling the satisfaction with which that great priest wrote, "While stacking brushwood / in the yard of my cottage / ... / how little is this year's end / like others I have seen!" He seems to be saying that people's desires can be satisfied with little.[133]

Already New Year's Eve:

324	aken toshi no	The eve of the day
	kyō no koyoi ya	the New Year begins—
	aratama no	soon I too will know
	kuru to iu hito no	if the things they say are true
	makoto shirubeki	about spirits coming back.[134]

Sixth Year of Daiei   1526

First Calligraphy of the New Year

New Year's morning. First calligraphy:

325   kuru to iu   The night they are said
       koyoi mo akenu   to return has now ended.
           tama no o no   If the cord
       taenaba kesa no   of my life had broken—
       haru no awayuki   light spring snow this morning.[1]

The next morning, I choked on a pepper and lost my breath:

326   nani mo ka mo   For this old man
       torikū oi no   who eats anything and everything,
           sanshō ni   it would be a pity
       musejini to iwan   to be remembered
       na koso oshikere   for choking to death on a pepper!

First month, twenty-eighth day—for Lord Ujiteru's linked-verse session:

327   fuji ya kore   Here is Fuji—
       kasumi no yomo no   Mount Sumeru circled
           kuni no haru   by lands in spring haze.

The verse is also meant to imply Suminoyama.² Lord Ujichika, Ōgimachisanjō Kin'e, and all the dignitaries participated.³

Verses at Asahina Yasumochi's Residence Before Departing

Second month, eighth day. Asahina Yasumochi's residence. I arrived the night before. A single sheet of linked verse to mark my departure for Kansai:

| 328 | nabete haru
itariitaranu
yado mo nashi | Everywhere spring!
There is not a single house
it has yet to reach.⁴ |

An Interview with Lady Kitagawa

On the ninth, after nightfall, I had an audience and celebratory wine with Lady Kitagawa.⁵ She favored me with relaxed conversation on various subjects. She was concerned about matters at home and tears wet her sleeves, which saddened me greatly. She said, "I have explained the situation and know you understand—by all means come back from Kyoto." I replied I would do so soon and presently took my leave. Her generous gifts left me at a loss for words.

Kogawa

Same month, tenth day. A night at my retreat in Mariko, at the foot of Utsunoyama mountain. I arranged for repairs. Set out early on the eleventh for Kogawa, where Hasegawa Motonaga had requested a thousand-verse session.⁶ As I could hardly refuse, we began on the thirteenth. Yasumochi accompanied us there. Three days for the thousand verses. My hokku:

| 329 | matsu no ha wa
hana zo mitsu shio
yamazakura | Pine needles
enhance the blossoms in the rising tide
of mountain cherries.⁷ |

It was such a pleasant gathering that I completely lost the unease that I had felt in this province until now.⁸ Two days later:

| 330 | tsubame tobu
ame honokeburu
yanagi kana | Slightly misty
in the rain through which swallows fly—
budding willow trees! |

Sixth Year of Daiei (1526)

| 331 | yuku to ku to
izuko mo kari no
nagori kana | Those coming and going
part no more permanently
than do the geese!⁹ |

I thought of this as a farewell session.

On the twentieth of the same month, as we were about to leave Kogawa, Yasumochi took me by the sleeve and recited this poem:

| 332 | tachiwakare
ima yori nochi wa
tarachine no
oya no isame to
tare o omowan | Now that we must part,
whom can I look to
in the days ahead
for the guiding counsel
that a loving parent gives? |

My reply:

| 333 | ōji chichi
kimi made oi ga
nagaiki o
awaremu ni tsukete
odorokarenuru | While reflecting
with esteem on the long lives
of your grandfather,
your father, and then yourself,
I am struck by my own age. |

Kanaya

We said our goodbyes, and I set out for Kanaya at the foot of Sayo no Nakayama, where I spent the night:

| 334 | iku tabi mo
mata koemu to zo
inoru nari
kimi o nezame ni
sayo no nagayama | On every journey
I say a prayer
that I will cross it yet again.
Wakeful thoughts of you—
Sayo no nagayama.¹⁰ |

Here I was thinking of that great man.¹¹ "I say a prayer" is an understatement!

Sayo no Nagayama Mountain

Concerning Nagayama mountain.¹² The great priest Saigyō came to this mountain in the company of an old man. In response to Saigyō's queries, the man explained that the mountain had formerly been called Nagayama [Long Mountain]. When the great priest asked why that was so, he answered that it was perhaps because it was so long that it covered four districts.[13] He added that he believed it also appeared in old poetry.[14] Saigyō thereupon removed his old short-sleeved travel robe and presented it to him. This is recorded in his *Travels in the Eastland*.[15] One therefore concludes that his poem "Long was my allotted span! / Sayo no nakayama" should actually be read "Sayo no nagayama."[16] I heard that the book was in the possession of Kasuya Nakatsukasa Matsutsuna, and so I borrowed it at Kogawa and read it.[17]

Kakegawa

Twenty-first.[18] To Kakegawa, the residence of Yasuyoshi. On the twenty-second, a linked-verse session:

335	hashitaka no	Are they the blossoms
	tokaeru hana ka	to which the molting hawks return,
	yamazakura	the mountain cherries?[19]

Various renovations have been carried out at this castle over the years. The moat is like a deep valley, and the mountain is thick with sweet acorns and oaks. Even from a distance one can tell sparrow hawks would nest on such a peak. I was captivated by the view out over the spring blossoms, which looked just like trailing clouds; I meant my verse to imply that the hawks too return to enjoy the blossoms and to molt.

Constant rain at Kakegawa from the twenty-first, continuing without pause until the first of the third month. We composed linked verse:

336	haru no ame no	Under light spring rains
	nodokeki maki no	among gentle evergreens,
	itaya kana	a planked-roof cottage![20]

Mitsuke

On the third, to the residence of Rokurō in Fuchū.[21] Tomorrow, linked verse. That day is an unlucky one, so this evening I composed this hokku:

337	hana sakite	The flowers are those
	naru chō mitsu no	said to bloom and ripen once
	chitose kana	in three thousand years![22]

This is a reference to today's date and to peach blossoms.

Book Two

Sixth
Year of   1526
Daiei

Suruga

Sixth year of Daiei, in Suruga, on the twenty-eighth of the first month:

338	ama no hara	The field of heaven
	fuji ya kasumi no	and Fuji—Mount Sumeru
	yomo no haru	circled by spring haze.¹

Brushwood Cottage

On the ninth of the second month of the same year, I left Sunpu for Izumi-gaya valley by Utsunoyama mountain, site of my Brushwood Cottage.² I made some improvements, setting in rocks, rerouting a stream, and planting plum trees. While I was about it, I laid down stones to make a fence through the bamboo beside the cedars and pines. Then I shaved three feet off the side of a pine and wrote:

339
    saioku no   I have made a path
  koke no shitamichi   of moss to my grave
      tsukuru nari   at my Brushwood Cottage.
  kyō o waga yo no   I will consider today
  kichinichi ni shite   a lucky day hereafter!³

BOOK TWO

I spent two days at my Brushwood Cottage. Thereafter off to Kogawa, three leagues south in the same province, where I had agreed to compose a thousand-verse sequence with a number of others who had received invitations from Asahina Sakyōnosuke Yasumochi to come down from the provincial capital.

340	matsu no ha wa hana zo mitsu shio yamazakura	Pine needles enhance the blossoms in the rising tide of mountain cherries.[4]

Concerning Sayo no nakayama Mountain

On the twentieth of the same month we all left Yasumochi's, and I set out for Kakegawa in Tōtōmi. I spent a night at the village of Kanaya, on the slope of Sayo no nakayama, then on the twenty-first, I crossed the mountain. In his *Travels in the Eastland*, the great priest Saigyō wrote of passing here in the company of an old man. As they went along, the man related that in the past the mountain had been called Sayo no nagayama, and he believed it appeared as such in old poetry. He spoke mixing fact and fancy. It would therefore appear that Saigyō's poem "Long was my allotted span! / Sayo no nakayama" should be read "nagayama." The account describes a long road running for three leagues through the mountains, with pines continuing for a long while along it, and it relates further that Saigyō presented his travel robe to his aged companion.

Kikugawa river and a village are nearby.[5] The white peaks of Kai Province are barely visible—it is this mountain that lies "between / with no thought for others" in the old poem.[6] Halfway over the mountain is a place called Nissaka.[7] Two leagues further is Kakegawa. I might in passing note this hokku, which I composed here in the tenth month more than ten years ago:

341	kai ga ne wa yuki ni shigururu yamaji kana	There is snow on the Kai peaks and cold rain on the mountain path![8]

This simply means that there is snow on the Kai peaks while here there is cold rain.

We held a linked-verse session at Kakegawa:

342	hashitaka no tokaeru hana ka yamazakura	Are they the blossoms to which the molting hawks return, the mountain cherries?[9]

Sixth Year of Daiei (1526)

This refers to the cherries among the sweet acorns and evergreen oaks that flourish in these mountains year after year. The hawks too enjoy the blossoms.

Mitsuke

Third month, third day. At the residence of Horikoshi Rokurō in Mitsuke, the capital of the same province.[10] His ancestor was Iyonokami Sadayo (called by his priestly name, Ryōshun), who is represented in the *Gyokuyōshū* and *Fūgashū* anthologies.[11]

343	hana sakite	The flowers are those
	naru chō mitsu no	said to bloom and ripen once
	chitose kana	in three thousand years![12]

Hamamatsu

West of Tenryūgawa river, at Hamamatsu Estate, residence of Iio Zenshirō, I composed this:[13]

344	sumire saku	The field where violets bloom
	no wa iku suji no	is crisscrossed by how many
	haru no mizu	springtime rivulets?[14]

Hikuma Field is famous in poetry.[15]

Hamana Bridge

I then went on to the site of Hamana Bridge.[16] It was washed away some years ago, and the rough waves make for a fearful crossing. Since this is my last journey, I felt somehow both anxious and sad.[17]

345	tabitabi no	Hamana Bridge,
	hamana no hashi mo	crossed on many a journey,
	aware nari	now gives rise to sadness
	kyō koso watari	at the thought that today will be
	hate to omoeba	the last time I pass over it.[18]

Zenrokurō Tamekiyo saw us to the crossing—I recited that on taking his sleeve when he was about to return home.[19]

Imahashi

Saw Makino Denzō, in Imahashi, Mikawa Province.[20] I was acquainted with his father and grandfather.[21] Border crossings are difficult, and so he came out with many well-equipped people to greet us.[22] It was impressive. Stayed one day. Kumagai Echigonokami stopped by.[23] Chatted well into the night.

Ina

Stayed in a place called Ina one night with Denzō and Heisaburō of the same family.[24]

Fukōzu

Linked verse at the residence of Matsudaira Ōinosuke:[25]

| 346 | sawa no ue no yama tachimeguru haruta kana | Encircling mountains above marshes, spring rice fields! |

This describes the local scenery.

Kira Tōjō

I paid my first call on Lord Tōjō.[26] Stayed two or three days. Linked verse. I initially refused the hokku, but when pressed, I composed the following:

| 347 | fujinami ya sakari kaeranu haru mogana | Waves of wisteria! Oh, for a spring that did not bloom and then depart![27] |

I meant this in reference to late spring. The following day, I composed this:

| 348 | nami ya yuku haru no kazashi no watatsuumi | The waves go out with spring—floss garlands on the great ocean.[28] |

Sixth Year of Daiei (1526)

Kariya

Kariya. Lodged with Mizuno Izuminokami.[29]

349	kaze ya haru	The spring wind—
	iso no hana saku	flowers blooming on the rocky shore
	okitsunami	and on ocean waves.

Moriyama

Twenty-seventh. Moriyama in Owari Province, residence of Matsudaira Yoichi.[30] A thousand-link sequence. From Kiyosu came Oda Chikuzennokami, Iganokami, others of the same family, and the deputy vice constable, Sakai Settsunokami.[31] It was my first time to compose verse with any of them, and I enjoyed it:

350	azusayumi	Along with catalpa bows,
	hana ni torisoe	the men carry blossoms—
	haruno kana	the springtime field!

Yoichi was granted new land. This in celebration.[32]

Atsuta

A pilgrimage to Atsuta Shrine.[33] All was still around the precinct and neighboring houses, and the wind in the pines lent a feeling of sacredness and awe, bringing to mind the age of the gods. It was the deity of this shrine, they say, who pacified the Eastern Seaboard.[34] The tide rises up to the fence of the shrine buildings. Through the pines I could see Narumi, Hoshizaki, and out over Ise Bay. The view was indescribable.[35]

A linked-verse session at our travel lodgings at Takinobō.[36] Chikuzennokami participated.

351	hototogisu	A waiting cuckoo
	matsu no hagoshi ka	seen through the pine boughs?
	tōhigata	The tidal pool.[37]

At the request of a priest, I composed this:

352	usumomiji	Waiting to turn
	matsu ni atsuta no	pale red, young ivy leaves
	wakaba kana	amid pines at Atsuta!³⁸

I seem to recall the line *koko mo atsuta no* from the *Latter Hundred-Waka Sequence at the Palace of the Retired Emperor Horikawa*.³⁹ Probably a misrecollection in my dotage.⁴⁰

Young men from the shrine, monks, and others went ahead to a pine grove four or five chō from here with various things to eat. From time to time there was singing and dancing to drums and flutes. It was quite merry. An entertainer-priest named Shin'eki was most amusing.⁴¹ All then regretfully parted:

353	okinoite	Sharper than the pain
	mi o yaku yori mo	of flesh seared by fiery coals
	oboyuru wa	is the memory
	kyō no atsuta no	of parting from you today
	miya no wakare zo	at the shrine of Atsuta.⁴²

In jest.

Kiyosu

In Kiyosu, lodged with Settsunokami. The garden was made by damming the moat of the old residence. Ancient willows, wisteria, and mountain roses on the banks, ripples on the pond, ducks wing to wing—it called out to be painted.⁴³

A linked-verse session:

354	saki sakazu	In the summer grove
	ki wa natsu kodachi	blooming and nonblooming trees,
	hana mo nashi	with none in flower.⁴⁴

That is to say that the green shade was better than blossoms. What I meant by *saki sakazu* is that the green shade was the same whether the tree was a blossoming variety or not.

This residence has been the headquarters of the constable for generations.⁴⁵ It is mentioned in Shōgetsuan Shōtetsu's *Travels in the Eastland*.⁴⁶

At the residence of Chikuzennokami:⁴⁷

355	asa kashiwa	In the morning oaks,
	nuru ya shinonome	dewy in the dawn, is it still asleep?
	hototogisu	The cuckoo.⁴⁸

Sixth Year of Daiei (1526)

At lodgings with Chikuzennokami's son Tōzaemon:[49]

356 natsu ya toki   The season, summer—
   uzuki bakari no   early in the fourth month
   yado no fuji   wisteria by the house.[50]

At the residence of Iganokami:[51]

357 unohana wa   Deutzia blossoms
   kiyosuru nami no at Kiyosu—waves breaking
   kakine kana   on the fence![52]

The wording happened by serendipity.
Lodgings with Takahata Magozaemon:[53]

358 kuina naku   The waterrail calls
   ashihara kuraki   in the dark field of reeds
   asato kana   outside the door at morning![54]

Tōzaemon asked me to write one or two poem strips for him. Nothing appropriate occurred to me, but I could not easily refuse, and so:

359 kanete yori   Even the letters
   miyako no tsute no you sent me from time to time
   fumi ni dani   in the capital
   utoki ima wa no now seem part of the distant past—
   oi zo kuyashiki   how abhorrent is old age!

This refers to having met him in person for the first time.

Tsushima

We set out for Tsushima in the same province.[55] Lodged at Shōgakuin.[56] The proprietor of these lands, Oda Sōdai, paid a courtesy call with his son, Saburō.[57] They brought many gifts. Linked verse at my lodgings:

360 tsutsumi yuku   Along the sides
   ieji wa shigeru   of the levee leading homeward,
   ashima kana   thick stands of rushes!

In these parts people go to and from their homes via levees. There is a bridge as well. Three chō in length, it is even longer than the Long Bridge of Seta.[58] The

BOOK TWO

place where Oyobigawa and Sunomatagawa rivers meet might be compared to the Sea of Ōmi.[59] At the end of the bridge a dozen or so boats lay ready for me and the young men and monks in my company. Along the banks of the river are villages without number. It was about three leagues by river to Kuwana, and on the way we danced, sang, and played pipes, hand drums, and large drums, "beating in time on the boatsides."[60] We were carried along by the current without poling. The boats coming to meet us from Kuwana approached, their boatmen singing lustily. All came together, and the boats that had taken us thus far and those that were to carry us thereafter merged into a single mass—it took me quite out of myself. The next morning I sent this to Shōgakuin with a reed:

361	tsunadenawa	While being pulled
	hikare wasureshi	by the tow rope I forgot
	oi no nami	the waves of old age,
	kyō wa tamoto ni	but I find they have returned
	tachikaeritsutsu	to moisten my sleeve today.[61]

Kuwana

I composed the following at the request of Tōun at this harbor of Kuwana:[62]

362	tobu hotaru	Flitting fireflies—
	momofune no tomaru	where the many boats are moored,
	ashibi kana	reed-kindled flames!

The port is located at the confluence of rivers flowing south through Mino and Owari.[63] It covers five or six chō and contains several thousand houses and temples. It might be the famous West Lake in China.[64] Thousands of boats lay moored beyond the bridge, and the lights from the inns looked just as they must have of old—"stars / on this clear night or . . . fireflies / by the riverbank."[65]

Crossing Eight Peaks Pass

There was a matter I wished to discuss with Seki Minbunotaifu, now called Kajisai, in Kameyama in the same province. I made the necessary arrangements for the journey and had already set out when word came suddenly of fighting—a contrary world this is—and so we turned back.

We proceeded instead to Eight Peaks Pass.[66] Cups of sake here and there with the monks and lay people seeing us on our way. When our escorts arrived from

Sixth Year of Daiei (1526)

Umedo, we set out to cross the peaks.[67] I had been told that horses and palanquins had for some reason not been allowed this way in years, but my aged feet could not manage it. Someone tried to carry me on his back, but it hurt my chest, cut off my wind, and put me in fear of plummeting into the valley below. So I hired a body of twenty or thirty palanquin bearers from Umedo to carry this old body of mine.[68] They marched past the huge rocks to the left and right and breasted through the waves that coursed down—from time to time I completely lost my nerve. I felt as though I were being borne right through the air. Finally we stopped for the night at a dwelling on the pass.

The following day we visited an *egedera* temple at Yamakami in Ōmi then took lodging while the sun was still high in a village called Takano at the foot of the slope.[69] A local acquaintance brought us food and sake and told some remarkable tales.

Through Ōmi

Gotō Tajimanokami in Kannonji sent a large number of palanquin bearers to meet us, and we again stopped early, at Chōkōji.[70] Tani Nakatsukasa and others came along with Nakae Tosanokami to visit.[71] The next day, to Shōrin'an in Yashima, a branch of Shūon'an in Takigi.[72]

On the way I wrote this haikai for my own amusement when I was told we were passing Mirror Mountain:

363	kagamiyama	I do not think I will
	iza tachiyorite	stop by and have a look
	mite yukaji	at Mirror Mountain.
	toshi henuru mi wa	I already know full well
	oshihakaru nari	I have become an old man![73]

Chuckling to myself I arrived at Shōrin'an. That morning a monk from the temple who guided us to Konohama Crossing requested a hokku.[74] For fun:

364	hototogisu	A cuckoo
	shigeru konohama no	at Konohama Crossing
	watari kana	through flourishing leaves![75]

I was sent this and that for my stay at Yashima from the master of Konrin'in in Sakamoto.[76] He arrived that night. They wanted to do a single sheet of verses the next day, but I could only send off a hokku, pleading haste to reach the capital:

365   kasaneage   Were others piled upon it,
       fuji no ne mo isa   this peak would still not match Fuji,
         hototogisu   but how high the cuckoo's cry![77]

Ōtsu

A night in Ōtsu. I could not refuse a request for a verse from the master of Jōkōin from Miidera temple:[78]

366   akenu to ya   Does it think dawn has come?
       yo fukaki tsuki no   Beneath the late moon
         kuina naku   the waterrail cries.[79]

My host in Ōtsu was Sōkei.[80] Again I could not refuse to compose linked verse, but my inspiration was nearly exhausted. I took for my subject the rocks and trees:

367   natsu no ame   Rain in summer—
       koke no mao naru   covered with moss of ramie fabric,
         iwaki kana   the rocks and trees!

Another request. Again difficult to refuse:

368   samidare wa   Summer rain—
       kumo no konata no   to this side of the clouds,
         yanagi kana   willow trees![81]

Tōenbō, eighty years old, came over from Miidera. Linked verse and then conversation and shakuhachi as the night deepened. The music was both inventive and sad, and I was deeply moved.

The Capital

We crossed the Mountain of Meeting and entered the capital at Awataguchi without meeting a soul.[82] This route used to be filled with horses and palanquins, everyone bumping shoulders and tilting hats to squeeze by. As I looked out over the city, I saw not one in ten of the houses that had been there formerly, either rich or poor. The sight of tilled fields around farmhouses, with the Imperial Palace in the midst of summer barley, was too much for words.[83]

Sixth Year of Daiei (1526)

At the house of an old friend of mine in Mushanokōji, I composed this on my feelings at the end of my long trip by palanquin:[84]

369	oi no koshi	Today I stretched out
	kyō zo nobetsuru	my aged, litter-bent back
	toki wakanu	and was brushed by breezes
	hana no miyako	from the capital that blooms
	kaze ni atarite	regardless of the season.[85]

It felt good to hear the word "capital."

Daitokuji Temple

Same month, twenty-eighth day.[86] Saw the Sanmon gate of Ryūhōzan Daitokuji at Murasakino, for which the posts were raised on the twenty-sixth of the first month of this year.[87]

The Death of Emperor Gokashiwabara

On the seventh of this past fourth month the emperor passed away.[88] The funeral was held at Sennyūji temple in Higashiyama.[89] It rained all day, and the trees and grasses by the road drooped beneath the drops, but that night they say the weather improved. The service on the forty-ninth day was held at Banjūzanmaiin, a mountain sanctuary in Fushimi.[90] I hear the emperor's posthumous name is Gokashiwabarain. In attendance at his funeral were the abbot of the Mountain, the prefect of the temple, and representatives from Daitokuji, Nanzenji, the temples of the Five Mountains, and the Ritsu and Pure Land establishments.[91] Incense filled the air, they say. During this time all activity ceased in the capital—it was as if a fire had gone out. I understand the accession took place last month on the third.[92]

Fifth month, sixth day. For a private linked-verse session at Gessonsai Sōseki's:

370	ama ga shita ya	All under heaven
	harema matsu toki	awaits the sun
	satsuki yami	in the fifth-month darkness.[93]

We wondered whether we needed special dispensation to meet for poetry and how often we might do so, but Lord Sanetaka favored us with the opinion that we might compose verse as often as we liked. He stated that everyone in the realm, even the poorest dweller in the mountains, was stricken with grief and that we might feel free to compose. We did two sequences in succession:

| 371 | asatsuyu ni
teru hi o utsusu
aoi kana | In the morning dew
they reflect the shining sun—
hollyhock blossoms! [94] |

| 372 | tokonatsu no
hoka wa kokoro no
chigusa kana | In addition to
the wild pinks, a thousand
flowers in my heart! [95] |

Spent the entire day at the residence of the former abbot of Daisen'in at Daitokuji; took morning and noon meals.

Twenty-third. Went to the Lower Capital.

Fushimi

Fifteenth.[96] A light meal at Shōun Hall, in the Jōkōin subtemple of Kenninji. I requested an audience with the retired abbots of Ikkein and Ryōsen'in.[97] That night I lodged in Fushimi with Tsuda Jujōken.[98] A mulberry bath and treatment for my sore back. Retired immediately thereafter.

In the night the mosquitoes encamped in the bamboo of the garden attacked in force, large and small alike, and filled the house. The war cries of the mosquito general's hordes were like thunder. I lit a smudge flame, but they swept in undeterred by the smoke. There was no way I could drive them from my old, paper-curtained fortress, and I spent the night in fruitless heroics with my fan. Just before dawn I was struck by the thought that this too is part of our melancholy world:

| 373 | kuretake no
shigeki fushimi no
ka no koe ya
harau ni kataki
chiri no yo no naka | The noise of mosquitoes
in Fushimi where *kure*
bamboo grows thick—
there is no way to sweep them
from this woeful world of dust! [99] |

Though it was a short summer night, I thought it would never end.

Sixth Year of Daiei (1526)

Takigi

The next day Jujōken accompanied me by boat up Ujigawa river. We disembarked at the bridge.[100] Two or three cups with Tōunken, commissioner for this province.[101] I composed this after telling him that we planned to cross the bridge and go down to Takigi:

374	waga io wa	My rustic hut
	miyako no tatsumi	lies southeast of the capital,
	shika mo sume	with dragons, snakes, and deer.
	yo o uji ni shi mo	So though called gloomy Uji,
	nani ka kurushimu	what could cause distress?[102]

At Shūon'an in Takigi, I paid my respects before Ikkyū's image and requested incense be lit:

375	suruga yori	Up from Suruga,
	isoganu hi naku	tarrying nary a day,
	yamashiro no	to Takigi
	takigi o oi no	in Yamashiro, where the weight
	ni o zo karomuru	of my old age is lifted.

I composed the following on the third of the seventh month, at a session with people from Izumigawa:

376	ima iku ka	How many more days
	kyō mikanohara	from today at Third-Day Moor?
	amanogawa	The River of Heaven.[103]

On the night of the seventh, I respectfully bowed before Ikkyū's vestments and composed this:

377	nori ni au	The religious law
	futatsu no hoshi no	that the two stars encounter
	karigoromo	in their borrowed robes—
	kyō no e ni te ya	will it be their chance today
	omoihanaren	to renounce their attachments?[104]

I construed "borrowed robes" as religious vestments and meant that the two stars might thus end their myriad years of karmic attachment.[105]

BOOK TWO

The Anniversary of the Death of Sōgi

Twenty-ninth. Anniversary of Sōgi's death.[106] Every year since his death, no matter where I have been at the time, I have composed votive linked verse, be it a single sheet or a thousand-verse sequence, but this year there seemed to be no one to participate. Then after making offerings of tea and hot water at Shūon'an, I was informed that the Abbot planned to hold a session that would involve even the locals.[107] At Shinden'an beyond the temple precincts, I composed this:[108]

| 378 | asagao ya
yume tsuyu hana no
hitosakari | A morning glory—
like dreams or dew, the flower
blooms but a moment.[109] |

Uji Shirakawa

Eighth month, fourth day. The Abbot departed for Shōrin'an in Yashima, Ōmi Province.[110] I could not accompany him, but on the eleventh I left for the capital to express my gratitude to Lord Sanetaka, who had completed a copy of *Kokinshū* for me in his own hand.[111] Stayed a night at Tsujinobō Bessho at Shirakawa in Uji.[112]

Tōunken

Twelfth. Tōunken.[113] Linked verse, by earlier agreement:

| 379 | kiri no asake
kawaoto kuraki
harema kana | In early morning,
the sound of the river
through dark gaps in the mist![114] |

This refers to the morning and evening views of Uji Bridge in the distance. Stayed up till the middle of the night. Sake and a bath. After it grew light on the morning of the thirteenth, our boat from Fushimi arrived at the bridge and we again embarked. Tōunken said he would come along to see us off. He had various things packed for us, and he arranged for tea.[115] It was all quite nicely done.

We rowed up to the eddies around Makinoshima and spent the day enjoying ourselves on the river.[116] I could not restrain my emotions and so composed this:

Sixth Year of Daiei (1526)

380	tsukihi nomi	The days and months
	mi ni zo hayase no	race by like the quick current
	ujigawa ya	of Uji River—
	kyō wa isayou	but today they slow their pace,
	oi no nami kana	the fleet waves of my old age!

We had no poem strips on board, so I wrote it on a fan, which I exchanged for Tōunken's. Insei and Shūkei had come from the capital, and they had a good time as well.[117] At Jujōken's, I took a restorative mulberry bath though thoroughly intoxicated. Left for the capital the next day. Jujōken took me by the sleeve and requested a hokku:

381	asatoake no	Outside the door at morning
	tanomo irozuku	the fields take on color—
	chisato kana	for a thousand leagues![118]

The Lower Capital

Fifteenth. I had a previous engagement for a linked-verse session on the night of the full moon with Gessonsai Sōseki, and he invited me to the Lower Capital. I then went to the Upper Capital, where I expressed my gratitude to Lord Sanetaka for the *Kokinshū* copy he made for me, and Sōseki and Shūkei accompanied me there. I returned to Sōseki's at day's end.[119]

Two or three days later, there was a monthly linked-verse session, where I composed this:

382	fukiaezu	Yet gently blows the wind,
	chiriaenu kaze no	and gently fall the leaves
	yanagi kana	from the willow trees!

Tea in the Lower Capital

The so-called Lower Capital Tea Coterie practices a style of tea called *suki*, which they hold in four-and-a-half-mat or six-mat rooms.[120] At Sōju's, there are great pines and cedars inside the gate.[121] All is clear and fresh within the fence. I noticed five or six fallen ivy leaves of deep color, and composed this:

383	kesa ya yo no	This morning
	arashi o hirou	I pick up last night's storm—
	hatsumomiji	the first colored leaves.

I must use this at a linked-verse session by all means.
Lodged at Hahakabe Hyōgonosuke's residence, where I composed this:[122]

384	ueshi yo ya	Long autumns ago
	aki to iu aki no	they were planted at this house,
	yado no kiku	these autumn asters.[123]

Tenth day of the same month.[124] Composed this at the mansion of Ise Bitchū-nokami:[125]

385	izuku moru	Whence did it come?
	chiyo no nokori no	dew dropped from asters
	kiku no tsuyu	that last a thousand years.[126]

Thirteenth. Composed this at the mansion of Isshiki Sōshū:[127]

386	aki no tsuki	The autumn moon—
	izuko terasanu	on what does it not shine down?
	kuma mo nashi	Nowhere a shadow.[128]

Lodged with Teramachi Saburōzaemon.[129] For a thousand-link sequence:

387	kari nakite	Geese are calling
	samuki sora sumu	in a cold and cloudless sky
	ashita kana	at the break of day!

Sanetaka sent a poem deploring the time it had been since we last met:

388	urami are ya	Have I angered you?
	miyako ni kite mo	Though you are in the capital,
	utsunoyama	it is as if you were
	yume bakari naru	back at Reality Mountain,
	au koto ni shite	since I see you only in dreams.[130]

This was an undeserved honor and left me completely at a loss for words. In my aged decrepitude I have not been fit for walking and have gone nowhere. But I was moved that his poem reflected my own humble thoughts, and so I had his poem recopied from the poem strip to formal paper, had it mounted, and sent it back to him to demonstrate my feelings.

Sixth Year of Daiei (1526)

Shinjuan

At Shinjuan, where I have recently been staying, they are constructing a handsome building called Plum Cottage.[131] A bamboo veranda, east and south wet verandas, running water in the washroom.[132] They put in four or five boulders, planted camellias, bamboo, and azaleas together with the plum, and spread sand as a ground cover. It has a cooling effect.

Gokokuji temple at Higuchi Aburanokōji is famous for its plums, and I asked that they send one to Shinjuan. They included in their answer a reference to the verse "Though it not suffice / I present this rock instead."[133] I composed this in response:

389	akanedomo iwa ni shi kaeba onajiku wa tsutsuji o mo nao soete tabe kashi	If plum trees in place of a rock "will not suffice," please send along (if it's all the same to you) some azaleas as well![134]

The Lower Capital

The night before I was supposed to go to Jujōken's in Fushimi for mulberry baths with the five trees and eight herbs, Lord Ise Hachirō, his brother, and Lord Isshiki Shinkurō invited me to visit them in the Lower Capital.[135] Eight or nine young men arrived at the residence late that night. I had cup after cup of relaxing sake and forgot my old age. The next morning:

390	hito shirezu mi ni shimesomeshi chishio o ba yoso ni sugiyuku hatsushigure kana	With no one else aware, it has dyed me deeply with hues of longing, but now it goes off elsewhere— the first chilling rain![136]
391	ika ni seba omoitaenamu wasurenamu kokoro no mama no kokoro to mogana	What am I to do— would that I could stop longing, that I could forget— how I wish my feelings would feel as I wish them to!
392	koyoi yori fushimi no sato no	When this evening comes, how much dew will I brush off

BOOK TWO

    kusamakura   my grass pillow
    iku tsuyukesa   here in Fushimi village
    haraiakasamu   before the night ends?[137]

Fushimi

Shinkurō sent these to me in Fushimi:

393   ika ni to mo   In my confusion
       obotsukanaki ni   about the state of my heart,
         ware mo mata   I too discover
       onaji kokoro no   that I share your feelings
       sode zo shigururu   as my sleeves are soaked by cold rain.

394   narekoshi wa   My time with you—
       yume ka utsutsu ka   was it a dream or reality?
         to bakari mo   How I wish that you
       kataramu hodo no   would tell me at least
       kokoro to mogana   the answer to that question!

395   shirazu sate   I have no idea
       kusa no makura no   to whom you will travel
         yomosugara   in dreams throughout the night
       tare ni fushimi no   on your pillow of grass
       yume kayouramu   in Fushimi Village.[138]

Sent by Lord Hachirō in answer to my letter:

396   iku yo ware   Can you not know
       fushimi no tsuki o   how many nights
         omou to mo   I have spent thinking of you
       shirade ya hito no   as you sleep beneath Fushimi's moon,
       sode no katashiki   alone on your outspread robe?

I replied after I returned to the capital:[139]

397   musubite wa   I fell asleep
       sameshi fushimi no   then awoke beneath the moon
         yowa no tsuki   of the Fushimi night,
       kimi kayowasuru   but did I have a dream, good sir,
       yume ni ya arikemu   in which you paid me a visit?[140]

Sixth Year of Daiei (1526)

The night I left for Fushimi, I exchanged my shakuhachi flute for Shinkurō's fan as we drank sake. Loath to put the fan down, I wrote this on it in appreciation:

398
  akanu yo no   This keepsake,
  semete shirushi ni   which I received in exchange
   torikaeshi   as a token
  wasuraregatami   of a night all too brief,
  oku kata zo naki   fills me with deep gratitude.

A week and more of mulberry baths at Jujōken's. The care he lavished on me at all times and places indeed reflected the "deep consideration" from which he took his name.[141]

Daigo

Kitamura Hyōgonosuke, of the same family as Jujōken, was good enough to invite me to Daigo for breakfast, and he accompanied me there in the same conveyance.[142] We left Fushimi at daybreak and enjoyed views of Uji, Yawata, and Kasugayama mountain.

Told we were passing the village of Kohata, I composed this:

399
  mukashi ware   Now in my old age,
  ochite tsue tsuku   bent over on a cane since
   oi no nare wa   a fall in the past,
  uma no aru sato no   simply the *name* of a place
  na sae osoroshi   with horses is frightening.[143]

I fell from a horse two or three years ago, and my legs and lower back have not been the same since.[144]

Cane in hand, I walked from the main gate of the Seven Yakushi Buddhas at Hino.[145] It was very lonely and sad—broken carts strewn here and there and fallen leaves driven helter-skelter by the wind up to the curtain before the Buddhas inside the temple hall. I began to feel the past about me, here near the site of Kamo no Chōmei's hermitage and the spot where Lord Shigehira paused, and my tears overflowed.[146] We pressed through the fallen leaves, here and there passing dilapidated monks' dwellings.

The meal at Daigoji was indeed of "superior taste."[147] Had a look at Bodaiin, which the late Jugō is said to have considered his hall of private worship.[148] The rocks called the "Nine Mountains and Eight Seas" are now completely overgrown with grass.[149] They looked even more impressive than I had heard. My late teacher, a monk called the Suruga Counselor, once served at this subtemple.[150] It was just as he always used to tell me.

We returned to our lodgings that morning in the cold rain that struck the slopes of Rain Hat Mountain and had rice in hot water.[151] They had made preparations for linked verse, laying out an ink stone and writing table, but I composed only a hokku:

400	hatsushigure	The first chill showers—
	kasa toriaenu	no time to don rain hats
	yamaji kana	on the mountain path!

Toba

We got back to Fushimi that day, then the next I went to spend the night with a friend in Toba.[152] Another hokku:

401	taga sato no	Where is a village
	shigure senu sora	beneath a sky with no cold rains?
	kaminazuki	The tenth month.

Jujōken sent me two canes, one short and the other long, which he said were for indoor and outdoor use. I sent this along in a letter:

402	kono tsue wa	These walking sticks
	taga ni wa arazu	are meant for you and me,
	kimi to ware	so that we may have
	yasoji no saka o	the pleasure of crossing
	koen ureshisa	the slope of four-score years.[153]

Eighty-year-old Tōenbō of Miidera temple has become famous as a shakuhachi player and also as a maker of those instruments. He sent one of his creations to me, with this poem:

403	susameoke	Take this bamboo,
	itsutsu no shirabe	which sounds the five tones so clear,
	sumu take no	to enjoy yourself,
	yowai yasoji no	and know that I fashioned it
	mi ni nasu o mite	at the age of eighty.[154]

Sixth Year of Daiei (1526)

It amazed me to think he had made such an instrument at his age. I replied with the following:

404	kimi ga nasu	To the thousand years
	itsutsu no shirabe	of the bamboo flute you made,
	sumu take no	good sir, which sounds
	chiyo ni wa yasoji o	the five tones so clear,
	torisoetekeru	you added eighty more!

The flute is therefore doubly felicitous.[155] It was so beautiful I could hardly bring myself to touch it.

405	take no yo no	This span of bamboo
	utsukushisa te ni	is so lovely it is hard
	furegatami	to take in the hands
	kimi ga shirabe o	until I have had the chance,
	kikanu kagiri wa	good sir, to hear you play it.

Daitokuji

I spent a day or two away from Daitokuji, at Gessonsai Sōseki's.[156] On the night of the twenty-fifth I stayed at Nōyū's, chief priest of Kitano Shrine.[157] Shūkei and some young men were invited. All night they played flutes and sang —it was most enjoyable. The next morning, I composed this hokku at the shrine:

406	kesa te ni mo	In my hands this morning,
	usuki awayuki	light snow thin as paper—
	kamiyagawa	Kamiya River.[158]

Then I returned to Daitokuji.

Linked Verse in Japanese and Chinese at Shinjuan

One night the young monks were having a few cups of sake as they composed linked verse in Japanese and Chinese in a small dormitory next to Shinjuan.[159] Feeling old and tired by evening, I was resting in the next building when they came and roused me, so I went out. Someone made what was apparently a comic verse:

BOOK TWO

<blockquote>

407   shichijūkyūnen   Seventy years and nine—
        korai mare nari   a rare age, past and present.[160]

</blockquote>

I have forgotten the first part of the poem. The young monks all laughed and agreed with the poet. They pressed me for a quick reply, but I was at a loss for words. It then occurred to me that lines from a field song would do perfectly, and I quoted them:[161]

<blockquote>

408   koishi no mukashi ya   How I yearn for bygone days!
        tachi mo kaeranu   The waves of old age roll away,
            oi no nami   never to return;
        itadaku yuki   like snow upon my head
            mashiraga no   lies my white hair,
        nagaki inochi zo   long as this life
            urami naru   that fills me full of woe.

</blockquote>

Though my years are fêted and celebrated, there is no joy in old age. I wanted to make that very, very clear.

An Exchange of Ten Poems with Sanjōnishi Sanetaka

Ten poems lamenting my old age of seventy-nine years:

<blockquote>

409   yasugenami   My body complains
        tachii ni tsukete   in discomfort whether
            nagekaruru   at work or at rest,
        waga mi wa oi mo   and I find it true indeed
        sazo na kurushiki   that old age is filled with pain.

410   yosekaeru   They keep rolling in
        izuko mo waga mi   over this body that is everywhere
            araiso ni   a ravaged strand—
        nani mutsumashiki   what is friendly about them,
        oi no shiranami   these white waves of old age?

411   yaku shio to   Quite as bitter
        ama no shiwaza no   as the work of the fisherfolk
            asayū no   who morning and evening
        karaki o iwaba   boil brine for bitter salt
        oi no shiranami   are the white waves of old age.[162]

412   yoshi ya oi   Let old age come—
        sa mo aranu yo ka to   there will be nothing to it!

</blockquote>

Sixth Year of Daiei (1526)

	omoedomo nageku wa waga mi ari no susami zo	So I used to think, but now I spend each day lamenting my condition.[163]
413	hito no ue ni tsune wa kikedomo waga shiranu nikuki mono to wa oi no tsurenasa	Although one always hears of it from others, one can never know just how hateful it is, the cruelty of old age.
414	kore mo mata toga zo to zo omou tsure mo naki oi no nikusa no kagiri shi mo naki	I cannot help but feel that this too is a sin: the hatred I feel for old age and its utter cruelty.
415	ima wa ware hito no tame sae wabishi chō koto o omou ni nageku oi kana	At this point in life I am aware not only of my own misery but that of others as well, as I lament old age.
416	wasurete wa nagakaranu oi o nageku kana kokoro ni kanau inochi naranu ni	At times I forget and resent old age, brief as it is, though I am well aware that life goes not as one would wish.[164]
417	kon to shirite hajime yosoji no kado sasaba yasoji ni itaru oi wa nagekaji	Had I locked the door at forty when first I knew it was bound to come, I would not be eighty now and lamenting my old age.[165]
418	kurikaeshi onaji koto nomi oinureba shizu no odamaki shizu no odamaki	When one grows old one repeats oneself over and over, like a spool of flaxen thread, like a spool of flaxen thread.

The reply from Lord Sanetaka:[166]

Our pleasant conversation yesterday was like none I have had in recent years.[167] It was deeply gratifying and will remain long in my memory. I eagerly anticipate another such occasion in the future.

BOOK TWO

    Your ten poems of jade and gold demanded a response, and I accordingly wrote out these verses by lamplight. I composed them in oil-taper style and send them to you as they are. I beg your indulgence![168] I look forward to seeing you again.

419
    oi no nami
tachite mi ite mi
    omou ni mo
kaeranu mono to
sugishi toshitsuki

    The waves of old age—
whether one watches them
    at work or at rest,
the months and years roll away
forever, wish what one will.

420
    oshikaeshi
omoeba oi zo
    mutsumashiki
ukimi o sutezu
shitaikinikeru

    Upon reflection,
I find the waves of old age
    friendly things indeed,
to come calling on you
and not forsake you in your pain.

421
    oi wa tada
ukime o mitsu ni
    yaku shio no
nani wa no koto mo
karaki yo no naka

    Old age knows only pain—
in every way this world
    is bitter as the salt
from the brine they boil
at the harbor of Naniwa.[169]

422
    nakute zo to
iwaremu koto wa
    shiranu mi no
itsu made oi no
ari no susami zo

    Although I am
not yet spoken of
    as one who is no more,
I now spend every day
wondering what time remains.

423
    hito no ue ni
nashite wa ika ni
    nikukaramu
ware dani oi wa
akihatenikeri

    I think I know
how hateful it is
    for others,
as I too have become
deeply weary of old age.

424
    nikukaranu
hito koso toga wa
    tsure mo naki
oi wa yo no tsune
nani ka kurushiki

    The sin lies instead
with those who hate it not—
    the cruelty of age
is natural in this life;
there is no harm in feeling so.[170]

425
    hito no tame
wabishigarade mo
    oi ga mi no

    How I wish
that instead of feeling pity
    for the plight of others

Sixth Year of Daiei (1526)

| | yasuraka ni shite | you might live out your remaining years |
| | yo o tsukusaba | in comfort and tranquillity! |

426 nagakaraji   When one simply knows
     to bakari shireba   how very brief life is,
        inochi nomi   it seems to me
     oi wa kokoro ni   that just to live on in old age
     kanau to zo omou   is all that one could wish.

427 sono kami wa   Earlier I passed my time
     kon to mo shirade   behind my cedar door
        sugi no kado   not knowing it would come,
     fukaku mo oi no   but now I find that old age
     iritachinikeri   has made its way deep within.[171]

428 oi no nochi   After one grows old,
     onaji koto to te   what one ought to say
        iubeku wa   and say again is
     Namu Amida Butsu   "faith in Amida,"
     Namu Amida Butsu   "faith in Amida."

The above were composed in exchange for your ten poems lamenting old age. I wrote them in haste with a frozen brush beneath the lamp.[172]

Asking Sanjōnishi Sanetaka to Critique a Hundred-Waka Sequence

While I was at my leisure in Suruga, in my Brushwood Cottage in Mariko, Utsunoyama, someone showed me a hundred-waka sequence Lord Sanetaka composed the previous winter on topics chosen by Iwayama Dōken from lines in *Kokinshū*.[173] I modelled a sequence on his and when last in the capital, I took it to him.[174] He was good enough to look it over, and he singled out forty-two for praise. His poem at the end:

429 ika ni shite   How did it happen
     shigure furinishi   that my leaf-like words,
        koto no ha o   rained on by chill showers,
     aranu iro ni mo   came to be so richly dyed
     somekaeshikemu   in these uncommon colors?[175]

I am undeserving of such praise.

BOOK TWO

The Lower Capital

On the twenty-third and twenty-fourth of the tenth month, violence broke out in the capital.[176] I have not heard about what. The chaos is disgraceful. The abbot of Shūon'an in Takigi had planned to go to Shōrin'an in Yashima at the end of the eighth month, but while he was engaged in this and that the present discord began, and he changed his plans. On the tenth of this month, he arrived in the Lower Capital and told me he was planning to go as far as Ōtsu tomorrow.[177] We spoke of various things and then said goodbye, promising to meet again soon. Whereupon I composed the following:

430	oinureba	The old cannot count
	asu wa ōmi to	on meeting on the morrow
	tanomanu ni	in Ōmi,
	yo wa fukenedomo	and though night has not grown late,
	sode zo shigururu	a cold rain moistens my sleeve.[178]

A haikai poem, in jest.

Shirutani Pass

I was warned of bandits in the area around Wakamatsu Pond and Shirutani, and so I traveled in a large company.[179] Shōzōbō of Miidera said he would come to Kazan in Yamashina to meet us, and he arrived with many people including some young men.[180] We rested there for a while and then sent back our escorts from the capital. When we passed Kaminabi Forest and saw the eaves of the gatehouse, "a cold rain began to fall, knowing that its time had come":[181]

431	utsusemi no	Cold evening rain
	usuki maroya no	on the frail, thatched-roof hut
	yūshigure	like a cicada's shell—
	tachiyoru bakari	it pauses but a moment
	ōsaka no yama	at the Mountain of Meeting.[182]

It seemed neither the rain nor the travelers would linger.

Sixth Year of Daiei (1526)

Ōtsu

A night's lodging with Tsuda Sōkei in Ōtsu.[183] Kendō came from Kyoto.[184] Shōzōbō played the shakuhachi.[185] We passed an amusing night.

Sakamoto

I went from Uchide Strand to Sakamoto by boat.[186] Had a number of cups of sake on board with Shōzōbō and Kendō. A brisk wind blew following the rain. We arrived at Hōsenji temple in Hieitsuji, drunk from both the boat ride and the sake, and then drank more at Einō's Chōgetsuken cottage.[187] Thereafter Shōzōbō returned to Miidera. Two nights rest at Einō's. His cottage reflected the utmost artistic sensitivity, even having facilities for tea. It showed unrivalled taste. That evening, snow fell. At dawn I went out of the gate and looked out over the lake, the slopes around Mount Hiei, and Yokawa Peak—the view was indescribable. I composed a haikai verse on it:

432	tachiwasure	While standing motionless,
	yasurau hodo no	having forgotten myself
	asaborake	at the break of day,
	mi mo te mo ashi mo	my arms, my legs, my whole body
	hie no ōyuki	froze in Hiei's deep snow![188]

In jest.

I was asked for a hokku incorporating Chōgetsuken [Listen to the Moon], the name of the cottage. I couldn't fathom what the name meant, but it struck me that it might perhaps relate to boughs breaking under heavy snow beneath the moon:

433	tsuki nagara	Beneath the moon,
	yukiore no take no	cottage eaves beside
	nokiba kana	bamboo broken by the snow!

This also evokes the feeling of listening to the moon.

Shōrin'an in Yashima

Then off to Yashima—we brought a brazier on board the Konohama ferry and crossed unfazed by the wind and snow. Had an interview with the Abbot

BOOK TWO

at Shōrin'an. Stayed at Myōshōan outside the temple precinct.[189] Though across the lake, I still heard news of the disruption in the capital:

434	koko mo koko mo	Even here, even here,
	mimi yasukaranu	those most distressing tidings
	shiranami no	do not cease to come
	miyako no kaze no	wind-borne from the capital
	tsute shi taeneba	across the white-capped billows.

Villagers here seem to be piling wealth upon wealth, having waited until just the right moment to load their rice onto horses and oxen and ship it to the storehouses. The voices of the girls lightheartedly singing rice-threshing *kouta* songs was a glad sound to my ears:

435	mimi yasuki	What *is* pleasant
	koto to wa koyoi	is hearing the sound this evening
	sato no ko no	of the voices
	inetsuki utau	of the country maids
	koe kikoyu naru	singing their rice-threshing songs.

Poems for the Great Thanksgiving Service that speak of "Rice from Sakata" perhaps refer to a place not far from this village.[190]

The cottage in which I am staying is badly run down and not fit to withstand storm or snow. I called in a carpenter and he shored it up, but I was a long way from the mountains and timber was scarce, so I had to order it from Katada and Sakamoto.[191] I fixed new reeds to the frame of the reed fence and enjoyed the carelessness of my preparations for my winter confinement:

436	azusayumi	Winter seclusion
	yashima no sato no	in Yashima, a name that brings to mind
	fuyugomori	catalpa bows.
	ima o harube to	I wish the plums would blossom now
	ume mo sakanamu	and proclaim to us the spring![192]

A certain person requested a hokku during a visit:

437	wataru se ya	Where are the shallows
	izuku yasugawa	of Yasu River safely crossed?
	asagōri	Thin ice at morning.[193]

I must decline such requests from this day forth.[194]

Sixth Year of Daiei (1526)

An Exchange of Poems with Nakae Kazutsugu

Nakae Tosanokami, an old friend, lives two or three leagues from here.[195] I contacted him, and he sent ten loads of charcoal and this and that. This area is far from the mountains, and it is not easy to acquire charcoal or firewood. His response to my letter about this difficulty was very kind. In my answer to him, I included this:

438	sono sato ni	I feel as though
	sumu kokochi sae	I were living in that village,
	shigaraki no	as the smoke rises
	maki no sumi yaku	from burning charcoal
	keburi tatetsutsu	made of wood from Shigaraki.[196]

One night I fell asleep at the *kotatsu* and did not notice when the untended flame set my clothing afire. I woke with a start:

439	toru tokoro	Morning dawned
	nakute zo akenu	with nothing to show for the fire
	katasuso mo	that coursed through my breast
	mune hashiribi no	and my robe as well—
	urameshi no yo ya	what an awful night![197]

A Visit from Suke Hyōgo

Suke Hyōgo, an old friend living close by, came to call with a keg of sake and other things.[198] The year before last he was one of those who traveled with me to Suruga in the company of the physician Sei Kunaikyō Hōin.[199]

Also received a keg of sake and two kinds of fish from Mikami Echigonokami, via his messenger Tsubota Chūemonnojō.[200]

Anniversary of the Death of Ikkyū

Eleventh month, twenty-first day, at Shōrin'an—the anniversary of Ikkyū's death.[201] Snow began fall before dawn:

440	niwa no matsu	The garden pines
	sora shi mo kyō o	did not expect today's weather,
	shirayuki no	and their branches bend

| | eda mo tawawa ni | beneath the white snow |
| | fureru akatsuki | that falls before dawn. |

The abbot replied:

441	tokaeri no	They might be covered
	hana to mo miete	with "centennial blossoms"
	kyō koto ni	today of all days—
	iku shirayuki no	the many snow-burdened branches
	niwa no matsu ga e	of the pine trees in the garden.²⁰²

I sent the abbot a small jug of good sake along with my usual haikai waka:

442	tamadare no	The jewelled flask's wine
	kogame wa mirume	is plentiful as sea plant;
	sono soko wa	pour what you will,
	utsusu ni tsukinu	still more remains in its depths—
	kō wa henubeshi	your life will last a *kalpa*!²⁰³

The abbot replied:

| 443 | anbai kiezu | Of its everlasting flavor, |
| | ikkō ryōzetsu nashi | one taste brings no two opinions. |

A Visit from Genshū

Genshū, a native of Nara recently living in the capital, called at Shōrin'an on the twenty-second of this month.²⁰⁴ He was returning from a journey to Tōtōmi and Suruga, after having called on a friend in Mikawa. He informed me that those provinces are at peace. He also conveyed to me a letter from the deputy vice constable of Owari, Sakai Settsunokami, who very thoughtfully sent one hundred hiki and two Akaike tea whisks.²⁰⁵

A Visit from Shōzōbō

On the twenty-third, Shōzōbō of Miidera arrived at sunset. Played shakuhachi together all night. Genshū happened to be here too. It was all most entertaining.

Twenty-fourth. To see Shōzōbō off, I invited two monks from Shōrin'an and some young men. We had sake, and then he departed. Before dawn I felt we should at least make a hokku:

Sixth Year of Daiei (1526)

444	sora wa tsuki akegata tozuru kōri kana	In the sky, the moon, and ice begins to form, freezing out the dawn!²⁰⁶

I composed the verse unable to restrain my emotion on seeing the cold moon in the sky near dawn. The waki verse:

445	yo fukaki tori ni sode no usuyuki	A cock's crow late at night, and light snow upon my sleeve.²⁰⁷

I wanted to continue thereafter and compose a single sheet of verses, but I was disappointed.

On the twenty-sixth, I entrusted someone going to the capital with this for Shōzōbō at Miidera:

446	hidari migi omou kimigimi tachihanare hitoyo mo yoso ya ideukaruramu	To take your leave from all the friends that esteem you at your left and right and come away for even one night must be difficult indeed!

He must be quite happy there, what with all those young men! My verse makes reference to the old poem composed at that temple, which goes "now I find how hard it is . . . ."²⁰⁸

Tormented by dreams during a long night:²⁰⁹

447	kokoro nomi madoromi sameba madoromade samenu yumeji ya taen to suramu	If my sleeping mind were finally to awaken, would these dreams in which I neither sleep nor wake finally come to an end?

Before dawn, troubled by a cough:

448	tare zo kono oi no shiwaza no shiwabuki o saki ni tatetsutsu tsune ni otosuru	Who is he, the one with an old man's habit of coughing noisily each time before he starts to speak?²¹⁰

My prophesied life span is seventy-nine years, and now, on the first of the twelfth month, I have only thirty nights remaining:²¹¹

BOOK TWO

449	eshinazu wa	If I do not die,
	shō kawareru ka	can the life that I now live
	ware nare ya	change to something new?
	kotoshi o kagiru	This year is the limit
	inochi narikeri	of my allotted span.²¹²

I sent this to the storehouse of Shōrin'an, on a cold morning:

450	oinureba	After one grows old,
	negaimono zo yo	this is what one wishes for:
	amazake no	to be drinking sweet
	minagara kuchi ni	*amazake* sip by sip,
	susuri ireba ya	down to the very last drop!²¹³

Hōgaiken Dōken has been in Noto Province for the last two years aiding the constable there.²¹⁴ Thinking I was in Suruga, he sent a letter there via a blind attendant.²¹⁵ I received it in a packet of letters forwarded to me here at Shōrin'an in Yashima, Ōmi Province. Dōken included a poem in his letter:

451	nao zo omou	I still think of it,
	koshi no miyuki ni	buried as I am beneath
	umorete mo	the snows of Koshi—
	fuji no takane no	sunrise in the springtime
	haru no akebono	over Fuji's soaring peak.²¹⁶

I sent a reply to Sōseki in the capital, asking him to forward it if he planned to write. It will be difficult to deliver through the snow at the end of the year.

452	mukashi kimi	In the past, good sir,
	fuji no ne wa miki	you admired Mount Fuji's peak.
	yukimoyo ni	But nothing compares
	shirayama no na ya	to White Mountain's renown
	tagū sora naki	when it lies beneath fallen snow!²¹⁷

Acquiring a Portrait of Ikkyū

I acquired a portrait of Ikkyū, one in which he is depicted with a sword:²¹⁸

453	uchiharau	How clear and bright
	yuka no atari ni	the sword in its scabbard that stands
	oku tachi no	on the clean-swept floor—

Sixth Year of Daiei (1526)

    sayaka ni izuko
    kumoru chiri naki

    nowhere is it clouded
    by a single speck of dust.

454   kumori naki
    yaiba suzushiki
    tsurugitachi
    togishi kokoro no
    masukagami kana

    A great sword,
    its brilliant blade
    utterly unclouded—
    the clear mirror
    of his fine-honed mind.[219]

A Dream

On the night of the fourth of the twelfth month, I had a dream before dawn. Asukai Masachika had come down to Suruga with Sōgi.[220] I believe it was at the provincial border, and I was seeing them off back to the capital. I seem to have made this poem to inquire why they had not gone to visit the site of Kiyomi Gate:

455   omoedomo
    kaeranu nami ya
    kiyomigata
    kyō wa iwa kosu
    iso uramuramu

    Though longed for,
    the men did not return
    to Kiyomi Strand—
    today do the waves that roll
    across the rocky beach resent them?

I do not know whether I was dreaming or awake. I thought it so strange that I rose and wrote it down.[221]

I heard people sweeping away the soot in the houses in preparation for the New Year:

456   susu hana wa
    makura ni sakite
    oi ga yume
    ibiki oroshi ni
    onore sametsutsu

    Flower-like cinders
    blossom on his pillow,
    and this aged one
    awakens from his dream-filled sleep
    in the winds from the Snore Mountains.[222]

In jest.

On the eighth of the twelfth month, I sent this to the abbot:

457   koyoi kore
    ika naru hoshi no
    akatsuki ni
    mireba sora nomi
    kirakira to shite

    Which star was it
    that he gazed upon this evening?
    In the sky above,
    all of them are twinkling
    in the light before the dawn.[223]

He replied:

458 chiin metsugo   Now that those who understood are gone,
       sara ni tare ka shirō   who can be the one to know?²²⁴

Just before the dawn after a night when I did not even doze:

459   tori no ne ni   The cock crows,
       me nomi sametsutsu   but only my eyes open—
           izuchi tomo   the dawn is wasted,
        yuku kata utoku   for I have no idea where
        atara akatsuki   I should go to truly wake.²²⁵

The cedar door of my travel cottage is filled with cracks. I composed this on deciding to fill the places where the snow and wind came in:

460   mi o tsumeba   Acute as a pinch
          itowaruru oi   is the pain of old age,
            kaze no oto   and I set my mind
        chiri no suki made   on keeping out the wailing wind
        fusegu kokoro ni   and the dust from the cracks.

A Visit from Nakae Kazutsugu

Nakae Tosanokami called at my travel lodging.²²⁶ He brought rice, firewood, money, and such. Spent two nights chatting beside the hearth. After he left, I sent him this:

461   hatsuboku ni   You came equipped
        takigi zōji nado   with rice and also with firewood
           torigushite   and coin of the realm—
        tabine no yoi o   we rested on our travels
         sake no yoiyoi   lit by evening's moonshine!²²⁷

The Suffering of Waterfowl

Near my travel lodgings, on the waters off Shina, Konohama, Yamada, and Yashima, boats without number rest their punting poles before their spread-out fowling nets.²²⁸ Watching the rain capes and hats bobbing up and down on the waves in the icy winds from the Ibuki and Hira Mountains, I cannot imagine the

Sixth Year of Daiei (1526)

evil of taking life to be any worse than the wretchedness of those who cling to it like this. In the dark before dawn, I hear the beating of the waterbirds' wings and the plaintive calls of geese, thwarted in their attempts to land, and I wonder which of them will be caught. Finally I hear them come to water and then their frantic screams as they are trapped in the waiting nets and killed. It is unbearable. I can only stop my ears, my pillow wet with tears:

462	aware naru kari no koe kana me mo haru ni ami okiwatasu nami no akebono	How pathetic, the crying of the wild geese! As far as the eye can see, waves spread with nets for waterfowl at the break of day.
463	nami no ue tachii makasuru ashigamo no ami no nawate ni kakarinuru kana	The ducks in the reeds, which once floated freely upon the waves, now lie snared in the meshes of the waterfowlers' nets!

The latter part of this verse may be duplicated elsewhere.

A messenger brought a keg of sake from Uhyōenojō Takayoshi, as well as other items too numerous to write down here.[229]

During the snow, a messenger from Kawai Matagorō brought money enough to buy eight kegs of sake and ten loads of charcoal.[230] I am deeply indebted to him. When I read his letter asking me to critique a renga sequence in memory of his late father Sunshū, I could not restrain my tears. The linked-verse session I attended at his residence (was it last summer?) kept coming to mind.[231]

Requests for hokku arrived continually from people going to and from Meeting Gate. This one would make a fine travel pass, I thought happily:

464	yuki ni hito taezu ōsaka yamaji kana	The Mountain of Meeting, where wayfarers keep meeting on the snowy mountain road!

Nothing could be more felicitous than this for Meeting Gate![232] In jest, in jest.[233]

A Visit from Yatarō of Suruga

On the last day of the eleventh month, Yatarō arrived from Suruga.[234] All well in Suruga and Tōtōmi.[235] That above all is a cause for rejoicing. He brought two *ryō* in gold (from Asahina Yasumochi and Tokishige) as tidings for the New Year, and another from Bōshū.[236] Had he meant to send this to me in the capital? His family forwarded it in accordance with his last will. I composed this:

465	waga tame ni	The sincere intention
	omoiokikemu	that he cherished in his breast
	karokaranu	from long ago
	kanete no kokoro	to do a favor for me—
	ika ni mukuin	how can I now repay it?

A Visit from Seki Kajisai

Seki, of the Popular Affairs Ministry, came from Kameyama in Ise to my travel lodgings in Yashima on the seventeenth of the twelfth month. He came in the snow, in the rush at year's end, and not simply because he happened to be passing by—I was touched by his sincerity. He had sent a letter by courier at the beginning of the month. I thought it was just a pleasantry, but when he went out of his way in the snow, I was speechless. On sending boxes of food to where he was staying, I wrote:

466	suzukayama	Through the driving snow
	sazo na furitsumu	that piled ever deeper
	yuki no uchi	on the Suzuka Mountains,
	ika ni koekeru	what feelings were in your heart
	kokoro naruramu	as you made your way across?

Soon came his reply:

467	suzukayama	Through the driving snow
	furiuzumoruru	that fell and covered
	yuki no uchi	the Suzuka Mountains,
	mimaku hoshisa no	I came searching out a path
	michi motometsutsu	in my desire to see you.

He came to visit after dark. Our words together piled deeper than the snow—we sat side by side at the hearth, eating tōfu with miso and taking cup after cup of sake. He then returned to his hostel. Five hundred hiki (the cost of five kegs of sake), six loads of charcoal, two baskets of oranges, and various dried foods. My lodgings were positively cramped. He stayed five days. During that time various people arrived day and night to help about the house.

Sixth Year of Daiei (1526)

At the hearth, sake cups in hand, we composed the first eight verses of a sequence, beginning with this:

468	furu ga uchi no	Beneath falling snow
	yuki ōmiji no	they meet one another
	yadori kana	in a hut in Ōmi![237]

This refers to one who has come from another province through the snow to visit. His rejoinder:

469	tabine wasururu	By the smouldering embers,
	uzumibi no moto	forgetting this is a night on the road.
		Sōtetsu[238]

Twenty-second, sunup. Kajisai returned to his fortress for a campaign in Hida. We had promised yesterday not to say goodbye this morning. But after he left and was about one chō away, I sent someone running after his palanquin with:

470	tanomanedo	Though naught is certain,
	haru to zo chigiru	I pledge to meet in the spring,
	yuku toshi no	drawn on as I am
	nokori ōkaru	by you, good sir, who have
	kimi ni hikarete	many years yet remaining.

This refers to the promise we made the day before to meet again next spring without fail.[239]

Year's end is commonly called "the season," and in this village too I hear families shouting as they pound glutinous rice in preparation for the festivities:

471	usu kine no	Here in this village
	oto ni nigiwau	that resounds with the pounding
	kono sato ni	of mortar and mallet,
	ikade tabine o	how is one to have the peace
	sumu kokoro kana	that comes from rested travel?

The Death of Wakatsuki Jirō

Recently Takakuni's forces chanced to be defeated in battle in Tanba, and Wakatsuki Jirō won fame for his matchless death on the field.[240] Years ago Jirō's father, Wakasanokami, had likewise won fame for his glorious death when he retired alone into the Kawarabayashi fortress.[241] I saw much of both father and son. They aspired to the poetic way and were frequent guests of Lord Sanetaka. What sadness and pity his lordship must have felt on hearing the news!

472	toritsutae	Those two who handed down
	wakatsukiyumi no	the way of the Wakatsuki zelkova bow—
	ika nare ya	how did it happen
	shinanu ga uchi no	that when they should have lived,
	aranu shinisuru	both so tragically perished?[242]

"Handing down the way" refers to the father's glory passing to the son.

'Setsubun'

Twenty-fifth, the night of *Setsubun*.[243] Hearing them throwing beans:

473	fuku wa uchi e	This night, when one throws beans
	iru mame no koyoi	and cries, "Good fortune in!"
	motenashi o	do all the demons
	hiroi hiroi ya	rush outside to scrabble up
	oni wa izuramu	the feast they are being offered?

In the capital, they have a practice for protecting against evil, in which one counts out his age in coins and tosses them out for beggars to pick up as they go by at night. Recalling that, I composed this:

474	kazoureba	Counting up the years,
	ware hachijū no	I find I have eighty—
	zōjisen	even to drive out evil,
	yaku to te ikaga	how could I possibly
	otoshiyarubeki	throw away that many coins?

The morning of the twenty-sixth, the first day of spring. Already my seventy-ninth year, prophesied to be my last, has ended:

475	kesa wa katsu	Morning's arrival
	yasoji ni iki o	means I have kept alive
	haetekeri	till the age of eighty!
	kōgaefumi no	The year of the prophecy
	toshi mo kureniki	has come to a conclusion.

Sixth Year of Daiei (1526)

The same morning:

476 kyō yori wa / ikite itsu made / itsu made no / isogu kata naki / yasotose no haru

How much longer / will I go on living from today? / How much longer? / Nowhere now to hurry to— / spring of my eightieth year.

Among the priest Tenmyō's poems:[244]

477 shinau to mo / ikite itsu made / arau to mo / mi ni irowaneba / wazurai mo nashi

Whether you want to die, / or whether you want to go on / living longer, / if you do not dwell upon it, / you will not suffer.

I must have had his verse in mind when I composed mine.
    The priest Sōbai sent me five bags of tea to mark the end of the year.[245] And Tanemura Nakatsukasa Sadakazu sent a horse-load of rice (white) from Kannonji.[246] Miyaki Nyūdō Shinkan heard I was needing a physic of sorrel roots and sent this with it:[247]

478 kimi ga tame / fuyu no no ni idete / shinone horu / waga kamiginu ni / yuki wa furitsutsu

For you, good sir, / I ventured out in winter fields / to dig sorrel roots, / and upon my paper robe / the snow never ceased to fall.[248]

My reply:

479 waga tame ni / motomuru shinone / yuki no uchi no / takana to koso wa / oi mo idekemu

The sorrel roots / that you went out and dug for me / must have been growing / under a cover of snow / like the bamboo shoots of old.[249]

Sōboku sent from Kyoto three bags of mustard seed as a souvenir from Ise, together with this poem:[250]

480 kuramazumi / onozumi koko ni / irikaware

Would this were full / of charcoal from Kurama / or Ono, not mustard,

BOOK TWO

    keshikaranu yuki no   for you in travel lodgings
    tabi no yadori ni   beneath this unseasonable snow.[251]

What a refreshing taste in my mouth!
On hearing families proudly pounding rice for New Year's rice cakes:

481   ōkata no   In my modest
    tabi no yadori ni mo   travel lodging
    kototarinu   I want for nothing,
    tonari no mochi o   and the sound of neighbors
    mimi ni tsukasete   pounding rice cakes strikes my ear.

New Year's Eve. Tonight the spirits of the dead return.[252] A sutra refers to this as well.[253] There is also a poem, in *Shikashū* I think, that goes ". . . so to the departing year / I offer these gem-like teardrops / to speed it on its way."[254] At seventy-nine, I made offerings of tea and hot water and lit incense for the many now departed. On kindling the flame:

482   ware zo kono   Here am I,
    michishirube shite   on the evening when I should be
    kubeki yoi   the one leading them back,
    mata takimukau   once again kindling the flame
    tomoshibi no kage   and sitting before its light.

Seventh Year of Daiei   1527

First Calligraphy of the New Year

Already the sixth year of Daiei has come to an end. Seventh year, first day of the first month:

483	azusayumi	O catalpa bow,
	yasoji no haru o	in this, my eightieth spring,
	chikara nite	bend back
	hito no sakai o	and from this world of men
	hikihanachite yo	release me with all your might![1]

Today I took my morning and noon meals at Shōrin'an. First calligraphy in celebration of New Year's:

484	ugoki naki	Steadfast for a thousand years,
	chitose no kage no	the protector that all extol
	haru ni au	as they greet the spring
	yo o hito mochii	round the mountain that recalls
	kagamiyama kana	mirror rice cakes!

This province is at peace.[2] I made this New Year's poem in reference to the great respect accorded in both town and country to the constable, whose will prevails. The word *mochiikagami* appears in the "Hatsune" chapter of *Genji monogatari*, I believe. It is *not* haikai.[3]

So, my eightieth year. Words fail me. For the last year or two I have kept a diary of things both serious and frivolous to console myself each day.[4] I know that the years have slipped away, never to return no matter how fully I am aware of their passing. So I will cast my brush into the waves of old age and write no more from this day forth.

485	makoto ni ya	I have tossed off these lines
	itsuwaru ni ya to	that may be the truth
	iisuteshi	or may then again be lies—
	tsumi saridokoro	where am I to turn
	izuku tazunemu	for that sin to be forgiven?

486	ori ni fure	These useless products
	nagusamefude no	of my brush, from time to time
	nani naranu	my consolation,
	ne wa musubu yume	are the stuff of dreams,
	yuku mizu no awa	the froth on water that flows away.

An Exchange of Poems with Sanjōnishi Sanetaka

Though I said I would write no more of these worthless lines after the New Year and throw away my brush, I received a letter with a poem by way of season's greetings from Lord Sanetaka that was impossible to ignore:

487	nagameyaru	As I gaze out toward
	yuki no fumoto no	the snow-covered mountain slopes,
	shiba no io	I wonder how hard
	ika ni fukuran	the wind from Hira's peaks
	hira no neoroshi	must be blowing on your brushwood hut.[5]

In my gratitude for his remembering me in my brushwood travel lodging, I replied:

488	ima zo omou	Now I feel that here,
	hira no neoroshi	where you gaze upon me
	nagamuramu	on my snowy slopes
	yuki no fumoto wa	blown by the wind from Hira's peaks,
	sumubekarikeri	is the right place for me to live![6]

Seventh Year of Daiei (1527)

A Renga Sequence with Sōboku

Sōboku requested a hokku from Lord Sanetaka. At my travel lodging we added to it a second and then a third verse. Our determination to complete the sequence was sustained by the deep impression made by the hokku, and we finally reached the hundredth link.[7]

| 489 | ume ga ka o
kieaenu yuki ya
niouramu | Is there a scent
of plum blossoms
in the lingering snow?[8] |

His conception of detecting the fragrance of plums in the snow when one is "deeply tinged with the desire for them" is a departure from the foundation poem.

The Departure of Sōsei

Sōsei, head of the repository at Yashima, suddenly left for Sakai in Izumi. Chinese poems were composed in honor of his departure. I presented two waka, using the third and fourth Chinese verses as my topics:

490	ryōchi kōzan ima hakutō	At both places, the rivers and mountains are now crowned with white.[9]
491	mataru na yo ima wakaru to mo haru no uchi ni kimi ni zo oi no wakaetsutsu mimu	Tarry no longer! Although we now must part, before spring ends I will see you again growing ever younger.
492	hansō tsuki ochi ittō kasuka nari	At the window, beneath the sinking moon, one lamp, dim.
493	wakarubeki koto o omou ni madoromanu tsuki wa ariake no yoi no tomoshibi	While I lie awake reflecting on the fact that you and I must part, the lamp of evening still burns beneath the moon at dawn.

I had gotten him to postpone his departure these last five or six days, despite letters having arrived earlier about sending an escort for him. Today, in my inability to detain him further, I composed this:

BOOK TWO

494
  shiite mina
 kanete wakare o
   todomezu wa
  niwaka ni mono no
  kyō ya kanashiki

Try as one might,
you will not be detained further
 from the parting that you planned,
and suddenly this day
is filled with sadness.

An Exchange of Poems in Japanese and Chinese with the Master of Jizōin

Chinese verse from the master of Jizōin near Shōrin'an.[10] Once again, I answered with a Japanese verse to harmonize with his third and fourth lines:

495
 bōen ya nari to iedomo
  tsutsushinde matsu ari
 seikō uki
  kōjō no yama

Though the miscanthus eaves fall to ruin,
 still one reverently waits.
When fair, beautiful; when rainy, mysterious—
 the mountains above the river.

496
 nami no ue no
 yama honokasumu
  ame narashi
 haru shi mo kimi o
 shiru hito ni shite

It seems to be raining
where the mountains shrouded
 in faint haze meet the sea,
for springtime has understood
the kind of man you are.[11]

From Kannonji, season's greetings from Hirai Uhyōenojō.[12] Two kegs of sake, a goose wrapped in reeds, etc.

A hokku I made at the request of Nakae Tosanokami last winter for his solo linked verse sequence for the new year:[13]

497
 asagasumi
 minami o yomo no
  tachido kana

The morning haze—
the south is the source from which
 it spreads in all directions![14]

One apparently refers to Ōmi Province in terms of north or south.

At Yashima, for a session held by Baba Hyōgonosuke:[15]

498
 ume yanagi
 niou ga ue no
  kasumi kana

The glow of the plums
and the willows is enhanced
 by the haze above![16]

A verse composed at the request of Miidera:

Seventh Year of Daiei (1527)

499   kaze ya haru   The wind of springtime—
        sazanami yosuru   waves rippling
           kōri kana   toward the ice![17]

Lord Mabuchi Kunainoshō, a person to whom I had given no thought and with whom I had had no communication, sent an extraordinary number of gifts.[18] They were delivered to me by my old friend Fukuda Hachirō, who bears the priestly name of Sōkan.[19] He requested a hokku for a thousand-link sequence at Tenjingū shrine in their domain.[20] Apparently for a private matter. He said it is to begin tomorrow, the twenty-fifth—quite a sudden request. Since they had favored me with so many gifts, I composed this:

500   ume sakite   Plums blossom and glow
        nioteru nami no   as do Lake Biwa's billows
           haruhi kana   in the springtime sun!

The Monthly Anniversary of Sōgi's Death

First month, twenty-ninth day: the first observance this year of Sōgi's death. After lighting incense:

501   tachikaeri   Spring goes backwards
        haru ya fuyugomoru   into winter seclusion—
           kesa no yuki   snow this morning.

502   haru ya toki   Is spring early?
        fuyugomorasuru   It was sent back into winter seclusion
           kesa no yuki   by snow this morning.[21]

I can see no difference between the two. His shade is no doubt laughing!

In the cold lingering since dawn the snow was falling on the pines and bamboo of Shōrin'an, bending them down. All morning, the cracking of breaking boughs. I was deeply struck by the matter of dreams and illusions:

503   nani ka sore   What is that?
        maboroshi to towaba   Were I to ask an illusion,
           yume ya kore   "It is a dream!"
        ware maboroshi no   the illusion might reply,
        nanorigao semu   to introduce itself.

504	wakite tare	Who was it
	futatsu ni nazuke	who separated them
	iiokishi	and gave them different names?
	yume ya maboroshi	A dream is an illusion,
	maboroshi ya yume	and an illusion, a dream.

On making deluded distinctions between life and death:

505	ika ni shite	As at Nakoso,
	nakoso to towaba	why do I say, "Stay away"?
	kokoro yori	It is, of course,
	hoka ni wa suenu	a barrier I erect
	seki ni zo arikeru	only in my own mind.[22]

506	otowayama	I have heard of it,
	kikite mo ika de	as of Otowa Mountain,
	ōsaka ya	but when will we meet?
	seki no konata ni	On this side of the Gate at the Mountain of Meeting
	yasoji henuramu	I have now passed eighty years.[23]

The monk Fukuda Hachirō sent a request in a poem:

507	hitofude no	Whenever you see
	ato miru tabi ni	this remnant of my brush,
	omoiidete	please remember me
	namu amida butsu no	and do not forget to chant
	tonaewasuru na	"faith in Amida."

My response:

508	nareshi yo o	The bond between us
	wasuregatami ni	will never be forgotten,
	omoide wa	but who will be the first
	izure ka saki no	to remember it and chant
	namu amida butsu	"faith in Amida"?

I heard that Matsudaira Ōinosuke lost his wife last autumn (was it in the ninth month?) and was in mourning, but I was not sure and could not send a letter of condolence.[24] Then this spring I heard for certain and sent this:

509	kozo no yume o	Since last year's dream
	katashiki koromo	you lie alone upon your robe—

Seventh Year of Daiei (1527)

	samushiro no	sweep the dust
	chiri uchiharau	from your cold, narrow mat
	haru no tamakura	and pillow your head on an arm this spring!²⁵

A humorous suggestion that he marry again!
One morning, on sending people off to town and countryside:

510	hitori futari	Dispatching one or two
	meshitsukau na o	servants on errands for me,
	inabune no	I called them "Rice,"
	ina to nazukete	just like the rice boats,
	kudashi nobosetsu	and sent them up and down.²⁶

On being discommoded by a negligent servant who allowed my money to be stolen:

511	kokomoto no	Such a bother
	fubin to ieba	here tonight—
	zōjisen	all my cash
	koyoi numoji ni	has been you-know-what
	tomoji seraruru	by a you-know-who.²⁷

War in the Capital

Hearing of the discord in the capital, I composed this:

512	kokimaze no	Though the cherries too
	sakura wa sakedo	blend in and bloom
	asamidori	in the capital,
	miyako wa yanagi	this spring there is nothing
	hitomoto no haru	but the light green of one willow.²⁸

Since last winter, the capital has been in an uproar—I can hardly believe what is happening. On the twelfth and thirteenth of the second month, seventh year of the Daiei era, a battle took place at Shichijō avenue. Takeda Izunokami was not blessed with one of the glorious victories of his forebears, and no one was left to challenge Yanagimoto Kataharu.²⁹ Kataharu and his ilk are nothing but woodcutters from the Tanba Mountains.³⁰

To review: in the Meitoku era Yamana Mitsuyuki led tens of thousands of troops to Uchino, and they spread over the capital like clouds and haze.³¹ But

Shogun Ashikaga Yoshimitsu confronted them, and in the space of a day and a night they were utterly destroyed.

Next, during the Ōnin era the constables of various provinces rose up against the shogun, and two-thirds of the capital was covered with great trenches.[32] The Eastern and Western Armies fought for ten years. Among them, Ōuchi Masahiro came to Kyoto on the enemy side.[33] He was finally defeated but was then pardoned, and he returned to his home provinces.[34] Thereupon the various constables retired one after another and soon peace was restored.

Then in the Eishō era, one named Miyoshi Yukinaga arrived in Settsu Province from Awa.[35] Castle after castle fell to him. Takakuni retired to Yamanoue in Ōmi, but he returned to the capital soon after, in the fifth month of that year.[36] Yukinaga and his sons and retainers were either killed, cut down and left for dead, or taken prisoner.

For a time thereafter it was uneventful, but then last winter the renegades in Tanba rose up. They crossed Katsuragawa river at Saga and advanced to the Shichijō crossing. Thereupon Shogun Yoshiharu deployed his troops at the Rokujō Ōmiya crossing.[37] Takakuni moved to the Great South Gate of Tōji temple and for a day and two nights there was a great battle at Katsuragawa. Hearing of the arrival of the shogun, the enemy lay down their shields, ceased shooting their arrows, and paid reverence.[38] As though awakening from a dream, Takakuni and the shogun went to Sakamoto on the fourteenth, then spent two or three days each at Shiga, Konohama, Yamada, Yabase, and Moruyama.[39] A temporary palace with an encircling wall was erected at Chōkōji temple, where the shogun took up residence. I understand that he plans to remain there for a time.

I composed this on the fact of the temple's essence being reflected in its name, "Long Light":

513	kono toki to	Is it not a name
	au ga zarame ya	that accords well with these times,
	haru no hi no	when the spring sun
	nagaki hikari o	shines forth its long-lasting light
	yomo ni shikitsutsu	on all both far and near?[40]

Warriors are flocking here from the Tōkaidō, Hokuriku, Saikoku, and Chūgoku areas.[41] Tens of thousands of men are announcing their arrival. The verse that refers to the old "palace of rough-hewn logs . . . who is it who takes his leave?" could describe Chōkōji at this moment.[42] I have given free reign to my brush here making a rough sketch of events.

Seventh Year of Daiei (1527)

Departure from Yashima

On the fourth of the third month I left Yashima.[43] A village called Minakuchi in Kōga continued for about ten chō, and I recalled the old palace built here once for an imperial pilgrimage to Ise.[44] There are many toll gates in these parts, and as we went along people would shout "Stop! Toll!" at every one, whereupon I composed the following:

514   minakuchi ni / ware ya miyuramu / kadogoto ni / seki ya seki ya to / morogoe ni yobu

I must have appeared / at the water's mouth, / for at every gate / "Stop! Toll!" is what / they cry together.[45]

Saji Nagamasa, now called Shōunken or San'unken, came out to meet us.[46] I stayed two days at his cottage. Too few people to compose more than a single round of eight verses:

515   yama kasumu / tani no to hiroki / tanomo kana

Hazy hills / with fields spreading out / from the valley's mouth!

This refers to Kōga Valley.[47]

In light of the great good will shown to me by the master of this house, I composed this:

516   koto ni fure / hito no nasake o / yasoji made / mishi mo kimi nomi / fukaki iro kana

Of the kindnesses / shown to me at every turn / through my eighty years, / I have known none that compare / with the deep color of your own!

His reply:

517   chigiri are ya / hitoki no kage no / koto no ha / hana ni towaruru / haru no yukusue

Was there a bond between us, / for you to call on me / with leaf-like words / beneath the blossoms of the same tree / now at the end of springtime?[48]

I also composed a hokku at the request of Kawai Matagorō of Ōmi for a sequence on the Holy Name for the first anniversary of the death of his father:[49]

518	naki ni shi mo	Far better had there
	shikaji yume chō	been none—these dream-like
	haru no hana	springtime blossoms.

Near Konohama, Iguchi Saburōzaemon came to escort me to Kameyama in Ise Province.[50] Afterward, when about to return, he requested a hokku:

519	sato tsuzuki	Throughout the town,
	kado utagai no	which gate is which?
	yanagi kana	Willow trees!

This refers to the many willows in the village.

Blinking and wiping my aged eyes while copying a crabbed document of fifty or sixty double pages, I found that my handwriting had begun to look like chicken scratchings.[51] Defeated, I lay down my brush and laughed to myself:

520	sumi fude mo	The ink and the brush,
	tsukue suzuri mo	the desk and the inkstone too
	waraubeshi	must find it funny!
	makoto ni tori no	These are indeed scratchings
	ato ni koso are	like those a bird might make!

Kameyama

Third month, seventh day. Crossed the Suzuka Mountains and stayed at Kameyama.

Fourteenth. A linked-verse session:

521	osozakura	These late cherry trees
	nochi zo sakamashi	are about to burst into bloom
	sakari kana	and then reach their height![52]

For a one-round waka sequence on twenty topics:[53]

522   EARLY SPRING HAZE

kasumumeri	Haze seems to cover all.
itsu yori haru no	It is impossible to tell

	akebono to	when dawn broke
	omoi mo wakanu	this spring morning,
	yomo no sora kana	what with such a sky!

Kajisai

523 BUSH WARBLER IN BAMBOO

    yuki tozuru   Snow that had frozen
isasamuratake   in the sparse stands of bamboo
    suzuka kaze   seems to have melted
fukitokinurashi   in the winds from Suzuka.
uguisu zo naku   A bush warbler sings.[54]

524 VIEW ACROSS THE BAY

    okitsunami   The waves of the offing
shiohi no kata no   look as though they are coursing back
    matsubara no   over the branches
kozue no ue ni   of the pines on the strand
kaeru to mo miyu   bared at low tide.

525 TO THE GODS, IN CELEBRATION

    nabete yo ya   For all in the world,
mo naku mo aran   I wish with my whole heart
    koto mo naku   for no calamities
negau kokoro wa   and no causes for mourning—
kami zo shirubeki   this the gods must know.[55]

Amidaji temple nearby has a statue which grew teeth just like a human being![56] To call it strange would be an understatement. The abbot of the temple is ninety-eight if he is a day, and he has grown a new set of teeth too. Is he a man, or is he a Buddha?[57]

Kanbe

For some time now the cherries have been in blossom, and the trees at the temples throughout Kameyama are past their prime. I passed through them on a mountain path flecked with green leaves and along the river for three chō or so.

    Stopped at the residence of Satō Nagatonokami in Kanbe.[58] On the second day there, I composed this hokku for a single round of linked-verse:

526 haru ya kono   Spring still—
    matsu ni kakareru   from the pines round the house
     yado no fuji   hangs wisteria.

After all the blossoms have gone, wisteria and kerria are all that remain.[59] The host provided this link:

527 sakuraba nokoru   The verdant growth of the garden
    niwa no kobukasa   where the cherry leaves remain.

The verse evokes the feeling of late spring in an indefinable yet elegant way.
  There was also a one-round waka sequence on twenty topics:

528 HAZE OVER THE SEA

    funabito mo   The seafolk in their boats
    kokoro yukurashi   also seem filled with good cheer.
     ise no umi   Out on the water
    uchihae utau   they sing "The Bay of Ise"
    asagasumi kana   over and over in the morning haze![60]

529 LOVE WITHOUT MEETING

    yosekaeru   Like an empty shell
    shiohi no kata no   that is washed by white waves
     shiranami no   that break then roll away
    utsuse ni nitaru   from a strand bared at low tide,
    mono omou kana   I am lost in love longing.

Takaokadera

We left Kanbe and were escorted for more than one league past Takaokadera by Nagatonokami. He brought along some young men, and we spent the day drinking sake, during which time I composed this:

530 nagaraeba   If I live long enough,
    kyō no kokoro mo   I will once again enjoy
     miyubeki ni   happiness like today's,
    oishisu mono wa   but for one now grown so old,
    kainakarikere   that hope seems forlorn.[61]

I also sent this to the young men:

Seventh Year of Daiei (1527)

531	sasowaruru	If there were some way
	hito naramaseba	I could convince you to come,
	fuji no ne no	I would cry, "We're off!"
	suruga e iza to	to the land of Suruga
	iwamashi mono o	where Mount Fuji stands.

A hokku at the abbot's request:

532	kesa wa tare	Who is it this morning
	waka no matsubara	at Waka Pine Strand? I cannot tell—
	asagasumi	haze at daybreak.[62]

The temple is near the pine strand of that name. I was concerned about using "this morning" with "haze at daybreak," but I was reassured by similar usages in such lines as "at daybreak this morning."[63]

Kuwana

We passed Hinaga, Long Day, at dawn, and at Kuwana Tōunken came a league to greet me along with a number of young men.[64] Toward evening, Tōunken's cottage. Next day a linked-verse session:

533	tanabikare	The departing spring
	yuku haru narashi	seems to trail away—
	yūgasumi	evening haze.

Tsushima

Twenty-sixth. To Tsushima in Owari.[65] Went about three leagues by boat. After the rain, people young and old came upstream with us in our boat from Kuwana. While we were having a few cups of sake another boat came to meet us from Tsushima, and we reembarked. Those that had brought us that far stayed for a while, and then we watched as they drew away in their boat, looking back at us.

At Shōgakuin we immediately composed a single sheet of verses:[66]

534	chiru o miyo	See the petals fall!
	aoba wa izuku	They obscure the green leaves
	hana mo nashi	as well as the blossoms.

147

BOOK TWO

The scribe was a young man; his calligraphy was beautiful.

Kiyosu

Twenty-seventh. Kiyosu in Owari.[67] Sakai Settsunokami arranged for my lodging.[68] Linked verse again the next day:

| 535 | haru ikue
iwa kakitsubata
kishi no fuji | Layers of springtime—
irises on the stone palisade—
wisteria on the cliffs.[69] |

The link by the host, Muramori:

| 536 | mizu ni kage sou
niwa no yamabuki | Their image doubled by the water,
the kerria in the garden. |

A linked-verse session at the residence of Oda Tanbanokami:[70]

| 537 | haru yo tada
akazu wa chiyo mo
koyoi kana | Spring has yet to pall,
and so too this last evening,
were it long as a thousand![71] |

This refers to the end of the third month.

Atsuta

Though I was asked to compose verses at various other places, I left on the first of this month. It was unconscionable of me to do so, but at my age I could not endure the repeated linked-verse sessions. Since Settsunokami escorted me to Atsuta Shrine, everyone there treated me very well. There was sake on the way. It was quite agreeable.

I had earlier refused to participate in a linked-verse session at my lodgings at the shrine, pleading the fatigue of old age, but since Settsunokami had accompanied me there it was unavoidable. I asked him to compose the hokku, though. After consulting me several times, he settled on this:

| 538 | hototogisu
hatsune zo hana no
osozakura | A cuckoo—
its first call among the blossoms
of the late cherries.[72] |

Seventh Year of Daiei (1527)

A fine effect—for a verse composed on such short notice, it showed considerable thought. I had absolutely no ideas for the waki verse, and could only provide this:

539	natsu to wa shirushi	It shows that it is summer
	haru ya kurenuru	and that springtime has passed by.

There were many young men in attendance, which was pleasant.

Rain Hat Temple

We left the shrine, and Settsunokami and the rest again accompanied us all the way to Narumi, where we parted with many regrets.[73] Between Narumi and the shrine is a place called Rain Hat Temple.[74] We saw many people going there to pray, and so we stopped by. The temple's main statue, a Kannon with puffed cheeks and a rain hat, was both mysterious and moving. The statue has been there for ages, and its puffed cheeks and rain hat no doubt gave the temple its name.[75]

Kariya

Mizuno Izumonokami's residence in Kariya, Mikawa Province. Stayed two days. Composed a single sheet of verses immediately on arriving:[76]

540	haru wa kurenu	Springtime has ended.
	hototogisu hata	There! The first call
	hatsune kana	of the cuckoo!

Five hundred hiki as a gift. Last year too when I left for Kyoto, I received one thousand hiki as a going-away present. Totalling these and other favors received from him to date, I find they amount to ten thousand hiki. Overwhelming! Just overwhelming!

Anjō

A night in Anjō.[77] Matsudaira Yoichi was there from Owari, and he stayed the night.[78]

BOOK TWO

Okazaki

From Anjō we crossed Yahagigawa river and reached Myōdaiji.[79] At the grave of Lady Jōruri only a pine remained.[80] Yoshitsune must have gazed at the same tree as he mourned her death, remembering their parting on the Tōkaidō road. The place is now called Okazaki and is the site of Matsudaira Jirōzaburō's castle.[81]

Fukōzu

On my way to the capital last year I spent a day in Fukōzu at the residence of Matsudaira Ōinosuke, and I stayed for a day on this trip as well.[82] For a linked-verse session:

| 541 | shigeriau
kozue no natsu no
toyama kana | The neighboring hills
in summer where the branches
are burgeoning! |

Nishinokōri and Ina

Nishinokōri, residence of Udono Saburō.[83] We stopped by during the day and had rice in hot water. We then stayed a day in Ina, at the castle of Makino Heisaburō.[84] Again, linked verse:

| 542 | unohana ya
nami moteyueru
okitsushima | Deutzia blossoms—
a garland of waves encircling
the ocean island.[85] |

Here, I was likening the castle and its environs to an island and the waves to deutzia blossoms that adorn the island's tresses. I was referring to the poem that goes: "It encircles itself / with a garland of white waves / such as the sea god / uses to decorate his hair— / the island of Awaji."

Imahashi

Imahashi. Lodged at Makino Denzō's for a day. Linked verse. I have been the recipient of the largesse of the Makino house over the years since the time of Kohaku.[86] During the linked-verse session I was moved to forget my aged decrepitude as I recalled the past:

543 kyō sara ni   Today once again
    satsuki matsu hana no blossoms awaiting the fifth month
    yadori kana   about my shelter![87]

The verse recalls the past. These blossoms, the ones that "await the fifth month," are deutzia.[88]

Utsuyama

Through the wind and rain for a day to Utsuyama Castle on the provincial border.[89] The sentries here keep watch day and night for possible attacks from Owari, Mikawa, or Shinano. Surrounding the castle to the north, south, and east is Lake Hamana; the water comes up between the hills like a moat and surrounds the castle ramparts. Boats large and small are moored below and can easily reach Horie Castle to the east, and Hamana Castle, Osakabe Castle, Inasa Mountain, and Hosoe Inlet to the north.[90] The west is solid mountains with no place for an enemy to gain access. Nagaike Kurōzaemonnojō Chikayoshi was ordered to oversee construction two years ago, and the work is now more than half completed.[91] The cliff walls of the main fortress have been dug straight down to the valley floor and provide no possible foothold. Since the castle is bordered by three hostile provinces, its watchmen shout constantly and the great drum sounds day and night.

Stayed one day. A renga session was planned, but I excused myself, pleading old age. I only composed the hokku. There were eight or nine people in the first round.[92]

544 nami ya kore   These waves
    kazashioru hana   are its crowning blossoms—
    natsu no umi   the sea in summer.

This refers to the view from the castle. The foundation poem is "The God of the Sea / did not begrudge giving it / to you, my good lords, / this sea plant that he treasures / as a garland for his hair."[93] The words "its crowning blossoms" are in praise of the castle, which will crown the surrounding provinces in perpetuity. By "the sea in summer," I was describing the cool waves, which are crowning blossoms now that spring has passed, and there are no flowers of any kind.

The link was composed by Chikayoshi:

BOOK TWO

545   matsu ni nokoreru   Floating seaweed washed up on the beach
      iso no ukimiru   still lies beneath the pines.

It made a refined connection to the foundation poem.[94]

Hikima

A night in Hikima.[95]

Kakegawa

We passed through the provincial capital of Mitsuke during the day, and I made a private request of Lord Rokurō.[96] Then a two-day stay at Kakegawa.[97]

Kanaya

As we proceeded through Sayonoyama, we met Sugihara Iganokami on his way to the capital.[98] We parted without exchanging any words worthy of note. I stayed in Kanaya that night and sent this to his lodgings in Kakegawa:[99]

546   yume nare ya   Was it but a dream?
      sayo no nakayama   Rather than being left
        nakanaka ni   as betwixt and between
      aimizu wa to zo   as Sayo the "Between Mountain,"
      tachiwakaretsuru   I wish we had not met at all.[100]

I sent him a few provisions as a small gift.
    While staying in Kanaya, I composed this:

547   iku tabi ka   How many times
      mata ya wa koyu to   have I passed this way thinking
        koete mata   will I come again?
      kyō wa yasoji no   Today again at eighty—
      sayo no nakayama   Sayo no nakayama.[101]

Mariko

We crossed Ōigawa river, passed through Fujieda, and reached my cottage in Mariko by Utsunoyama mountain.[102] I left last year at seventy-nine thinking it was to be the last time, but I have once again come through "the narrow path of ivy," my fears instead disappearing.[103] I can only wonder with shame why I have lived so long and how I will die. Aside from Lord Ujichika, Lords Bōshū and Zushū have passed away as well—how is it that I too did not awake from this dream in the past year?[104]

548
 kazoureba   A count of my years
 ware taga tame mo   shows me to be older
  kono kami no   than the others
 shiniokurekinu   who have gone before me,
 kore ika ni semu   and I can do nothing.

Some visitors said they wanted to see the site of the old Kiyomi Gate, and I gave them a letter of introduction to take with them to Seikenji temple.[105] When they returned, they said nothing about the trip to me, so I appended this poem to an answer to a letter from Okitsu Hikokurō:[106]

549
 iza saraba   If they would be so,
 waga na o kaete   I will try calling myself
  yobite mimu   something different—
 sōchō yue ya   was it the name "Sōchō"
 tsurenakaruramu   that made them so unresponsive?[107]

550
 miyakobito ni   Know that in place of
 tachikawaritsutsu   the people from the capital,
  kiyomigata   the waves that wash
 iwa shiku nami mo   the rocks at Kiyomigata
 omou to o shire   will convey my feelings.

I sent this to Miidera temple:[108]

551
 kaeru ni wa   Returning home
 fuji no ne mo shikaji   is even better than Mount Fuji
  hototogisu   for the cuckoo.[109]

An Exchange of Poems with Matsudaira Tadasada

I sent a letter to Matsudaira Ōinosuke of Mikawa on behalf of a blind master and two or three of his blind attendants regarding lodging and horses.[110] They were staying for two nights at Bishamondō next door. When I saw them off on their way back, I had nothing at all to present to them, so I sent these on a single fan to Sonjō Kōtōbō:[111]

552	hoka hoka no	From the brushwood hut
	takaki kikoe no	near the peak of Fuji,
	fuji no ne no	which elsewhere
	shibaya wa keburi	is of such high renown,
	tatewabinu to te	smoke rises but fitfully.[112]
553	sabishi to yo	"A poor thing it is—
	mata mo tazunu na	do not come to call again,
	tazunu na	do not come to call,"
	shirushi no sugi zo	says the gate marked by the cedar,
	saioku no kado	here at Brushwood Cottage.[113]

The First Anniversary of Imagawa Ujichika's Death

Sixth month, twenty-third day—first anniversary of the death of Imagawa Ujichika. I composed a solo hundred-verse sequence, beginning each verse with a syllable from the first five syllables of twenty of his poems:

554	kaze wa nao	Its breeze
	wasuregatami no	makes him harder still to forget—
	ōgi kana	this keepsake fan!

I tried to order a fair copy but could find no one to do it for me. There was nothing for it but to entrust the work to my own aged brush:

555	sarade dani	These remnants
	yukitodokōru	from this eighty-year-old's brush,
	mizukuki	which in any case
	yasoji no ato mo	never moved but haltingly,
	tamuke to zo omou	will serve as a parting prayer.

Correspondence with Iwaki Yoshitaka Regarding Taishō

I have corresponded with Iwaki Minbunotaifu Yoshitaka in Michinoku for many years and have helped send blind masters and assistants to him a number of times.[114] Recently I wrote him to arrange for Taishō's visit to Shirakawa.[115] Taishō stayed there from last summer through the New Year, then returned here in the sixth month. Yoshitaka did a great deal for him, including providing travel supplies and horses for his return. I was immediately envious and sent this poem to him together with one from Taishō:

556	yasoji zo yo	I am now eighty—
	moshi mo nao moshi	if I chance to live longer,
	nagaraeba	if I have that chance,
	iwaki no oku no	I think I will hide myself
	naka ni kakuremu	deep among the rocks and trees.[116]

A haikai lament in my old age—in jest.

Poetry in Sunpu

Impromptu waka at Ujiteru's residence:

557   MOUNTAIN VIEW

	tsuki izuru	They remain till dawn
	akatsuki kakete	beneath the rising moon
	wakarete wa	then depart
	irihi ni kaeru	to return with the setting sun—
	mine no yokogumo	the clouds trailing around the peak.[117]

558   LISTENING TO CHIRPING INSECTS

	yūkaze ni	In the autumn field
	suzu no kikoeshi	one heard the tinkle of little bells
	aki no no wa	in the evening wind—
	furisutegataki	how hard to turn one's back
	mushi no koe kana	on the chirping of the crickets![118]

At the same gathering for the first anniversary of Ujichika's death, a poem was presented in Chinese by the Abbot of Chōrakuji.[119] I composed a verse to harmonize with it, using the third and fourth lines of his poem as the topic:[120]

559	nao jin'ai o todome	His benevolence and love remain still,
	ringaku ni amaneshi	everywhere in forest and valley.[121]
	hana onozukara kōkō ni shite	The blossoms by themselves turn red;
	kusa onozukara aoshi	the grasses by themselves turn green.[122]

| 560 | omokage wa | Their appearance |
| | sanagara akashi | is so like him! |

iroka ni te　　　　　　The hue and fragrance
michi no kusa shigeki　　of the flowers by the roadside
hana zo kanashiki　　　fills me with sadness.

For the same anniversary, Lord Nakamikado sponsored a waka sequence on the *kana* syllabary.[123] For the syllable *ri*, I composed:

561　MOUNTAIN DWELLING

rin'e seba　　　　　If he is reborn,
mizu kusa kiyoki　　his heart still thirsting for more
yama no i no　　　　of the pure water and grass
akanu kokoro wa　　at the mountain well,
sa mo araba are　　it is good that it be so.[124]

562　ryū no sumu　　　　The headwaters
minakami tsune ni　where the dragon dwells
haruru hi mo　　　　flow down from a mountain
kumo kaze ame no　where even on clear days below
taenu yama kana　　there are always clouds, wind, and rain![125]

Festival of the Weaver Maid (Tanabata)

For the Festival of the Weaver Maid, at Ujiteru's residence:

563　THE FESTIVAL OF THE WEAVER MAID AT FAMOUS PLACES

tago no ura ya　　　Tago Bay—
ama no kawara no　unlike at the River of Heaven,
toshidoshi ni　　　there is no day in the year
tatanu hi mo naki　when the waves cease to rise up
koinu hi mo nami　or the heart ceases to long.[126]

564　ISLAND CRANES

yo to tomo ni　　　By the pines
nami yoru matsu no　where waves roll in through the ages,
koto no ha no　　　the cranes cry
shikishima no michi o　as if seeking the leaf-like words
tazu no morogoe　　of the way of Shikishima.[127]

See note.[128]

Seventh Year of Daiei (1527)

565 THE GODS

chihayaburu	The display
kami no shimenawa	of the sacred rope of the mighty gods
kakemaku mo	is an ancient rite
ima ya kashikoki	that now fills one with awe
tameshi narubeki	even to put into words.[129]

During the Festival of the Weaver Maid, as I sighed over the length of my old age:

566 negaikinu	I have often wished
negau ni taenu	upon them but now at eighty
yasoji nari	wishing does no good.
kyō zo waga yo wa	Today ends the two stars' tryst,
aihate no hoshi	the last one that I will see.

A haikai, in jest.[130]

On the same day, I sent this to someone together with bush clover from my garden:

567 motoara no	Their sparse branches have bloomed!
hana sakinikeri	Was this bush clover cut
amanogawa	to make garlands for him
hagi kariagete	to wear while crossing Heaven's River,
wataru kazashi ka	his robe rolled above the shins?[131]

Mariko

At Mariko. Early in the morning of the ninth of the seventh month I heard voices next door. I was told they were mourning a lovely little child who had died of a stomach ailment. That evening I composed this:

568 kyō ika ni	Today one hears
ne nomi tatsuramu	the sound of so much grief.
yoso ni te mo	Here too one mourns
omoikurashi no	at day's end with the cicadas,
sode zo tsuyukeki	his sleeves damp with dew.[132]

I attached the verse to some baby's breath and sent it over.[133]

A few years ago the guest house at my Brushwood Cottage was blown down.

BOOK TWO

I understand it happened in a storm on the morning of the fourteenth of the seventh month (I was in Echizen at the time).[134] I left it that way after I returned to Suruga, until the winter before last, when I replaced it with a thatched building of about one-third the original size.[135] On the ninth of the seventh month of this year I came back here again to take up residence. I removed the encircling fence and the rush blinds, and I also took out more than half the stones in the garden creek and in the short cogon grass to use in the retaining wall for the stream outside the gate. I gave instructions for the rest of the stones, which had been strewn here and there, to be rearranged to allow the creek to flow clear. The garden is a great comfort to me. In the evening cool I composed these:

569	kage mo te mo	Aged and bent
	oikagamarinu	are my hands and my reflection,
	aratamuru	although the water
	asaji no soko no	around the new shoots of short grass
	mizu wa moto mizu	is the same as that of old.

570	sumiutsuru	I am filled with shame
	kage hazukashi no	at the ancient face
	uzumoreshi	so clearly reflected
	yomogi ga moto no	in the water I ladle
	mizu wa kumu made	from the place hidden in the mugwort.[136]

After the Festival of the Dead, on the sixteenth, I composed this:

571	kono tabi no	On their return
	kaerusa ni dani	this time too I have been
	suterarete	abandoned by the spirits,
	mata kyō asu no	again left behind to await
	oi o shi zo omou	my end today or tomorrow.[137]

At my Brushwood Cottage by Utsunoyama mountain, I dug up some of the rocks about the pond in the garden and converted more than half of it into dry field. There, I planted seeds for young greens:

572	mabikina wa	How hard it is,
	sazareishi ma no	the ground of this mountain field
	yamabata no	where I plant young greens
	katashi ya oi no	between the stones—
	nochimaki no tane	the late-sown seeds of my old age.[138]

Seventh Year of Daiei (1527)

How I do love a garden!¹³⁹ In the same dry field I put up a small hut, then hung a rain cape and rain hat in the alcove and laid straw mats on the floor:

573	omoiyare	Keep me in your thoughts
	waga yamabata no	here in my brushwood cottage
	shiba no io	in the mountain field
	shika no naku ne o	where I listen to the deer calling
	oi no akatsuki	before dawn in my old age.¹⁴⁰

This is a response to Saigyō's verse, "The coming of autumn / to distant fields in mountains / cloaked with clouds— / simply the thought of it . . ."¹⁴¹

The Anniversary of Sōgi's Death

On the twenty-seventh of the seventh month, for the anniversary of Sōgi's death, I composed this:

574	asagao ya	The morning glory—
	hana to iu hana no	a flower that is a flower's
	hana no yume	flower dream.¹⁴²

A solo verse, on hearing men shouting as they chased deer over the mountain fields across from my Brushwood Cottage:

575	shika no ne ya	The cries of the deer—
	tōyamabata no	in the distant mountain fields,
	yūarashi	a harsh evening wind.¹⁴³

In my garden I planted soy and adzuki beans, put up a small hut, rigged a bird-rattle, and spent my mornings and evenings in contentment:

| 576 | mamemameshiku mo | An old man full of beans |
| | nareru oi kana | to plant in his garden!¹⁴⁴ |

On picking greens from my garden to send to someone:

577	tsumade koso	You should have seen
	misubekaritsure	these greens before they were picked!
	asana asana	Morning after morning
	waga yamabata no	in my mountain field,
	aki no tsuyukesa	the autumn dew!¹⁴⁵

BOOK TWO

Rain brought out the singing frogs in the "mountain and river" part of my garden. On hearing their song:

578	sekiiruru	Chirping in water
	niwa no yamamizu	that chortles down its channel
	korokoro to	into my garden,
	ishibushi kajika	*ishibushi* singing frogs
	ame susamu nari	frolic in the rain.[146]

Gradually the wind has begun to blow cold of nights, and in the wakefulness of old age my mind keeps returning to painful thoughts about my various wants:

579	ama ga shita	How I wish
	ari to aru mono	that everything under heaven
	naku mogana	simply did not exist,
	sate ya hoshisa no	for if that were so
	tsukuru to omoeba	then all my wants would disappear!

Though I live in quiet retirement, I do indeed hear of events in both the capital and the provinces from pilgrims and travelers who pass by:

580	tabi goto ni	Every time they come
	sate mo te o nomi	to Reality Mountain,
	utsunoyama	I just clap and say, "Really?"
	utsutsu to mo naki	though there is nothing real
	koto o kiku kana	in anything they tell me![147]

Hokku composed at someone's request:

581	no wa aki no	In the autumn field
	tsuyu mushi hana no	the dew, insects, and flowers,
	sakari kana	all at their height!

582	sora midare	Over a troubled sky,
	kumo nowakidatsu	clouds come and go
	yukiki kana	in the gathering storm![148]

While collecting the poems of Imagawa Noritada, I came across verses of his among poems composed on each of the twenty-eight chapters of the *Lotus Sutra* for the thirty-third anniversary of the death of Ryōshun.[149] Both mourner and mourned are now men of old:

Seventh Year of Daiei (1527)

583   namida nomi   Tears come to my eyes
       tokiaenu himo no   and I am sunk in sadness
       makimaki no   at each of the words
       koto no ha goto ni   in scroll after scroll,
       musubōretsutsu   whose strings I humbly untie.

A hokku in my thatched mountain cottage:

584   shika no ne ya   The cries of the deer—
       tōyamabata no   in the distant mountain fields,
       yūarashi   a harsh evening wind.[150]

Okitsu

At the residence of Okitsu Hikokurō, on his garden view:

585   shigure sae   The cold rains
       someakanu yado no   cannot tint them too much—
       kozue kana   the branches round the house!

On the water birds in the same garden:

586   shimo wa kesa   The frost this morning—
       harau mo oshi no   a pity mandarin ducks
       uwage kana   brush it off their feathers![151]

Self-Exoneration

A courier bringing news of the death of Imagawa Ujichika on the twenty-third of the sixth month, sixth year of Daiei, arrived at Shūon'an in Takigi from Rinsen'an on the twenty-ninth of the seventh month.[152] I should have gone to pay my last respects on hearing of Ujichika's death, but I was already in my seventy-ninth year and thought it was to be my last, so I had requested leave to prepare for my end at Daitokuji or Takigi. Having done so, how could I simply rush back again? Nevertheless, I knew that the prediction might not come true, and so I first of all carried out the rites for the forty-ninth day after his death, making daily offerings of tea, water, and rice gruel for a week at Takigi. In addition, I sent a letter to Ujichika's foster brothers Yasumochi and Tokishige to the effect that if I outlived the prediction that year I would venture down to Suruga the following spring.¹⁵³ In the eighth month I asked Lord Sanetaka if he would be good enough to arrange for each of the various courtly houses to present a poem on a book of the *Lotus Sutra* as a prayer for the repose of the deceased, but I then left Takigi because of the disruption in the capital, and it was not until the sixteenth of the second month of this year that I received them in Yashima.¹⁵⁴ Soon thereafter, on the fourth of the third month, I left Yashima and in the fourth month arrived in Suruga and presented them. Lord Nakamikado and his son had just arrived from the capital at the time.¹⁵⁵ The reading of the sutra poems was particularly appreciated, fulfilling my deepest hopes. I received sake, numerous other gifts, and a document from his lordship Ujiteru expressing his thanks.

I also brought a copy of *Kokinshū*, personally completed last year by Lord Sanetaka, which I had requested eight or nine years previously.¹⁵⁶ I had already presented to Ujiteru as a little memento three books and a box of loose papers on the secret traditions of that collection when I left for the capital last year. They were given to me by Sōgi.¹⁵⁷ Over the years I gave various writings to Lord Ujichika as well, either presenting them personally or sending them by messenger.

Though I was in no special service of Lord Yoshitada, I was close to him day and night for years. No one knows that now, though Lady Kitagawa may remember it. She said as much when she summoned me into her presence—when was it? At that time Asahina Yasumochi was also in respectful attendance on her.¹⁵⁸

When Lord Ujichika was a child, I took my leave to spend time at Daitokuji. He showed me great consideration. For twenty years I came and went from the capital and enjoyed his special favor. Everyone must know that. Moreover from time to time I was of service to him.¹⁵⁹

Then when I returned in the fourth month of this year, I learned of events in the province and saw things for myself. Nothing seemed real. Not a year had passed since his lordship's death. I can only wonder in amazement how all could have changed so. I wrote all this down giving free rein to my brush, though it may give the impression that I know more than I do.

A Letter to Yasumochi

At the beginning of the seventh month of this year I finally returned to my place of retirement in Mariko and sent this off to Yasumochi:¹⁶⁰

Seventh Year of Daiei (1527)

587	sa mo araba	Though I told myself
	are to omoedo	if it must be it must be,
	me ni mimi ni	my eyes and ears
	kikite mo mite mo	are surfeited in sight and sound
	amaru kuchi zo yo	with many too many mouths.[161]

I am saddened by the falsehood I encounter everywhere.[162] I have heard nothing but doubts voiced about judgments and policies made after Lord Ujichika suffered his stroke ten years ago. Lord Ujiteru, they continue, is a boy not yet twenty, unstable and willful with those in his service. When I returned to this domain I heard nothing but slander, groundless rumor, and outrageous insolence, some directed even at me. Were it meant for me alone I would not be bothered. It may seem that I am defending them to all and sundry, but I wanted at the very least to plead their case, and I gave free rein to my brush.[163] But I can do nothing about the ever-present rumors, protest them though I will. Anyone can imagine my vexation. I pressed for an investigation several times but it had no effect. Moreover the slanderers came out in the open. In the end nothing could be done, and so I prepared to meet my end at my Brushwood Cottage in Mariko. But Mariko is only just across the river from Tegoshi, and people are always coming and going. What painful matters for these aged ears!

Okitsu

At the residence of Okitsu Saemon, brine baths were prepared for me.[164] I underwent treatment for a week, then took the waters in Atami.[165] I had hoped thereafter to call on an old friend in the east, but I have recently been suffering cruelly from the flux, and to make matters worse I have been having numbness in the legs.[166] I crawl along like a dog crushed by a cart, completely unfit for travel. In any case the year will soon be over. I have decided to go east as soon as the new year begins, should I live so long, and have taken up travel lodgings at the "Hall of No Renunciation," near the Okitsu manor.[167] I thought the temple's name curious and made this poor attempt:

588	oi no nochi	After one grows old
	sute sutezu to mo	it is just as difficult
	iigatami	to renounce as not,
	shibashi na ni nomi	so for the moment I will enjoy
	mezuru yado kana	the cottage's name alone![168]

The Hall of No Renunciation needs to have its roof repaired. One evening, when I was wondering what would happen should it rain or hail, I composed:

589 kozo kotoshi   This year and last,
sugi no itaya no   beneath the moon that shines
mabara naru   through the gaps in the cedar planks
tsuki ni shigure o   of this cottage, I have listened
kikiakashitsuru   until morning to the cold rain.[169]

Last year at this time I was staying in travel lodgings at Myōshōan, outside the gate of Shōrin'an in Yashima. I recalled how the wind from the Ibuki and Hira Mountains would blow the snow and hail through the thin cedar-plank door of my time-worn cottage, and engaged by the memory, I wrote the poem above to express my aged emotions.

My eightieth year is drawing to a close. In the last days of the tenth month, in distress as I continue to linger on in this life, I composed this:

590 hakanasa wa   If you would know
tsuyu yume awa no   of something evanescent
maboroshi no   as the illusions
hoka o tazuneba   of dew, of dreams, and of froth,
waga mi narikeri   there is this life of mine.

Lord Nakamikado is now in Suruga.[170] I have been taking the brine baths in Okitsu, and he was kind enough to include this verse in a letter to me here:

591 samuki yo wa   In the chilly night,
mukau uchi ni mo   sitting across from embers
uzumibi no   smoldering in the ashes,
okitsu no koto zo   it is to Okitsu
omoiyararuru   that I find my thoughts are straying.

My humble response:

592 akatsuki wa   Before the break of dawn,
ikeru bakari no   as I sit barely alive
okiitsutsu   like the glowing coals
omou koto to wa   at Okitsu, my thoughts dwell
oi no samukesa   on the coldness of old age.[171]

Seventh Year of Daiei (1527)

Composed in the darkness before dawn at my travel lodging, the Hall of No Renunciation:

593   yosoge ni mo / sugi no nokiba no / itama arami / moranu shigure ni / fukasetarikeri

    Even from afar / one saw the rough gaps between / the eaves' cedar shakes, / so I had the roof repaired / to keep out the chilling rains.

I composed this on request for a hokku to begin a votive sequence for someone who was ill:

594   toshi no uchi wa / fuyu koso matsu no / fukamidori

    Of all the seasons, / it is in winter that the pine / is deepest green.[172]

For a single sheet of linked verse at a place near the site of the old Kiyomi Gate:

595   towataru ya / matade mo shiramu / sayochidori

    Without waiting / for the nighttime plovers to fly across, / day starts to break.[173]

I received a letter from the chief assistant priest of the Inner Shrine at Ise, regarding the thirteenth anniversary of the death of the previous holder of that office, Moritoki.[174] His friends in Uji and Yamada have planned a memorial linked-verse session to be held in Saigyō Valley on the seventeenth of the second month of next year and urgently requested a hokku, so I took up my brush at once and sent them this:[175]

596   ai ni ainu / sono kisaragi no / hana no haru

    A rare chance meeting / in that same second month / of spring amid blossoms.[176]

Lord Ōgimachisanjō Sanemochi graciously stopped at my Brushwood Cottage in Mariko on his return from a trip. He saw that I had turned half the garden into dry field, built a watchman's hut, and put in a clapper, so he left the following verse on a pine post. The master of the cottage was taking the waters in Okitsu at the time:

BOOK TWO

597 yamabatake no   The loneliness
   shika no naku ne no   of the sound of the deer calling
    sabishisa o   in the mountain field
   omou ni sazo na   must seem all the more so
   oi no akatsuki   in one's old age before the dawn.

I have long felt that way, and now I do all the more, on winter mornings in my eightieth year:

598 okiwakare   The cock's crow,
   uramu mono chō   hated by lovers who must rise
    tori no ne no   and leave each other—
   oi no akatsuki   why is it now so slow in coming
   nado mataruramu   before the dawn in one's old age?[177]

A hokku for a votive linked-verse sequence at Chōzenji temple for my new guest cottage:[178]

599 noki no matsu   On pines by the eaves,
   yuki no shiratama   the jewelled whiteness of snow
    tsurara kana   and gem-like icicles!

The Seventh Anniversary of the Death of Yoshikawa Yorishige

Yoshikawa Jirōzaemon Yorishige, the son of the deputy constable of Awa, came with me to Suruga to escape the animosity of his stepmother.[179] Neither with master nor without, he went to Kai Province in the company of reinforcements for the Imagawa forces there, where he was cut down.[180] He died seven years ago, on the twenty-third of the eleventh month. I sent these to his son Tōgorō:[181]

600 awajishima   Far, far away
   awa to haruka ni   from the island of Awaji,
    shionoyama   upon Sashiide Strand
   sashiidenoiso o   by Mount Shio
   terasu tsukikage   moonlight shines.[182]

601 nanatose no   How melancholy
   fuyu zo kanashiki   is this winter, the seventh
    usuyuki no   since he passed away

Seventh Year of Daiei (1527)

ha bakari no koto mo	without receiving a boon
awade kiekemu	even light as the snow on a leaf.

How sad that without receiving a stipend light as the dew he was cut down side by side with those who did. I composed the second verse on recollecting the saying "life is frail as a leaf."

A Linked-Verse Session Before Taishō's Departure

Taishō came to see Mount Fuji two or three years ago.[183] He went on to Mount Tsukuba thereafter.[184] In the sixth month of this year he returned to Suruga. Though he had planned to stay through the new year, escorts suddenly arrived from Jibunokyō Hokkyō Taiken in Higashiyama.[185] He will be leaving in four or five days. Ohara Hyōgonokami Takachika, who had met him on his earlier visit, sponsored a farewell session.[186] I could not refuse the request to compose the hokku:

602	saki sakazu	The blooming and nonblooming trees
	matsu to shirakawa	know not that one awaits
	hana no haru	Shirakawa's springtime blossoms.[187]

603	toshi ni narenuru	Evening under snow,
	yuki no kuregata	well known for many a year.[188]
		Taishō

604	yukikaeri	It looks like a cottage
	takigi koritsumu	where men come and go,
	yado narashi	cutting and stacking firewood.
		Takachika

The mention of Higashiyama recalled to my mind Saishōji temple in Shirakawa, where Lord Masatsune composed the following verse:

605	narenarete	Long a friend it was—
	mishi wa nagori no	how did I not guess that this spring
	haru zo to mo	would be the last time
	nado shirakawa no	I would know the shade
	hana no shitakage	of its blossoms at Shirakawa?[189]

This refers to the cherry tree by the kickball field there. Taijin, father of Taiken and Taishō, was a friend of mine for more than forty years. It was because of our

BOOK TWO

particularly close friendship that Taishō came to call on me in Suruga, and now he is leaving to return to the capital. My verse suggests that Shirakawa does not know that he has promised to return again soon next spring.

First of the twelfth month, before dawn—an auspicious verse on my wish at eighty:

606   negawaku wa   This is my request
kyō gannichi no   on this day, the first
toshi no kure   of the last month of the year:
ima komu haru wa   let the coming spring
koke no shita ni te   find me beneath the moss.[190]

I composed this while Taishō and I sat side by side at the kotatsu before dawn that morning:

607   kimi inaba   If after you leave,
kaze no tsute ni mo   good sir, you chance to hear
akatsuki wa   that I died before dawn,
negaishi koto to   know it was what I wished for,
sode nurasu ga ni   and let tears wet your sleeve.

His reply:

608   narenareshi   If you, my old friend,
kimi ga kokoro no   have your wish to pass away,
akatsuki no   how could I forget
orifushigoto o   those many times that we spent
ika ni wasuremu   together before the dawn?

Lord Nobuhide deigned to send me a goose together with this poem:[191]

609   furusato ni   How does it feel
kaeru kokoro no   to make one's way back
sue o kike   to one's native place?
ima otozururu   Ask the goose messenger
kari no tamazusa   who now calls upon you![192]

My reply:

610   mi ni amaru   Your words, good sir,
kimi ga koto no ha   far too grand for such as I,
kakesouru   and the letter-bearing goose

kari no tamazusa	that you sent with them
oku kata zo naki	both fill me with gratitude.

An Exchange of Poems with Bōjō Toshina

Someone brought a branch of early plum, laden with clusters of blossoms. I sent it on to Lord Bōjō:[193]

611	mono wa mina	All things are better
	hitotsu futatsu ka	when they are in one's and two's—
	hana dani mo	even with blossoms,
	sakikoru eda wa	a branch that is all in bloom
	midokoro no naki	has nothing to catch the eye.

Winter plums are most moving when they have only one or two faintly fragrant blossoms. They are not fit to be seen when they look like the blossoms children make of pounded rice and attach to branches for New Year's Day.[194]

Piqued by angering events in my declining years, I wrote them down one by one, then facing the paper exclaimed, "Katsu! Katsu!" and mentally consigned them to the flames, laughing away the troubles of my old age. Someone heard me and sent me a poem saying that now my heart must be free from care. I responded with this:

612	kiku hito no	How true it is
	yoso ni hashiru chō	that one who hears another's words
	kotowari yo	will take them amiss
	omou bakari wa	even when the speaker says
	iihatenu to mo	all of what was on his mind!

Far too many lies are spread about nowadays. I hear people doing nothing but slandering others and, being in their company, I wonder if I will become like them.[195]

613	yoki ni tsuke	About the good
	ashiki wa mashite	and even more about the bad
	yo no hito no	people everywhere
	kotoba mugomugo	spread endless gossip
	shima ni kanetsutsu	full of conjecture and innuendo.[196]

BOOK TWO

At the Imagawa residence, Lord Sanemochi provided the topics for a waka sequence for the end of the year. I composed the following:

614 THATCHED COTTAGE IN THE RAIN

    kokoro are ya   Have pity on me,
    kario no kuraki   rain that raps in the dark night
      yoru no mado   upon the window
    utsu oto wa shite   of my makeshift cottage
    suguru ame kana   and then passes me by.

I received a short-sleeved robe from Asahina Shimotsukenokami Tokishige. A poem was included. It contained an allusion to the verse that goes "so deeply colored by / the desire for them."[197]

My reply:

615 kokorozashi   Now I know how deep
    kieaenu yuki mo   are the colors of your goodwill
      ima zo shiru   and of the blossoms
    fukaku someteshi   that one so desired
    hana no iro to wa   in the lingering snow![198]

I received a letter with a single narcissus from someone. My reply:

616 ajikinaya   There is naught for it—
    kotoshi mo arite   I have lived another year
      tsure mo naku   doleful to relate,
    seibo no fumi o   and I again exchange letters
    kakikawashitsuru   to commemorate its end.

On receiving greetings at year's end from a grandfather, father, and grandchild:

617 ōji chichi   Greetings at year's end
    mumago no toshi no   from grandfather and father
      kure ni shite   and also grandchild—
    arite nasake wa   I am both glad and ashamed
    ureshi hazukashi   to have lingered on so long.[199]

Appendixes

APPENDIX A

The Imagawa House

The following summary is meant to elaborate on Sōchō's list of Imagawa daimyo and their dates of birth and death found on *JS*: 12. For an abbreviated Imagawa house lineage, see Appendix A of the companion volume to this translation, *Song in an Age of Discord: The Journal of Sōchō and Poetic Life in Late Medieval Japan*. For a more extensive treatment of the cultural history of the Imagawa house, see Horton 1993.

Originally a branch of the Ashikaga house, the Imagawa were awarded the constableship of Tōtōmi and then of Suruga in the time of Imagawa Norikuni 今川範国 (Jōkōjidono 定光寺殿, 1295?–1384), in recognition of his role in Ashikaga Takauji's victory in the wars at the end of the Kenmu Restoration (1333), in which three of his brothers were killed. Norikuni also enjoyed a reputation as a poet, and a famous anecdote relates that he rejected a request to submit samples of his poetry for inclusion in the *Fūgashū* imperial poetic anthology, protesting that he composed verse only to "cultivate the spirit." In his pursuit of excellence in the ways both cultural (*bun*) and martial (*bu*), he established an ideal that was respected and pursued by his Imagawa descendants.

Imagawa Noriuji 今川範氏 (1316–65?) was the eldest son of Norikuni and second-generation head of the Imagawa house. He was far less important to Imagawa history than his younger brother Imagawa Sadayo 今川貞世 (Ryōshun 了俊, 1326–1420), the most accomplished literatus the Imagawa were to produce. Skilled in both cultural (*bun*) and martial (*bu*) pursuits, Ryōshun spent years in Kyushu as inspector (*tandai*), warring with the enemies of the shogunal government (*bakufu*), and he also held the constableship of Tōtōmi and later that of Suruga, while concurrently producing important literary works in a variety of

Appendix A

genres. He studied waka with a member of the Reizei family of court poets and renga with Nijō Yoshimoto and Kyūsei, and his work was included in several imperial anthologies. He also produced poetic treatises, a private poetry anthology, diaries, and a body of house injunctions, *Imagawajō*, that became so famous that the name "Imagawa" subsequently became a generic term for such documents. Ryōshun was also an influential teacher, his most important student being Shōtetsu. Shōtetsu's student Shōkō thus brought with him long-standing ties to the Imagawa when he called on Ryōshun's descendant Imagawa Yoshitada in 1473 (*JS*: 57–58, 175).

The third head of the Imagawa house, Noriuji's son Yasunori 泰範 (1334–1409), was not as important to Imagawa history as his son Norimasa 範政 (1364–1433), another prominent man of letters. The latter studied waka with Reizei teachers, furthering the Imagawa connection to the Reizei family that continued in Sōchō's time. Like Ryōshun, Norimasa composed poetry that was included in an imperial anthology, copied dozens of literary classics, and authored *Genji monogatari teiyō*, a six-volume study of *Genji monogatari* that is still useful today (see Yonehara 1979: 819–25). In his old age he hosted the entourage of Shogun Ashikaga Yoshinori (1391–1455), and he is thought to have written *Fuji goran nikki*, one of the poetic diaries that document that trip. Sōchō later wrote a postscript to that work for Norimasa's descendant Imagawa Ujiteru 今川氏輝 (1513–36; *JS*: 176).

The shogun's journey to the Imagawa domain, however, was primarily motivated by military, not literary, concerns, for the area was becoming increasingly marked by violence and division (see Harrington 1985). As a direct collateral of the Ashikaga, the Imagawa house was central to subsequent bakufu efforts to retain control of the Kantō area, but in 1433 the house was rent by its first internal dispute, the Succession Conflict of the Eikyō Era (Eikyō no naikō 永享の内訌), brought about by Norimasa's death. His eldest son, Noritada 範忠 (1408–61?), triumphed, but thereafter distinguished himself more by military than by cultural activity. He nevertheless found time for literary pursuits, and Sōchō writes in his journal of coming across poetry composed by Noritada to commemorate an anniversary of Ryōshun's death (*JS*: 160).

Five years after he succeeded to the headship of the house, Noritada took up arms at the direction of the bakufu against its erstwhile viceroy in the east, the "Kantō Shogun" (Kantō Kubō) Ashikaga Mochiuji 足利持氏 (1398–1439), who had long been at odds with his own ostensible deputies, the Uesugi. Imagawa and Uesugi forces defeated Mochiuji in the following year, 1439, and caused him to commit suicide. This dispute, the Discord of the Eikyō Era (Eikyō no ran 永享の乱), was premonitory of the subsequent collapse of central authority in the region and the competition between individual daimyo and provincial warrior (*kokujin*) houses in the ensuing power vacuum. Imagawa Noritada is said to have been awarded the title of vice shogun (fuku shogun) by Ashikaga Yoshinori for his role in putting an end to the Discord of the Eikyō Era (Wakabayashi 1970: 133–34).

The history of the Imagawa role in subsequent Kantō history is briefly related by Sōchō in his journal, and he witnessed many of the events personally. A year after Sōchō was born, one of Mochiuji's sons, Shigeuji 成氏 (1434–97), was installed as the new bakufu deputy for Kantō, with the blessing of the Uesugi, now the predominant power in the immediate Kantō region. Predictably, he soon rose against his own deputies as his father had, only to be driven from Kamakura in 1455 by Imagawa Noritada, who put the city to the torch. The defeated Shigeuji fled to Koga in Shimōsa Province (modern Ibaraki Prefecture), where he established a local power base. The bakufu then ordered the Uesugi to reinforce their holdings against this "Koga Kubō." Edo Castle was built by Ōta Dōkan 太田道灌 (1432–86), an Uesugi lieutenant, as part of that enterprise in 1456–57. When preparations were complete, the bakufu sent Ashikaga Masatomo 足利政知 (1435–91), brother of the new shogun Yoshimasa, to defeat the Koga Kubō, Shigeuji, but he was unable to advance beyond Horikoshi (or Horigoe) in Izu, where he installed himself, becoming known as the "Horikoshi Kubō" in consequence. Dwindling bakufu power in Kantō was now divided between competing viceroy houses. The Uesugi also divided into several branches at this time, the Yamanouchi Uesugi and the Ōgigayatsu Uesugi being the two most important. The part played by the Imagawa in the struggle for Kantō supremacy between the two Uesugi houses figures prominently in the historical passages of Sōchō's journal.

Suruga, meanwhile, remained securely under Imagawa control, and when Noritada died, headship of the house passed to his son Yoshitada 義忠 (1436–76?), Sōchō's first patron. As related in Appendix B, Yoshitada directed his energies to the recovery of Tōtōmi Province, which had passed into the hands of the rival Shiba house in the early fifteenth century. Yoshitada also pursued the arts, though in a more limited way than his illustrious literary forbears Ryōshun and Norimasa. Though his poetic accomplishments were exaggerated in a later house history, it is true that Sōgi's first collection of personal verses, *Wasuregusa*, includes lines that the poet composed at Yoshitada's manor in 1466. It was at that

Appendix A

point that the fledgling poet Sōchō guided the older master to Kiyomi Strand (*JS*: 56–57).

When Yoshitada was killed in Tōtōmi, his son Ryūōmaro 竜王丸 (also read Tatsuōmaro), later called Imagawa Ujichika 氏親 (1471?–1526), was still a minor, which brought about another division within the house, the Succession Conflict of the Bunmei Era (Bunmei no naikō 文明の内訌). Ujichika and his mother, Lady Kitagawa, took refuge and waited for her brother, who was later known as Hōjō Sōun, to effect a settlement with the more mature claimant, Yoshitada's cousin. It was agreed the cousin would serve as interim head until Ujichika achieved his majority, and Ujichika and his mother went to live in Mariko, where Sōchō would later build his Brushwood Cottage. The cousin predictably refused to step down at the stipulated date, and in 1487 Ujichika killed him with the help of Sōun and took over the headship of the house.

Ujichika established local control over his domains, instituted cadastral surveys, and promulgated house rules (*Kana mokuroku*), which Nagahara Keiji (1975: 154–55) sees as the first mature Sengoku-period house laws. The cadastral surveys and house laws constituted a renunciation of the subordinate role of bakufu constable. Ujichika was one of Sōchō's major patrons, and his death, which is treated in depth near the end of *The Journal of Sōchō*, seems to have precipitated a decline in Sōchō's fortunes. Ujichika's son Imagawa Ujiteru succeeded to the headship on Ujichika's death, and he too figures in *The Journal of Sōchō*. For more on the military and cultural careers of Yoshitada, Ujichika, and Ujiteru, see *Song in an Age of Discord*.

After Ujiteru's premature demise, his younger brother, who had taken holy orders, returned to secular life and adopted the name Imagawa Yoshimoto 今川義元 (1519–60). Under his rule the Imagawa experienced their greatest efflorescence. He was aided by his mother, known as the nun Jukei 寿桂 (1490–1568), and his advisor, the monk Sessai 雪斎 (1496–1555). Yoshimoto's defeat and death at the hands of Oda Nobunaga 織田信長 (1534–82) at Okehazama 桶狭間 (Toyoake 豊明 City, Aichi Prefecture), however, sent the house into a decline, and its influence came to an end eight years later when Takeda Shingen 武田信玄 (1521–73) drove Yoshimoto's son Imagawa Ujizane 今川氏真 (1538–1614) out of Suruga.

APPENDIX B

The Historical Context of the "Asahina Battle Chronicle"

Sōchō's account of Kakegawa and the Asahina and Imagawa is elliptical and chronologically disorganized, and an overview of the relevant historical background may be useful. The Imagawa (see Appendix A), originally a branch of the Ashikaga, had been invested with the constableship of Tōtōmi and then Suruga in the time of Imagawa Norikuni in return for their services to Ashikaga Takauji 足利尊氏 (1305–58), the first Ashikaga shogun. They thereafter came to consider the office of constable of those two provinces theirs by tradition. Imagawa Ryōshun, however, was implicated in a plot against the bakufu, and he lost that office. In 1405 it was awarded instead to the Shiba house, which (by and large) held it into the next century. But Ryōshun's descendents in Tōtōmi, who later took the surname Horikoshi 堀越, were well established in that province and continued to live there after the Shiba acquired the constabulary. Horikoshi Norimasa 堀越範将, the head of the family in the mid-fifteenth century, rose against the Shiba in 1459 along with other kokujin. This was part of the Central Tōtōmi Uprising (*Chūen ikki* 中遠一揆, see Ogi 1979). The movement was suppressed by the Shiba with the consent of the bakufu, Norimasa was killed, and his Horikoshi Castle (Fukuroi 袋井 City, Shizuoka Prefecture) was awarded by the bakufu to the Kanō, assistant vice constables to the Kai, instead of to the Imagawa. The Kanō were a branch of the Izu Kanō and were headquartered in Mitsuke Castle in the provincial capital (Iwata City, Shizuoka Prefecture). They controlled central Tōtōmi under the protection of their Shiba overlords. Owada (1986: 82), on the basis of *Imagawaki* (*Furokuki*), theorizes that in 1465 Kanō Suke Nyūdō 狩野介入道 and his son Kanō Shichirōemonnojō 狩野七郎右衛門尉 (given in *Imagawaki* [*Furokuki*] [196]) as Kanō Shichirōzaemonnojō 狩野七郎左衛門尉) were attacked

Appendix B

at Mitsuke Castle by Kanō Kaganokami 狩野加賀守. Kaganokami, Owada holds, was reinforced at the behest of the bakufu by the Yokochi and the Katsumata, kokujin of east Tōtōmi. Defeated, the Mitsuke Kanō both took their own lives, and Kanō Kaganokami occupied their fortress at Mitsuke. The descendants of Horikoshi Norimasa, however, were anxious to recover their property, and in 1474 Norimasa's son Horikoshi Sadanobu 堀越貞延 (also known by the surname Sena 瀬名) invaded the province. The region had long been vulnerable as its overseers, the Shiba, held the constableships of Echizen and Owari as well and were overextended, and their vice constables for Tōtōmi, the Kai, were also vice constables in Echizen, where a power struggle of both houses with the Asakura demanded much of their attention. Sadanobu's campaign in Tōtōmi was probably backed by Sōchō's patron Imagawa Yoshitada, who had secured rights to a bakufu estate in Kakegawa in that province in 1473, in return for service in the Ōnin War (*JS*: 13). Yoshitada thereafter had his trusted vassal Asahina Yasuhiro (d. 1513) construct Kakegawa Castle, and the daimyo used it as a base for subsequent incursions (*JS*: 8). He thereafter took Mitsuke Castle from Kanō Kaganokami, a victory that marked the end of Kanō resistance. Horikoshi Sadanobu, however, was killed by the Yokochi and the Katsumata at Sayo no nakayama. Yoshitada subsequently withdrew to Suruga, and Yokochi Hidekuni 横地秀国 and Katsumata Motonaga 勝間田元長 moved into the vacated Mitsuke Castle. In 1476 Yoshitada took back the castle, then for good measure reduced the home fortresses of the Yokochi and Katsumata as well, effectively destroying both kokujin houses. Horikoshi Sadanobu's son Sadamoto 貞基 was given command of Mitsuke. But Yoshitada himself was killed by surviving Yokochi and Katsumata partisans at Shiokaizaka as he returned homeward from that campaign (*JS*: 9, 13). Yoshii (1985: 55) adheres to the same general chronology, but he believes that it was not Kanō Kaganokami but Kanō Suke Nyūdō and his son Shichirōemonnojō (Hisachika 久親, who may also have been called Kunainoshō, assistant vice constable to Kai Nobuhisa 甲斐信久) who were defeated at Mitsuke by Yoshitada in 1474 and then committed suicide. This version is closer to Sōchō's account on *JS*: 12–13, but the details are unclear. The *GSRJ* ms. of *The Journal of Sōchō* (259) identifies Kunainoshō as Shichirōemonnojō and the date as 1465, and it states that Yoshitada was accompanied on his campaign by the Katsumata and the Yokochi. As the events in *The Journal of Sōchō* cannot have taken place before Yoshitada was invested with the Kakegawa Estate in 1473, it would appear that the *GSRJ* interlinear commentator conflated the campaign of the Yokochi and Katsumata against Kanō Shichirōemonnojō and Kanō Suke Nyūdō, dated 1465 in *Imagawaki* (*Furokuki* 196), with the later attack of Yoshitada against the Kanō in Mitsuke in 1474.

Yoshitada's son, Ujichika 氏親 (c. 1471–1526), one of Sōchō's most important patrons, also had designs on Tōtōmi. His armies advanced into the province in 1494, and by 1501 they had penetrated even into Mikawa. Shiba Yoshitō 斯波義寛 initiated a concentrated effort to restore Shiba influence in 1499, but his army was defeated at Yashiroyama in 1502 (*JS*: 8). Ujichika's troops occupied the Shiba strongholds of Hikuma and Murakushi in the next year and essentially controlled the province by 1504. Ujichika was considerably aided in his campaigns in the region by his uncle, Hōjō Sōun 北条早雲 (1432–1519). When his western flank was secured, Ujichika was able to reinforce Sōun, by that time master of Izu, in the latter's northern expansion. The support of Sōun and Ujichika was instrumental in the victory of Ōgigayatsu Tomoyoshi 扇谷上杉朝良 (d. 1518) over Yamanouchi Uesugi Akisada 山内上杉顕定 (d. 1510) in Musashi Province in 1504 (*JS*: 9–10). The Imagawa thereafter again turned west and reduced the castle at Imahashi (Toyohashi City 豊橋市) in Mikawa in 1506. Ujichika then managed to have the constableship of Tōtōmi transferred to him in 1508 in return for a sizeable monetary gift to the weakened bakufu. In the same year the Shiba lost the constabulary of Echizen to the Asakura and were left with only Owari. Shiba partisans, however, continued to hold out in parts of Tōtōmi, and in 1510 they were rallied by Shiba Yoshitatsu 斯波義達 (d. 1521), who like Imagawa Ujichika felt the province was his by traditional right. Yoshitatsu established himself in Mitake Castle (Inasachō 引佐町, Inasa District 引佐郡, Shizuoka Prefecture) in territory held by the Ii family north of Lake Hamana. The Ōkōchi, Shiba allies, concurrently took over Hikuma Castle (Hamamatsu 浜松 City, Shizuoka Prefecture, *JS*: 10–12). The Shiba, however, were defeated at their Mitake fortress by Ujichika in 1513 (some sources say 1514) (*JS*: 10–11). The Imagawa thereafter again felt their western flank secure enough to take sides in an intra-house conflict in 1515 between Takeda Nobutora 武田信虎 (1494–1574) of Kai (Yamanashi Prefecture) and his brother Nobutsuna (*JS*: 11). Ōkōchi Sadatsuna 大河内定綱 (d. 1517) then took that conflict as an opportunity to once more move into Hikuma Castle and organize resistance to Imagawa hegemony. Ujichika, with Sōchō's help, arranged a truce with his opponents among the Takeda in Kai and marched on Hikuma, reducing it in 1517, killing all the Ōkōchi and forcing Shiba Yoshitatsu to take holy orders (*JS*: 11–12). That marked the end of Shiba resistance in the province.

Sōchō's account is heavily biased in favor of his patrons, the Imagawa and

Appendix B

Asahina, and he overemphasizes the role of the Ōkōchi so as to emphasize the victories over them by the Asahina. For more on this period of Imagawa history see Akimoto 1984, Kurosawa 1977, Ogi 1979, Owada 1983, id. 1986, and Yoshii 1985, to which the above summary is indebted. Much of the history of these events, however, remains obscure.

APPENDIX C

*Chronology of
'The Journal of Sōchō'*

Book One

1522

5. Sōchō departs from Sunpu in Suruga Province, domain of Imagawa Ujichika, intending to call on the Asakura in Echizen regarding a donation for Daitokuji in Kyoto, temple of his late spiritual master, Ikkyū. He passes Sayo no nakayama mountain, an emblematic *utamakura* for his journey made particularly famous by a verse of the earlier poet-priest Saigyō, and then he stays at Kakegawa Castle of the Asahina, retainers of the Imagawa and vice constables of Tōtōmi. Here he inserts into the journal a chronicle of the recent military history of the Asahina in the service of the Imagawa. He then journeys toward Kansai, staying with various warrior acquaintances and participating in renga sessions. Fighting makes it impossible for him to visit the Eight Bridges (Yatsuhashi), an utamakura connected with another earlier poet traveler, Ariwara Narihira, in *Ise monogatari*. Several days later he takes a boat across Ise Bay and visits Ise Shrine.

8:4 to 8:8. Sōchō and his disciple Sōseki compose *Ise senku*, a thousand-link votive sequence commissioned by the warlord Hosokawa Takakuni, master of Kyoto.

8:16. He departs from Ise for Echizen and after missing connections and losing his way is escorted to the residence of Seki Kajisai in Kameyama in Ise Province, where he stays for more than ten days. He then tries to continue north but fighting makes the route impassable, and he abandons his attempt to reach Echizen, returning instead to Kameyama. He thereafter sets out for Takigi and the capital via a southern route. He stops first at Anonotsu and spends a night on the beach composing verse and enjoying sake and music with young men (wakashu).

Appendix C

9:1 to c. 9:22. The poet returns to Anonotsu then reaches Yamada (the location of Ise Shrine) on the second and stays until after the twentieth. He thereupon decides to visit Saigyō Valley, site of Saigyō's hermitage, after which he returns to Yamada.

10. After staying for two or three days in Take and composing renga, Sōchō makes a pilgrimage to Hatsuse (Hasedera temple), where he stays several days. He next goes to Tōnomine, where he spends an evening with the nō actor Konparu Shichirō. The next day he visits Tachibanadera temple, and then two days later he arrives in the ancient capital of Nara, where he stays for more than ten days and participates in renga sessions. In Nara he also hears news of the suicide of his old friend, the shakuhachi musician Jōsū, whom he had seen only weeks before in Yamada. He then makes a pilgrimage to the Great Buddha at Tōdaiji, enjoys a picnic at Hannyaji Hill, and finally, after falling when getting out of his palanquin, he arrives at Shūon'an temple in Takigi. At Takigi he corresponds with Sanetaka and Sōseki before the year ends.

Also in this year Ōuchi Yoshioki wars with Amako Tsunehisa in Aki Province, and Rokkaku Sadayori lays seige to the castle of Gamō Hidenori in Ōmi. It is the latter conflict that interrupts Sōchō's journey to Echizen. Regular poetry meetings for waka and renga are held at Kitano Shrine.

1523

1. Sōchō greets the new year at Takigi, beginning his account of that year with exchanges of poems with the courtier Sanjōnishi Sanetaka and other acquaintances in the capital. During this period he also discovers correspondence at Shinden'an (near Shūon'an) relating to his son Jōha, a novice monk. The widow of the warrior Nose Yorinori, now a nun in residence at Shinden'an, had at one time offered to raise Jōha. The memory prompts Sōchō to recall a thousand-verse memorial sequence, *Higashiyama senku*, which he had arranged in 1518 in memory of her late husband and in which Sanetaka and the renga master Shōhaku had participated.

3. Sōchō goes to the capital by way of Shirakawa in Uji.

3 (intercalary). The abbot of Shūon'an asks Sōchō to set out again for Echizen and pursue the matter of a donation from the Asakura daimyo to rebuild the Sanmon gate of Daitokuji. Sōchō relates that he had traveled to Echizen on a similar errand in 1519, but that the project had subsequently been held in abeyance.

Chronology of 'The Journal of Sōchō'

3 (intercalary):15 to year-end. Sōchō arrives in Echizen, and Asakura Norikage, an old friend, promises to make a donation. Sōchō adds parenthetically that he himself had donated to that point thirty thousand *hiki* toward rebuilding the temple of his late master. Sōchō stays in Echizen until the eighth month, and he records hokku he composed there and on his return trip to the capital. He then takes the waters in Arima, and subsequently returns to Takigi, where he and a number of friends compose haikai renga at the end of the year. Some of the verses were composed by Yamazaki Sōkan, compiler of the early haikai anthology *Shinsen inu tsukubashū*.

Also in this year Hosokawa Takakuni (deputy of the current shogun, Ashikaga Yoshiharu) and Ōuchi Yoshioki both send China trade missions to Ningbo, where their representatives fight each other and are ejected from the country by Ming officials, who close the port to the Japanese. Sanjōnishi Sanetaka's son Kin'eda begins a lecture series on *Genji monogatari* for Prince Fushinomiya Sadaatsu, and Konoe Hisamichi presents a copy he made of *Shuten Dōji ekotoba* to Hōjō Ujitsuna, son of the early Sengoku daimyo Hōjō Sōun.

1524

1:1. Sōchō greets the new year at Takigi, and again exchanges felicitations with various acquaintances. He travels to Yawata and then to the capital, where he composes linked verse with a friend from Miidera temple, Shōzōbō.

3:17 to 3:21. Sōchō, Sanetaka, and Sōseki compose *Iba senku*, otherwise known as *Gessonsai senku*, at Sōseki's residence in the capital. Thereafter he exchanges poetry with the court musician Toyohara Muneaki and the courtier Nakamikado Nobutane, and he sends poetry to Asakura Norikage congratulating him on having two hawks born in captivity, an event also chronicled in *Yōyōki* (An Account of Raising Hawks).

4:11. Sōchō leaves the capital for Suruga. He calls first on an acquaintance in Fushimi to arrange for carting lumber to Daitokuji, then travels by boat up Ujigawa river toward Uji Bridge, the passengers singing songs as they are towed upstream.

4:12. When he reaches Takigi, he pays his respects to the memory of Ikkyū and announces his departure for the east. He is met by Shōzōbō from Miidera temple.

Appendix C

4:13. Shōzōbō escorts Sōchō to Ōtsu and Miidera, where he is subsequently met by Sōseki the next day.

4:15 to 4:22. Sōchō crosses Lake Biwa then spends several days composing linked verse with warrior-literati.

4:22 to 6:7. Sōchō sets out across the Suzuka Mountains then reaches Kameyama and calls on Seki Kajisai, with whom he visits Washinosuyama mountain and composes linked verse. His sojourn ends when he receives word from the Imagawa in Suruga that he must accompany the physician Sei Kunaikyō back to Sunpu to treat Ujichika, who has fallen ill.

6:7 to 6:16. Sōchō and company hurry back to Suruga, staying with some of the same hosts Sōchō had visited in his trip to Kansai in 1522.

7:27 to 7:29. Sōchō guides the visitors from the capital to the site of the old Kiyomi barrier, where they compose poetry. Sōchō recalls taking Sōgi and later the poet Shōkō (disciple of Shōtetsu) to the same spot more than a half century earlier. The party then returns to Sunpu.

9. Early in the month Sōchō falls from his horse while on a short ride out from the Suruga capital. It becomes a chronic injury. Sōchō writes to Takigi informing them that he hopes to spend his last days there.

10. Sōchō visits Okitsu, where he takes brine baths and composes verse.

Also in this year Hōjō Ujitsuna defeats Uesugi Asaoki at Edo Castle and becomes master of Musashi, and Enryakuji monks attack members of the Nichiren sect. The Imagawa carry out cadastral surveys in Suruga. The *Goseibai shikimoku* (*Jōei Code*), house laws of the Kamakura Bakufu and foundation of later warrior house laws, are printed for the first time.

1525

1 to 6. Sōchō participates in poetry gatherings in Sunpu and in Okitsu, composes a long poem on hermitage life in Sunpu, corresponds with acquaintants, and composes hokku by request.

8:20. He composes votive waka for the first anniversary of the death of his friend, the court musician Toyohara Muneaki, and he records them along with waka made for the same occasion by the courtiers Sanjōnishi Sanetaka and Ōgimachisanjō Sanemochi. Sometime thereafter Sōchō composes votive verses on the suicide of the impoverished samurai Osada Chikashige, who was likely the son-in-law of the donor of Sōchō's Brushwood Cottage, Saitō Yasumoto. He also sells his copy of *Genji monogatari* to raise money to contribute to the rebuilding of the Sanmon gate at Daitokuji.

9:30. Imagawa Ujichika, Ōgimachisanjō Sanemochi, and other important figures in Sunpu compose poetry in honor of Sōchō's longevity. Later Sōchō composes a poem to mark the anniversary of his father's death.

11:25. Sōchō composes poetry in honor of Imagawa Ujiteru's coming-of-age ceremony and presents him with lecture notes on *Kokinshū*, recalling his own study of that anthology with Sōgi.

11 (intercalary):17. Sōchō composes poetry to mark the first month after the death of the courtier Nakamikado Nobutane.

Year-end. Sōchō expresses to Asahina Tokishige his views on success in business, charity to pilgrims and people in poverty, and laxity in Zen practice.

Also in this year there is unrest in Tango and plague in the capital. The painter Tosa Mitsunobu and the bakufu *dōbōshū* Sōami die.

1526

1. Poetry for the New Year in Sunpu.

2.9 to 2:20. Sōchō has an interview with Ujichika's mother, Lady Kitagawa, before setting out again for Kansai. He stops at his Brushwood Cottage in Mariko, then departs on 2:11 for Kogawa. There he composes a thousand-verse sequence with Asahina Yasumochi and other warriors on 2:13–15. On 2:17 he composes more linked verse with them, considering it a "farewell session." He stays until 2:20, then leaves for Sayo no nakayama and presents a disquisition on the etymology of that place name.

2:21 to 3:3. Sōchō arrives at Kakegawa, site of the Asahina castle, and on 2:22 composes linked verse. He then departs and reaches Mitsuke on 3:3. Here Book One of the journal ends.

Book Two

1526

Sōchō reviews events from the beginning of the year, then carries on his account from Mitsuke.

Appendix C

3:4. He composes verse at the residence of Horikoshi Rokurō, a descendant of Imagawa Ryōshun, then continues west past Hamamatsu and Lake Hamana, which he believes he is viewing for the last time. He then stays with warrior acquaintances, including Iio Zenshirō in Hamamatsu and then Makino Denzō in Imahashi, Mikawa Province. Denzō's father and grandfather were also patrons of his. Sōchō then composes verse with the Matsudaira and the Kira Tōjō; this is his first linked-verse session with the latter. After a pilgrimage to Atsuta Shrine, he continues to call at the lodgings of warrior acquaintances, where he composes linked verse. At Tsushima he meets Oda Nobuhide, father of Oda Nobunaga. He then travels to Kuwana by boat, enjoying the dancing and singing on board. He attempts to visit Seki Kajisai as he had on his journeys to and from Kansai in 1522 and 1524, but his plans are frustrated by fighting en route, and so he proceeds instead to Eight Peaks Pass, where he makes a dangerous crossing by palanquin. Sōchō calls at Shōrin'an in Yashima, another temple of the Daitokuji lineage connected with Ikkyū, but he pauses only briefly before continuing on to Miidera temple in Ōtsu, where he composes verse and plays shakuhachi with the same friends who had hosted him in 1524.

4. Sōchō crosses Ōsaka, the Mountain of Meeting, and enters the capital, which is more desolate than he remembered. He notes the progress on the rebuilding project for the Sanmon gate at Daitokuji. He also learns that Emperor Gokashiwabara died on 4:7, and he writes a second-hand account of the funeral ceremonies. The new emperor is Gonara.

5:6. Sōchō and Sōseki compose two sequences of one hundred verses each, after being assured by Sanjōnishi Sanetaka that they might do so during the mourning period for the late emperor. Sōchō stays at Daitokuji.

5:23. He goes to the Lower Capital, then on 6:15 visits Tsuda Jujōken in Fushimi, where he writes a mock heroic anecdote about his trials with mosquitoes. The next day he and Jujōken travel by boat to Uji Bridge, where he again calls on the vice constable of the province, Tōunken. He then proceeds to Takigi.

7:7. On the Festival of the Weaver Maid, Sōchō composes ceremonial verse in memory of Ikkyū, then on 7:29 does the same for Sōgi on the anniversary of his death in 1502.

8:11. Sōchō departs for the capital to thank Sanjōnishi Sanetaka for a copy of *Kokinshū* he had asked the courtier to make. On 8:12 he again stops at the residence of Tōunken, who arranges for a boat to take Sōchō to Fushimi. On

Chronology of 'The Journal of Sōchō'

8:15 he composes linked verse with Sōseki in the Lower Capital, then travels on to the Upper Capital, where he calls on Sanetaka. Some days later he visits a wabi-style tea house used by Murata Sōju and the "Lower Capital Tea Coterie" (Shimogyō chanoyu).

9. He stays with several warrior patrons and composes linked verse, then returns to Daitokuji, where he lives for a time in Plum Cottage and notes improvements to its garden. He then returns to Fushimi, where he lodges with Jujōken for more than ten days, taking medicinal baths. During that time he enjoys a day trip to Daigoji and recalls the Suruga Counselor, a monk affiliated with that temple who had instructed him in religious matters. Sōchō is moved to think how close he is to the site of Kamo no Chōmei's hermitage and the place Taira Shigehira in *Heike monogatari* visited his wife on the way to execution. He subsequently returns to Fushimi, and then to Daitokuji via Toba. He later stays with Sōseki for a day or two and participates in the monthly poetry meeting at Kitano Shrine on 9:25. In the tenth month, Sōchō visits Sanjōnishi Sanetaka.

10:24. Violence breaks out in Kyoto in connection with the uprising of Yanagimoto Kataharu. Sōchō subsequently leaves Kyoto for Shōrin'an temple. On the way he visits Shōzōbō at Miidera and then proceeds by boat from Uchide to Sakamoto, stays for two days with another acquaintance, then crosses Lake Biwa and reaches Shōrin'an. Throughout that winter, he is visited there by various friends, including Shōzōbō (11:23–24) and Seki Kajisai (12:17–22). During that time he dreams of Sōgi and acquires a portrait of Ikkyū.

Also in this year Imagawa Ujichika promulgates his *Kana mokuroku* (Kana Code). He dies later in the year and is succeeded by his son Ujiteru. Takeda Nobutora defeats Hōjō Ujitsuna in Suruga. Members of a peasant uprising (*tsuchi ikki*) in Yamashiro march on the capital to demand release from debt (*tokusei*); the bakufu later issues a *tokusei* decree.

1527

1.1. Sōchō composes New Year's verse, having outlived the prophecy that he would die in his seventy-ninth year (1526). He thereupon resolves to throw away his brush, but he is drawn back to writing when he receives New Year's verses from Sanjōnishi Sanetaka. He composes *Yashima Shōrin'an naniki hyakuin* with Sōboku (1:18), and he records in his journal poetic exchanges with various acquaintances, verses made by request, and waka. Word reaches him of more fighting in Kyoto, prompting him to write a short history of violence in the capital over the previous century and a half. Hosokawa Takakuni and the shogun, Ashikaga Yoshiharu, are defeated by Yanagimoto Kataharu and his allies, and they retreat to a place very near Yashima, which may have been what prompted Sōchō to return to Suruga at this time.

3:4. Sōchō leaves Shōrin'an and reaches Kameyama, residence of Seki Kajisai, on 3:7, where he stays for a week, composing waka and renga. He records another exhilarating trip by boat at Tsushima, then more linked-verse sessions at the residences of various acquaintances.

4:1. Sōchō visits Atsuta Shrine in the company of Sakai Muramori, where they compose linked verse. He then stops at Rain Hat Temple and stays in Kariya with Mizuno Chikamori, a particularly generous patron. After lodging with the Matsudaira, he pauses at the grave of Lady Jōruri, lover of Yoshitsune and eponymous heroine of the puppet theater, then again visits the Makino. He subsequently sojourns at Utsuyama, where he remarks on the castle's constant readiness for war, and thereafter arrives at his Brushwood Cottage in Mariko.

6:23. Sōchō composes a hundred-verse solo sequence for the first anniversary of the death of Imagawa Ujichika. He composes poetry in Sunpu for such formal events as Ujichika's death anniversary and the Festival of the Weaver Maid.

7:9. Sōchō returns to his Brushwood Cottage and carries out renovations to the house and the garden. Later he goes to nearby Okitsu, where he takes brine baths and writes a long account of his service to the Imagawa in self-exoneration for criticism he appears to have received after returning to Suruga. He corresponds with the courtiers Ōgimachisanjō Sanemochi and Nakamikado Nobuhide, both of whom are in Sunpu, and he later returns there himself to attend year-end poetry gatherings.

Also in this year peasants rise up in Sakamoto in Ōmi demanding release from debt. The troops of Yoshiharu reenter the capital later this year from Ōmi, as does Yoshiharu's ally Asakura Norikage from Echizen, and they continue to battle the armies of Yanagimoto Kataharu and his allies. The renga master Shōhaku dies.

Reference Matter

Notes

BOOK ONE: *Second Year of Daiei (1522)*

1. "Northland" refers to *hokuchi* 北地, which can also explicitly mean the Hokuriku 北陸 region, in which Echizen Province (Fukui Prefecture) is located. There, Sōchō intended to call on Asakura Tarōzaemon Norikage 朝倉太郎左衛門教景 (1474–1555), also known as Sōteki 宗滴. He was the brother of the head of the Asakura house, Ujikage 氏景, and advisor to three generations of Asakura leaders. The Asakura had become constables of that province in 1508. Respected for both his martial and literary accomplishments, Norikage commanded the Asakura forces sent to the capital during the Yanagimoto uprising in 1526 (*JS*: 120, 141–42), and he died of illness while on a campaign against the Ikkō ikki 一向一揆 in Kaga (Ishikawa Prefecture). He recorded his experiences in his *Asakura Sōteki waki* (Asakura Sōteki's Anecdotes, 1555) (Yoshida 1983: 108–40). He was also dedicated to linked verse, and Sōchō provided the first verse (*hokku*) for his *Norikage (Sōteki) senku* (Kawai 1985: 275).

Sōchō first visited the Asakura at their fortress at Ichijōdani 一乗谷 with Sōgi in 1479 (see Sōgi's *Oi no susami* [Aged Consolation, 1479]), and he enjoyed a close relationship with the house for nearly a half-century thereafter. Sōchō also mentions them in his earlier diary *Utsunoyama no ki* (Account of Utsunoyama, 1518) (398–99) of 1518 and his second personal poetry collection, *Nachigomori* (Beneath Nachi Falls, 1517) (13–16, 163–64), covering poetry from 1515–17. They were active patrons of the arts (see Suitō 1981: 55–60, Tsurusaki 1969b, and Yonehara 1979: 215–354). Ichijōdani was a model of the Sengoku castle town (*jōkamachi* 城下町), and it has been extensively excavated (see Ishii 1974 and Suitō 1983).

2. Kaeruyama 帰山, the Mountain of Returning, is an utamakura in Echizen Province, Sōchō's intended destination. It frequently figures in parting poems (*ribetsu no uta*), e.g., *Kokinshū* 8: 370:

Sent to a person leaving for Koshi:

Notes to Book One (1522), Page 7

> kaeruyama
> ari to wa kikedo
> harugasumi
> tachiwakarenaba
> koishikarubeshi
>
> Though I hear
> of a Mountain of Returning there,
> if you now depart
> amid the haze of springtime,
> I will miss you nonetheless.

See also *JS* no. 22. Utsunoyama 宇津山, now called Utsunoya tōge 宇津谷峠, is an utamakura located in Shizuoka Prefecture, at the border of Abe 安部 and Shida 志太 Districts. Sōchō's cottage in Mariko 丸子, just west of the Suruga provincial capital (now Shizuoka City), was nearby. Utsunoyama is given particularly famous mention in *Ise monogatari* (Tales of Ise) (*JS*: 279, n. 130).

Sayo no nakayama 小夜の中山 (also called Saya no nakayama, Sayo no nagayama, etc.) is an utamakura in Tōtōmi Province, northeast of what is now Kakegawa 掛川 City, Shizuoka Prefecture. The *honka* foundation poem is *Shinkokinshū* 10: 987, Saigyō:

> toshi takete
> mata koyubeshi to
> omoiki ya
> inochi narikeri
> sayo no nakayama
>
> Did I ever think
> I would pass this way again
> in my old age?
> Long was my allotted span!
> Sayo no nakayama.

This poem may in turn be related to *Kokinshū* 2: 97:

> haru goto ni
> hana no sakari wa
> arinamedo
> aimimu koto wa
> inochi narikeri
>
> There will always be flowers
> bursting into glorious bloom
> whenever springtime comes,
> but whether I shall see them
> rests with my allotted span.
>
> (trans. McCullough 1985)

See *JS*: 91–92 and 96 for Sōchō's discussion the etymology of the name Sayo no Nakayama. Oi no saka (the hill of old age) may derive from *Goshūishū* 7: 429:

> Composed by Saki no Daisōjō Myōson on the advent of his ninetieth year, when he received a bamboo staff from Uji Saki no Daijō Daijin Yorimichi:

> kimi o inoru
> toshi o hisashiku
> narinureba
> oi no saka yuku
> tsue mo ureshiku
>
> Since the years in which
> I have prayed for you, my lord,
> are now so many,
> pleasing even is the staff
> I use to climb the hill of old age.

3. For the background of the following historical passages, see Appendix B. Kakegawa 懸川 (now written 掛川) was the seat of the Asahina 朝比奈, vice constables (*shugodai*) of Tōtōmi and important Imagawa vassals. The head of the house in 1522 was Asa-

Notes to Book One (1522), Pages 7–8

hina Yasuyoshi 朝比奈泰能 (d. 1557), who was related by marriage to the current Imagawa daimyō, Imagawa Ujichika 今川氏親 (also refered to by Sōchō in his journal by such names as Shōsaku 匠作, Kyōzan 喬山, Jōki 紹僖, etc., c. 1471–1526). Matsumoto (1980: 117) states that Kakegawa Castle was begun in the Bunmei era (1469–87) by Asahina Yasuhiro 朝比奈泰熈 (d. 1513?), father of Yasuyoshi, at the behest of Imagawa Yoshitada 今川義忠 (c. 1436–1476?), father of Ujichika, after Yoshitada returned from Kyoto, where he had gone to reinforce the Eastern Army of Hosokawa Katsumoto 細川勝元 (1430–73) at the outbreak of the Ōnin War in 1467. Katsumoto had ordered Yoshitada back to the east to counter the Shiba 斯波, constables of Tōtōmi, who supported the Western Army. Sōchō refers to the project hereafter (*JS*: 7–8). A second castle (Shinjō, New Castle) was being added to the older castle (Honjō, Main Castle) when Sōchō visited in 1522. Work on the second castle appears to have been begun at least by 1513, and there is evidence that construction was carried out in the Meiō (1492–1501) and Bunki (1501–4) eras as well in conjunction with Ujichika's Tōtōmi campaign (Seki 1981: 216). It was at Kakegawa Castle that Asahina Yasutomo 朝比奈泰朝, son of Yasuyoshi, sheltered Imagawa Ujizane 今川氏真 (1538–1614), grandson of Ujichika, when Ujizane was driven from Suruga by Takeda Shingen 武田真玄 (1521–73) in 1568. Yasutomo and Ujizane held off a Tokugawa army of superior numbers for nearly half a year at Kakegawa, after which the besieged forces were allowed to retire to Hōjō lands to the east. On the Asahina, see Matsumoto 1980.

4. Sōchō measures the circumference in *ken* 間, one of which loosely equalled two yards, though with considerable regional variation.

5. The old castle, built on a hill called Tennōzan 天王山 (65 m.), included three compounds. The new castle, which also contained three compounds, was located at the foot of the mountain, about five hundred meters to the southwest, bordered by Sakagawa 逆川 river. Kakegawa Castle was thus of the "flatland-hill castle" (*hirayamajō*) type.

6. The hokku is included in Sōchō's third personal linked-verse collection, *Oi no mimi* (Aged Ears, 1526) no. 18. *Kishi* (cliffs) is a metaphor for the castle walls, high enough to pierce the clouds. *Kishi* and *yanagi* (weeping willows) are kindred words (*engo*), and the poet draws a parallel between the streaks of rain and the thin, hanging branches of the willow trees. The water metaphor has a correlative in the English "weeping" (cf. *JS* no. 368).

7. Sōchō draws a flattering classical parallel between his host's fortifications and the pond in the garden of Xingqing Palace 興慶宮 of Emperor Xuanzong 玄宗. It figures in such well-known poems as the following by Li Qiao, (*Wakan rōeishū* no. 81), where it is associated with willows:

> The sound of the bell of Changle Palace
>   fades beyond the blossoms;
> The color of the willows of Dragon Pond
>   deepens in the rain.

8. This is a felicitous hokku in praise of the castle's pond, which Sōchō compares to the Sumiyoshi (Suminoe) coast with its splendid cliffs. A kakekotoba pivots between *sumi* (clear) and Suminoe; *kishi* and Suminoe are kindred words. The season of the verse is problematic, however, since Sōchō composed it in midsummer. Perhaps the verse compares the summer pond to Suminoe in springtime.

9. Sōchō's "four or five years" is problematic, as he is ostensibly writing in 1522, and the castle is believed to have been begun in the Bunmei era (1469–87). He may have visited the castle in 1517 during the travels recorded in *Utsunoyama no ki* and heard the following account there at that time. Or "four or five" may be a scribal error for "forty or fifty," which roughly corresponds to the start of construction.

10. *Sōchō Kojiden* (Biography of the Lay Priest Sōchō), the earliest extant biography of Sōchō, written by Kurokawa Dōyū 黒川道祐 in 1668, states that Sōchō and Yasuhiro were close friends, an assertion corroborated by the linked-verse sequence entitled *Jukkai hyakuin dokugin* (A Solo Hundred-Verse Sequence in Lamentation), which Sōchō composed in Yasuhiro's memory (ms. in Ijichi 1975: 244–48).

11. The well, which still exists, is actually forty-two meters deep. "Feet" translates *shaku*, a roughly equivalent unit of measure. There is a legend that during a campaign in 1568–69 the well belched forth mist that cloaked the castle and saved its defenders from defeat. The fortress was also known as the Castle of Clouds and Mist (Kumogirijō 雲霧城) in consequence.

12. The Undiggable Well, Horikane no i 堀兼井, is an utamakura in Musashi Province (Sayama 狭山 City, Saitama Prefecture). The name is used in poetry to mean either a shallow well or one of great depth. Sōchō of course uses it in the latter sense.

13. Sakagawa river. Kakegawa loosely translates as "upon the river."

14. Owada (1983: 97) suggests *tohi* 都鄙, lit., capital and hinterlands, here means Kyoto and Kamakura.

15. The following chronicle amplifies or abbreviates much of the material found in *Imagawa kafu* (Lineage of the Imagawa House) and an alternate text, *Imagawaki* (Imagawa Chronicle), the latter not to be confused with a second *Imagawaki* also known as *Furokuki* (Chronicle Beneath Mount Fuji). The postscript of *Imagawa kafu* relates that Sōchō transcribed the document from Sino-Japanese (*kanbun*) into a more easily readable style mixing Chinese characters and *kana* syllabary (*wakankonkōbun*) in 1526. Sōchō's work was later lost in a fire and rewritten from memory in 1576 by a descendant of the person who had originally requested the wakankonkōbun from Sōchō. The extant work includes material from after 1526. It is possible that *The Journal of Sōchō* itself was used to recreate the original *Imagawa kafu*.

16. An interlinear note in the Shōkōkan ms. of *The Journal of Sōchō* (Shimazu 1975: 8) states that Saemonnosuke 左衛門佐 was a vassal of the Imagawa who later bore the surname Futamata 二俣. The Shōkōkan ms. says his surname was Kanbara 蒲原 (Shimazu 1975: 8). Shimazu identifies him as Futamata Masanaga 二俣昌長 (ibid.) Yama-

Notes to Book One (1522), Page 9

moto and Owada (1984: 345) hold that he was lord of Yashiroyama 社山 Castle (Toyookamura 豊岡村, Iwata 磐田 District, Shizuoka Prefecture,) and later the builder of Futamata Castle (Futamata, Tenryū 天竜 City, Shizuoka Prefecture), to which he subsequently moved. They add that he was confined in 1502 for involvement with the Shiba (ibid.). Akimoto (1984: 123–24), however, points out that there is no real reason to assume Saemonnosuke was an Imagawa vassal; he may in fact have been on the Shiba side. Akimoto suggests that he may have been Shiba Saemonnosuke Yoshio 斯波左衛門佐義雄 and that he was taken prisoner by the Imagawa and exiled to Futamata Castle (ibid.). Yoshii (1985: 50–51) concurs.

17. Horie Shimotsukenokami 堀江下野守 was an important Shiba vassal. Murakushi 村櫛 is a peninsula that protrudes into Lake Hamana in western Shizuoka Prefecture.

18. These events occured in 1501 (Akimoto 1984: 123). Hōjō Sōun 北条早雲 (1432–1519) was the founder of the Gohōjō 後北条 house and eventual lord of Izu and Sagami. His younger sister, known as Lady Kitagawa 北川 (c. 1442–1529), became the wife of Imagawa Yoshitada and also a confidante of Sōchō (*JS*: 90, 162).

19. Yoshii (1985: 50) states that the castle fell in the spring of 1502.

20. Ōkōchi Bitchūnokami Sadatsuna 大河内備中守貞綱 was proprietor (*ryōshu* 領主) of Hikuma 引馬 (Hamamatsu City, Shizuoka Prefecture) and deputy (*daikan*) for the Kira 吉良, the Hamamatsu proprietors (Shimazu 1975: 9). The Ōkōchi were residents of Mikawa (Aichi Prefecture), who traced their descent to Minamoto Yorimasa 源頼政 (c. 1103–80). The Kira were based in the Kira area, in what is now Hazu 幡豆 District, Aichi Prefecture. They later supported the Imagawa in 1505 by attacking Anjō 安城 (Anjō City, Aichi Prefecture) and, in 1506, Okazaki 岡崎 (Okazaki City, Aichi Prefecture) during Ujichika's Imahashi campaign in eastern Mikawa (see Appendix B).

21. Iio (or perhaps Inō) Zenshirō Katatsura 飯尾善四郎賢連 was a peripheral member of the Miyoshi 三善 (Shimazu 1975: 9). The context suggests that Katatsura assumed the office of commissioner (*bugyō*) of the Hamamatsu Estate when Ōkōchi Sadatsuna vacated it.

22. Iio Zenzaemonnojō Nagatsura 飯尾善左衛門尉長連.

23. Yoshitada was killed in a skirmish in 1476 at Shiokaizaka 塩買坂 (Shizuoka Prefecture, Ogasachō 小笠町) after suppressing the Yokochi 横地 and Katsumata 勝間田, two provincial warrior (*kokujin*) houses in eastern Tōtōmi, at Mitsuke 見付 Castle (Iwata 磐田 City, Shizuoka Prefecture).

24. Iio Zenzaemon Katatsura 飯尾善左衛門賢連, probably the same as Iio Zenshirō Katatsura, became lord of Hikuma Castle when Ōkōchi Sadatsuna was killed in 1517; Iio Zenshirō Noritsura 飯尾善四郎乗連 was commissioner of the Hamamatsu Estate and was visited by Sōchō on his journey to Kyoto from Suruga in 1526 (*JS*: 97); Iio Zenrokurō Tamekiyo 飯尾善六郎為清, Katatsura's younger brother and Noritsura's uncle, took part in a renga sequence, Eishō 1 [1504] (Eishō 3? [1506?]) *Nanibito hyakuin* (A Hundred-Verse Sequence Entitled "A Kind of Person"), composed at Sōchō's hermitage in Mariko

Notes to Book One (1522), Page 9

in 1504 (or 1506, depending when the hermitage was built; see Shigematsu 1979), visited Sōchō at that hermitage in 1517 (*Utsunoyama no ki* 401), and saw Sōchō off as far as Hamana Bridge on the latter's journey to Kyoto in 1526 (*JS*: 308). The Iio were thus Sōchō's close acquaintances, and he was perhaps moved to make special mention of their names in this chronicle with the expectation that they would see it.

25. In 1504 Ōgigayatsu Uesugi Tomoyoshi 扇谷上杉朝良 (d. 1518) was in conflict with Yamanouchi Uesugi Akisada 山内上杉顕定 (d. 1510) and had gradually been pushed back to his castle at Kawagoe 川越 (Kawagoe City, Saitama Prefecture). To save him, Imagawa Ujichika and Hōjō Sōun mobilized. Akisada learned of this and abandoned his attack on Kawagoe Castle to face them. The battle that Sōchō describes took place in the ninth month of 1504 at Tachikawa 立川 in Musashi Province (Tachikawa City, Tokyo Metropolitan Prefecture), but it resulted in no clear victory. It is said 1,800 died in the conflict (Owada 1984b: 27). Fighting between the Yamanouchi and Ōgigayatsu is also mentioned in Sōchō's *Sōgi shūenki* (The Death of Sōgi, 1502) (103). For background on their conflicts, see Sugiyama 1974: 56–60; 72–77. Though Sōchō is writing as an Imagawa partisan here, he was well acquainted with both Yamanouchi and Ōgigayatsu leaders; he and Sōgi stayed with Yamanouchi Akisada for over twenty days at Uwado 上戸 (Kawagoe City, Saitama Prefecture) in 1502 (*Sōgi shūenki* 109). In 1509, Sōchō visited the Yamanouchi at their castle at Hachigata 鉢形 (Yoriimachi 寄居町, Ōsato 大里 District, Saitama Prefecture) during his journey described in *Azumaji no tsuto* (Souvenir of the Eastland, 1509)(778), and he also sent Akisada renga composed in that year (Ōshima 1963–64, 35: 77). But in 1502 he and Sōgi remained with the Ōgigayatsu as well for over ten days at Kawagoe Castle and later at Edo Castle, where there was a linked-verse session (*Sōgi shūenki* 109). Sōchō and Tomoyoshi also took part in a three-hundred-verse session at Edo Castle in 1509 (*Azumaji no tsuto* 779).

26. This is Ōgigayatsu Tomoyoshi, not Tomonaga 朝長 as given in the interlinear notes of the Shōkōkan ms. (Shimazu 1975: 9). *Imagawaki* gives Tomoyoshi (237).

27. A "Kantō league" (*bandōri* 坂東里) was six *chō* 町 in length (somewhat under 700 m.). Three Kantō leagues thus equalled approximately two kilometers.

28. Hōjō Sōun had already gone to reinforce Ōgigayatsu Tomoyoshi. In Sōchō's postscript to his celebratory thousand-verse sequence, *Shutsujin senku* 出陣千句 (A Thousand-Verse Sequence for the Campaign, 1504)(564), composed soon after the battle, he writes that Ujichika set out on the twelfth of the ninth month, not the eleventh as indicated in *The Journal of Sōchō*. Inasmuch as Sōchō most likely wrote the postscript soon after composing the sequence but composed the account in *The Journal of Sōchō* eighteen years later, the dating in the former would seem the more reliable.

29. Fukushima Saemonnojō 福島左衛門尉 (read Kushima in Yamamoto and Owada 1984: 338) is probably Fukushima Sukeharu 福島助春, lord of Takatenjin 高天神 Castle in Tōtōmi and a major Imagawa vassal.

30. Masukata 益形, in Musashi Province (Tokyo Metropolitan Prefecture).

31. The context makes this the twenty-fourth of the ninth month. Owada (1984b: 27), however, gives it as the twenty-seventh. The latter date is corroborated in the postscript of *Shutsujin senku*.

32. The text appears to be corrupt here, as the battle itself took place at Tachikawa, and Akisada had no castle there. *Imagawa kafu* (156) states that he retired to Hachigata, which seems much more likely.

33. Nirayama 韮山 (Tagata 田方 District, Shizuoka Prefecture) is famous for its hot springs, as is Atami 熱海, on the northeast coast of the Izu peninsula. Nirayama was also the site of Sōun's main castle.

34. Mishima 三島 Shrine is located in Mishima City, Shizuoka Prefecture. Ujichika perhaps petitioned the god of Mishima because of the shrine's connections with the Minamoto clan, from which the Imagawa claimed descent. Minamoto Yoritomo had prayed for success at Mishima before warring with the Taira.

35. This is *Shutsujin senku*, also known as *Saiokuken senku* 柴屋軒千句, *Mishima senku* 三島千句 (the latter not to be confused with Sōgi's *Mishima senku* of 1471), or *Shin Mishima senku* 新三島千句. Sōchō says in his journal that he began the solo sequence on the tenth of the tenth month, but the postscript of the sequence itself says that it was completed on the twenty-seventh of that month. As a formal thousand-verse sequence conventionally required three days to complete, it follows that the dates of the sequence were most likely 1504:10:25–27. That is corroborated by the dates affixed to the ten hokku: nos. 1–3, 10:25; nos. 4–7; 10:26; nos. 8–10, 10:27. It must be noted, however, that in view of the fact that the battle occurred on the twenty-seventh of the ninth month, Sōchō's mention of the twenty-seventh of the tenth month in the postscript is suspiciously fortuitous; he may indeed have completed the work earlier and later affixed appropriately auspicious dates to the document itself. The sequence was commissioned to thank the god of Mishima for the victory and to pray for peace thereafter. It was not commissioned to pray for victory, as Yamada (1980: 196) has indicated. Harada (1979: 338) argues that Ujichika did not request the sequence as related in Yamada (1980: 150), but that Sōchō initiated it himself for Ujichika's benefit. For the background of *Shutsujin senku*, dating problems, and discussion of the first eight and last seven verses of the first hundred-verse sequence as well as other select couplets, see Harada 1979: 310–56.

36. The work is a "four-season, thousand-verse sequence" (*shiki senku* 四季千句); thus the first hokku begins with spring, despite having been composed in the tenth month. The seasonal arrangement of hokku is nos. 1–3, spring; nos. 4–5, summer; nos. 6–8, autumn; nos. 9–10, winter.

37. The spring haze at Mishima Shrine reaches over the surrounding province, now at peace. Ujichika may have composed the hokku himself, or Sōchō may have composed it for him as a proxy poem.

38. This is the hokku for the second hundred-verse sequence. *Yūkazura* is a vine (*kazura*) with white mulberry paper (*yū*) affixed to it, the garland then being dedicated to a

god. *Aoyagi* (light-green willow) and *kazura* (vine) are kindred words. Here willows are added to the garland, making an even more elegant dedication. *Kakesou* also has overtones of *kage sou* (added divine presence), which suggests the god himself is present in the willows. *Kage* is also a kindred word with *kazura*.

39. Yokoyama (1978: 362) identifies the date as 1512:5, and Kurosawa (1977: 172) as 1512, c. the fourth month. Akimoto (1984: 129), however, interprets Sōchō's *mata hachi, kyūnen shite* as "Again, in the eighth or ninth year of Eishō," which equates to 1511 or 1512. Ōkōchi Bitchūnokami is Sadatsuna (*JS*: 195, n. 20).

40. Asahina Sakyōnosuke Yasumochi 朝比奈左京亮泰以 (n.d.) was the younger brother of Yasuhiro, and he served as regent for his nephew Yasuyoshi for approximately a decade. He composed the hokku for Eishō 15 [1518]:1:3 *Yamanani hyakuin* (A Hundred-Verse Sequence Entitled "A Kind of Mountain"), a solo sequence by Sōchō for which Imagawa Ujichika provided the waki verse. He also sponsored a sequence at his residence in which Sōchō took part in 1526 (*JS*: 90) and appeared in connection with a thousand-verse sequence later that year (*JS*: 90, 96). He was one of Sōchō's closest and most influential patrons. For the names and dates of the most important Imagawa vassals from 1480 to 1580, see Ōtsuka 1977.

41. This not a new Ōkōchi campaign but an amplification of their rise in support of Shiba Yoshitatsu 斯波吉達 (d. 1521), who had begun his attempt to retake Tōtōmi in 1510 (Akimoto 1984: 129).

42. Ryōgonji 楞厳寺 was a Zen temple (Sōtō sect, now defunct) in the Kasai 笠井 Estate, which was located to the west of Tenryūgawa 天竜川 river, now in Hamamatsu City, Shizuoka Prefecture. Shimazu (1975: 10) suggests it may have been on a sandbar in the river. Daibosatsu 大菩薩 Mountain, in Mikataharachō 三方原町, Hamamatsu City, is now known as Utōzaka うとう坂.

43. Ii Jirō 井伊次郎 was a local warrior from Tōtōmi. Mitake 深嶽 Mountain is in Mitake 三岳, Inasachō 引佐町, Shizuoka Prefecture, northeast of Iinoya 井伊谷. "Martial Defender" (Buei 武衛) was the Sinitic style for *Hyōefu* 兵衛府, standing for Sahyōenokami 左兵衛督, hereditary office of the Shiba constable, here Yoshitatsu. Ujichika set out for Hamamatsu and made camp at Ryōgonji in the Kasai Estate. His forces met those of Shiba Yoshitatsu and Ii Jirō, based at Mitake Castle, and those of Ōkōchi Bitchūnokami Sadatsuna, based at Hikuma Castle, and drove them from the Hamamatsu area (Kurosawa 1977: 173). Asahina Yasumochi led the vanguard. Akimoto (1984: 129) cites sources that date the fall of Mitake Castle to 1513:3:7, and he feels these discredit the 1514 date in the *GSRJ* ms. (258). Kurosawa (1977: 173) likewise gives 1513.

44. Okunoyama 奥山 is in Inasachō, Inasa District, Shizuoka Prefecture.

45. The Kai were vice constables of Tōtōmi.

46. Takeda Jirō Nobutsuna 武田次郎信綱 fell out with his brother Takeda Nobutora 武田信虎 (1494–1574), daimyō of Kai (Yamanashi Prefecture). *Imagawaki* (238) relates that "In the third year of Eishō [1506, *sic*] Takeda Jirō Nobutsuna of Kōshū and his brother

had a falling out which led to war." Interlinear notes in the Shōkōkan (Shimazu 1975: 11) and *GSRJ* mss. (258) of *The Journal of Sōchō* date this Eishō 12 (1515), "three" and "twelve" being orthographically similar when written vertically. Akimoto (1984: 130) dates Ujichika's involvement to the tenth month of that year. Nobutsuna's ally was Ōi Nobutatsu 大井信達. When Nobutsuna was attacked by Takeda Nobutora, Ujichika sent troops under Ihara Tangonokami 庵原丹後守 in Nobutsuna's support, but they themselves were besieged at Katsuyama 勝山 Castle (Higashiyatsushiro 東八代 District, Yamanashi Prefecture). They were near to being annihilated when in 1516 Ujichika dispatched Sōchō to negotiate for the siege to be lifted (see *Song in an Age of Discord*, 85–86). Because of Sōchō's success, the beleaguered army was saved, and Ujichika could turn his attention to a fresh rising by Ōkōchi Bitchūnokami Sadatsuna at Hikuma.

47. The Martial Defender, Yoshitatsu, was headquartered at Hikuma Castle.

48. This is the winter of 1516. The preface to the hokku Sōchō composed in celebration of the new shrine, which appears in Sōchō's second personal collection of linked verse, *Nachigomori* no. 1690, is dated to that year. The verse also appears below as *JS* no. 6.

49. *Iwashimizu* (rock-pent spring) is also the name of a famous Hachiman shrine south of Kyoto, which Sōchō invokes here to give the verse added topicality and loftiness and to elevate by association the new Asahina shrine of the same name. Hachiman 八幡 shrines are dedicated to the worship of the gods of war. "Flows on without freezing" (*kōranu nagare*) implies the never-ending blessing of the gods.

50. Asahina Shimotsukenokami Tokishige 朝比奈下野守時茂 was the brother of Yasumochi and another of Sōchō's closest friends and supporters. He and Sōchō enjoyed a year-end discussion in 1525 recorded later in *The Journal of Sōchō* (*JS*: 84–86). He participated with Sōchō in a session linking Japanese and Chinese verses (*wakan renku*) in 1525 (*JS*: 82), and he and his brother contributed to Daiei 5 [1525]:9:21 *Nanibito hyakuin* (A Hundred-Verse Sequence Entitled "A Kind of Person")(Yonehara 881–87). He and Yasumochi also sent money to Sōchō when the poet was in Kansai in 1526 (*JS*: 359).

51. 1517 (Kurosawa 1977: 174). Ujichika used Kakegawa Castle as a base of operations for his assault on Hikuma Castle, further west.

52. This verse also appears in *Utsunoyama no ki* (401) and in *Nachigomori* (Kitano Tenmangū ms., no. 2982). The "Waterless Month" (*minazuki* 水無月) is the sixth, and despite the fact that the waters are actually in flood, the soldiers cross the river as though walking on solid ground. There is a pun on *kachibito*, meaning both "victors" and "people on foot."

53. Sōchō perhaps preferred the alternate version, which reads *minazuki wa / mina kachibito no / watari kana*, because of the pleasing sound repetition of the first two parts of the verse.

54. One chō variously equalled about 110 meters or about 100 ares. The castle in question is Hikuma.

Notes to Book One (1522), Page 12

55. The Shōkōkan (Shimazu 1975: 12) and *GSRJ* (259) mss. give Eishō 13, but that is a mistake for Eishō 14 (1517). See Akimoto 1984: 131.

56. The Abeyama gold mines covered a large area at the upper reaches of Abekawa river. They and other mines at the upper section of Ōigawa 大井川 river were a primary source of Imagawa wealth and vital to the ability of the house to conduct military campaigns. See Owada 1984a: 107–9.

57. Like the Ōkōchi, the Ōmi 巨海 had been long opposed to the Imagawa. In 1473 Ashikaga Yoshimasa had made over to Imagawa Yoshitada the rights to estates which had been held by Ōmi Shinzaemonnojō 巨海新左衛門尉. Sōchō reviews this further on in this account (*JS*: 13). The Ōmi were situated in the town of that name, now part of Shinshiro 新城 City, and the Takahashi 高橋 were located in the village of that name, now part of Toyota 豊田 City, Aichi Prefecture (Shimazu 1975: 12). *Nagoya kassenki* (Nagoya Battle Chronicle) (105) identifies Ōmi as Shinzaemonnojō Michitsuna 巨海新左衛門尉道綱, younger brother of Ōkōchi Bitchūnokami Sadatsuna, and Takahashi as Saburōbyoenojo Masasada 高橋三郎兵衛尉正定.

58. Iio Katatsura was put in charge of Hikuma Castle on Sadatsuna's defeat.

59. *Nagoya kassenki* (105) relates that the Martial Defender signed a pledge never again to take up arms against the Imagawa. Fusaiji 普斎寺 is a Sōtō Zen temple in Tomizukachō 富塚町, Hamamatsu City.

60. The account goes back in time here to the beginning of the fifteenth century. In 1400 Imagawa Yasunori 今川泰範 (1334–1409) was made constable (*shugo*) of Tōtōmi in addition to Suruga. In 1405 the office of Tōtōmi constable was transferred to Shiba Yoshinori 斯波義教 (or Yoshishige 義重, 1371–1418), who held it until 1407. Thereafter it may have been that Shiba Yoshinori and Imagawa Yasunori shared constabulary duties in Tōtōmi until the death of the later in 1409, but the facts are unclear, as Sōchō suggests in the following sentence (Yoshii 1985: 32–33). Shiba Yoshinori then served as *shugo* until his death in 1418. His descendants held the office thereafter until 1508. The Imagawa may, however, have retained jurisdiction over what is now the Kitō 城東 District even after Yasunori's death (Yoshii 1985: 35–36).

61. For the background of Sōchō's remarks here on the Imagawa house, see Appendix A, "The Imagawa House."

62. The Shōkōkan (Shimazu 1975: 12–13) and *GSRJ* (259) mss. give the interlinear note, "The Imagawa returned after the Martial Defenders had been in the province eighty-five years." The dating is imprecise, however, as Yoshitada was granted rights to lands there in 1473 (see following).

63. In 1473 Yoshitada was made deputy (*daikan*) of Kakegawa 懸革 or 掛川 Estate. The document recording the grant survives (Owada 1983: 135). Presumably the grant of the Kawawa 河匂 Estate was made at the same time, though no document is extant. The latter estate was located in what is now Kawawachō 川輪町, Hamamatsu City (Shimazu 1975:

165). Shimazu remarks that the grant was made by the bakufu because of Imagawa help in suppressing the "Koga Shogun" (Koga Kubō 古賀公方), Ashikaga Shigeuji 足利成氏 (Shimazu 1975: 13). Yoshii (1985: 55) concurs. Fukōin 普広院 was the family temple of Ashikaga Yoshinori. Shimazu adds that both estates were taken from Ōmi Shinzaemonnojō and given to Yoshitada, who occupied Kakegawa in 1474. The Kakegawa Estate was near Kitō District, which the Imagawa may have held all along (Yoshii 1985: 55).

64. Ōmi Shinzaemonnojō held the estates as *shugouke* properties, having ceded them to the constable in return for various rights.

65. Kanō Kunainoshō 狩野宮内少輔. Actually the Kanō assisted the vice constables, the Kai. The constable at the time was Shiba Yoshisuke 斯波義良 (who later changed his name to Yoshitō 義寛) of the Eastern Army in the Ōnin conflict, but real Shiba power in the province was held by the forces of Shiba Yoshikado of the Western Army (Yoshii 1985: 55).

66. An interlinear note in one manuscript identifies the date as 1465, but 1474 seems more likely. For the background of this campaign, see Appendix B, "The Historical Context of the Asahina Battle Chronicle."

67. It would appear the narrative has gone back in time here.

68. A "district constable" *gundai* 郡代 administered one or more districts (*gun*). They were sometimes called "vice constable" (*shugodai* 守護代; note Sōchō earlier refers to Kanō Kunainoshō as such [*JS*: 12]), but the term *shugodai* more commonly referred to a vice constable under a *shugo*.

69. Kanō Jirō 狩野次郎.

70. The relationship between Kanō Suke of Abe 安部 and Kanō Suke of Izu is unclear.

71. Imagawa Yoshitada went to Kyoto in 1467 to lend his support to the Eastern Army (Tōgun) under Hosokawa Katsumoto 細川勝元 (1430–73). The shogun, Yoshimasa, notified Yoshitada through shogunal advisor Ise Sadachika 伊勢貞親 (Isenokami, 1417–73) that he should join with Hosokawa Sanukinokami 細川讃岐守, likewise of the Eastern Army, who held Mikawa, and oppose Shiba Yoshikado 斯波義廉 (n.d.), constable of Tōtōmi, Owari, and Echizen. If successful, Yoshitada was to be rewarded with the constableship of Tōtōmi (as mentioned earlier, the Imagawa had already been granted estates in Tōtōmi by the bakufu for earlier military service). Yoshitada obeyed the order and sent troops to Hikuma in west Tōtōmi, then returned to Suruga in 1468. He was no doubt willing to comply with the bakufu directive because by opposing Yoshikado he stood not only to protect his current holdings but to expand them. The Shōkōkan (Shimazu 1975: 13) and *GSRJ* (260) mss. identify Hosokawa Sanukinokami as Yoshiyuki 義之. Owada (1981c: 987) believes he was Shigeyuki 成之. He was being opposed in Mikawa by his vice constable, Tōjō Ōminokami Kuniuji 東条近江守国氏, a member of the Kira Tōjō 吉良東条 house. While in Kyoto, Yoshitada married the younger sister of

Hōjō Sōun. She was the daughter of Ise Morisada 伊勢盛定, of the same Ise family as the bakufu advisor, Sadachika. Yoshitada returned to Kyoto in 1470, then went back to Suruga later that year.

72. Sōchō's account, as indicated by Shimazu (1975: 13), suggests "twelfth month" refers to Yoshitada's return from Kyoto in the second year of Bunmei (1470 or early 1471). But as noted by Owada (1986: 84–85), that date seems unlikely, as the next sentence, beginning with "the next year," refers to events which could only have happened after Yoshitada invaded Tōtōmi to subdue the Kanō in 1474. He succeeded in overcoming Kanō resistance in the eleventh month of that year, as Sōchō wrote earlier (*JS*: 12).

73. *Imagawaki* (236) identifies those freebooters as the Yokochi and Katsumata kokujin houses. Interlinear notes in the Shōkōkan (Shimazu 1975: 13) and *GSRJ* (260) mss. identify Mutsunokami as Sena Sadanobu, another name for Horikoshi Sadanobu. Owada (1986: 84) cites *Kansei chōshū shokafu* (Kansei Continued Lineage of the Various Houses, 1812)(2: 232) to show that Sadanobu was killed in 1474, but he admits that the work provides no source for its information. The account in *The Journal of Sōchō* says he was killed in the following year, which was 1475, if 1474 is the correct date for this campaign. In another work, *Suruga Imagawa ichizoku*, Owada agrees with the 1475 date (Owada 1983: 137).

74. Yabe Saemonnojō 矢部左衛門尉 was an Imagawa vassal and Tōtōmi resident. Higonokami Yasumori 肥後守泰盛 was a member of the Asahina house who the *Imagawaki* (236) states died in battle. Okabe Saemonnojō 岡部左衛門尉 was another Imagawa vassal and Tōtōmi resident.

75. Sōchō may be implying that a curse was at work. Yoshitada defeated the Yokochi and Katsumata, but as pointed out earlier, he was killed in a skirmish with their surviving partisans in what appears to have been 1476. Other sources place his date of death at 1475 or 1479, but Shimazu (1975: 14) and Owada (1983: 140) agree on 1476.

76. The editing in Shimazu (1975: 14) connects the first part of this sentence, "it was over twenty years after Yoshitada's untimely death," to the previous paragraph. That passage should instead introduce the next paragraph as it does in the translation, since it was twenty-one years after Yoshitada's death that Ujichika made his first major moves into Tōtōmi.

77. Shimazu (1975: 14) identifies Tahara Danjōnochū 田原弾正忠 as Toda Munemitsu 戸田宗光, resident of what is now Taharamachi 田原町, Atsumi 渥美 District, Aichi Prefecture, and Suwa Shinanonokami 諏訪信濃守 as a local Tōtōmi resident. Funakata ふなかた (舟方), was located in what is now Toyohashi 豊橋 City, Aichi Prefecture.

78. Tame Matazaburō 多米又三郎 was an Imagawa partisan.

79. Due to an earthquake in 1498, Lake Hamana, which had been landlocked, was opened to the ocean. Asahina Yasumochi was a younger brother of Yasuhiro and regent to Yasuhiro's son, Yasuyoshi.

80. "The interior" (*okugun* 奥郡) may refer to Funakata and environs.

81. The "Asahina Battle Chronicle" ends here.

82. Iio Noritsura's grandfather Nagatsura was honored in the "Asahina Battle Chronicle" (*JS*: 9) for having been appointed commissioner of the Hamamatsu Estate and later for having died in defense of his lord Imagawa Yoshitada in Tōtōmi. The Hamamatsu 浜松 Estate had previously been under the control of Ōkōchi Bitchūnokami Sadatsuna, who was killed in the siege of Hikuma Castle in 1517 (*JS*: 11–12).

83. Yamazaki 山崎 is in Yūtōchō 雄踏町, Hamana 浜名 District, Shizuoka Prefecture. The residence of Hamana Bitchūnokami 浜名備中守 was Saku 佐久 Castle in Mikkabichō 三ヶ日町, Inasa 引佐 District. The Hamana were vassals of the Imagawa (Abe and Nishimura 1990: 640).

84. Shigematsu Hiromi (1978: 10) suggests Sōchō may have in mind the following verse (no. 696) from *Horikawa hyakushu*, by Minamoto Shunrai:

karigane mo	The wings of the geese
hane shioruran	must be dripping with moisture.
masuge ouru	They too should dress for rain
inasa hosoe ni	at the Inlet of Inasa
amatsutsumi seyo	where the fine sedge grows.

Sedge was used to make rain capes and hats. For commentaries on this poem, see Hashimoto and Takizawa 1977: 62. Sōgi's commentary quoted therein expressly indicates that the uncommon word *amatsutsumi* means "[don] rain gear." The hokku suggests that the rain on Lake Hamana has stopped, as if the sky itself were wearing a rain cape.

85. Honsaka 本坂 is a pass at the border of Tōtōmi and Mikawa Provinces. The Saigō 西郷 were Mikawa kokujin, possibly based at Wachigaya 月ケ谷 Castle in Suse 嵩山, Toyohashi City, Aichi Prefecture. On the Saigō, see Ōkubo 1987. The Uri Kumagai 宇利熊谷 were lords of Kachiyama 勝山 Castle in Ishimaki 石巻, Toyohashi City, three kilometers from Wachigaya Castle. On Sōchō's activities in Mikawa, see Shingyō 1977.

86. The verse appears in *Oi no mimi* (no. 23) as *kumo kakaru / chiri no fumoto no / ōchi kana*. The verse implies that the slopes stand in the mundane, dust-covered world, while the pinnacle, covered in purple *ōchi* blossoms, approaches the Western Paradise.

87. Yawata 八幡 is northeast of Kō 国府 in Aichi Prefecture. Makino Shirōzaemonnojō 牧野四郎左衛門尉 was lord of Ichida 市田 Castle. Honnogahara 本野が原 is northwest of Hoi 宝飯 District, Toyokawa 豊川 City; it is also mentioned in *Tōgoku kikō* (Journey to the Eastern Provinces, 1545), the travel diary of Sōchō's disciple Tani Sōboku 谷宗牧 (d. 1545).

88. *Oi no mimi* no. 24. There the verse appears in corrupt form as *yuku sode o / kusaba no take no / natsuno kana*.

89. "This province" refers to Mikawa. Yahagigawa 矢作川 river runs by Okazaki 岡崎 City in Aichi Prefecture. Eight Bridges (Yatsuhashi 八橋) is a famous utamakura located in Chiryū 知立 City, Aichi Prefecture. The spot is given particularly famous mention in

Notes to Book One (1522), Page 15

Ise monogatari (21): "They reached Eight Bridges. It bears that name because of the eight bridges spanning the river that branches out there like the legs of a spider."

90. Mizuno Izuminokami Chikamori 水野和泉守近盛, also called Tōkurō 藤九郎, was one of Sōchō's main patrons. Sōchō records a hokku composed in 1516 for a thousand-verse sequence at Chikamori's residence in *Nachigomori* (168) and *Utsunoyama no ki* (400), and he stayed at his castle in Kariya 苅屋 (Kariya 刈谷 City, Aichi Prefecture) on each of the four trips between Suruga and Kansai recounted in *The Journal of Sōchō* (*JS*: 15, 55, 99, 149). It was also for Chikamori that Sōchō wrote a commentary in 1520 on Sōgi's second personal collection of linked verse, *Wakuraba* (Blighted Leaves, 1481, rev. 1485). Sōchō added his commentary to one that Sōgi had written for the work earlier, hence the combined title for the two commentaries (*Guku Wakuraba* (My Ignorant Blighted Leaves). For more on the Mizuno family, see Suzuki Mitsuyasu 1973.

91. Mizuno Kisaburō 水野紀三郎 was another warrior literatus of the Mizuno house, and his name appears in a preface to one of Sōchō's hokku in *Nachigomori* dated 1516 (168). Tokoname 常滑 City, Chita 知多 District, is on the west coast of the Chita Peninsula, Aichi Prefecture.

92. Noma 野間, south of Tokoname, was the site of the death of Minamoto Yoshitomo 源義朝 (1123–60), the father of the founder of the Kamakura Bakufu, Yoritomo.

93. Ōminato 大湊 is in Ise City, at the mouth of Miyagawa 宮川 river. Yamada 山田 is also in Ise City, where the Outer Shrine (Gekū 外宮), more formally Toyouke (or Toyuke) Daijingū 豊受大神宮, is located. *Ise senku* 伊勢千句 (also known as *Yamada senku* 山田千句) is one of the most important thousand-verse sequences in the body of renga literature, and numerous commentaries have been written on it. Two that have been printed are the Jingū Bunko ms., *Daijingū hōraku onsenku* 大神宮法楽御千句, to which Senda Ken added the commentary of the *Daijingū hōraku onsenkuchū* 大神宮法楽御千句註, also in Jingū Bunko (see Senda 1964–69) and the Naikaku Bunko ms. (Kaneko 1974: 340–422). Sōchō recorded a large number of his *Ise senku* verses in his personal poetry collection *Oi no mimi* (see Iwashita 1985).

94. Gessonsai Sōseki 月村斎宗碩 (1474–1533) was a disciple of both Inō Sōgi 飯尾宗祇 (1421–1502) and Sōchō, and he succeeded to Sōgi's Shugyokuan 種玉庵 cottage in the capital when Sōgi died. He and Sōchō were present at the master's death at Hakone Yumoto 箱根湯本 (Kanagawa Prefecture) in 1502, and he figures in Sōchō's account of the event, *Sōgi shūenki*. Sōchō and Sōseki composed an extant two-poet hundred-verse sequence as well, *Sōseki Sōchō ryōgin nanimichi hyakuin* (A Hundred-Verse Sequence Entitled "A Kind of Path," by Sōseki and Sōchō, n.d.), and Sōchō also made several judgments of Sōseki's work. Sōseki also frequently appears in the pages of *The Journal of Sōchō*. His account of the composition of *Ise senku* in his *Sano no watari* (Sano Crossing, 1522) reads as follows:

My journey to Ise had its beginnings at the end of last year, when the Zen priest Sōchō sent a letter to me from Suruga saying that he had been planning to compose a solo thousand-verse sequence as an invocation at the Grand Shrine of Ise. But as he was of great age, two or three years had passed without his being able to carry it out, and he asked whether I would be inclined to make it a two-poet sequence if I happened to be visiting the Shrine in the spring. At first I was too overwhelmed to reply, but he continued to inquire, and it occurred to me that such a composition might serve as a lasting memorial to the way of linked verse. So I wrote that I would set out when he reached Yamada and that I looked forward to catching up since seeing him last.

Soon the New Year arrived, but we were both detained, and more time went by. At the beginning of the sixth month he came up from Suruga. Though he presently notified me by courier, I was just then building my hermitage, and the noise of the adzes in my ears disconcerted me so that I could give no thought to renga. I decided that the earliest I could set out would be about the twentieth of the seventh month. Someone from Owari Province was visiting me in the capital just then, so I invited him to accompany me as far as Ise . . . .

My accommodations at the Shrine were in the residence of Ajiro Tarōzaemonnojō Hirosada, but this trip was to see Sōchō, so we chatted at the house of Takabuku Jirōdayū [Mitsusada] about events since we had seen each other last, then immediately began to make plans for the linked-verse sequence. It was to be a solemn votive composition for the peace of the realm, and the Deputy [Hosokawa Takakuni] supplied the hokku. A hokku for the tenth hundred-verse sequence was provided by Lord Shōyōin Chōsetsu [Sanjōnishi Sanetaka]. As the fourth of the eighth month was auspicious, we began composing it on that date and finished on the eighth of the same month. We had earlier agreed to proceed at a deliberate pace to ensure that the sequence would be all it should be.

After the senku there was a session held by Mitsusada. On the fifteenth there was another by Hashimura Shinjirō Kiyomasa. On the sixteenth Sōchō, having business in Ōmi, set off over the Suzuka Mountains. (*Sano no watari* 1282–84)

95. Hosokawa Takakuni 細川高国 (1484–1531), the deputy (*kanrei*), fought his way back to Kyoto in 1520 after having been defeated in the second month of that year by Hosokawa Sumimoto 細川澄元 (1489–1520) (like Takakuni an adopted son of Hosokawa Masamoto) and Sumimoto's ally Miyoshi Yukinaga 三好之長 (1458–1520). Takakuni in turn drove them out in the fifth month. Sōchō records the history of these events in detail later in the journal (*JS*: 141–42).

96. Shinjuan 真珠庵, at Daitokuji 大徳寺 temple in Murasakino 紫野 (Kita 北 Ward, Kyoto City), was established in memory of Ikkyū Sōjun 一休宗純 (1394–1481), the great Zen prelate with whom Sōchō studied intermittently for several years after leaving Suruga after Yoshitada's death in c. 1476. Sōchō venerated Ikkyū's memory for the rest of his life, and Daitokuji figures in both trips recorded in *The Journal of Sōchō* (*JS*: 22,

Notes to Book One (1522), Page 15

105, 111, 115–16). Sōchō also frequented two other temples connected with Ikkyū in the Daitokuji network. Those were Shūon'an 酬恩庵 at Takigi 薪 in Yamashiro Province (Tsuzuki 綴喜 District, Kyoto Prefecture) and Shōrin'an 少林庵 (also 小林庵, or Shōrinji) in Yashima 矢島, across Lake Biwa from Kyoto, in Ōmi Province (Moriyama 守山 City, Shizuoka Prefecture). Sōchō stayed at Shūon'an on both trips to the Kansai in *The Journal of Sōchō* (*JS*: 22–29, 34–43, 47, 103, 107–8) and three times in the work expressed his desire to die there (*JS*: 23, 60, 161). He stayed at Shōrin'an during the winter of 1526–27 (*JS*: 121–43). On Ikkyū, see Nakamoto 1967, Covell 1980, Sanford 1981, and Stevens 1993.

97. One of the two Hiroshima University manuscripts of *Ise senku* (*Kōdai kōhon* 廣大甲本) and the Kokkai Toshokan manuscript label this a proxy poem (*daisaku*), composed for Takakuni by Sōchō. See Kaneko 1974: 123. Iwashita Noriyuki (1985: 308) likewise sees it as a proxy poem. But it may indeed be by Takakuni, as Sōchō deliberately writes that it was sent from Kyoto. The commentary in the Naikaku Bunko ms. reads in part, "The sun is mentioned in the hokku because Ise is the seat of the Sun Goddess. The haze spreads out in all directions, glowing in the light of the morning sun. The underlying meaning refers to Takakuni's authority over the realm" (Kaneko 1974: 340). A different commentary sees the sun as a metaphor for the virtue of the Sun Goddess (Senda 1964, 63: 30). The honka is *Shinkokinshū* 1: 98, by Fujiwara Ariie:

asahikage	The cherry blossoms
nioeru yama no	on the mountains aglow
sakurabana	in the morning sun
tsurenaku kienu	might be mistaken for snow
yuki ka to zo miru	that does not deign to melt.

This is in turn based on *Man'yōshū* 4: 495. The hokku is listed in Sōchō's third personal verse collection, *Oi no mimi*, together with his waki verse:

| 151 | yuki wa nokoreru | There is no mountain crest |
| | yama no ha mo nashi | where snow yet lingers. |

The title of the first hundred-verse sequence is *Nanifune*, "[what] kind of boat." The answer is found by taking the word *asa* (morning) from the hokku and combining it with *fune* (boat) to form *asabune* (morning boat).

98. *Oi no mimi* no. 37. The underlying metaphor of the verse is that the world bends to Takakuni's will. This is the hokku for the second hundred-verse sequence. There is a kakekotoba pivoting between *arashi mo nabiku* (even the wind abates) and *nabiku yanagi* (bending willows). The *fushimono* title is *Sanji chūryaku* 三字中略, in which the middle syllable of a three-syllable word in the hokku is deleted to make another word relating to "boat." Here *arashi* (brisk wind) becomes *ashi* (reed), which refers to *ashibune* (reed boat).

Notes to Book One (1522), Pages 15–16

99. During his stays in Yamada, Sōchō also composed a number of poetry handbooks, such as *Sōchō kawa* (Sōchō's Talks on Waka; also entitled *Mikawa kudari* [Down to Mikawa] 1490), the first draft of the Okitsu half of *Sōchō renga jichū* (Personal Commentary on Sōchō's Linked Verse, in or after 1523), and possibly *Nagabumi* (Long Letter, 1490). The preface of *Sōchō kawa* (9) says it was written for Ise poets: "While I was staying for more than twenty days at Yamada in Ise, some young people came to brighten my hours in my travel lodging. During our talk, they inquired about . . . renga in the capital."

He also stopped in Ise on the journey recorded in *Utsunoyama no ki* (400) and *Nachigomori* (167–68). The Ise literary circle centered around Arakida Moritake 荒木田守武 (1473–1549), author of the famous thousand-verse haikai sequence *Moritake senku* (for a commentary on that work, see Iida 1977). For overviews of the renga activity at Ise Shrine, see Okuno Jun'ichi 1975 and Tsurusaki 1997.

100. It is now the eighth month. Sōchō intends to visit the Asakura in Echizen.

101. Kumozugawa 雲津川, now written 雲出川, in central Mie Prefecture. Anonotsu 阿野の津 (or 安濃津) is present-day Tsu 津 City.

102. Seki Minbunotaifu 関民部大輔 was Seki Toshimori 関俊盛, who bore the sobriquet Kajisai 何似斎. Sōchō also refers to him in his journal as Ikkan 一閑 and Sōtetsu 宗鉄. He was lord of Kameyama 亀山 Castle and one of Sōchō's patrons and close friends. See Tsurusaki 1971a and 1979. Kajisai had dealings with many other men of letters besides Sōchō, notably Asukai Masayasu 飛鳥井雅康 (1436–1509), son of Masayo 飛鳥井雅世 (1390–1452) and adopted son of Asukai Masachika 飛鳥井雅親 (Eiga 栄雅, 1417–1490), the last of whom is mentioned in *The Journal of Sōchō* (*JS*: 127). The relationship between Kajisai and Masayasu is touched upon in Masayasu's own travel journal, *Fuji rekiranki* (Account of Sightseeing at Fuji, 1499).

103. Shimazu (1975: 16) conjectures that Miyahara Shichirōbyōenojō Moritaka 宮原七郎兵衛尉盛孝 was a subordinate of the Kitabatake 北畠 house. Tsurusaki (1971) details the friction between the Kitabatake, the Seki, and other forces in the region. Sōchō did, in fact, stay with Moritaka for three days after leaving Kajisai's residence in 1522, but he did not mention it in his journal, possibly for political reasons. Take たけ (or 多気), in Ichishi 一志 District, Mie Prefecture, was the site of the Kitabatake castle. Sōchō also stopped there in 1516 (*Utsunoyama no ki* 400). Yawata 八幡 is in Tsu City; Hirao 平尾 is east of Matsuzaka 松坂 City.

104. Three Crossings refers to Miwatari みわたり, which Shimazu (1975: 16) notes is mentioned in Kamo no Chōmei's *Iseki*.

105. According to Sugimoto Kōjirō (1970: 193), the initial reason for the ruin of Anonotsu may have been a major earthquake in 1498. But the continual fighting among Ise barons no doubt hindered rebuilding.

106. "League" translates *ri*, a distance equal to about four kilometers. Kubota 窪田 is north of Tsu City.

107. Sōchō links the upper and lower halves of the poem through the kindred words

207

Notes to Book One (1522), Pages 16–17

naru (become / ring) and *suzu* (Suzuka Mountains / bell). The poem recalls *Shinkokinshū* 17: 1613, by Saigyō:

Composed on a journey to Ise:

suzukayama	In the Suzuka Mountains
ukiyo o yoso ni	I cast aside
furisutete	this world of sorrow—
ika ni nariyuku	what will come to pass
waga mi naruran	in this life of mine henceforth?

The Suzuka Mountains (Suzukayama 鈴鹿山) represent the division between the secular world and the sacred approach to Ise Shrine.

108. The present Kameyama Castle, in Kameyama 亀山 City, Mie Prefecture, was begun by Okamoto Munenori 岡本宗憲 in 1590. The foundations are extant. West of them, on the same chain of hills, in the area called Nomura 野村, was the old castle that the Seki used.

109. Jōjuin 成就院. A *ritsuin* 律院 was either a temple of the Vinaya (Ritsu) Sect or a temple that stressed the study of monastic discipline (*vinaya*). Kajisai's own retirement dwelling was there. Shinpukuji 新福寺 was burned in a battle in 1472 and rebuilding was begun in 1511. It was therefore relatively new when Sōchō stopped there in 1522. Three chō equalled about a third of a kilometer.

110. *Oi no mimi* no. 40. "High" refers both to the visual and the auditory aspects of the scene.

111. *Man'yōshū* 12: 3156:

suzukagawa	For whose sake
yasose watarite	do I cross the eighty rapids
taga yue ka	of Suzuka River
yogoe ni koemu	and travel the nighttime roads,
tsuma mo aranaku ni	since my wife is nowhere near?

Suzuka River (Suzukagawa 鈴鹿川) flows east through the Suzuka Mountains past Kameyama and then empties into Ise Bay.

112. According to the conventions of linked verse, the guest composes the hokku of the sequence and the host, the waki. *Nagare* (current) is associated with *yaso no se* (eighty rapids).

113. The castle of the Gamō 蒲生 house was in Gamō District, Shiga Prefecture. The constable (*shugo*) at the time for the southern part of Ōmi was Rokkaku Sadayori 六角定頼 (1495–1552). Sadayori besieged Gamō Hidenori 蒲生秀紀 at Hino 日野 Castle and defeated him (Shimazu 1975: 17). For the background of that conflict, see Tsurusaki 1983.

114. Here Sōchō attempts to set out from Kameyama, but he must turn back. He thus temporarily abandons the attempt to go to Echizen, the original purpose of the trip.

Notes to Book One (1522), Pages 17–18

115. The verse is a haikai reworking of *Kokinshū* 1: 20:

azusayumi	Today fell spring rain,
oshite harusame	recalling catalpa bows
kyō furinu	that one bends to string.
asu sae furaba	If it but falls tomorrow,
wakana tsumitemu	we will be picking young greens.

(Adapted from McCullough 1985.) Sōchō retains the double kakekotoba pivoting between *yumi oshite* (bend the bow) and *oshite* ([fall] all about) and then between *oshite haru* (bend to string) and *harusame* (spring rain).

116. Rokudaiin 六大院 is a Shingon temple of the Daigoji lineage. The hokku was the most important verse in a linked-verse sequence and the most difficult to compose. It was therefore common practice to request the hokku from a skilled poet when possible, for it raised the artistic level of the entire composition. Hokku by renga masters were in particular demand for formal votive sequences meant for a temple or shrine. Such may have been the case here. Sōchō was not physically present at the session, but his verse nevertheless evokes the time, place, and level of formality (*ji-sho-i* 時所位) of the session, as stipulated by the conventions of hokku composition. Hokku by request appear throughout *The Journal of Sōchō*.

117. The verse is based on *Kin'yōshū* (Sansōbon) 4: 262, by Sesshōke no Mikawa (the daughter of Minamoto Nakamasa):

On "cold rain":

kaminazuki	Beneath the cold rain
shigure no ame no	that continues to pour down
furu mama ni	during the tenth month,
iroiro ni naru	the Suzuka Mountains
suzukayama kana	take on such varied hues!

Shimazu (1975: 18) notes that Sōchō's verse refers as well to the teaching that the Bodhisattva Kannon has multiple means to save mankind. This hokku is also mentioned in *Nikonshū*, a collection of waka, renga, and poetic lore by Arakida Morihira (d. 1597), a priest at the Inner Shrine at Ise (see Arakida Morihira 1: 66).

118. Sakamoto 坂本 (Ōtsu 大津 City, Shiga Prefecture), is located on the east slope of Mount Hiei 比叡山. Sakamoto was a "temple town" (*monzenmachi* 門前町) associated with the Tendai temple Enryakuji 延暦寺 atop Mount Hiei. It was also a trade center well-known for its sake wholesalers and teamster activity. The passage very likely relates to Sōchō's change of plans regarding his visit to the Asakura.

119. *Oi no mimi* 38. *Shiranami* functions as a kakekotoba, pivoting between *shira[nu]* (do not know) and *shiranami* (white waves).

120. The quotation is from *Ise monogatari* (20): "As he went along the shore at the border of Ise and Owari, he saw the waves rising up brilliantly white."

121. "Young men" translates *wakashu* (or *wakashū*) 若衆, youths who were often male prostitutes.

122. The foundation poem to which Sōchō refers is *Shinkokinshū* 4: 363, by Fujiwara Teika:

Composed for a hundred-waka sequence inaugurated by Saigyō:

miwataseba	Far as I might gaze,
hana mo momiji mo	neither cherry blossoms
nakarikeri	nor colored foliage.
ura no tomaya no	Thatched-roof huts beside the bay
aki no yūgure	on an evening in autumn.

123. "Pillowed on the waves" means to sleep near the water's edge. The figure may also convey a dreamlike meeting, as in the nō play *Eguchi*:

kawabune o	Mooring the boat
tomete ōse no	on the river for a meeting
namimakura	pillowed on the waves,
tomote ōse no	on the river for a meeting
namimakura	pillowed on the waves,
ukiyo no yume o	accustomed to the dream
minarawashi	of this fleeting, floating world.

(Koyama, Satō, and Satō 1973, 1: 266). Sōchō may also be recalling Genji's exile in Suma, where Genji sleeps near the waves (*nami*), his pillow awash with tears of loneliness (*Genji monogatari* 3: 48–49).

124. The poem is a rhetorical tour de force: *seze no nami* (never-ceasing waves) and *shiku* (wash [the beach] again and again) are kindred words, as are *shiku*, *ashi* (reeds), and *karine* (brief rest), and finally *nami* (waves) and *nagori* (trace left behind).

125. Like the opening passage to *The Journal of Sōchō* (*JS*: 7), this poem is based on the utamakura Returning Mountain (Kaeruyama) in Echizen. The foundation poem, however, is not *Kokinshū* 8: 370 (*JS*: 191–92, n. 2), where "returning" implies to the capital, but rather *Kokinshū* 8: 382, where it means back to Echizen:

An acquaintance who had gone to Koshi came back after some years to the capital. This was composed on his return again to Koshi:

kaeruyama	What is the point
nani zo wa arite	of the name Returning Mountain?
aru kai wa	People call it that
kite mo tomaranu	for even if one leaves,
na ni koso arikere	one must go back again.

Sōchō's *koshiji ni zo / nani zo wa ari to* means "what good is its being in Koshi [when I must return instead past the Suzuka Mountains?]," meaning "What has happened up in Koshi?" Koshi (which includes Echizen Province) was the location of the Asakura domain.

126. Kenkokuji 建国寺 was once located in Ise City. Shimazu (1975: 19) notes it had close ties with *kanjin hijiri*, a term that referred in specific to holy men who traveled to raise religious subscriptions, or to beggar monks in general. The Inner Shrine (Naikū 内宮) is Ise's Kōtai Jingū 皇大神宮.

127. Saigyō 西行 Valley is in Ise City, south of Mount Kamiji 神路山. Saigyō went to Ise in 1180 at the outbreak of the Genpei War and lived there for about seven years.

128. The Isuzu Mimosusogawa 五十鈴御裳濯川 river flows through the precinct of the Inner Shrine at Ise.

129. Sōchō's hokku and the waki, perhaps by the abbot of Kenkokuji, are linked by a mutual reference to a foundation poem in Saigyō's personal poetry contest (*jikaawase*) *Mimosusogawa utaawase* (no. 36). It also appears as *Senzaishū* 20: 1278, with the following preface:

> After sojourning at Mount Kōya, he traveled to a mountain temple at Futaminoura in Ise Province, where he composed this. Kamiji is the name of the mountain of the Grand Shrine of Ise, which he construed as a manifestation of Dainichi Nyorai:

> fukaku irite   I made my way
> kamiji no oku o   deep into the recesses
>   tazunureba   of Mount Kamiji,
> mata ue mo naki   and on the highest peak of all,
> mine no matsukaze   wind in the pines.

130. This is the same route that Sōseki followed in the opposite direction in *Sano no watari*.

131. Hasedera 長谷寺 is an utamakura and major Shingon temple in Hase (or as here, Hatsuse 泊瀬), Sakurai 桜井 City, Nara Prefecture. It was a center for mountain ascetics and a popular pilgrimage temple for Heian courtiers, particularly women.

132. The foundation poem is *Senzaishū* 17: 1154, by Fujiwara Ariie:

> After the death of the lay priest Shigeie, vice commander of the Dazaifu, his son composed this on the theme "recalling the past at a mountain temple":

> hatsuseyama   At Mount Hatsuse,
> iriai no kane o   when I hear the sound
>   kiku tabi ni   of the temple's vesper bell,
> mukashi no tōku   I am moved to sadness
> naru zo kanashiki   by the ever more distant past.

133. Tōnomine 多武峰 Shrine, on the mountain of the same name in Sakurai City, Nara Prefecture, is said to be the place where Fujiwara Kamatari 藤原鎌足 (614-69) and Emperor Tenji 天智天皇 (c. 614-71) planned the overthrow of the Soga. The peak is also called Katariyama 談山 (Plot Mountain) in consequence. It is known for its autumn foliage and its connection to *Tōnomine Shōshō monogatari*, a Heian-period poetic diary. The festival referred to is the "Eight Sermons on the *Lotus Sutra* at Tōnomine" (*Tōnomine hakkō*), which traditionally took place on the thirteenth and fourteenth of the tenth month. *Sarugaku* (nō) performances by the Konparu (or Komparu) and other Ōmi Sarugaku troupes were held as well.

134. Shimazu (1975: 21) suggests that An'yōin 安養院 was associated with Gokokuin 護国院 of Myōrakuji temple 妙楽寺, located on the mountain.

135. Konparu Shichirō Ujiaki 金春七郎氏昭 (or 氏照, also called Sōzui 宗瑞) was the son of Konparu Zenpō 金春禅鳳 (1454-1532) and sixtieth head of the Konparu school of *sarugaku* performers.

136. Tachibanadera 橘寺, in Asukamura 明日香村, Takaichi 高市 District, Nara Prefecture, is located at what is said to be the birthplace of Prince Shōtoku. It was once a major complex with more than sixty structures. Yagi 八木, in Kashihara 橿原 City, was the headquarters of the Ochi 越智, constables of Yamato Province.

137. Shiratsuchi 白土 is in Yamato Kōriyama 大和郡山 City, Nara Prefecture. The identity of Hōgen Chōei 法眼澄英 is unknown. *Hōgen* was a medieval ecclesiastical rank awarded to doctors, Buddhist artisans, renga poets, and others.

138. Shimazu (1975: 21) notes that Senjuin 千手院, affiliated with Kōfukuji temple 興福寺, was then located at Wakakusayama 若草山 (Mikasayama 三笠山), Senjudani 千手谷, in the eastern part of Nara City. The Southern Capital (Nanto 南都) is Nara.

139. The hokku incorporates the locale of the session, Wakakusa Mountain, located to the north of Kasuga 春日 Mountain. The name of the latter may also be read *haruhi* (spring sun). Wakakusayama also includes overtones of *waka[razu]* (I do not know [when winter will come]). This is a felicitous verse implying that though the season is now winter, the pleasant sunlight gives the appearance of spring.

140. Jison'in 慈尊院 was also affiliated with Kōfukuji, as was Rengein 蓮花院, which follows.

141. *Oi no mimi* no. 48. The snow is likened to cherry blossoms, which are classified as "faux blossoms" (*nisemono no hana*) in the renga rules.

142. *Oi no mimi* no. 47. Again, these are "faux blossoms." The hokku is appropriate to the Rengein (Lotus-Blossom Hall) because it calls to mind the practice of scattering lotus blossoms (*sange* 散華) at religious rituals.

143. Sōchō refers to the Great Buddha (Daibutsu 大仏) of Tōdaiji temple 東大寺 in Nara.

144. Hannyajizaka 般若寺坂, also called Narazaka 奈良坂, is north of Hannyaji temple

in Hannyajichō, Nara City, at the border of Yamashiro Province on the Kyō kaidō road connecting Kyoto and Osaka. Hannyaji temple was very prosperous at the time.

145. Sōchō refers to an elegant practice mentioned in a popular couplet in *Wakan rōeishū* no. 221, by Bo Juyi:

> We warm wine in the woods, burning fallen leaves;
> We write verses on the stones, wiping off green moss.

146. This is a *kyōka* (lit., crazy poem) based on a kakekotoba pivoting between *oi no musa* (old warrior) and *musa to* (carelessly). The verse is a parody of the language of war tales: *tsukiorite* recalls *ya tsuki katana ore* (arrows gone and blade broken) frequently encountered in such works.

147. Ikkyū built this hermitage on the site of the long-ruined Myōshōji 妙勝寺, founded by Daiō Kokushi 大応国師 (1235-1309), patriarch of the Daitokuji/Myōshinji school of Zen (see Sanford 1981: 16, 59-60). The name means "Hall of Repayment of Debt."

148. Jōsū 紹崇 is unknown. Sōchō too was a fine performer on the shakuhachi bamboo flute. Ryōzen 霊山 refers to Shōhōji 正法寺 temple, headquarters of the Ryōzen branch of the Ji 時 sect, located in Higashiyama 東山, Kyoto.

149. Jōfukuji 常福寺, located at Gojō Higashinotōin 五条東洞院, is unknown. After the Ōnin war, the port of Sakai, in Osaka Prefecture, prospered through its trade with Ming China and was self-governing. The renga master Botanka Shōhaku 牡丹花肖柏 (1443-1527) lived there in his last years and became the central figure in its literary community. On Sakai, see Morris 1977.

150. Futami 二見 Bay is off the Ise coast.

151. Sōchō's poem may be a straightforward question, expressing dismay and the desire to know what drove Jōsū to his fatal decision. But it may also be asking how the poet's friend could have been enlightened through the *shakuhachi* piece "Perceiving the Law of Change" (*Mujōshin* 無常心) and yet be driven to despair.

152. Sōchō refers to *Kokinshū* 18: 990, by Lady Ise:

> Composed when she sold her house:

asukagawa	Though not a deep pool
fuchi ni mo aranu	in Tomorrow River,
waga yado mo	my home as well,
se ni kawariyuku	having been exchanged for funds,
mono ni zo arikeru	has turned into a shallows.

153. The courtier Sanjōnishi Sanetaka 三条西実隆 (1455-1537) was the doyen of Kyoto letters during the years covered by *The Journal of Sōchō*, and he figures frequently in the work. He and Sōchō were close friends. They collaborated in numerous linked-

Notes to Book One (1522), Page 23

verse sequences and other literary works. For more on Sanetaka, see Haga 1960 and Hara 1978. Sōchō also refers to him in his journal as Shōyōin 逍遙院 and Gyōkū 堯空.

154. Sanetaka makes a pun on *takigi*, meaning both "firewood" and the village of Takigi, where Sōchō is staying at Shūon'an. Though the name "takigi" is sufficient for the winter season, "the flowery name of the capital" will be the more appropriate when spring arrives.

155. *Shikashū* 3: 83, by Sōzu Seiin 僧都清胤:

When Sōzu Seiin was residing in Tsu Province, Ōe Tamemoto's term of office in the province expired, and he returned to the capital. Seiin composed this and sent it to him:

kimi sumaba	Were you here, good sir,
towamashi mono o	then I would call upon you.
tsu no kuni no	In the Wood
ikuta no mori no	of Ikuta in Tsu Province,
aki no hatsukaze	the first wind of autumn.

156. The Wood of Iwata (Iwata no mori), in Ishida 石田, Fushimi Ward, Kyoto Prefecture, had been a famous utamakura since *Man'yōshū* times. Shimazu (1975: 23) suggests Sōseki may have been in Iwata at this time. But the point is rather that Iwata is close to Sōchō in Takigi, just as its near-homonym Ikuta no mori is close to Seiin in the honka, the recipient of the poems in both cases being far away.

157. The foundation poem is *Sankashū* no. 77, by Saigyō:

negawaku wa	This is my request—
hana no moto ni te	let me die in springtime
haru shinamu	beneath the blossoms,
sono kisaragi no	when the moon is at its fullest
mochizuki no koro	in that same second month.

"That same second month" refers to the time the Buddha entered nirvana. Sōchō's poem also incorporates the phrase *takigi o kiru* ("cut firewood"), which also refers again to the place name Takigi as well as to the phrase *takigi o koru* (*Sōchō michi no ki* [206] gives that version, in fact), a conventional metaphor for the pursuit of the Buddhist Law. It is based on a passage from the "Devadatta" chapter of the *Lotus Sutra*, in reference to a past life of the Buddha when as a king he sought to learn the Dharma from a holy man: "When the king heard the seer's words, he danced for joy, then straightway followed the seer, tending to whatever he required: picking his fruit, drawing his water, gathering his firewood . . ." (Hurvitz 1976: 195). This then became the source for such poetry as *Shuishū* 20: 1346, attributed to Gyōki 行基 (669–749):

hokekyō o	The means by which
waga eshi koto wa	I mastered the *Lotus Sutra*
takigi kori	were cutting wood,
na tsumi mizu kumi	picking greens, and drawing water—
tsukaete zo eshi	serving thus, I mastered it.

Genji monogatari also makes reference to the phrase (e.g., the "Sakaki" chapter of *Genji monogatari* 1: 168). Sōchō's verse takes on added resonance in view of the belief that the Buddha attained nirvana on the day the firewood ran out in Crane Grove.

BOOK ONE: *Third Year of Daiei (1523)*

1. These poems appear in Sanetaka's personal poetry collection, *Saishōsō* (Grasses of Recrudescence, 1501–36).
2. The underlying meaning of the verse is that because Sōchō is living in a temple at Takigi, he is far from mundane concerns.
3. According to poetic convention, the bush warbler flies out from the mountain valley to the village and sings.
4. Mount Fuji and Kiyomi Strand (Kiyomigata 清見潟) are *utamakura* in Suruga, Sōchō's home province. The latter, located in Okitsu 興津, Shimizu 清水 City, Shizuoka Prefecture, was the site of the ancient Kiyomi Gate (Kiyomigaseki 清見関) as well as Seikenji temple (also read Kiyomidera 清見寺). Cf. *Shikashū* 7: 213, by Taira Suketaka:

mune wa fuji	Is my breast Fuji?
sode wa kiyomi ga	Are my sleeves Kiyomi Gate?
seki nare ya	There is no time
kemuri mo nami mo	when smoke from this smouldering love
tatanu ma zo naki	and waves of tears cease to rise.

Suketaka's poem is in turn based on another (*Kokinshū* 11: 489) that deals with Suruga (*JS*: 237, n. 24).

5. Sanetaka's poem is based on a line in the *Kokinshū* preface: "The style of Ōtomo no Kuronushi's poems is countrified. It is, as it were, like a mountain dweller with a load of firewood, who is resting beneath the blossoms."
6. "Charcoal" here refers to "torment amid the mud and charcoal" (*totan no kurushimi* 塗炭の苦しみ), an expression of suffering. It also relates to firewood (*takigi*), which follows. "The firewood of the Good Law" (*nori no takigi*) is the firewood that the Buddha gathered during his austerities (cf. *takigi o koru*, *JS* no. 37).
7. The "old man of Brushwood Cottage" (Saioku rōjin 柴屋老人) refers to Sōchō, whose elegant epithet was *Saioku*, taken from the name of his cottage in Mariko. The Shōkōkan ms. (Shimazu 1975: 24) links "on a journey of Zen meditation" with Sanetaka

(who signs himself Shōyōshi 逍遙子 here), but since Sōchō was at the Zen temple of Shūon'an, it clearly relates instead to him, as shown by the *GSRJ* ms. (265).

8. The Shōkōkan ms. (Shimazu 1975: 24) gives 上毛, which is unclear. The context implies a date, which suggests the characters may be *jōshun* 上春, one name for the first month, which looks very similar to 上毛 in cursive script.

9. Sōchō's poems respond to the sentiments expressed in Sanetaka's.

10. The verse points out, in response to Sanetaka's observation about Sōchō's retreat from the world into a holy temple (*JS* no. 38), that he has not in fact retired from the secular world and its trials.

11. *Shirayuki* is a kakekotoba pivoting between *shira[zu]* (know not) and *shirayuki* (white snow).

12. Mount Hiei is northeast of Kyoto, and the temple at its summit, Enryakuji, guards the capital from malign influences thought to enter from that quarter. "The crossing at Uji" (*Uji no watari*, in Uji 宇治 City, Kyoto Prefecture), located south of the capital not far from where Sōchō is at the moment in Takigi, figures in such classics as *Genji monogatari* and *Heike monogatari*. These two Kyoto utamakura, one a mountain and one on water, correlate with the two in Suruga that Sanetaka mentions.

13. Sōchō responds to Sanetaka's reference to the *Kokinshū* preface with *yasumu* (rest) from the same quotation.

14. Mirror rice cakes (*kagamimochii*) were glutinous rice cakes made round and flat, resembling mirrors, for festive occasions (*JS* no. 484).

15. I have emended *mimouki* in the Shōkōkan ms. (Shimazu 1975: 25) to *mimauki* on the basis of the *GSRJ* ms. (266).

16. Kozu 木津 is the old name for Kizu (Kizuchō, Sōraku 相楽 District, Kyoto Prefecture).

17. As this is a request from Kozu, Sōchō works in a mention of Izumi River (Izumigawa 泉川), another name for Kotsugawa 木津川 (now Kizugawa) river.

18. Sao 佐保 is a place name in Nara City. It also refers to Saokaze, variously the wind that blows at Sao, or the east wind, or the wind of the Goddess of Spring, Saohime. *Somekakuru* (begin to tint) includes the word *kakuru* (to hang up), which though it does not enter into the surface meaning of the poem is a kindred word for Sao through the homonym *sao* (pole). Cf. *Man'yōshū* 10: 1847:

asamidori	Looking almost as though
somekaketari to	they had been tinted light green
miru made ni	then hung out to dry,
haru no yanagi wa	the spring willows
moenikeru kamo	are coming into bloom!

19. Cf. *Gosenshū* 3: 131:

uguisu no	Jewelled willow branches
ito ni yoru chō	that the bush warblers are said
tamayanagi	to twist into strings—
fuki na midari so	do not blow and tangle them,
haru no yamakaze	mountain wind of springtime!

20. Rikijū 力重 was a monk of the Ji (Time) sect. Gokokuji 護国寺 (or 其国寺) was located at the intersection of Higuchi 樋口 and Aburanokōji 油小路 streets, at the south side of the Lower Capital.

21. The poem is a play on one in *Ise monogatari* (22):

toki shiranu	Fuji must be
yama wa fuji no ne	a mountain that cannot tell the season—
itsu to te ka	when does it think it is,
kanoko madara ni	for snow to fall upon it
yuki no fururamu	like the dappling of a fawn?

Sōchō puns on *fuji no ne* (Fuji's peak) and *fushi no ne* (lie down to sleep).

22. Tsujinobō 辻坊 was a religious establishment located in what is now Shirakawa 白川, Uji City, Kyoto Prefecture. Shimazu (1975: 25) notes that Shirakawa Shrine is now on the site. It was affiliated with Hakusan Shrine in Ishikawa Prefecture (*JS*: 223, n. 56). Sōchō later visited there (*JS*: 29, 47, 108).

23. The underlying meaning is "how inconsequential seems this 'Willow' sake and the rest, in light of your constant consideration." The poem includes the kindred words *yanagi* (willow) and *ito* (string) (*JS* no. 52 and *Gosenshū* 3: 131, above [*JS*: 216, n. 19]), and it puns on *ito* as well, which also means "very."

24. Sōchō writes "two barrels" with poetic license, so as to introduce the homonym *futa* (lid).

25. "Novice" translates *kasshiki* 喝食, an untonsured boy serving in a Zen temple. Here and elsewhere Sōchō's style is elliptical, and he only later identifies the person who made the offer. Like Ikkyū, Sōchō was not celibate despite his priestly status, and he had a daughter (b. 1505) and a son (Jōha 紹巴 [b. 1507]), of whom he wrote in *Utsunoyama no ki* (404) (see Chapter One of *Song in an Age of Discord*).

26. Shinden'an 心伝庵 was also in Takigi. It was built, as Sōchō writes, by the nun Jikō 慈香, widow of Nose Inabanokami Yorinori 能勢因幡守頼則, a vassal of Hosokawa Takakuni and lord of Akutagawa 芥川 Castle in Takatsuki 高槻 City, Settsu Province (Osaka Prefecture). Yorinori was a devoted patron of Sōgi and Sōchō, a poet represented in *Shinsen tsukubashū*, and the sponsor of two important thousand-verse sequences, *Shin Sumiyoshi senku* 新住吉千句 of 1485 and *Settsu senku* 摂津千句 of 1488, the latter a particularly grand event including Sōgi, Shōhaku, and Sōchō. He is also mentioned in Sōchō's second linked-verse collection, *Nachigomori* (162). Yorinori was also a disciple of Ikkyū

(Tsurusaki 1971b: 14). His widow built Shinden'an near Ikkyū's Shūon'an to pray for her departed husband. See also Yoshikawa 1955: 3–6. *Diamond Sutra* translates *Kongōkyō* 金剛経.

27. The verse involves a kakekotoba pivoting between *haha* (mother) and *hahaso* (oak).

28. This is *Higashiyama senku*, composed at An'yōji 安養寺 in 1518. It involved Hosokawa vassals and a brilliant array of literati, including Sanetaka, Shōhaku, Sōseki, and of course Sōchō himself.

29. Sanetaka wrote the postscript to the sequence (*Saishōsō* 12: 239–40). Teramachi Saburōzaemon 寺町三郎左衛門, Hahakabe Morikuni 波々伯部盛郷, and Kawarabayashi Tsushimanokami Masayori 河原林対馬守正頼 were all vassals of the Hosokawa. The latter two are represented in *Shinsen tsukubashū*. Shimazu (1975: 26) gives Morikuni's name as Masamori 正盛. Morikuni also contributed along with Sōchō to Chōkyō 2 [1488]: 4 *Nanimichi hyakuin* (A Hundred-Verse Sequence Entitled "A Kind of Path"), and he figured in the famous incense competition of 1501, *Meikōawase* 名香合 (*GSRJ* 19: 596–600), in which Sanetaka and Shōhaku also took part. Sōchō composed with Kawarabayashi Masayori on the occasion of *Settsu senku* sponsored by Yorinori (Ōshima 1963, 28: 38), and he called on Masayori at his castle in Ashiya in 1516, on the journey chronicled in *Nachigomori* (no. 162).

30. The host of a thousand-verse sequence, here Sōchō, traditionally composed the tenth hokku. The *GSRJ* ms. (267) renders the first line *tsuki ni aware*. The verse refers to the "moon of truth" (*shinnyo no tsuki* 真如の月), a metaphor for Buddhist illumination. Beneath the moon of Buddhist truth, one recognizes that all mundane desires are inimical to final enlightenment. The hokku is appropriate to a sequence in Yorinori's memory.

31. Opinion is divided regarding whether Jikō actually helped bring up Jōha after Saitō Yasumoto raised him in Suruga or whether she simply made the offer to do so (cf. Nakamoto 1967: 265 and Kaneko 1969: 40).

32. Sōchō refers here to a poem from the abbot in Uji to Nakanokimi in the "Sawarabi" chapter of *Genji monogatari* (9: 20):

kimi ni to te	Spring after spring
amata no haru o	I would pluck them to present
tsumishikaba	to your honored father,
tsune o wasurenu	and these first ferns
hatsuwarabi nari	continue to remember.

From Uji, the Shirakawa retreat was across the river, hence the reference to "the temple across the way" (*mukai no tera*). But that passage appears in the "Agemaki" chapter, not "Sawarabi":

The day was darkened by falling snow, and Kaoru spent it looking out from his room lost in thought. When he rolled up the blind to gaze at the moon shining

Notes to Book One (1523), Pages 29–30

bright and clear, that moon of the twelfth month said to be so chilling, he heard the faint sound of the bell of the temple across the way . . . and thought "this day too has come to an end." (*Genji monogatari* 8: 250–51)

The passage in turn relates to *Shūishū* 20: 1329:

yamadera no	With every stroke
iriai no kane no	of the bell tolled for vespers
koegoto ni	at the mountain temple,
kyō mo kurenu to	I note with sadness
kiku zo kanashiki	that this day too has come to an end.

33. The foundation poem is *Kokinshū* 2: 73:

utsusemi no	Are they like this life,
yo ni mo nitaru ka	fleeting as the cicada?
hanazakura	Even as I watched
saku to mishi ma ni	the cherries come into bloom,
katsu chirinikeru	their petals began to fall.

Utsusemi no (fleeting as the cicada or empty as the cicada husk) is a *makurakotoba* (fixed epithet) for "life" (*yo*), and it echoes the *usu* of *usuhanazakura* in the hokku. Sōchō's verse is also found in *Hokku kikigaki* (34), a collection of hokku and linked-verse sequences dating from 1515 to 1528 compiled by Senchō 仙澄, of Sugawara Shrine in Yasu 野洲, Shiga Prefecture.

34. Yamashina 山科 refers to Yamashina Ward in the eastern part of Kyoto City, on the main road to Ōtsu.

35. *Oi no mimi* no. 55. As Shimazu (1975: 27) notes, there is an Otowa Falls 音羽の滝 located near the Okunoin 奥の院 of Kiyomizu Temple 清水寺 in Higashiyama Ward, just across the border of what is now Yamashina Ward. Its source is Kiyomizuyama mountain, also known as Otowayama mountain. But there is another falls of the same name within Yamashina Ward itself, on the border of Shiga Prefecture, also known as Nunobiki no taki 布引の滝, and it may be that to which Sōchō refers, given the location of those making the request. It is likewise located on an Otowayama mountain. It is this Otowayama that is indicated on the map of the Kyoto area that accompanies this volume. Cf. *JS* no. 506. The name of the falls incorporates the word *oto* (sound), and *taki* (falls) functions as a kakekotoba pivoting between *otowa no taki* (Otowa Falls) and *takitsu haru no mizu* (surging springtime waters).

36. Tango 丹後 Province in Kyoto Prefecture.

37. *Oi no mimi* no. 56. Yosa no umi 与謝海 or 与佐海 was the old name for Miyazu 宮津 Bay, the western part of Wakasa 若狭 Bay, off Tango Province. It surrounds Ama no hashidate 天橋立, traditionally designated one of the Three Sights of Japan for its white sand and green pines. As the request came from Tango Province, Sōchō refers to

those elements in his hokku. He also includes a kakekotoba pivoting between *nami ya yosu* (waves approach) and *yosa no umi* (Sea of Yosa).

38. *Hokku kikigaki* (34). The third month in particular is the time to view the blossoms, and in this case, because of the intercalary month, one can enjoy them yet again.

39. *Oi no mimi* no. 59. Sōchō suggests the spirit of the deceased has returned as a butterfly, and he puns on *tama* (jewel / spirit). This was a standard metaphor; it hearkens back to the "dream of a butterfly" in the "Qiwulun" chapter of *Zhuangzi*, in which the speaker wakes and cannot tell whether he is a person who dreamt he was a butterfly or a butterfly now dreaming he is a person. See Chapter Three of *Song in an Age of Discord*.

40. Miidera 三井寺, also called Onjōji 園城寺, is in Ōtsu City. It is the headquarters of the Jimon 寺門 (Temple Gate) branch of Tendai Buddhism, traditionally in competition with the Sanmon 山門 branch (Mountain Gate) centered at Enryakuji on Mount Hiei to the northwest. Sōchō stopped here a number of times in the years covered by *The Journal of Sōchō*.

41. *Oi no mimi* no. 61. There is a kakekotoba pivoting between *tare sugi* (who passes) and *sugimura* (stand of cedars). The Ōsaka Gate was located in Shiga Prefecture, Ōtsu City (location of Miidera), on the road to the capital. Sōchō's use of "cuckoo" (*hototogisu*) in the verse shows that he is writing in the summertime, since the bird is a "seasonal word" (*kigo*) for that season. By poetic convention, the cuckoo sings in a stand of cedars; cf. *Shinkokinshū* 3: 217, by Saigyō:

kikazu to mo	Though I hear you not,
koko o se ni semu	here I will await your call,
hototogisu	cuckoo,
yamada no hara no	by this stand of cedars
sugi no muradachi	in Yamada field.

Sōchō's verse implies that the cuckoo's voice is as effective as a barrier for stopping passers-by, for all pause to hear its call.

42. The Daitokuji complex sustained massive damage in a fire in 1453 and again in the Ōnin War. Rebuilding the temple was one focus of Ikkyū's last years. After Ikkyū's death, his disciples, among them Sōchō and Nose Yorinori, continued the campaign to raise funds, concentrating in particular on donations for the thirteenth and thirty-third anniversaries of Ikkyū's death (observed in 1493 and 1510, respectively, see Yoshikawa 1955: 6–11). Sōchō saw work begun on the new Sanmon 山門 gate in 1526 (*JS*: 105). Soshin Jōetsu 祖心紹越 (d. 1519) was the fourth abbot of Shinjuan and Shūon'an and the founder of Shingakuji 深嶽寺 at Ichijōdani, seat of the Asakura house (Miyamachō 美山町, Asuwa 足羽 District, Fukui Prefecture). He was acquainted with the court literati Ichijō Kaneyoshi (or Kanera) 一条兼良 (1402–81) and Sanjōnishi Sanetaka (Yonehara 1979: 289). Asakura Norikage, on whom Sōchō set out to call at the beginning of *The Journal of Sōchō*, was his cousin. Two leaders of the Asakura house, Norikage's father, To-

shikage 敏景 (1428–81), and brother, Ujikage 氏景, had been disciples of Ikkyū, and the Asakura were thus devoted patrons of Daitokuji. One reason for their support of Zen was their opposition to the Amidist Ikkō 一向 (Single Minded) sect, whose followers controlled neighboring Kaga Province (Ishikawa Prefecture). Sōchō became one of the intermediaries between the Asakura and Daitokuji. Shingakuji is also mentioned by Sōchō in *Nachigomori* no. 14. On the Asakura and Daitokuji, see Tsurusaki 1969b: 8–12 and Yokota 1957.

43. Jōetsu died on 1519:4:16 (Yonehara 1979: 289).

44. The new abbot was Tōgaku Jōhō 桐岳紹鳳 (1451–1534). Another Ikkyū disciple, he was fifth abbot of Shinjuan and Shūon'an, and also abbot of Shōrin'an in Yashima. Legend holds that Shōrin'an was established by Ikkyū in 1470, but Tsurusaki (1983: 269–70) cites good evidence that it was actually founded by Jōhō himself. Jōhō figures a number of times in *The Journal of Sōchō*.

45. Myōshōji 妙勝寺 was the first temple built by Daiō Kokushi 大応国師 (Nanpo Jōmin 南浦紹明, 1235–1308/9), one of the founders of Ōtōkan 応燈寒 Zen, the school to which Daitokuji belongs. It was then destroyed during the wars of the Kenmu Restoration. Ikkyū rebuilt it, finishing in 1456, and located his Shūon'an (Cottage of the Repayment of Obligation) beside it. See Nakamoto 1967: 262–63, and Sanford 1981: 16, 59–60. It became a substitute Daitokuji when the latter was ravaged during the Ōnin war. Fifty *kanmon* 貫文 equalled five thousand *hiki*. As one hiki was worth 1.5 liters of rice in 1522 (*Dokushi biyō*), Sōchō's donation equalled 75 kiloliters of rice. It must again be borne in mind, however, that there was great latitude in Sengoku period weights and measures.

46. In 1520 Sōchō returned to Suruga, where he spent the next two years or so until setting off on the journey that begins *The Journal of Sōchō* in 1522. The narrative now takes up at the present, 1523. *Oi no mimi* records two links (nos. 1134/35; 1138/39) composed for Daiei 3 [1523] 4:4: *Nanibito hyakuin* (A Hundred-Verse Sequence Entitled "A Kind of Person") at Sōseki's residence. *Sanetakakōki* states Sōchō left for Echizen on 1523:4:10.

47. Shimazu (1975: 28) suggests that this passage is saying that the abbot was right to suspend the project. But in light of the success in raising funds, it is perhaps more likely that Sōchō means that the abbot was correct in deciding to press for donations again despite Sōchō's misgivings.

48. Teraki Shirōzaemon 寺木四郎左衛門 is unknown.

49. *Oi no mimi* no. 65. Sōchō employs a kakekotoba pivoting between *au* (meet) and *ōchi* (bead tree). Shimazu (1975: 29) interprets the subject of "coming and going" as "people" rather than "clouds," but one conventionally interprets the basic meaning of a verse only on the basis of the elements specifically stated within it, making "clouds" seem the more appropriate subject (cf. *JS* no. 582). On clouds and bead trees, see *JS* no. 9.

50. *Oi no mimi* no. 64. The verse recalls *Kokinshū* 3: 139:

Notes to Book One (1523), Pages 31–32

satsuki matsu	When I catch the scent
hanatachibana no	of the orange blossoms
ka o kageba	that await the fifth month,
mukashi no hito no	it is so like the fragrance
sode no ka zo suru	of the sleeves of one now gone!

51. *Oi no mimi* no. 66. *Yūdachi* (evening shower) relates to the name of Norikage's villa, Sakuuken 昨雨軒 (Cottage of Yesterday's Rain), the villa of Asakura Norikage. There is a kakekotoba pivoting between *iwa kosu* (lit., go over rocks) and *iwakosuge* (rock-pent sedge).

52. *Oi no mimi* no. 67. Again without indicating specific dates, the diary progresses to early autumn (leaves) from summer in the previous verse (*iwakosuge*). *Hitoha* (single leaf) usually refers to pawlonia. The foundation poem is *Shinkokinshū* 5: 534, by Princess Shokushi:

An autumn poem from a hundred-waka sequence:

kiri no ha mo	Pawlonia leaves
fumiwakegataku	now lie so deep that it is
narinikeri	hard to walk through them,
kanarazu hito o	though I am not necessarily
matsu to nakeredo	expecting someone to call ....

53. *Oi no mimi* no. 68. *Matsumushi* (lit., pine crickets) are thought to be today's bell crickets (lit., *suzumushi*) and vice-versa (Katagiri 1983: 373). I have retained Sōchō's terminology. The foundation poem is *Shinkokinshū* 16: 1560, by Fujiwara Shunzei:

Composed well after his eightieth year, on being commanded to present a hundred-waka sequence:

shimeokite	Mark that plot for me,
ima ya to omou	for I feel my end is near—
akiyama no	in the mugwort
yomogi ga moto ni	of the autumn mountains,
matsumushi no naku	pine crickets call.

54. *Oi no mimi* no. 70. A *nowaki* is a typhoon. Sōchō had an apparent affinity for the stillness after a tempest—compare *Yuyama sangin* (225–27):

31	shika no ne o	The cry of a deer
	ato naru mine no	in the mountains behind
	yūmagure	at evening twilight.
		Shōhaku

Notes to Book One (1523), Page 32

32	nowaki seshi hi no	After the tempest,
	kiri no awaresa	how moving is the mist!
		Sōchō

55. *Oi no mimi* no. 72. According to the lunar calendar, the fourteenth was the day before the moon became completely full. The full moon of the eighth month, the "famous moon" (*meigetsu* 名月), was considered particularly impressive. The poet feels that because the moon is shining so brightly on the fourteenth, it will surely continue to do so on the following night as well. *Kuma mo nashi* means both "without shadow" and "without a shadow of doubt."

56. Heisenji 平泉寺 temple, in Katsuyama 勝山 City, Fukui Prefecture, affiliated with Hakusan 白山 (White Mountain) Shrine on Hakusan mountain, was a historical center for mountain asceticism and renga activity. Hakusan mountain, more poetically read Shirayama, is an utamakura. It straddles Ishikawa, Toyama, Fukui, and Gifu Prefectures.

57. *Oi no mimi* no. 71 (where it appears *tsuki o okite*). The foundation poem is *Kokinshū* 9: 414, by Ōshikōchi Mitsune:

Composed on seeing Shirayama while on a journey to the land of Koshi:

kiehatsuru	Since no season
toki shi nakereba	sees a thaw,
koshiji naru	the name White Mountain
shirayama no na wa	in the land of Koshi
yuki ni zo arikeru	was given by its snow!

58. Kannonji 観音寺, in Azuchichō 安土町, Gamō District, Shiga Prefecture, was the site of the castle of the Rokkaku (*JS*: 17). While at Kannonji, Sōchō also directed Daiei 3 [1523]:9:2 *Yamanani hyakuin* (A Hundred-Verse Sequence Entitled "A Kind of Mountain"). *Oi no mimi* records Sōchō's hokku (no. 76) as well as several of his *tsukeku* (nos. 1598–1607). Sōboku also participated in the session. For more on the contemporary political situation in Ōmi, see Tsurusaki 1983.

59. *Oi no mimi* no. 75.

60. *Oi no mimi* no. 77, where it appears as *mishi ya minu*.

61. *Oi no mimi* no. 78. Deer are often poetically associated with hilltops or highlands (*onoe*), e.g., *Kokinshū* 4: 218, by Fujiwara Toshiyuki:

Composed for Prince Koresada's poetry contest:

akihagi no	The autumn bush clover
hana sakinikeri	has come into bloom!
takasago no	Now upon
onoe no shika wa	the Takasago heights,
ima ya nakuramu	might the deer be calling?

Notes to Book One (1523), Page 33

62. Shiga 志賀 refers to Shigamura 志賀村, Ōtsu City, Shiga Prefecture.

63. *Oi no mimi* no. 80, where it is prefaced by "At Sakamoto." *Chigusa* (a thousand flowers) is a seasonal word for autumn. The phrase "on whose billows blossom / a thousand flowers" (*hana saku nami no / chigusa*) brings to mind *nami no hana* (blossoms of the billows, i.e., white froth; cf. *Kokinshū* 5: 272 (*JS*: 228, n. 90). "The sea" refers to Lake Biwa, also called Nio Sea (Nio no umi 鳰の海). Cf. *Shinkokinshū* 4: 389, by Fujiwara Ietaka:

For a contest for the Bureau of Poetry, on "the moon on the lake":

nio no umi ya	Since the Nio Sea
tsuki no hikari no	is reflecting the light
utsuroeba	of the moon,
nami no hana ni mo	autumn's tints are seen as well
aki wa miekeri	in the blossoms of the waves.

"Blossoms of the waves" are white, but here they too have taken on autumn's tints since they reflect those the poet professes to see in the light of the autumn moon.

64. Bōnotsu 坊の津 is Bōnotsuchō 坊津町, Kawanabe 川辺 District, Kagoshima Prefecture. It was a center for trade with Ming China and one of the "Three Ports of Japan" (*Nihon sanshin*) along with Anonotsu (Tsu City in Mie Prefecture, *JS*: 16, 18, 61) and Hakatanotsu 博多津 (Hakata City, Fukuoka Prefecture).

65. Shijō Bōmon 四条坊門 was the avenue running east and west two blocks north of Shijō Avenue in the Lower Capital.

66. *Oi no mimi* no. 81, where the preface reads "Bōmonchō" 防門町.

67. Arima 有馬 hot springs, also known as Yuyama or Yunoyama 湯山, in Arimachō, Kōbe City, Hyōgo Prefecture, is the oldest spa in the Kinki region. It was there that Sōchō, Sōgi, and Shōhaku composed Entoku 3 [1491]:10:20 *Nanibito hyakuin* (*Yuyama sangin*). Koyadera 児屋寺 (昆陽寺), in nearby Itami 伊丹 City, is an ancient temple said to have been erected by Gyōki 行基 (668–749). Koya 昆陽, an important stop on the route west from the capital, was located between Mukogawa 武庫川 and Inagawa 猪名川 rivers.

68. *Oi no mimi* no. 82. *Shinagadori* (grebes side by side) is a makurakotoba for Inano 猪名野 (Itami City, Hyōgo Prefecture), an utamakura in the Yuyama region. Sōchō includes a kakekotoba pivoting between *Inano o yuki* (off to Inano) and *yuki* (snow). He may have had in mind *Shinkokinshū* 10: 910:

shinagadori	Off to Inano,
inano o yukeba	a name recalling grebes side by side,
arimayama	I find as evening mist
yūgiri tachinu	rises round Mount Arima
yado wa nakushite	that I have no place to stay.

69. *Oi no mimi* no. 84. Sōchō provides a personal commentary on the verse in the *Okitsuate* 興津宛 section of *Sōchō renga jichū* (156–57):

> Withered pampas grass under the crescent moon before dawn. Here one gazes at the moon with the thought that it too seems withered in the sky:

mireba ge ni	Gazing out,
kokoro mo sore ni	I feel my heart growing ever more
nari zo yuku	at one with the scene—
kareno no susuki	pampas on the withered moor,
ariake no tsuki	the moon before dawn.

The foundation poem Sōchō quotes is *Saigyō Shōninshū* no. 555. As Sōchō's commentary explains, *sora ni shimogare* (frost-withered against the sky) applies both to *ariake [no tsuki]* (the moon before dawn) and *hanasusuki* (ears of pampas grass). Shigematsu (1973: 29) believes that the *Okitsuate* section of *Sōchō renga jichū* was begun in 1522 while Sōchō was in Ise and that it was completed at about the time he entered this poem in his journal, at the end of 1523.

70. Nose Gengorō Kuniyori 能勢源五郎国頼, vassal of the Hosokawa, was either the younger brother or the son of Nose Yorinori. Shiroyama 城山 may refer to Shiroyama (Takatsuki City, Osaka Prefecture) at the headwaters of Akutagawa river (Tsurusaki 1971b: 15–19).

71. *Oi no mimi* no. 85. In this felicitous hokku (cf. *JS* no. 11), Sōchō plays on *kurete* (to end, as in a day, season, or year, and also to darken, thus "sunset of the year" in the translation) and *hikari* (light). *Toshi no hikari* refers to the passage of time.

72. Fourteen verses from this rare early collection of Sengoku-period haikai renga were later included in various versions of *Shinsen inu tsukubashū* (Newly Selected Mongrel Tsukubashū), attributed to Yamazaki Sōkan 山崎宗鑑 (1465–1553), with additions by later compilers. Two of the verses in *The Journal of Sōchō* appear under his name. It is as yet unclear whether the pairs of verses recorded in *The Journal of Sōchō* were originally composed as such (*maekuzuke*) or whether they were culled from a single long sequence, each tsukeku having been selected from among various candidates composed at the session. It is also unclear whether Sōchō was responsible for all or only some of the links he included here. For more on those questions as well as on the relationship between these verses and *Shinsen inu tsukubashū*, see Araki 1947: 95–99, Harada 1979: 356–70, Inazawa 1973, Keene 1977, Kidō 1984: 340–50, Shimazu 1969: 176–81, and Tani 1952. Many of the verses are obscure and have invited a variety of critical interpretations to date.

73. The verse plays on *tama kagiru* (faintly glitter), a makurakotoba usually modifying subjects more elevated in tone than edible seaweed, and *kagiri* (limited), evoking the poverty of the household on New Year's Eve. There are also overtones of *aratama* (New Year) and *arame* (coarse or rough, relating to the quality of the meal). Araki (1947: 96) relates *tama* (gem) to *tamatama* (as it happens or by chance).

Notes to Book One (1523), Page 34

74. Though about to greet her first spring as a wife, her face is lined with year's end labor in her straitened household. The verse includes a kakekotoba pivoting between *shiwasu* (twelfth month) and *shiwa* (lines or wrinkles).

75. The wisteria was the crest of the courtly Fujiwara house.

76. Minamoto Yoshitsune 源義経 (1159–89), also called Genkurō 源九郎, was the half-brother of the founder of the Kamakura Shogunate, Yoritomo. The verse accordingly may mean that while he is dressed as elegantly as a Fujiwara courtier, his ornamented saddle proclaims him a warrior general after all. It could, however, refer to the Fujiwara family in the Tōhoku region, whose protection Yoshitsune received as a young man after being exiled by the Taira. The northern Fujiwara were a provincial house of great wealth, famous in particular for having built the gold-leaf Konjikidō mausoleum in 1124. Shimazu (1975: 31) interprets the verse in reverse and assumes the rider *is* a Fujiwara courtier, though his golden saddle resembles that of Yoshitsune. Araki (1947: 96) points to the added haikai interest derived from the marked internal rhyme of the two verses.

77. The verse by itself means: "One leading the next, they are / moving slowly as syrup." This perhaps refers to a Buddhist ritual procession (*gyōdō* 行道). It takes on its second meaning when connected to the tsukeku.

78. *Yamamono* is another word for *yama no imo* 山の芋 or *jinenjo* 自然薯, a potato used in the glutinous potato dish *tororo*. This then links with the *nebari* (sticky) in the maeku, implying a sticky dish of syrupy tororo at one's bedside. "Hot potato" in the translation is not strictly accurate, but is added to evoke the ribald secondary meaning of the verses, based on a pun involving Yunoyama hot springs in Arima (*JS*: 96–97) and *yuna* 湯女, hot-spring girls who often doubled as prostitutes. Those at Yunoyama were particularly famous. The phrase *jinenjo o horu* (dig a potato) was also a common euphemism for sleeping with a prostitute. Thus the verses also mean: "Bring one along with you and / she will stick to you like glue" and "Sharing one's pillow / with a hot-spring girl from / Yunoyama in Tsu."

79. *Kōya hijiri* 高野聖, "Kōya holy men," were monks affiliated with the Shingon monastery of Kongōbuji 金剛峰寺 on Mount Kōya in Wakayama Prefecture. Many traveled to raise funds for the temple, and some were more or less beggars (cf. medieval European Beghards, a mendicant brotherhood, from which the English "beggar" may derive). Often traveling merchants with no ties to monastic life donned clerical robes and the appropriated the title Kōya hijiri to pass through the numerous barriers erected on main thoroughfares in that period (cf. *JS* nos. 133–34). See Anrakuan Sakuden, *Seisuishō* 2: 129–30, and Gorai 1965. Kōya monks often begged lodging in the evening, and it was believed that anyone who heard their call and did not offer them lodging would be cursed (Kimura and Iguchi 1988: 148).

80. The tsukeku includes a kakekotoba pivoting between *kayadō* (thatched hut) and *kaya* (mosquito net). Mendicant Kōya monks normally begged for lodging ostensibly

for ascetic discipline, but here one does so in the prosaic hope of finding a place with more protection from insects. Cf. *Shinsen inu tsukubashū* (Tōkyō Daigaku Toshokan ms., Suzuki 1965: 35):

80	kōya hijiri no yado o karu koe	The voice of a beggar monk from Kōya craving lodging.
	ōki naru kasa kite tsuki mo fukuru yo ni	He wears a big hat during the deepening night beneath the haloed moon.

This tsukeku is based on a pun on *kasa* (rain hat / halo around the moon). The *kasa* rain hat was one of the identifying characteristics of the Kōya monk. Harada (1979: 360) points out that a halo around the moon means rain is likely, thus increasing the urgency of the monk's calls for lodging.

81. For Hannyaji Hill (Hannyajizaka), see *JS*: 21. The central image of Hannyaji temple is the Bodhisattva Monju 文殊 (Sk. Manjusri), and the Hannyaji Monjue 般若寺文殊会 religious festival is now held annually on April 25 (originally on the twenty-third of the third month). Cf. *Shinsen inu tsukubashū* (Tōkyō Daigaku Toshokan ms., Suzuki 1965: 61):

161	hitori to saka o niguru nara chigo	Alone he escapes over the hill— a temple lad from Nara.
	hannyaji no monjushirō ga tachi nukite	Monjushirō from the Hannyaji temple has unsheathed his sword.

The Daiei ms. of that collection, entitled *Haikai rengashō* 誹諧連歌抄, reads *hirari to saka o* (nimbly over the hill) (Kimura and Iguchi 1988: 181). Monjushirō 文殊四郎 suggests either a monk with a name based on that of the deity Manjusri, or that deity himself, in human form. It was also the name of a famous swordsmith (Kimura and Iguchi 1988: 181). The humor derives from the pederastic double meaning of sword and the pun on the Japanese pronunciation of Manjusri, *Monjushiri* 文殊師利, which includes the word *shiri* (rear end).

82. *Sechiben* 世智弁 is a Buddhist term meaning "parsimonious." The tsukeku derives its humor from the image of secularity and stinginess, theoretically far removed from the ken of the selfless priest devoted to contemplation of the hereafter. The word has been here rendered Sechibenbō to resemble the name of a priest or his temple residence.

83. The moon has gone down, and with it, their main topic of romantic conversation. There may be a ribald double meaning behind this pair of verses as well, involving *tsuki* (moon/thrust) and *ireru* (set/insert).

84. Again, the verse involves an indecent pun on *tsuki*, which gives the verse this second meaning: "Feeling fore and aft / then thrusting it in, beneath / the late-rising moon."

According to poetic convention, nights with the late moon are particularly dark, hence the gender confusion.

85. The humor derives from a pun on *koshiore*, meaning "bent back" and a "bent-backed poem" whose third and fourth stanzas do not mesh. The word also applies in general to any poor verse. Harada (1979: 367) assumes the two already composed their poems and are congratulating themselves on their way home, blithely ignorant of their lack of skill.

86. This is the meaning of the verse in connection with the tsukeku. By itself, the verse means "How many people have come / to frolic 'neath the blossoms." The pun is on *gozaru* (to be present / to spoil).

87. Shimazu (1975: 32) instead suggests that *gozareta* should be read *kosareta* (strained or filtered) in the context of *ocha no mizu* (water for tea) and that *umekae* should be read *umegae* (plum branch), here the name of a temple lad bringing the water.

88. The verse refers to *Kokinshū* 2: 56, by Sosei:

Composed on looking out over the capital at the trees in bloom:

miwataseba	Far as I might gaze
yanagi sakura o	willows and cherry trees
kokimazete	blend in profusion—
miyako o zo haru no	the Imperial City
nishiki narikeru	has become a spring brocade.

(Adapted from McCullough 1985.) Here willows and cherries are further blended with the "cherry" (*sakuragasane*) and "willow" (*yanagigasane*) color combinations of the boys' kimono.

89. The verse has an obscene double meaning based on *nyake* (now *niyake*, i.e., buttocks/anus, synecdoche for temple lad or catamite) and *kiku no hana* (chrysanthemum [rendered aster for paronomastic reasons] or anus). Thus: "Between the buttocks / is the anus."

90. The poem is related to *Kokinshū* 5: 272, by Sugawara Michizane:

A poem attached to an aster in a *suhama* centerpiece for a contest held in the same [Kanpyō] reign. The poem was based on the fact that the aster centerpiece was modelled on Fukiage Strand:

akikaze no	The white asters
fukiage ni tateru	that stand in gusts of autumn wind
shiragiku wa	at Fukiage—
hana ka aranu ka	are they flowers
nami no yosuru ka	or instead approaching billows?

The haikai tsukeku link pursues the homoerotic *double entendre* of the maeku.

91. *Seisuishō* (Laughs to Wake One, 1623)(2: 38–39) relates a story as well of a temple

Notes to Book One (1523), Page 36

lad nicknamed "Subari" (Tight Ass) whose father is humorously ignorant of the sexual mores of monastic life.

92. *Ichijō* 一帖 is usually twenty sheets of paper, which roughly corresponds to a quire. *Suiharagami* 杉原紙 was a high-quality paper originally made in Taka 多可 District, Harima Province (Hyōgo Prefecture) and primarily used for the official documents. As it came into common use, it began to be produced in various places. It is also mentioned in *Seisuishō* (1: 226–27), "A Letter from the Buddha" (*Shaka no tegami*), where it is called the best in the land.

93. Paper was often the prize in competitive linked-verse sessions. Here the poet sits beside the paper he won and fans himself in a self-satisfied way. Yoshida Kenkō also mentions prizes won in renga competition in *Tsurezuregusa* (Essays in Idleness, c. 1330?) no. 89 (150–53).

94. The verses are linked by the poetic convention that in spring the geese wear a robe of haze. Cf. *Shinsen inu tsukubashū* (Tōkyō Daigaku Toshokan ms., Suzuki 11):

1	kasumi no koromo suso wa nurekeri	The robe of haze is soaked at the hem.
	saohime no haru tachinagara shito o shite	Spring has come and the goddess Saohime pisses where she stands.

Cf. *Kokinshū* 1: 23, by Ariwara Yukihira:

haru no kiru　　　　　　The robe of haze
kasumi no koromo　　　that springtime wears
　nuki o usumi　　　　　is of such fragile weft
yama kaze ni koso　　　that it will surely be disarrayed
　midaruberanare　　　　by the mountain wind.

Saohime 佐保姫, the goddess of spring, is here personified to humorously vulgar effect. Tani (1952: 66) takes the name to refer to a country girl too busy at work in the fields to relieve herself in private.

95. Gojō, the Fifth Ward in Kyoto, was a popular place to hire prostitutes, many of whom dressed as nuns. *Goke* 後家 means both "widow" and "prostitute." *Shichijūichiban shokunin utaawase* (Poetry Competition in Seventy-One Rounds on the Professions and Trades) depicts two such "nuns" soliciting in the Fifth Ward (522–23). In *Genji monogatari*, Gojō was the residence of Yūgao, mistress of Tō no Chūjō and then of Genji, and the tsukeku contains overtones of Yūgao's rustication. Also cf. *Shinsen inu tsukubashū* (Tōkyō Daigaku Toshokan ms., Suzuki 1965: 26):

51	gojō watari ni tateru amagoze	In the Fifth Ward stands someone in a nun's habit.

Notes to Book One (1523), Pages 36–37

yūgao no	She wears over her head
hana no bōshi o	a hood as white
uchikazuki	as a moonflower.

The *Shinsen inu tsukubashū* verse pursues the *Genji monogatari* theme by connecting the lady Yūgao with her eponymous "moonflower" (also translated "evening faces"), and it puns on *hana no bōshi* (flower hat) and *hanada bōshi*, a nun's hood.

96. Like so many of the verses preceding it, the maeku here is a *nanku* (difficult verse or poser), designed to elicit a clever solution in the tsukeku. *Hara no uchi* also means "the heart of a wife."

97. This is again a nanku, as the autumn, usually melancholy according to poetic convention, is here characterized as "interesting" or "exciting" (*omoshiroge*).

98. The Festival of the Weaver Maid (Tanabata 七夕) on the seventh day of the seventh month, when according to legend the Weaver Maid and the Herdboy have their one annual meeting, does indeed evoke excited anticipation. The Weaver Maid is said to weave elegant garments for the occasion on many looms, e.g., *Man'yōshū* 10: 2034:

tanabata no	The first autumn robe
iohata tatete	made of cloth woven
oru nuno no	by the Weaver Maid
akisarikoromo	on her myriad looms—
tare ka torimimu	who will be the one to see it?

The former Ebara ms. of *Shinsen inu tsukubashū* (entitled *Renga haikaishō*, Suzuki 1965: 237) gives this:

omoshirosō ni	The autumn wind blows with it
akikaze zo fuku	a feeling of excitement.
tanabata no	The rhythm of feet
iohata oreru	weaving on the many looms
ashihyōshi	of the Weaver Maid.

Someone else composed:

uchimawasu	A field of kudzu
heta sarugaku no	with inept sarugaku
makuzuhara	on a curtained stage.

Here the second tsukeku is linked by the relationship between "autumn wind" and "kudzu," demonstrated in such poems as *Man'yōshū* 10: 2096:

makuzuhara	With every gust
nabiku akikaze	of autumn wind that ripples
fuku goto ni	the field of kudzu,

Notes to Book One (1523), Page 37

| ada no ōno no | blossoms fall from bush clover |
| hagi no hana chiru | here on the vast Ada moor. |

Kimura and Iguchi (1988: 143) point out that *makuzuhara* may be a proper noun, as there was a field of that name in Kyoto's Higashiyama Ward, near what is now Maruyama Park, where various entertainments were held.

99. Harada (1979: 368) renders the verse: "A heavy, one-sided load / can never be carried." The humor again is in the vagueness of the verse; it can also mean "never nestle up against a heavy one."

100. The verse relates to *Shinkokinshū* 20: 1963:

On the commandment proscribing adultery (*fujainkai*):

saranu dani	Even by themselves
omoki ga ue	they are quite heavy enough,
sayogoromo	your nighttime garments—
waga tsuma naranu	do not lay on top of them
tsuma na kasane so	robes that are not your spouse's.

The link also more generally refers to the heavy sin of sleeping with a woman (*nyobon* 女犯)—one ought never commit it, even if one were paid. Harada (1979: 368) suggests the couplet means that one-sided love is as futile as trying to carry a load on one side of a shoulder pole—who could do it even for wages? Perhaps there are overtones in the couplet as well of the *nō* play *Koi no omoni* (The Heavy Burden of Love), a revision by Zeami of *Aya no tsuzumi* (The Damask Drum), where this appears: "On one shoulder then the other, I try to carry it but cannot—why is love so heavy?" (Yokomichi and Omote 1972, 1: 328).

101. The humor of this link derives from the pun on *ana* (respectfully/hole): "All of one's emotions are / concentrated on a hole." Suzuki (1965: 54) points out that the ribald comedy is further increased by a play on *nasake* (emotions) and *nasakedokoro* (place of emotions / feelings, slang for the female genitals). Here the salacious potential of the maeku is so obvious that the challenge for the tsukeku is to avoid it.

102. The tsukeku links *kashiko* to *ana* in the maeku to form *ana kashiko* (with awe and respect), the standard closing salutation for women's letters of the period. The poet thus on one level coyly frustrates the potential for ribaldry in the maeku, but on another pursues it through a pun on *kashiko*, which means not only "deep respect" but also "That's the place!" Cf. *Shinsen inu tsukubashū* (Tōkyō Daigaku Toshokan ms., Suzuki 1965: 54):

141	hito no nasake ya	All her emotions
	ana ni aruran	in the word "Respectfully."
	tamazusa o	The billet doux
	koyoi nezumi ni	would seem to have been carried off
	hikarekeri	tonight by a mouse.

Here too the the tsukeku "defuses" the ribald maeku, through a pun on *ana* (respectfully / [mouse] hole).

103. The ribald humor is based on the double meaning of the tsukeku, which employs the language of warrior battle accounts. Translation after Keene 1977: 275.

104. The humor is based on a pun on *seitaka* (tall of stature) and Seitaka 勢多迦 (Sk. Cetaka), an attendant of Fudō Myōō 不動明王 (Sk. Acala), one of the five "Bright Kings," and here cast as the object of Fudō's unrequited affection. Also implied in the link is the name of the other of Fudō's two closest attendants, Kongara 金伽羅 (Sk. Kinkara), and the facts that Seitaka is iconographically associated with a childlike mien, and Fudō, with a nimbus of flames. The couplet is reversed in the *GSRJ* ms. (270). Cf. *Shinsen inu tsukubashū* (former Eizan Shinyo ms., entitled *Haikai renga* 俳諧連歌, Suzuki 1965: 177):

104	ware yori mo	How he longs with love
	seitaka wakashu	for the lad Seitaka,
	koiwabite	taller than himself.
	ōki ni semi no	He cries just like
	ne o nomi zo naku	a cicada on a big tree!

Ōki ni semi (a cicada on a big tree) was a metaphor for a great difference in size.

105. *Zungiri* refers to cutting a large tree straight off at the trunk, sometimes to ornament a teahouse gate.

106. Mount Miwa 三輪山, in Sakurai City 桜井市, Nara Prefecture, is the object of worship of Ōmiwa 大神 Shrine and is traditionally associated with cedars. The foundation poem is *Kokinshū* 18: 982:

waga io wa	My rustic hut
miwa no yamamoto	lies at the foot of Mount Miwa.
koishikuba	If you long for me,
toburai kimase	come and pay a call
sugi tateru kado	at the gate where the cedar stands.

The venerable tone of the maeku and the awe-inspiring makurakotoba that begins the tsukeku are literally and figuratively undercut by the plebeian vision of a teahouse priest (*chayabōzu*), whose head is shaped like a flat-topped *zungiri* tea container made from one of the ancient cedars. Teahouse priests operated places of refreshment near temples and shrines. The same tsukeku appears in *Shinsen inu tsukubashū* (former Ebara ms., entitled *Haikai rengashō*, Suzuki 1965: 209) and is expressly credited there to Sōchō.

107. There is a pun on *oenu* (nothing to be done / impotent).

108. The verse is a puzzle (nanku); by itself it reads: "The haze hangs delicately, / drawn about like a curtain."

109. *Hōzukimayu* are eyebrows painted on with pigment made from ground cherries (*hōzuki*). It was a practice children particularly enjoyed. *Hikimawasu* by itself can mean

Notes to Book One (1523), Page 38

"hang a curtain around," but in the context of the tsukeku it means *mayu o hiku* (paint on eyebrows). The Shōkōkan (Shimazu 1975: 34) and *GSRJ* (270) mss. give *bōbomayu*, which may be a variant of *bōbōmayu* 茫茫眉, "shaven eyebrows." Harada (1979: 368), however, takes *bōbō* in the context of *hige bōbō* (wild growth of beard) and believes *bōbomayu* refers instead to the *un*shaven eyebrows of a youth. The variant in the Shōkōkan and *GSRJ* manuscripts may have been the result of a copyist's error in which the cursive character for *tsuki* in *hōzukimayu* was confused for the similar *hentaigana* character for *ho*. *Marugao* (round face) and *mawasu* (here, [draw] on) are kindred words, as are *mayu* (eyebrows) and *hiku* (here, draw).

110. The grandeur of the mounted Hitomaro, the great *Man'yōshū* poet, is deflated in the second verse by the fact that his retinue includes only a single man. The verse may also refer to the *Kokinshū* preface: "Hitomaro did not stand above Akahito; nor did Akahito stand beneath (*shimo ni tatamu*) Hitomaro." Suzuki (1989: 143) suggests that this verse may derive its humor from the fact that Hitomaro was not conventionally portrayed on horseback. There may be homoerotic overtones.

Cf. *Shinsen inu tsukubashū* (Tōkyō Daigaku Toshokan ms., Suzuki 1965: 35):

81   uma ni noritaru   Look at Hitomaro
      hitomaro o miyo   as he sits astride his horse!

      honobono to   Vaguely in the dawn
      akashi no ura wa   beneath the moon of Akashi Bay,
      tsukige ni te   on a dappled gray.

The *Shinsen inu tsukubashū* verse is based on *Kokinshū* 9: 409, attributed to Hitomaro:

      honobono to   Dimly, dimly
      akashi no ura no   at daybreak in the mist
         asagiri ni   of Akashi Bay,
      shimagakure yuku   my thoughts pursue the boat
      fune o shi zo omou   that disappears behind the island.

The tsukeku then strengthens its link to the preceding verse by employing *tsukige*, meaning both "moonlight" 月気 and "dappled gray" 月毛. *Honobono* (dimly) and *tsuki* (moon) are also linked in earlier poetry, such as *Shinkokinshū* 6: 591, by Minamoto Saneakira, which uses *Kokinshū* 9: 409 as its foundation poem:

      honobono to   Dimly, dimly
      ariake no tsuki no   in the light of the late moon
         tsukikage ni   on an early morning,
      momiji fukiorosu   the colored leaves are scattered
      yamaoroshi no kaze   by the wind from off the peaks.

111. Sōkan puns on *oitsuku* (catch up / pierce his backpack). Harada (1979: 357) sees

homosexual overtones in the verse. The couplet appears in *Shinsen inu tsukubashū* (Tōkyō Daigaku Toshokan ms., Suzuki 1965: 62) with the maeku given as *oitsukan / oitsukan to ya / omouran*.

112. The maeku appears only once in *The Journal of Sōchō*, but the different points of view of the two tsukeku necessitate a recasting of the verse in English.

113. Sōchō's tsukeku does not appear in *Shinsen inu tsukubashū*. Sōchō also puns on *oitsukan* (catch up / thrust), with obvious ribald intent. Kōya monks were popularly associated with lechery (see also *JS* no. 88). Thus Harada (1979: 358) construes the verse as "'I'll catch up with her, / I'll catch up'—is that / what he thinks, running?" Tani (1952: 62) believes that the "young girl" (*himegoze*) is in fact a prostitute, who like the "monk" is affecting more respectable dress. In that case she surely will not mind being overtaken. Kaneko (1987: 406) believes the verse is from the girl's point of view, but he thinks the grammar and tone of the link imply that she is afraid of being overtaken. The translation follows this interpretation.

114. This couplet appears in *Shinsen inu tsukubashū* (Tōkyō Daigaku Toshokan ms., Suzuki 1965: 12), no. 4. The maeku is a puzzle, and the couplet is generally interpreted two ways. Suzuki (1965: 12) sees it as a description of a *tokonoma* centerpiece for New Year's, made in the shape of a nesting warbler, which then relates to "nesting crane" (*tsuru no sugomori*), a move in the game of *go*. Sōkan altered "crane" to "bush warbler" because the latter is a seasonal word for spring and thus ties to the maeku. Such centerpieces, moreover, were often displayed atop go boards and were sometimes made of food, which was later consumed. Harada (1979: 358), by contrast, believes a game is actually in progress, and that Sōkan conceived of the go stones as bush warbler eggs and of their layout on the board as a decorative centerpiece. Kimura and Iguchi (1988: 120–21) also believe a game is in session and point out that in addition to its main meaning of "centerpiece," *tsukurimono* is also a go term for a series of moves, which further strengthens the link to the maeku.

115. *Asagasumi* (morning haze, an image related to the spring season) functions as a preface (*jo*) to introduce the phonetically related *sumizumi* (four corners), which in the verse by itself would mean "the morning haze has yet to reach to the corners of the landscape." But in connection with the maeku, *sumizumi* also refers to the four corners of a go board. Harada (1979: 358) believes that Sōchō is simply comparing the arrangement of white and black go stones on the board to a painting in which the white spring haze does not penetrate to the corners. Kaneko, however, believes that in the word *asagasumi* Sōchō is also implying *kasumiwari*, "territories," a term denoting spheres of influence of, for example, rival mountain ascetic sects or blind performers (personal communication). According to that interpretation, the link would read, "In the morning's haze / he has not reached the corners of / the other's holdings."

Notes to Book One (1524), Pages 41–43

BOOK ONE: *Fourth year of Daiei (1524)*

1. This verse is a kyōka based on *Kokinshū* 1: 1, by Ariwara Motokata:

    Composed when spring arrived before the old year was out:

toshi no uchi ni	It seems that spring has come
haru wa kinikeri	before the year has ended.
hitotose o	Though one and the same,
kozo to ya iwamu	should we call it last year,
kotoshi to ya iwamu	or should we call it this?

    Sōchō's parody plays on *kozo* (last year / scamp) and on *koshami* (novice monk) / *kotoshi* (this year).

2. "Testing the brush" (*shihitsu*) refers to the first writing of the New Year.

3. A child was traditionally considered one year old at birth, and everyone became a year older on the first day of the first month. Here and elsewhere the translation retains the traditional counting system (*kazoedoshi*) because of the wordplay on numbers Sōchō sometimes employs.

4. This is the kanbun preface to the abbot's return poem, which follows.

5. The abbot, Tōgaku Jōhō, became seventy-four years old by the Japanese count on New Year's day, 1524. In the latter half of his verse he expresses the hope that he will live as long as Sōchō has.

6. It was believed that the spirit could leave a person's body while he or she was still alive. Love poetry in particular often refers to the idea that the strength of a person's longing could cause his or her spirit to appear to the loved one in a dream.

7. The poem plays on *tama* (spirit / coins, or here, for paronomastic reasons, "change"). Sōchō then repeats the word in "irikawari*tama*e" (change).

8. Nakamikado Nobutane 中御門宣胤 (1442–1525) was the father-in-law of Imagawa Ujichika and a close friend of Sōchō. He also figures in Sōchō's *Utsunoyama no ki* and *Nachigomori* (Kitano Tenmangū ms. 163).

9. Again, the poem plays on the toponym Takigi and its homonym, "firewood." Firewood is not necessary in the springtime warmth of the capital. *Hiroisute* more accurately means picking up certain branches and discarding others.

10. *Oi no mimi* no. 1.

11. Cf. *JS* no. 29. There is a partial kakekotoba pivoting between *waka[razu]* (do not know [here implied by "whence"]) and *wakakusayama* (Mount Wakakusa). There is also a pun on *wakakusayama* and *waku* (to spring forth or to appear).

12. A single sheet (*hitoori*) contained twenty-two linked verses, with eight on the front and fourteen on the back of the folded sheet. Yawata 八幡, in Tsuzuki 綴喜 District, Kyoto Prefecture, is the site of Iwashimizu Hachiman Shrine, in which Umenobō 梅坊 hall was located.

13. *Oi no mimi* no. 86.
14. A reference to *Shinkokinshū* 6: 701, by Fujiwara Sanefusa:

   For a hundred-waka sequence:

isogarenu	How heavy my heart
toshi no kure koso	now that I am not caught up
aware nare	in New Year's bustle.
mukashi wa yoso ni	In springtimes past would I
kikishi haru ka wa	have simply listened from afar?

15. *Oi no mimi* no. 87. The foundation poem is *Kokinshū* 1: 20 (*JS*: 209, n. 115).
16. Shōzōbō 勝蔵坊, also called Shōjun 正純, was a monk affiliated with Miidera (*JS*: 30). Skilled at both shakuhachi and renga, he appears in *The Journal of Sōchō* several times. Extant hyakuin involving Shōzōbō and Sōchō include Daiei 7 [1527]:1:19 *Yamanani hyakuin* (A Hundred-Verse Sequence Entitled "A Kind of Mountain") and Daiei 7:4:2 *Nanibito hyakuin* (A Hundred-Verse Sequence Entitled "A Kind of Person"), the latter composed when Shōzōbō was accompanying Sōchō back to Suruga. The text is garbled here, and the hokku is missing. The translation supplies the likely verse on the basis of a passage later in the journal (*JS* no. 163). This verse also appears as *Oi no mimi* no. 89 with the preface, "At a linked-verse session with someone who came up to the capital from Miidera." The missing verse may have been deleted here because it was repeated later in the text.
17. *Shinkokinshū* 16: 1504, by Fujiwara Norikane:

   After going to Miidera and spending several days there, he prepared to return and composed this for those lamenting his departure:

tsuki o nado	Why did I used think
matare nomi su to	of nothing but how long the wait
omoikemu	till the moon appeared?
ge ni yama no ha wa	Now I find how hard it is
ideukarikeri	to forsake the mountain crest!

18. The "Shogunal Deputy's Thousand Verses in One Day" (*Kanrei ichinichi senku* 管領一日千句) was an annual event sponsored at Kitano Shrine by the shogunal deputy (on this occasion, Hosokawa Takakuni; see *JS* no. 11) on the twenty-fifth of the second month. See Kaneko 1971.
19. *Oi no mimi* no. 90. This is a felicitous hokku; "every blade of grass" refers to the nation's people (*tamikusa*, lit., people-grasses) who bow (*nabiku*) to the will of the ruler.
20. *Iba senku* is a famous thousand-verse sequence in which Sōchō, Sōseki, and Sanetaka participated. Held on 1524:3:17–21, it was sponsored by the warrior-literatus Tanemura Nakatsukasanojō Sadakazu 種村中務丞貞和 (also called Iba Sadakazu 伊庭貞和,

Notes to Book One (1524), Pages 44–45

hence the title of the sequence), who was a lieutenant of Rokkaku Sadyori, constable of south Ōmi. Sadakazu also contributed a token number of verses to the sequence. The work is also called *Gessonsai senku*, as it was held at the residence of Gessonsai Sōseki. The work is extant. See also Tsurusaki 1969a and 1976. Sōchō included a large number of verses from the sequence in *Oi no mimi* (see Iwashita 1985). Sōchō had also composed verse in the company of Tanemura Sadakazu at Kannonji during his trip to Echizen in 1523.

21. This is the hokku for the second hundred-verse sequence. The foundation poem is *Kokinshū* 20: 1081:

aoyagi o	These plum-blossom hats
kataito ni yorite	are the ones said to be sewn
uguisu no	by the bush warblers
nū chō kasa wa	from light green willow branches
ume no hanagasa	that they weave into strings.

Cf. *JS* no. 52.

22. Toyohara Muneaki 豊原統秋 (also read Sumiaki or Tōshū, 1450–1524), referred to here and elsewhere by Sōchō as "Bun no Utanokami" 豊雅楽頭 (Bun [Sinitic style for Toyohara], Head of the Bureau of Gagaku Music), was a court musician, poet, and close friend of both Sanetaka and Sōchō. He was the author of the musical treatise *Taigenshō* 体源抄, and his personal poem anthology is entitled *Shōkashō* 松下抄. Muneaki appears with Sōgi, Sōchō, and others in the extant Meiō 8 [1499]:2:19 *Nanibito hyakuin* (A Hundred-Verse Sequence Entitled "A Kind of Person"). For more on Muneaki, see Itō Kei 1969.

23. This may be a reference to the legend that the tincture of eternal youth was to be found on Mount Penglai (J: Hōrai 蓬莱). Two basic sources of that legend are *Liezi* 列子 (215) and *Shijing* (336–37). According to the latter, Qinshi Huangdi 秦始皇帝 dispatched one thousand boys and girls to find it.

24. The foundation poem is *Kokinshū* 11: 489:

suruga naru	Though there are days
tago no uranami	when the waves do not rise up
tatanu hi wa	upon Tago Bay
aredomo kimi o	in Suruga, on no day
koinu hi wa nashi	do I cease to long for you.

Tago Bay is an utamakura in Suruga, Sōchō's home province. Here Nakamikado Nobutane uses the waves on Tago Bay as a metaphor for Sōchō himself (cf. *JS* no. 563).

25. *Yōyōki* (An Account of Raising Hawks) relates that a pair of Norikage's hawks produced two superb chicks, a rare event for birds not in the wild. The offspring were later given to Takakage 孝景 (1493–1548), head of the Asakura house, and Hosokawa

Notes to Book One (1524), Pages 45–46

Takakuni (both of whom include a homonym for "hawk" [*taka*] in their names). The account, written in *kanbun*, states that Sōchō had heard of the hawks while he was a guest of Norikage and that he asked for the story to be written down and presented to his host. Though the author's name is not recorded in *Yōyōki* itself, the passage in *The Journal of Sōchō* suggests that it was most likely Gesshū Jukei 月舟寿桂 (1460–1533). An important figure in the Gozan Zen literary establishment, Gesshū Jukei had received the patronage of the Asakura and during the years covered by *The Journal of Sōchō* was living in retirement in Ikkeken 一華軒 at Kenninji 建仁寺. He also became the guardian of the child of the linked-verse master Kensai when the latter left on his last journey north in 1501 (Kaneko 1977b: 159). For more on Gesshū Jukei, see Tsurusaki 1969b.

26. The source of the invitations is unclear; Shimazu (1975: 38) suggests they came from the Oda family.

27. In the Ōnin War the capital was reduced to a fraction of its previous size. The Kyoto that Sōchō knew, in the north-central part of the present city, was divided into halves called the Upper Capital (Kamigyō) and the Lower Capital (Shimogyō). Hōshōji 法性寺, a temple founded by Fujiwara Tadahira 藤原忠平 (880–949), was located on the west side of the Fushimi Road, near the north gate of the present Tōfukuji 東福寺. Fukakusa 深草 is an utamakura in the north of Fushimi Ward.

28. This unorthodox *zareuta* is puzzling, as indicated by the reference to a note, which unfortunately does not survive. It may have pertained to the last line, *koto shi aru rō*, in which *rō* is perhaps a pun on "old one" (more normally read *oi*) and *arō*, a colloquial rhetorical question.

29. The identity of the Tsuda Bizen Lay Priest 津田備前入道 is unclear; Tsuda may be a surname, a place name, or both. This passage refers to arrangements for rebuilding Daitokuji in Murasakino, to which Sōchō contributed so much time and effort out of veneration for his late teacher, Ikkyū. Lumber would have been transported from Takigi as far as Fushimi by boat, been offloaded there, and then taken to the Upper Capital by cart.

30. The verse means that the protective shade is perpetual, as bamboo has no seasonal fluctuation. It is a felicitous poem for Fushimi; *kuretake* and *yoyo* are both kindred words for that area (cf. *JS* no. 373). The foundation poem is *Ise monogatari* (74):

waga kado ni	Since bamboo
chihiro aru kage o	for endless shade has been planted
uetsureba	here at my dwelling,
natsu fuyu tare ka	who in summer or winter
kakurezarubeki	will fail to find shelter beneath it?

31. Uji Bridge (Ujibashi 宇治橋), which spans Ujigawa 宇治川 river at Uji City, was the site of a famous battle during the Genpei war portrayed in *Heike monogatari*. Mizu mo mimaki 美豆の御牧, an utamakura in Fushimi Ward, Kyoto Prefecture, had long

been imperial pastureland. Yawata 八幡 Mountain is the site of Iwashimizu Hachiman 岩清水八幡 Shrine.

32. Kotsugawa river joined with Ujigawa and Katsuragawa 桂川 rivers at Yodo 淀 (Pool) (*JS* no. 50). Sōchō is describing Ogura Pond (Ogura no ike 巨椋池), since filled in.

33. "Beating in time on the boatsides" refers to tapping on the gunwales of the boat in time to music, and is a quotation from *Wakan rōeishū* no. 503, by Liu Yuxi:

> The mountains are like a painted screen,
>> the river is like a bamboo mat;
> beating in time on the boat sides, we ply to and fro,
>> while the moon shines bright.

"Pipes" refers to transverse flutes, versus the shakuhachi. The popular song (*kouta*) referred to here is *Kanginshū* no. 64:

uji no kawase no	Water wheels revolving
mizuguruma	in Uji's rapids—
nani to ukiyo o	are they turning over thoughts
meguro	of this woeful world?

Note the kindred words *uji* (Ujigawa river) and *ukiyo* (woeful world), as well as *mizuguruma* (water wheel), *omoimegurasu* (turn over thoughts), and *meguru* (revolve). Sōchō's interest in popular song, demonstrated here and elsewhere, led to the traditional attribution to him, now largely discredited, of *Kanginshū* 閑吟集 (1518), a collection of such songs.

34. The phrase quoted from the song, *noboriwazurau tsunadenawa*, also appears in *Shinkokinshū* 18: 1775, by Fujiwara Yorisuke:

kawabune no	Like a river boat
noboriwazurau	struggling against the current
tsunadenawa	at a tow-rope's end,
kurushikute nomi	I make my way through this life,
yo o wataru kana	prey to constant sorrow.

35. The image of the waterrail flying in tight circles because of the narrow valley and steep walls is slightly unorthodox, but the reason Sōchō considers this verse haikai is otherwise unclear. *Toyama* (nearby hills) is aurally related to *to* (door), which is a kindred word to *kuina* (mudhen) (cf. *JS* no. 165).

36. Shimazu (1975: 39) identifies Tōunken 東雲軒 as the artistic name of the vice constable (*shugodai*) of Yamashiro Province. Sōchō stayed with him on his second trip to Kansai as well (*JS*: 107–9). The constabulary was located near Uji Bridge.

37. Sunrise Mountain (Asahiyama 朝日山) is located to the east of Uji. *Oi no mimi* no. 94.

38. Jōkōin 上光院 is a subtemple of Miidera.

39. The Hakone Bettō 箱根別当 (Commissioner of Hakone Gongen Shrine) was Hōjō Gen'an 北条幻庵 (1493–1589). The third son of Hōjō Sōun, he went to Miidera in 1522 and studied there for approximately three years, living in Jōkōin. "Youth's attire" (*tōgyō* 童形) was a term used in reference either to a young man without dressed hair or to any youth of noble blood before his coming-of-age ceremony. Some affected the fashion well into young manhood, as appears to have been the case with Gen'an. After leaving Miidera, he became the fortieth Hakone Bettō. He was a connoisseur of tea, gardens, and poetry, and his hermitage was located near Odawara, Kanagawa Prefecture. For more on Gen'an, see Shima 1980: 77. It would appear from the context in *The Journal of Sōchō* that he was no longer in residence when Sōchō arrived.

40. This passage is vague; I have followed the punctuation in the Hayashi ms. of the text, entitled *Sōchō Suruga nikki* (49). The identity of Hyōbukyō 兵部卿 is unclear, as is the relationship between him, Gen'an, and the master of the Jōkōin subtemple. It may be that it was Hyōbukyō and not the Hakone Bettō who took his vows that spring.

41. Sōchō modestly implies that he was compelled to accept the honor of composing the hokku.

42. *Oi no mimi* no. 95, where it is prefaced with "At Miidera." *Yama no i* (a mountain well) relates the verse to Miidera, "Three Wells Temple." The foundation poem is *Kokinshū* 8: 404, by Ki no Tsurayuki:

Composed while crossing the Shiga Mountain Pass, as he took leave of one with whom he had spoken at a rock-pent spring:

musubu te no   As one thirsts for more
shizuku ni nigoru   at a mountain well too soon
yama no i no   muddied by the drops
akade mo hito ni   that fall from hands cupped to drink,
wakarenuru kana   so now do I part from you.

43. Shimazu (1975: 40) suggests that this may mean that Hyōbukyō was the master of Jōkōin, as it was conventional for the guest to compose the hokku and the host to respond with the waki verse. Hyōbukyō 兵部卿, "Minister for Military Affairs," would have been a hereditary title passed down through a family, and it does not necessarily suggest that the person to whom it refers had not taken holy orders.

44. The foundation poem is *Kokinshū* 6: 324, by Ki no Akimine:

Composed while crossing the Shiga Mountain Pass:

shirayuki no   As the glistening snow
tokoro mo wakazu   falls and covers all about
furishikaba   without distinction,

| iwao ni mo saku | flowers seem to be blooming |
| hana to koso mire | even on the rocky cliffs! |

Hyōbukyō's poem, however, treats the flowers literally, not metaphorically. Sōchō misquotes the foundation poem, giving *iwa ni mo sakeru*. The tsukeku is linked to the maeku through the standard association between *unohana* (deutzia) and *hototogisu* (cuckoo), which is noted in Ichijō Kaneyoshi's linked-verse handbook *Renju gappekishū* (Collection of Linked Pearls and Joined Jewels, 1476 [hereafter cited as *RJGPS*], no. 364), and also by the fact that both verses are based on foundation poems composed at Shiga Mountain Pass.

45. Shimazu (1975: 40) notes that this refers to the festival at Hie 日吉 Shrine in Sakamoto, held on the day of the monkey in the middle of the fourth month.

46. Tōenbō 東円坊 was a shakuhachi virtuoso (*JS*: 318). The "Eighty-Year Staff" is another word for the Dove-Tipped Staff (*hato no tsue*), a cane capped with a dove ornament, originally presented by the court to a meritorious subject on the attainment of his eightieth year.

47. *Hyōjō* 平調 is a musical mode beginning on the note *ho* ホ (Western E or mi).

48. *Shinkokinshū* 16: 1560 (*JS*: 222, n. 53).

49. This is Tsuda Sōkei 津田宗珪 (or 宗桂, see also *JS*: 104, 121).

50. Motosu Yamatonokami 本須大和守 was a member of the Nasu 那須 house. Konohama 木の浜, in Moriyama 守山 City, Shiga Prefecture, was a center of Lake Biwa trade.

51. The verse is actually *Shinkokinshū* 16: 1504 (*JS*: 236, n. 17).

52. This is an allusion to a passage in *Genji monogatari* (3: 72): "The same wind came up again, and they arrived at Akashi as if they had flown. It was the work of a moment, the place being but a short walk away."

53. Mirror Mountain (Kagamiyama) is an utamakura located in Shiga Prefecture at the border of Ryūōchō 竜王町 and Yasuchō 野洲町.

54. *Oi no mimi* no. 97. *Muranae* pivots between *mura* (village) and *muranae* (rice shoots).

55. Kawai Suruganokami 河井駿河守 (d. 1526) was a lieutenant of Rokkaku Sadayori, constable of south Ōmi. His residence was in Gamō 蒲生 District, Shiga Prefecture.

56. Moruyama もる山 is an utamakura in Moriyama 守山 City.

57. *Oi no mimi* no. 96.

58. For Tanemura Nakatsukasanojō, see *JS*: 44; for Kannonji, see *JS*: 32.

59. Kawai Gorō 河井五郎 may be the same person as Kawai Matagorō 河井又五郎 who appears on *JS*: 129 and *JS*: 144. It was not uncommon for a son to bear a different surname from that of his father.

60. Sakanoshita 坂の下 is in Sekichō 関町, Suzuka 鈴鹿 District, Mie Prefecture, at the southern foot of the Suzuka Mountain chain, just to the east of Suzuka Pass (Suzuka Tōge 鈴鹿峠).

61. Inohana ゐのはな (猪鼻) is in Tsuchiyamachō 土山町, Shiga Prefecture; Tsuchi-

yama is at the north foot of Suzuka Pass; Uchi no Shirakawa 内の白川 is the old name for Tamuragawa 田村川; and Soto no Shirakawa 外の白川 is the old name for Matsuogawa 松尾川.

62. Cf. *Shinchokusenshū* 8: 517, by Fujiwara Michitoshi:

A travel poem composed at the Suzuka temporary palace during the vestal's progress:

isogu to mo	Though we are in haste,
ima wa tomaramu	for a moment let us pause—
tabine suru	at the reed shelter
ashi no kario ni	where we rest on our journey
momiji chirikeri	the autumn leaves have fallen.

The vestal's palace gave its name to the present Tongū 頓宮 (Temporary Palace) in Tsuchiyamachō.

63. The cuckoo, associated with the fifth month, was believed to live in the mountains and to fly rarely to settled areas, where its call was prized. The bird was also believed to come from the Mountain of the Dead (Shide no yama), and its call brought intimations of the afterlife (see also *JS* no. 202 and *JS* no. 217).

64. The source of the association is unclear. It may simply be that the cuckoo, because of the sound of its call, is related to the Suzuka Mountains through the word *suzu* (bell). The Shōkōkan ms. gives *shino ni nakikeru* in the poem and *shino ni nakitsuru* in the following phrase (Shimazu 1975: 42). The *GSRJ* text (274) gives *shino ni naku naru* in the poem.

65. *Shinkokinshū* 17: 1613, by Saigyō (see also *JS* no. 13).

66. The haikai verse includes a pun on *koshi* (back / palanquin).

67. The foundation poem on which this haikai is based is *Man'yōshū* 12: 3156 (see *JS*: 208, n. 111).

68. Sōchō last saw Seki Kajisai at Kameyama in the eighth month of 1522 (*JS*: 16-18).

69. Nomura Ōinosuke 野村大炊介 was a retainer of the Seki house.

70. Shōhōji 正法寺, a temple affiliated with Daitokuji, was built by Kajisai just west of Washiyama 鷲山, where it was protected on three sides by Onogawa 小野川 river. Kajisai was accordingly also known as Lord Shōhōji. The temple site remains today. Washiyama is located in Suzuka District, two kilometers north of the center of Sekichō. See Tsurusaki 1971 and 1979.

71. Either Sōchō means the twenty-fourth here or he was mistaken about leaving Kannonji on the twenty-second (*JS*: 49), because he spent one night at Sakanoshita and one more at Nomura Ōinosuke's residence.

72. The Shōkōkan ms. is garbled here; the translation follows the Saiokuji ms.

73. A quotation from *Wakan rōeishū* no. 319, by Du Xunhe:

Four or five mountain peaks painted in rainy colors;
Two or three flights of geese dotting the autumn clouds.

74. Jingoji 神護寺 is located on Mount Takao 高雄山 in Ukyō 右京 Ward, Kyoto City.

75. Dairyōji 大竜寺 is no longer extant.

76. Toganoo 栂尾 is the site of Kōzanji 高山寺 temple. Takao 高尾 (or 高雄), Toganoo, and Makinoo 槇尾, places known together as the Sanbi 三尾, are all famous for fall foliage.

77. A legend in *Shuyiji* 述異記 relates that Wang Zhi 王質, who lived during the Jin dynasty (265–419), become so engrossed in watching a game of chess played by immortals in the mountains that he did not notice the passage of time until the handle of his axe had rotted away.

78. This is a repetition of *JS* no. 14.

79. The honor of providing the hokku usually went to an exalted guest. Sōchō takes credit for the verse in *Oi no mimi* (no. 98), and he may in fact have composed it as a proxy poem for Kajisai. Iwashita (1985: 307) is of that impression.

80. *Yaesakaki* are the many *sakaki* evergreens to the left and right of the Nakanoe Torii gate of the Inner Shrine at Ise. *Sakaki toru* (break off evergreen boughs) is a summer seasonal word; one breaks sacred *sakaki* boughs from Kamiyama 神山 mountain to prepare for the Aoi festival of the Kamo Shrines in the middle of the fourth month. Cf. *Goshūishū* 3: 169, by Sone no Yoshitada:

> sakaki toru   In the fourth month
> uzuki ni nareba   when one breaks off *sakaki* boughs,
>   kamiyama no   no old leaves remain
> nara no ha kashi ha   on *nara* oaks or *kashi* oaks
> mototsuha mo nashi   on Kamiyama mountain.

The word *takashi* in the hokku skillfully relates it to the hokku of two years before.

81. Ikkan 一閑 was another sobriquet of Seki Kajisai.

82. Sōchō links to the Shintō sentiment of the hokku through *yū kakete*, which has the secondary meaning "hang sacred mulberry paper" on the *sakaki* trees to make shrine offerings. Cf. *Shokusenzaishū* 3: 214, by Lady Sanuki:

> kami matsuru   The deutzia
> uzuki no hana mo   are in bloom in the fourth month
>   sakinikeri   when we worship the gods.
> yamahototogisu   Sing throughout the evening,
> yū kakete nake   mountain cuckoo!

See also *JS* no. 5.

83. Washinosuyama 鷲の巣山 (Eagle Nest Mountain) is called Haguroyama 羽黒山 today; it is northwest of Washiyama. But Sōchō may be using the name as simply a common noun.

84. Kōzenji 興禅寺 is a Rinzai temple affiliated with Tōfukuji 東福寺, one of the great Gozan temples in Kyoto.

85. The verse is a play on Washinosuyama (Eagle Nest Mountain) and Eagle Peak, Ryōjusen 霊鷲山, where the Buddha preached the *Lotus Sutra* in India. It is possible that the verse also implies that the cuckoos keep their distance because of the eagles. Note *to ya* (quotative and interrogative particles) are homophonous with *toya* (hawk's cage / molting).

86. The abbot links his five-character verse to the previous through "fifth month," the time of the year associated with the cuckoo. Hearing the name of the mountain where the Buddha preached the great sutra, one feels a refreshing coolness.

87. "Acolyte" translates *shakatsu* 沙喝, which in the Zen sect denotes a young monk who while tonsured still wears the robes of a *kasshiki* (novice) (cf. *JS*: 28).

88. Jionji 慈恩寺 was located to the north of the present temple of the same name. Sōchō is still near Kajisai's residence.

89. *Oi no mimi* no. 100. The verse contains a play on *masu* (build or increase) and *masuge* (sedge grass).

90. *Hanatachibana* (orange blossoms) includes embedded the word *tachi* (to rise). The foundation poem is *Kokinshū* 3: 139 (*JS*: 221–22, n. 50).

91. Shirō Tanemori 四郎種盛 (or 胤盛) was Seki Kajisai's successor and heir to his title of Minbunotaifu. He may have been one of the "three fine sons" referred to on *JS*: 22.

92. "Waka sequence" translates *tsugiuta* 続歌, in which topics are written down and then drawn by the participants, who thereafter compose on them one after the other. Short sequences of only one round, such as this one, are called *hitotsugi*. The sequence of which Sōchō speaks is of the impromptu variety (*tōza* 当座 or *sokudai* 即題), where composition takes place immediately after the topics are distributed. Sequences where the topics are distributed beforehand are known as *kendai* 兼題 or *shukudai* 宿題.

93. Jirō Moriyoshi 次郎盛祥 (or Masayoshi 正祥) was another of Kajisai's sons. *Meidaishū* 明題集 may refer here to *Meidai waka zenshū* 明題和歌全集, a collection of more than twelve thousand waka from the *Kokinshū* period to 1446, classified by poem topic. It is thought by some to be an expanded version of Imagawa Ryōshun's *Nihachi meidaishū*, a personal anthology of selections from the first sixteen imperial poetic anthologies.

94. I have emended *waga* in the *Shōkōkan* ms. (Shimazu 1975: 45) to *ware* on the basis of the *Saioku* ms. The poem includes a pun on *ware to shi takasago* and *toshi taka* (full of years). The foundation poem is *Kokinshū* 17: 909, by Fujiwara Okikaze:

tare o ka mo	Is there no one left
shiru hito ni semu	of those that I once knew?
takasago no	Not even the old pine
matsu mo mukashi no	of Takasago is among
tomo naranaku ni	my friends of long ago.

The verse also appears as *Hyakunin isshu* no. 34, and it forms the central motif of the nō play *Takasago*.

95. Sōchō puns on *kari (ni)* (goose / for a moment).
96. The poems read like a love exchange.
97. Kanbe Ukyōnoshin Morinaga 神戸右京進盛長 was one of the three heads of the Seki house (Shimazu 1975: 46). Mon'ami 聞阿弥 was a shakuhachi virtuoso also mentioned in Konparu Zenpō's *Zenpō zōdan* (506).
98. Isonokami 石上 is a shrine in Tenri 天理 City, Nara Prefecture. It is often used as a makurakotoba for *furu* (old). Embedded in the word is *sono kami* (the past).
99. "Rice cakes" here translates *sasachimaki*, glutinous rice balls (*mochi*) wrapped in bamboo leaves, hence Sōchō's reference to "abundant as mountain bamboo" in the verse that follows.
100. Sōchō plays on *senshū senbei* (a thousand autumns of rice crackers) and *senshū banzei* 千秋万歳 (lit. a thousand autumns, ten thousand years), used when wishing someone a long life. There is a kakekotoba pivoting between *kokorozashi mi* (I see your kindness) and *miyama* (mountain).
101. Sugihara Iga Nyūdō Sōi 杉原伊賀入道宗伊 (1418–86), also known as Sugihara Katamori 杉原賢盛, was one of the "seven sages" of linked verse anthologized by Sōgi in *Chikurinshō*.
102. Sugihara Takamori 杉原孝盛 was Sōi's son and heir (Shimazu 1975: 46).
103. On Jionji 慈恩寺, Shinpukuji 新福寺, Amidaji 阿弥陀寺, and Chōfukuji 長福寺, see Tsurusaki 1971: 12–13.
104. Sei Kunaikyō Hōin 清宮内卿法印 was a famous court physician. He may have been a member of the Kiyohara 清原 family.
105. Tsurusaki (1979: 11) suggests that Kajisai's generosity may have been due not only to his esteem for Sōchō but to family connections. The physician was being sent to treat Ujichika, whose mother, Lady Kitagawa 北川, was the sister of Hōjō Sōun, who in turn was an ally of the Imagawa and possibly himself originally of the Seki house in Ise. Sōun's earlier name, Ise Nagauji 伊勢長氏, suggests his geographical origins.
106. Mori Hayatonosuke 森隼人佐 was a retainer of the Seki.
107. The phrase "at the border of Ise and Owari" again recalls *Ise monogatari* (20); see *JS*: 18.
108. The poem again includes the famous phrase from *Ise monogatari* quoted in the previous note and bears overtones of Narihira's composition made at the same place:

itodoshiku	In my longing,
sugiyuku kata no	which grows ever stronger
koishiki ni	for the place I left,
urayamashiku	how I envy the waves
kaeru nami kana	that can return whence they came!

The verse is also referred to in the "Suma" chapter of *Genji monogatari* (3: 39).

109. Ōno 大野 in Chita 知多 District is now in Tokoname 常滑 City, Aichi Prefecture.

110. See *JS*: 19.

111. Dora Ikkōdō 土羅一向堂, in what is now Fukuokachō 福岡町, Okazaki 岡崎 City, was a branch temple of the Honganji lineage. It was destroyed in 1562 (Shimazu 1975: 47).

112. See *JS*: 19. Makino Denzō Nobushige 牧野田三信成 (d. 1529) was an Imagawa ally and lord of Imahashi 今橋 Castle, located in what is now Toyohashi 豊橋 City, Aichi Prefecture.

113. Kibi 吉美 is in Kosai 湖西 City, Shizuoka Prefecture.

114. See *JS*: 10.

115. Kakegawa was the site of Asahina Yasuyoshi's residence (*JS*: 7).

116. Kiganji 鬼巌寺 temple is now Ryōgonzan Kiganji 楞厳山鬼岩寺, a Shingon temple in Fujieda 藤枝 City, Shizuoka Prefecture.

117. Fuchū 府中, i.e., Sunpu 駿府, the Imagawa capital in Suruga, now Shizuoka City.

118. See *JS*: 8.

119. The "ten dumplings" (*tōdango*) were a famous product (*meibutsu*) of the spot through the Edo period (see Shimazu 1975: 165).

120. Ryūōmaro 竜王丸 (also read Tatsuōmaro, 1513–36) was the childhood name of Ujichika's son, who took the name Gorō Ujiteru 五郎氏輝 on reaching adulthood. Ujichika likewise used the name Ryūōmaro during his minority.

121. Okitsu Tōbyōenojō Masanobu 興津藤兵衛尉正信 was lord of Okitsu Castle and an Imagawa retainer. It was for him that Sōchō composed the Okitsu half of *Sōchō renga jichū* in or after 1523.

122. Ōgimachisanjō Sanemochi 正親町三条実望 (1463–1530) was a high-ranking court noble married to Ujichika's elder sister Kitamuki 北向. He retired to Suruga in early 1524, where he took religious vows and adopted the Buddhist name Jōkū 浄空. Sōchō also refers to him in his journal as Jikōin 慈広院.

123. Ohara Chikataka 小原親高 is identified by Matsumoto (1980: 105) as Bizennokami 備前守. He also participated in Daiei 5 [1525]:9:21 *Nanibito hyakuin* (A Hundred-Verse Sequence Entitled "A Kind of Person"), some verses of which were incorporated into *Oi no mimi* (nos. 2192–2201).

124. A misunderstanding prevented Chikataka from participating in the waka sequence. Sōchō apologizes in his reply (*JS* no. 189) for the missed connections.

125. This is a very complicated verse: Sōchō casts himself as the aged billows and asserts that they forgot their promise (with overtones of Sōchō's promise to Chikataka) to rise with the morning tide (i.e., to meet at Kiyomi) until the noon / ebb, *hiru* (noon) then introducing *hirune* (nap).

126. Sōgi died on the last day of the seventh month, 1502. For an account of his last years see Sōchō's *Sōgi shūenki* (The Death of Sōgi). Sōchō first met Sōgi in 1466, when

Notes to Book One (1524), Pages 56–59

Sōgi stopped at the residence of Imagawa Yoshitada. Sōchō was nineteen (by the Japanese count). At that time the young Sōchō (who had yet to adopt that name) guided the older poet to the Kiyomi Strand utamakura.

127. *Oi no mimi* no. 102 and *Rengashū* no. 1334 (in Iwashita and Kishida 1978).

128. Sōgi thought enough of this verse to include it in both *Wasuregusa* 萱草 (1474) and *Wakuraba* 老葉 (1481, rev. ed., 1485), his first two personal poetry collections. The *Jingū* ms. of the former includes the headnote, "Made for a single sheet of verses at daybreak, after spending the night with a number of others, gazing at the moon over Kiyomi Gate."

129. *Shinkokinshū* 15: 1333, by Fujiwara Masatsune.

130. Zuiun'an 瑞雲庵.

131. Sōchō is humorously describing the lonely natural scene in terms of a temple sleeping alone, in keeping with monastic strictures.

132. Unpa (雲波 or 雲坡) went to Suruga in early 1503 (Yonehara 1979: 902).

133. Matsushita Shōkō 松下正広 (1412–94) was the closest student of the waka poet Shōtetsu 正徹 (1381–1489), who in turn had studied with Imagawa Ryōshun 今川了俊 (1325–1420). Shōtetsu and Shōkō were acquainted with Imagawa Yoshitada's grandfather, Norimasa 今川範政 (1364–1433). Shōkō visited Imagawa Yoshitada in 1473 and left a record of the journey in his travel journal *Shōkō nikki* 正広日記, 643–47.

134. Mihogasaki 三保が崎 is a cape extending east from Kiyomi Strand. Also known as Miho no matsubara 三保の松原, it is renowned for its superb beach lined with pine trees, behind which rises Mount Fuji across the bay.

135. The temple fell to ruin in the medieval period but was restored by the abbot Kankoku 関国 (various sources give also give Kanchi 関智 or Kanshō 関聖 [Kanaoka 1970: 170]). At that time it received the patronage of Ashikaga Takauji (Tōjiin 等持院), founder of the Ashikaga shogunate, who changed it from a Tendai to a Rinzai Zen temple. A portrait sculpture of him, which survives, was installed in the image hall. The temple had been destroyed by warfare when Shōkō visited it.

136. Unlike *JS* nos. 196 and 199, this waka is found neither in *Shōkō nikki* nor in either of Shōkō's personal poetry collections, *Shōkō eiga* and *Shōkashū*.

137. The constable of Noto Province (Ishikawa Prefecture) was Hatakeyama Yoshifusa 畠山義総 (1491–1545). He acceded to the headship of the Hatakeyama house in 1515 and initiated the golden age of Hatakeyama cultural activity. He was acquainted with Reizei Tamekazu, Sōseki, and Sanetaka, and Sōboku wrote linked-verse commentaries for him, including the well-known sequence he composed with Sōchō that is mentioned in the journal, Daiei 7 [1527]:1:18 *Yashima Shōrin'an naniki hyakuin* (A Hundred-Verse Sequence Entitled "A Kind of Tree" Composed at Shōren'in in Yashima) (*JS*: 137). For a detailed study of the cultural history of the Hatakeyama house in Noto, see Yonehara 1979: 49–214.

138. Fujimasu 藤増.

Notes to Book One (1525), Pages 59–61

139. The Ichikawa 市川 were an old family in Ihara 庵原 District.

140. The passage demonstrates the nature of medieval *Man'yōshū* scholarship. The poem in question, *Man'yōshū* 1:19 (attributed in some texts to Princess Nukada), appears to have been read in Sōchō's time as:

somakata no	My love holds my eye
hayashihajime no	fast as a robe holds color
sanohagi no	made from bush clover
kinu ni tsukunasu	growing straight as timber
me ni tsuku waga se	and just beginning to flourish.

The *Man'yōgana* 綜麻形乃林始乃狭野榛能 is now generally read:

hesokata no	My love holds my eye
hayashi no saki no	fast as a robe holds color
sanohari no	*made from the alders*
kinu ni tsukunasu	*at the outer reaches*
me ni tsuku waga se	*of Hesokata forest.*

The Shōkōkan (Shimazu 1975: 50) and *GSRJ* (279) texts render the first line of the *Man'yōshū* quotation as *somabito no* 杣士の, but Sōchō, as seen from his use of *somagata no* 杣形の in the line following the quotation, clearly read it *somakata*, and that is the reading in the Saiokuji manuscript. Meaning "timber" or "timberland," the word here refers to bush clover growing sparsely and thus, like timber, straight and tall. Hesokata is a place name, thought to have been in Kurita 栗太 District, Shiga Prefecture.

141. *Oi no mimi* no. 101. Sōchō's verse refers to the fact that while the capital's own tall mountain, Hiei, has no snow on it in the autumn, Sunpu's Fuji already does.

142. The verse involves a pun on *hototogisu* and *hedo* (vomit). The humor of the *kyōka* is largely based on a reversal of the classical convention of taking pleasure in the cuckoo's call. The bird is also linked with death (*JS*: 217).

143. On the connotations of *takigi koru* (cut [fire]wood), see *JS* no. 37. The word "moving" derives from the fact that Sōchō's life span had been prophesied by a diviner to be seventy-nine years, by the Japanese count (*JS*: 125, 161). He therefore expected to die at Takigi.

144. The poem is based on a pun on *mekarenu* (cannot take my eyes from / unwithered buds).

BOOK ONE: *Fifth Year of Daiei (1525)*

1. This is Daiei 5 [1525]:1:25 *Naniki* (or *Nanibito*) *hyakuin* (A Hundred-Verse Sequence Entitled "A Kind of Tree" [or "A Kind of Person"]). Except for Ujiteru's verse, it is a solo sequence (*dokugin*) by Sōchō.

2. *Uguisu* ([bush] warbler) links to *ume* (plum) (*RJGPS* nos. 300, 363). Sōchō puns on *hatsune no hi* (First Rat Day) and *hatsune no hi* (day of the [warbler's] first song). On the first Day of the Rat of the new year, it was the custom to go into the fields and pluck young pines (*ne no hi no matsu*) and young greens (*ne no hi no wakana*). Sōchō may also have in mind *Shūishū* 1: 22:

> When Kunai of the Palace of the Dowager was a child, she composed this on the first Day of the Rat of the first month, when while serving the Emperor Daigo she heard a bush warbler singing in the pine outside:
>
> | matsu no ue ni | It now strikes me that |
> | naku uguisu no | the name *hatsune no hi* |
> | koe o koso | ought to mark instead |
> | hatsune no hi to wa | the time one hears the call |
> | iubekarikere | of the bush warbler in the pines. |

3. *Ne no hi* (Day of the Rat) links with *[hatsu]haru* ([early] spring)(*RJGPS* no. 56). Three spring verses have continued in succession, marked by *ume*, *uguisu*, *haru* (spring), and *kasumu[ran]* (haze). This is a felicitous verse expressing the expectation that like this spring, so will springs hereafter be accompanied by gentle haze.

4. *Oi no mimi* no. 103. For Anonotsu, see *JS*: 18. Akogi Bay 阿漕の浦 is an utamakura lying off Tsu (Mie Prefecture). It was once a preserve for fish for Ise Shrine. The verse employs a kakekotoba pivoting between *Akogi* and *kogu* (row).

5. *Oi no mimi* no. 104. Mount Shio (Shionoyama 塩山) is an utamakura in Kai Province (Enzan 塩山 City, Yamanashi Prefecture). There is a kakekotoba pivoting between *shio* (tide) and Shionoyama. The connection between *shio* and Shionoyama is homophonic, there being no beach near the mountain.

6. Sōchō established his residence beside Abekawa river in the Teramachi 寺町 district of Sunpu sometime after returning from Kyoto in 1496. It later became Sōchōji 倉長寺. See Nakagawa 1981: 1310–19. He later built his Brushwood Cottage (Saioku 柴屋) in Mariko, several kilometers to the west of the provincial capital. See Shigematsu 1979.

7. *Oi no mimi* no. 105.

8. No note survives.

9. Okitsu Masanobu's Yokoyama 横山 Castle in Okitsu. Yokoyama means "long line of mountains."

10. Sōchō refers to Ogimachisanjō Sanemochi (*JS*: 56) and his son Kin'e 正親町公兄 (1494–1578; Sōchō also calls the latter Onkata in his journal). Kin'e lived in Suruga for a total of twenty-three years, having most recently arrived from Kyoto in 1522 (see Owada 1981a: 1219).

11. *Oi no mimi* no. 106, where it appears as *hototogisu / makoto wa kyō o / hatsune kana*. The term *hatsune* (first song) usually applies to the first call of the bush warbler (cf. *JS*

no. 207). Here the call of the cuckoo, traditionally associated with early summer, has so moved the poet that he feels the term should apply to it instead.

12. *Oi no mimi* no. 110. Sōchō includes a pun on *mi mo hi mo* (the day and I) and *mimoi* (drinking water). The verse is based on *Saibara* no. 8, "Asukai":

asukai ni	At Asukai
yadori wa subeshi	we ought to take our lodging.
ya oke	Ya! Oke!
kage mo yoshi	So fine is the shade,
mimoi mo samushi	so cool the drinking water,
mimakusa mo yoshi	so fine the horses' fodder.

(Usuda and Shinma 1976: 129.) Saibara are ancient folksongs set to court *gagaku* music. The same verse is referred to several times in *Genji monogatari* (e.g., 1: 68; 3: 61).

13. The "Waterless Month" is Minazuki 水無月, the sixth month.

14. This is a reference to the "Yūgao" chapter of *Genji monogatari* (1: 106):

"The white ones blooming over there are called 'evening faces,'" he said. "The name sounds so like a person's, yet here they are blooming on this dilapidated fence." Indeed it seemed a poor neighborhood, chock-a-block with huts.

Sōchō may also have been thinking of a line in Yoshida Kenkō's *Tsurezuregusa* (44): "In the sixth month one is moved to see the evening faces blooming so white by the poor houses and smoke rising from the smudge fires," itself possibly based in part on the *Genji monogatari* passage.

15. Nakagawa Yoshio (1981: 1316) suggests Sōchō is referring here to *Kokinshū* 18: 990 by Lady Ise (*JS*: 213, n. 152) to imply that he was hoping for a change in his financial situation that was not forthcoming, and that in consequence he could only sit and watch as summer passed by. Araki Yoshio (1947: 70), however, believes the changes spoken of in the passage refer to Sōchō's not knowing when his life will end. Harada Yoshioki (1979: 379) combines both interpretations. The pun on *se ni* ([become] a shallows) and *zeni* (money) was apparently common; Kensai in *Kensai zōdan* (415) takes issue with the opinion that the usage was only fitting for haikai verse, citing *Kokinshū* 18: 990 as a locus classicus. He then continues: "Lady Ise composed the verse when she sold her house. One theory holds that *se ni kawaru* means 'as times change' and that it is inappropriate [in formal poetry] to use it in the sense of 'exchange for money,' but this opinion is wrong."

16. The quotation "not been able to poke my head outside" refers to the "Akashi" chapter of *Genji monogatari* (3: 65), which likewise takes place during a storm.

17. I have emended *izuko mo ga* in the Shōkōkan ms. (Shimazu 1975: 54) to *izuko mo ka* on the basis of *Sōchō michi no ki* (219). *GSRJ* (280) gives *izuku moru*.

18. *Urabon* 宇蘭盆 refers to the Festival of the Dead, in which services are held for the repose of the deceased. It comes to a climax on the fifteenth of the seventh month.

Notes to Book One (1525), Pages 64–65

19. The cuckoo was thought to guide the spirits of the dead to the underworld, and its cry constantly reminds Sōchō of his own end. Sōchō in consequence humorously asks the cuckoo to stop waiting for him and to serve instead as a guide for those already dead. The classical treatment is found in poems such as the following exchange from Saigyō's *Sankashū* (nos. 750–51):

Sent by Horikawa no Tsubone, lady-in-waiting to Taikenmon'in:

> kono yo ni te
> katarai okan
>   hototogisu
> shide no yamaji no
> shirube to mo nare

> Let us make a pact
> while I am still of this world,
>   cuckoo,
> that you will serve as my guide
> across the Mountain of the Dead.

[Saigyō's] reply:

> hototogisu
> naku naku koso wa
>   katarawame
> shide no yamaji ni
> kimi shi kakaraba

> The cuckoo
> will cry and cry
>   as it shows you the way
> when the time comes for you
> to cross the Mountain of the Dead.

20. The verse appears in the Shōkōkan ms. (Shimazu 1975: 54) as *nokoshitsuru / yo ya wa wasururu / aki no kaze* (Could we ever forget / the night he left us behind? / The wind of autumn). I have altered it on the basis of the *Sōchō Suruga nikki* (72), *GSRJ* (280), and Saiokuji texts. It appears in *Oi no mimi* (no. 2128) as *nokoshitsuru / yo ya wa wasururu / tsuki no kage* (. . . The light of the moon). While *kaze* (wind) is indeed what makes the flowers blossom and so works with *asagao* (morning glory) in the next verse, *tsuki* (moon) is more effective with *yume* (dream).

Ujichika had been present at a memorial gathering in Suruga soon after Sōgi's death in 1502, and he composed a waka at that time that was very similar to his hokku of 1525. It appears in Sōchō's account of Sōgi's death, *Sōgi shūenki*:

> During a session with fixed topics that same night, on "under the moon, longing for an old friend," the constable composed this:
>
>> tomo ni min
>> tsuki no koyoi no
>>   nokoshiote
>> furubito to naru
>> aki o shi zo omou
>
>> I think back upon
>> this autumn when he became
>>   a man of old
>> and left behind the evening moon
>> we would have viewed together.
>
>>   Ujichika

Might this mean that though he waits for Sōgi, he does so in vain? (Kaneko 1976: 120).

This passage suggests that *aki no tsuki* may be the most accurate version of the problematic third phrase (*ku*) in Ujichika's hokku of 1525.

21. Jōki 紹僖 was Imagawa Ujichika's Buddhist name.
22. *Oi no mimi* no. 2129.
23. Sōseki had been with Sōchō when Sōgi died. One linked-verse sequence Sōseki and Sōchō composed soon thereafter survives (Bunki 2 [1502]:8:6 *Sōgi tsuitō nanibito hyakuin*. It too is mentioned in *Sōgi shūenki* (Kaneko 1976: 119–120).
24. For Toyohara Muneaki see *JS*: 44.
25. The letter was dated 1524:8:19 (*JS*: 69).
26. The verse contains a pun on *kakaru* (linger / like this). The foundation poem is *Shinkokinshū* 8: 757, by Sōjō Henjō:

sue no tsuyu	Dew on leaf tips,
moto no shizuku ya	and water drops on stems—
yo no naka no	those are reminders
okure sakidatsu	that sooner or later
tameshi naruran	all living in this world must part.

27. I have emended *kagiri arikeru* in the Shōkōkan ms. (Shimazu 1975: 55) to *kagiri arikeri* on the basis of the *GSRJ* (281) and Saioku mss.
28. I have emended *kieshi to kiete* in the Shōkōkan ms. (Shimazu 1975: 55) to *kieshi to kikite* on the basis of the *GSRJ* ms. (281).
29. The upper phrase (*ku*) is missing in all manuscripts save *Sōchō michi no ki* (220). Sōchō sent messages to Kyoto via a messenger, whom he arranged to meet at Sayo no nakayama (see *JS*: 192, n. 2). Sayo no nakayama also functions rhetorically to introduce *nakadachi mo* (someone . . . to convey).
30. Sōchō's last mention in his journal of writing to Muneaki occurred when he was in Kansai in 1524 (*JS*: 44).
31. See *JS* no. 151.
32. Muneaki was actually two years younger than Sōchō. The poem is similar to *JS* no. 548.
33. The holograph of these thousand waka, entitled *Toyohara Muneaki senshu* 豊原統秋千首 (read *Toyohara Sumiaki senshu* in *KSSMR*), is in Tenri Toshokan (see Shimazu 1975: 56). It was composed in the seventh month of 1496 and presented to Sanetaka for his judgments (*gatten*). See *Sanetakakōki* 1496:7:20, 3a: 259.
34. The connection between a wheel and turning over thoughts was a common conceit (cf. *JS*: 46 [also *Kanginshū* 64]). Sanemochi may also have had in mind here the wheel of transmigration, *samsara*.
35. Sanemochi responds to Sōchō's verse *JS* no. 222.
36. This responds to Sōchō's verse *JS* no. 223.

Notes to Book One (1525), Pages 68–70

37. This responds to Sōchō's verse *JS* no. 224. Sanemochi's verse involves a number of kindred words (e.g., *ori*, *nare*, *karakoromo*, *haru*), much in the manner of *Ise monogatari* (21):

karakoromo	How I miss my wife,
kitsutsu narenishi	to whom I have grown accustomed,
tsuma shi areba	as to a well-worn robe
harubaru kinuru	of Chinese cut,
tabi o shi zo omou	now that I am come so far.

38. *Kumoi* (clouds) contains overtones of "above the clouds," a conventional reference to the imperial court, which Muneaki served.

39. *Kusa no kage* (grassy shade) is a standard euphemism for the grave.

40. Utsunoyama mountain (translated here for paronomastic reasons as "Reality Mountain") is invoked as a reference to where Sanemochi and Sōchō reside.

41. Sanemochi responds to Sōchō's verse, *JS* no. 221. The poem involves a kakekotoba pivoting between *mi* (see) and *mizukuki* ([writing] brush).

42. Sanemochi is addressing Sōchō here. Mount Meet-Again (Nochiseyama or Nochisenoyama 後瀬山) is an utamakura in Obama 小浜 City, Fukui Prefecture.

43. This verse is not in the *GSRJ* ms. It was possibly an appended personal lament (*jukkai*).

44. The letter was written in kanbun by an amanuensis a year earlier; Sōchō has inserted it in his journal in the appropriate place. Sōchō's letter reached Muneaki on 1524:8:19.

45. Sōchō arrived in Suruga on 1524:6:16.

46. Goose-skin paper (*ganpi no kami* or *ganpishi* 雁皮 [の] 紙), known as "the king of papers" (*kami no ō*) for its superb quality, is made from the *ganpi* tree, a relative of the *jinchōge* (*Daphne odora*).

47. Sōchō received the poems weeks after Muneaki's death anniversary and inserted them in the appropriate place in his journal, which returns to the proper chronology at the end of the Muneaki sequence.

48. This introduction is by Sanetaka. Muneaki was an adherent of the Nichiren sect, hence Sanetaka's decision to begin each of his poems with a syllable of the title of that sect's main scripture, the *Lotus Sutra* (*Myōhō rengekyō*).

49. "One . . . who knew the music" recalls the compound *chiin* 知音, lit., "knows sounds," which also means "friend." The word is based on a Chinese legend related in *Liezi* 列子 about Zhong Ziqi 鍾子期 of the Spring and Autumn period (722–481 B.C.E.), who understood the music of the *qin* 琴 player Bo Ya 伯牙; when Zhong Ziqi died, Bo Ya cut the strings of his qin, as no one was left whom he felt could truly appreciate his playing.

50. The verse refers to "the darkness of ignorance" (*mumyō no yami* 無明の闇), also

called "the long night of ignorance" (*mumyō jōya* 無明長夜), the cycle of reincarnations in the world of suffering before enlightenment. Related is the concept of "the darkness of births and deaths" (*shōji no yami* 生死の闇), also called "the long night of births and deaths" (*shōji jōya* 生死長夜).

51. This is a reference to the "Song that Opens the Blossoms" (*kaika no shirabe*) that was believed to have the power to bring buds into blossom. Sanetaka apparently possessed the drum as a keepsake.

52. The shrine in question is Isonokami, which was associated with great age (see *JS* no. 183). Cf. *Man'yōshū* 4: 501, by Hitomaro:

otomera ga	For as long
sode furuyama no	as there has been a sacred shrine fence
mizukaki no	on Mount Furu,
hisashiki toki yu	a name recalling a maiden's waving sleeves,
omoiki ware wa	I have longed for you.

Furu 布留 is an utamakura in Tenri 天理 City, Nara Prefecture. It is the site of Mount Furu (Furuyama), on which Isonokami Shrine is situated, and is homophonous with *furu* (to wave / to grow old).

53. Sanetaka includes a kakekotoba pivoting between *omoi* (think) and Omoigawa, the "River of Longing," an utamakura thought to be in Tsukushi 筑紫 District, Fukuoka Prefecture. The foundation poem is *Gosenshū* 9: 515, by Lady Ise:

The lady left without telling anyone, and when the man learned of her whereabouts, he wrote saying, "I have not been able to call on you recently and thought you might have passed away," whereupon she replied:

omoigawa	My tears flowed
taezu nagaruru	like the ceaseless River of Longing—
mizu no awa no	would I ever
utakata hito ni	pass away like the river's froth
awade kieme ya	without seeing you again?

54. The "Since I" hymn (*Jigage* 自我偈) is a *gatha* of praise in 102 five-character lines that appears at the end of the "Nyorai juryōbon" 如来寿量品 chapter of the *Lotus Sutra*. The hymn, which takes its name from its first line, "Since I attained Buddhahood," deals with the efforts the Buddha makes in this world to lead believers to salvation. See *Hokekyō* 3: 28–37 and Hurvitz 1976: 242–44.

55. Gyōkū 尭空 was Sanetaka's Buddhist name.

56. The moon disappearing behind the clouds is a conventional metaphor for death. The poet includes a pun on *kasuka* (faint) and *hatsuka* (twentieth). Sanetaka's section ends here.

57. *Hagi* (bush clover) is usually associated with *tsuyu* (dew), and *ogi* (reeds) with *kaze*

Notes to Book One (1525), Pages 72–75

(wind). Both are evocative of evanescence. Here the poet is hard-pressed to choose which of the two poetic combinations is the more moving.

58. Sōchō may have had in mind this passage from the "Suzumushi" chapter of *Genji monogatari* (7: 81): "Her Majesty said that of all the autumn insects, she particularly favored the pine cricket, and she sent people to remote fields just to bring back those with particularly good voices to set free at her palace. But few sounded as fine as they had in the wild."

59. Sōchō quotes a well-known proverb saying that just as a tiger dies and is still valued for its skin, so must the warrior live so that his reputation will continue to be revered after his death. The proverb also appears in *Jikkinshō* (62–63).

60. The poems were perhaps sent to Chikashige's father-in-law.

61. Mitsuse River (Mitsusegawa 三つ瀬川) is another name for Sanzunokawa 三途の川, the river on the way to the underworld. It has three crossings depending on the burden of sin of the deceased. Cf. *Shūishū* 9: 542, by the daughter of Sugawara Michimasa:

mitsusegawa	There is no pole
wataru mizao mo	to propel the boat across
nakarikeri	Mitsuse River.
nani ni koromo o	Upon what then will they hang
nugite kakuran	the garments that they remove?

62. It is one's normal fate (*jun'en* 順縁) to die before one's children and a reversal of fate (*gyakuen* 逆縁) to be predeceased by them.

63. Saitō Kaganokami Yasumoto 斉藤加賀守安元 (n.d.), lord of Mariko Castle, was one of Sōchō's most important patrons. The context of this passage suggests he was the father-in-law of Chikashige.

64. Only the tsukeku (no. 265) is Sōchō's. The verses are also found in *Sōchō renga jichū*, both in the *Okitsu* section (131–32) and the *Mibu* section (177), with minor changes in the maeku. It appears as well as *Renga tsukeyō* no. 1021.

65. On the reconstruction of the Sanmon gate at Daitokuji, see *JS*: 30–31. There is a legend that the copy was in the hand of Fujiwara Teika. See Takeuchi Gengen'ichi 1987: 214.

66. The foundation poem is *Kokinshū* 18: 990 (*JS*: 213, n. 152). It is likely that *nani ni kawaramu* also means "what can I [now] exchange?" and that *kono se o hate* also means "the end of my money," the implication being that now that he has sold his last remaining article of value, he can donate nothing more. Cf. *JS*: 22 and *JS* no. 215.

67. Sōchō criticizes himself in his poem for his insensitivity toward another living thing.

68. *Oi no mimi* no. 113. Sōchō did not return to his Brushwood Cottage in Mariko until the twenty-sixth of the twelfth month (*JS*: 86).

69. Okitsu Hikokurō Chikashisa 興津彦九郎親久 was the heir of Okitsu Masanobu (*JS*: 55) and subsequently lord of Yokoyama Castle. Sōchō also refers to him in his journal as Sōtetsu 宗鉄.

70. I have emended *akemaku hoshiki* in the Shōkōkan ms. (Shimazu 1975: 63) on the basis of *Sōchō michi no ki* (228). Cf. the sequence of poems (*JS* nos. 190–92) Sōchō records earlier. Kiyomi Strand is famous for its moonlit view and ancient gate, both of which are artfully combined in the poem.

71. Here, Sōchō states that he is seventy-eight (seventy-seven by the Western count) in the ninth month, on the tenth day of the month's last third (*gejun*). Thus he counts off the days of his old age: 7, 8, 9, 10. The ninth month of 1525 was a "long month" of thirty days (a "short month" had twenty-nine). The last day of the ninth month was particularly poignant, as it marked the end of autumn.

72. Sōchō borrows imagery from poems such as this from *Ise monogatari* (41):

inishie no	Like a spool of flaxen thread
shizu no odamaki	that rolled round and round
kurikaeshi	in days gone by,
mukashi o ima ni	would there were a way to roll
nasu yoshi mo ga na	the past back to the present!

73. For Ōgimachisanjō Sanemochi, see *JS*: 56; for Kin'e, see *JS*: 62; for Imagawa Ujichika, see *JS*: 9. Sekiguchi Ujikane 関口氏兼, Ohara Chikataka (*JS*: 56), and Yui Hōgo 由比保悟 (also known as Mimasakanokami 美作守) were retainers of the Imagawa; Shueki 珠易 was one of Sōchō's disciples. Ujikane, Chikataka, Hōgo, and Shueki all participated in Daiei 5 [1525]:9:21 *Nanibito hyakuin* (A Hundred-Verse Sequence Entitled "A Kind of Person") along with Asahina Yasumochi (*JS*: 10), Asahina Tokishige (*JS*: 11), and others. Shueki also took part with Sōchō in Eishō 2 [1505]:8:22 *Tamanani hyakuin* (A Hundred-Verse Sequence Entitled "A Kind of Gem") at Kōfukuji in Nara, after which he returned with Sōchō to Suruga. He also accompanied him on the journey chronicled in Sōchō's *Azumaji no tsuto* (1509). He appears in *Utsunoyama no ki* and in Arakida Morihira's poetic miscellany *Nikonshū* (2: 32).

74. The aster (or chrysanthemum) was believed to have properties conducive to longevity.

75. There is a kakekotoba pivoting between *hatsuka* (faint) and *hatsukarigane*, "the first call of the geese" that are flying south for the winter.

76. The *udonge* 優曇華 (Skt. *udumbara*) is a mythical flower that according to Buddhist legend blooms once every three thousand years and announces the appearance of a Buddha or powerful ruler.

77. Nasu Suketarō 那須助太郎 is unknown.

78. Mount Kōya 高野山 in Wakayama Prefecture is the location of Kongōbuji 金剛峰寺 temple, a center of Shingon Buddhism.

79. The implication here is that the story is too painful for Suketarō to relate personally.

80. Cf. *Senzaishū* 19: 1236, by Jakuren:

Composed at Kōya:

akatsuki o	Awaiting the dawn
takano no yama ni	of realization
matsu hodo ya	on Mount Kōya,
koke no shita ni mo	he is resting beneath the moss
ariake no tsuki	under the late-night moon.

"Takano no yama" is the poetic reading of Mount Kōya. The verse refers to Kōbō Daishi, who lies in his tomb at Mount Kōya awaiting the arrival of Maitreya, Buddha of the future. The verse relates to *sono akatsuki* (that dawn), which refers to the advent of Maitreya's appearance on earth, or in more general terms to the moment when delusion will give way to Buddhist enlightenment (cf. "the darkness of ignorance," *mumyō no yami*, JS no. 244).

81. Miura Yatarō 三浦弥太郎. The Miura and the Asahina were the "house elders" (*shukurō*) of the Imagawa.

82. Saitō Shirō 斉藤四郎 is unknown; possibly he was a relative of Saitō Yasumoto (JS: 272, n. 64).

83. *Gosenshū* 4: 197:

hototogisu	The cuckoo
akatsukigata no	with a single cry
hitokoe wa	in the dawn twilight
ukiyo no naka o	passes on its way
sugusu narikeri	through this melancholy world!

84. "Paper robe" translates *kamiko* 紙子 or 紙衣, a cold-weather garment made of thick paper treated with persimmon bitters then repeatedly exposed to the dew, dried in the sun, and kneaded for softening.

85. *Fuji [no] wata* is silk floss produced in Susono 裾野 in Suruga Province. *Susono* also means "foothill fields," here in reference to anywhere near Fuji, including Sōchō's cottage. *Wata* here also implies *watabōshi* (silken cap), which is used as well as a metaphor for Fuji's snow-covered peak. The poem in addition involves a kakekotoba pivoting on *tokaku suru* (can do anything or want for nothing) and Suruga. Sōchō means that while Fuji is covered with snow like a silken cap all year long, he himself did not have a cap for the winter snow, despite the fact that in Suruga one should be able to obtain most anything, particularly in view of the proximity of the place of production of *Fuji [no] wata*.

86. Hōgo suggests that since snow has only recently fallen on Mount Fuji, adding to its white cap, the foothills too will wear a cap of snow before long, and Sōchō will now have a cap of silk floss to protect himself as well.

87. Sōchō is believed to have been a younger son of Gojō Yoshisuke 五条義助, head of what would become a major house of swordsmiths in Suruga.

88. Cf. *Shinkokinshū* 16: 1586, by Fujiwara Shunzei:

oinu to mo	Though I have grown old,
mata mo awanu to	I trust we shall meet again,
yuku toshi ni	so to the departing year
namida no tama o	I offer these gem-like teardrops
tamuketsuru kana	to speed it on its way.

Usually on the death anniversary (*shōtsuki meinichi* 祥月命日) of one's father one hires priests to hold a religious service. Sōchō does not, hence his tears "without a spark of luster."

89. Sōchō puns on *hitatare* (warrior's robe) and *hita[sura] tare[ru]* (have diarrhea). The name Kusoichi resembles samurai names but literally means "shit once," and *komeru* (contain or subdue) has a martial tone. A more literal translation would be "Unexpectedly / I donned a warr7ior's robe / (have diarrhea) — / would the name Kusoichi (Shit Once) / help to subdue it?"

90. Shiki Suruganokami Yasumune 志貴駿河守泰宗, also called Kunainoshō 宮内少輔, was the head priest of Sengen 浅間 Shrine in Sunpu (Miyagasakichō 宮ヶ崎町, Shizuoka City). The shrine stands on Shizuhatayama 志豆機山 mountain.

91. *Ato tareshi* (lit., spread traces) refers to the doctrine of *honji suijaku* 本地垂迹 (manifestation from the original state), which holds that Japan's indigenous Shintō gods are manifestations of Buddhist deities.

92. For Gorō Ujiteru 五郎氏輝 see *JS*: 55.

93. *Oi no mimi* no. 116. During a youth's coming-of-age ceremony (*genpuku*), his hair was for the first time arranged in adult style. The foundation poem for Sōchō's verse is *Kokinshū* 14: 693:

kimi kozuba	If you do not come,
neya e mo iraji	I will not enter my bedroom,
komurasaki	even if frost
waga motoyui ni	should settle on the deep purple cord
shimo wa oku to mo	with which I bind my hair.

94. Sōgi conferred the secret traditions of *Kokinshū* (*Kokin denju*) on Konoe Masaie 近衛政家 (1444–1505) and his son Hisamichi 尚通 (1472–1544), and on Sanjōnishi Sanetaka. He also bestowed a considerable part of the traditions on the renga master Shōhaku, who in turn passed them on to disciples in the Sakai area (in present-day Osaka). The

Shōhaku lineage of the secret traditions came to be known as the *Sakai denju* in consequence. Sanetaka, however, received the most complete version of the traditions and was recognized as Sōgi's "first disciple." His lineage was called the *Gosho denju* (Palace Traditions).

95. The lectures to which Sōchō so diffidently refers were in fact a very serious affair taking place over three months in 1492–93. Taijin 泰諶 (d. 1518), of Shōren'in 青蓮院 imperial temple (*monzeki*), attended the sessions with Sōchō, and a portion of his notes survives (see Arai 1976: 49). Taijin (also called Jibukyō Hōgan 治部卿法眼) had five renga verses chosen for inclusion in *Shinsen tsukubashū*. He also took part with Sōgi, Sōchō, and others in *Hamori senku* in 1487 and appears with Sōchō in many other extant renga sequences.

96. *Oi no mimi* no. 118.

97. *Kokinshū* 1: 2, by Ki no Tsurayuki:

Composed on the first day of spring:

sode hichite	Will the ice on the water
musubishi mizu no	I once cupped in my hands,
kōreru o	soaking both my sleeves
haru tatsu kyō no	melt off in the spring wind
kaze ya tokuran	that begins to blow today?

98. Hasedō 長谷堂 refers to Shinhasedera 新長谷寺, in Otowachō 音羽町, Shizuoka City.

99. *Oi no mimi* no. 117.

100. Sōchō quotes a five-character line from a *gatha* in the *Lotus Sutra*, "Kanzeon Bosatsu Fumonbon" (*Hokekyō* 3: 262; trans. Hurvitz 1976: 316):

Even if someone whose thoughts are malicious
　　Should push one into a great pit of fire,
By virtue of constant mindfulness of Sound-Observer
　　The pit of fire will turn into a pool.

　　　(trans. Hurvitz 1976: 316)

101. Kenchōji 建長寺 is one of the Kamakura Gozan temples. Sōchō may have resided there in 1529 (Ōshima 1962: 51). For Asahina Tokishige, see *JS*: 11.

102. Chōrakuji 長楽寺 is a Rinzai temple located in Fujieda 藤枝 City.

103. Yōtokuji 養得寺 is unknown. It may be a mistake for Zentokuji 善得寺 in Fuji 富士 District. The abbot at the time was Shun Kinkei 舜琴渓 (d. 1530). It is not to be confused with Zentokuin 善得院, later Rinzaiji 臨済寺, in Sunpu. Tenryūji 天竜寺 is one of the Kyoto Gozan temples.

104. Paperers (*hyōhoishi* 表布衣師 or 表補衣師) like Saburōgorō 三郎五郎 replaced the

paper or silk on *fusuma* sliding screens, scrolls, and the like. He lived in Kyoto at Ayano-kōji 綾小路, one block south of Shijō Avenue, and Muromachi 室町, one block west of Karasuma Avenue.

105. Sōchō makes a pun on Tema no seki 手間の関 (lit. Hindrance Gate), an ancient barrier in modern Tottori Prefecture, and *tema* 手間, an abbreviation for *temachin* 手間賃, payment for work. *Tema no sekimori* is thus "keeper of Hindrance Gate" and "keeper of payments." Cf. *Kokin waka rokujō* no. 1026:

yakumo tatsu	Like Hindrance Gate
izumo no kuni no	in Izumo Province,
tema no seki	where banks of clouds rise,
ika naru tema ni	what manner of hindrance,
kimi sawaruran	is keeping you away?

106. The poem was probably meant for Nobutane's daughter Jukei, wife of Ujichika. As Sōchō was not shown the poem for a month, it is unlikely the "one in the east" (*higashi naru hito*) could be he. *Saranu wakare* (lit., unavoidable parting), furthermore, usually refers to the parting between parents and children.

107. This was a *kanpenjō* 勘返状, a letter received and returned with the reply written directly on it.

108. The chronology of this passage is problematic. It would seem that *JS* nos. 304–5 were a private correspondence between Sōchō and the nurse and that *JS* nos. 306–8 were in formal mourning, but that Sōchō's three poems were all sent at about the same time, a short while after seeing Nobutane's death poem and holding the poetry session. For Isonokami, see *JS* no. 183.

109. Tsuge et al. (1931, 1: 370) suggest the following points were raised by Sōchō in answer to Tokishige's questions. For a discussion of this passage, which is reminiscent of *zuihitsu* miscellanies like Yoshida Kenkō's *Tsurezuregusa*, see Harada 1979: 385–93.

110. What is translated here as "near and dear" would more literally be "fail to be moved 'because of one shoot of *murasaki* grass,'" from *Kokinshū* 17: 867:

murasaki no	Because of one shoot
hitomoto yue ni	of *murasaki* grass,
musashino no	I feel fondness
kusa wa minagara	for all the plants and grasses
aware to zo miru	on the plain of Musashino.

The poem suggests that the love that one bears another extends to all those connected with that person. The people Sōchō describes reject the appeals from even those with claims upon them in order to make money.

111. Such landowners will not succeed in commerce because they will be inexperienced amateurs dividing their attention between their land holdings and their business,

Notes to Book One (1525), Pages 84–86

competing with professionals who have spent their lives at their occupations and who have no other obligations.

112. Sake dealers often doubled as moneylenders.

113. These are jobs traditionally confined to the lowest orders of society.

114. Sōchō would seem to have Osada Chikashige in mind (*JS*: 72–74).

115. Harada (1979: 391) interprets this sentence as "Those who beg by the roadside and wait by houses and gates are still better off [than these starving samurai]."

116. I have substituted the version in *GSRJ* (289) for that in the Shōkōkan ms. (Shimazu 1975: 71), which is irregular and repetitive: *tare zo kono / me oshinogoi / tateru hito / hito no yo wataru / michi no hotori ni.* Jichin 慈鎮 (also known as Jien 慈円, 1155–1225) was a major *Shinkokinshū* poet. But the poem is not found in *Shūgyokushū* 拾玉集, his personal poetry collection.

117. The phrase contrasts those who are able to support themselves and those who are not.

118. *Kokinshū* 5: 292, by Sōjō Henjō. It bears the preface, "Composed as he stood under the shade of a tree at Urin'in temple." Sōchō construes *wabibito* in the poem as "forlorn one," but Henjō perhaps simply meant a monk forgotten by the world.

119. This passage pursues the subject of the preceding. Lion dancers wore lion headdresses; monkey trainers sang songs and chanted poetry while leading monkeys from house to house; bell ringers and bowl beaters begged while chanting sutras to rhythms beaten out on bells or bowls (for a picture of the last, see *Shichijūichiban shokunin utaawase* 101).

120. "Separate transmission outside the teachings" (*kyōge betsuden* 教外別伝) and "nonverbalization" (*furyū monji* 不立文字) are Zen teachings that stress the necessity of intuitive mind-to-mind transmission of religious truth without reliance on written or spoken words.

121. Sōchō's excoriation of the lax Zen clergy reflects the attitude of his outspoken religious master, Ikkyū, who wrote such lines of poetry as, "Who of Linji's [Rinzai's] descendants passes on his Zen properly?" and "There are no true masters, only false ones" (*Kyōunshū* 93, 159 [nos. 8 and 169]). Linji 臨済 (d. 867) was the founder of Ikkyū's Zen sect. Sōchō's mention of those who meditate on the Holy Name is a reference to adherents of the Pure Land (Jōdo) sects. Note that Ikkyū too professed at one point to have abandoned Zen for Pure Land beliefs: "In an earlier year I humbly received the portrait of [the Zen priest] Daitō Kokushi. Now I exchange my robes for those of the Pure Land sect" (*Kyōunshū* 181).

122. *Bon* (*Urabon*) is the annual Festival of the Dead, observed in the seventh month (*JS*: 250, n. 18); *Higan* 彼岸 refers to the seven days of rituals in observation of the spring and autumn equinoxes.

123. This passage is reminiscent of the house laws (*kakun*) of warriors. Sōchō himself

is mentioned in one such document, *Asakura Sōteki waki* (125), written by his Echizen warrior patron Asakura Norikage (*JS*: 191, n. 1):

> A man can accomplish nothing if he has no reserves. It is said, though, that unlike the world's rich, a warrior must never put wealth ahead of all else and hoard gold and coin. Hōjō Sōun of Izu saved everything, even needles, in his storehouses, but when it came to his campaigns he would not have stopped at smashing gemstones. Sōchō always spoke of this. (125)

124. Sōchō was in the capital from 1518 to 1520, then again in 1522–24; the sentence suggests that it has been five or six years since Sōchō spent time at his Brushwood Cottage (Saioku 柴屋) in Mariko 丸子, five kilometers southwest of Sunpu. The source of the name Saiokuken is unclear; Sōchō himself always uses Saioku. The traditional date given for its construction is 1504, based on the phrase "In the beginning of the Eishō era [1504–21]" (*Eishō hajime no koro*) in *Utsunoyama no ki*. Shigematsu (1979), however, argues that the date was actually 1506. The cottage was located on the fief of Saitō Yasumoto (*JS*: 73).

125. See *JS* no. 37. Sōchō is suggesting that ideally he would be pursuing the Buddhist law in Takigi, site of Ikkyū's hermitage, but he has only managed to reach his hermitage by Utsunoyama, "Reality Mountain."

126. Sōchō contrasts the religious world of Takigi to the world of ephemeral secular reality in which he now lives. Though he cannot reach Takigi, he will instead place his hopes for salvation in the Utsunoyama pines.

127. The verse combines elation at being back with a deflated sense of loneliness because no one has come to greet him.

128. The snow looks like cherry blossoms amid the rocks and trees, and it hides the rougher spots of the garden from view. Sōchō refers to *Kokinshū* 6: 324 (see *JS*: 240–41, n. 44).

129. Sōchō contrasts the rusticity of his environment with the elegance of Bo Juyi's "Three Friends of the Northern Window" ("Beichuang sanyou" 北窓三友), poetry, wine, and the *qin*. See Saku 1978, 3: 290–91.

130. Sōchō refers to *Ise monogatari* (21–22): "Going on, they came to the province of Suruga. When they reached Utsunoyama, the path they must follow was dark and narrow, and overgrown with ivy and maples [*tsuta kaede wa shigeri*], filling them with apprehension."

131. Cf. *Man'yōshū* 14: 3442:

azumaji no	Unable to cross
tego no yobisaka	Maiden-Calling Slope
koeganete	in the eastland,
yama ni ka nemu mo	am I to sleep in the mountains,
yadori wa nashi ni	without any lodging?

Notes to Book One (1526), Pages 88–90

Maiden-Calling Slope (Tego no yobisaka 手児の呼坂) is unknown; it may be one of the seven steep slopes east of Kanbarachō 蒲原町 in Ihara 庵原 District, Shizuoka Prefecture, or Satta Pass 薩埵峠 in Okitsuchō 興津町, Shimizu 清水 City, also in Shizuoka Prefecture. Sōchō was a native of Shimizu.

132. There is snow-white hair on Sōchō's head and now the old cottage is covered with snow as well.

133. Saigyō's poem, *Shinkokinshū* 6: 697, reads in its entirety:

mukashi omou	While stacking driftwood
niwa ni ukiki o	in the yard of my cottage
tsumiokite	I recall the past—
mishi yo ni mo ninu	how little is this year's end
toshi no kure kana	like others I have seen!

The interpretations of this poem by Tanaka and Akase (1992: 206) and Minemura (1974: 220) are, however, different from that of Sōchō. Both modern commentators believe Saigyō is unhappily comparing his comfortable life before taking holy vows to his present rustication. The interpretation of Kubota Jun (1976–77: 552–53), however, is in agreement with Sōchō's.

134. Sōchō is suggesting that he will soon die and become a spirit himself. *Tsurezuregusa* (19) refers to a similar belief: "The practice of worshipping the spirits of the dead that return on New Year's eve has disappeared from the capital, but it continues in the east. I find that very moving."

BOOK ONE: *Sixth Year of Daiei (1526)*

1. The poem refers to *Shinkokinshū* 11: 1034, by Princess Shokushi:

In a hundred-waka sequence, on "Concealing Love":

tama no o yo	Jewelled cord of life,
taenaba taene	if you are to break, then break!
nagaraeba	If I live on,
shinoburu koto no	I will weaken from the strain
yowari mo zo suru	of concealing my longing.

Had Sōchō not survived the night, he would have been like the light snow of spring, becoming one with all things.

2. *Oi no mimi* no. 120, where the verse appears as *ama no hara / fuji ya kasumi no / yomo no haru* (cf. *JS* no. 338). Suminoyama is Mount Sumeru, center of the Buddhist cosmos. The poet has included it through a kakekotoba pivoting between *kasumi* (haze) and *sumi* (Sumeru), then through slant rhyme on *yomo* (in all directions or circling) and *yama*

(mountain). "Circled by lands" (*yomo no kuni*) refers to the four lands said to surround Mt. Sumeru. Sōchō thus locates Suruga, the province in which Mt. Fuji is located, at the center of the world.

3. Ōgimachisanjō Kin'e (*JS*: 62) was the nephew of Imagawa Ujichika (*JS*: 9–13).

4. Based on *Kokinshū* 2: 93:

haru no iro no	It is not as if
itariitaran	spring comes to some villages
sato wa araji	and not to others.
sakeru sakazaru	Why then are some flowers blooming
hana no miyuran	and others failing to bloom?

(Translation after McCullough 1985)

5. Lady Kitagawa 北川 (c. 1442–1529) was the wife of Imagawa Yoshitada and the mother of Ujichika. Her elder brother was Hōjō Sōun (*JS*:11). She was one of Sōchō's most devoted patrons. For more on Lady Kitagawa, see Nagakura 1978.

6. Kogawa 小川 is in Yaizu 焼津 City, Shizuoka Prefecture. Hasegawa Motonaga 長谷川元長 was the son of Hasegawa Masanobu 長谷川正宣 (1430–1516), who had sheltered Lady Kitagawa and her young son Ryūōmaro (later Imagawa Ujichika) during the Succession Conflict of the Bunmei Era (*Bunmei no naikō*) after Yoshitada's death in 1476 (see Appendix A). Motonaga's younger sister was the wife of Asahina Jūrō Yasutsugu 朝比奈十郎泰次, who Nakagawa (1981: 1330) believes may have been Yasumochi (*JS*: 10).

7. *Oi no mimi* no. 124. The verse means that the pines set off the cherries to mutual advantage, with both being reflected in the water. The hokku is appropriate to Kogawa's coastal location.

8. Sōchō apparently means the unease that customarily accompanied the start of a journey.

9. *Oi no mimi* 125. The verse expresses the conviction that just as one will see again in the fall the geese that now fly north in the spring, so will the friends meet again who now bid each other goodbye. Since Sōchō says he thought of this as a farewell session, he may mean they will meet in the Western Paradise (cf. Nakamikado Nobutane's farewell verse to his daughter, Jukei, *JS* no. 303). There is a pun on *kari* (geese / temporary).

10. Sōchō refers to *Shinkokinshū* 10: 987, by Saigyō (*JS*: 192, n. 2). Sayo no nakayama appears in the poem as Sayo no nagayama 小夜の長山 (Sayo Long Mountain), for etymological reasons which Sōchō subsequently explains.

11. Sōchō refers to Saigyō.

12. Sōkyū 宗久 (n.d.) also demonstrated interest in the etymology of this toponym in his *Miyako no tsuto* (350) of 1367:

> I reached Saya no nakayama. I was moved by the recollection that this was where Saigyō composed ". . . I would pass this way again." Opinions differ on whether

to pronounce it Saya no nakayama or Sayo no nakayama. Chūnagon Moronaka wrote that when he was on his way to take up his post in this province, the natives pronounced it Sayo no nakayama, and earlier poets perhaps did so as well. I recall having seen it so in anthologies. Minamoto Sanmi Yorimasa wrote it Nagayama 長山. When I asked an old man here, he immediately replied, "Saya no nakayama."

koko wa mata	When I inquired
izuku to toeba	of the name of this place,
amabiko no	the sound
kotouru koe mo	of the echo answered too, saying
saya no nakayama	Saya no nakayama.

13. Shimazu (1975: 77) notes that the mountain now lies between only two districts, Ogasa 小笠 and Haibara 榛原, but that there is a Four District Bridge to the east of nearby Kyūenji 久延寺 temple, referring to Shūchi 周智, Sano 佐野, Haibara, and Kikō 城飼 Districts. The Shōkōkan ms. (Shimazu 1975: 77) reads, "It was in four districts *in the mountains*," which would seem instead to justify calling the mountain Nakayama (in the mountains), thus missing the point of the anecdote. I have emended the text on the basis of the GSRJ (292) and Saiokuji mss., which employ the character for "long" (*nagai* 長), making the line read "it was so long that it covered four districts." Sōchō equivocates in his rewritten version of the account in Book Two (Shimazu 1975: 80), where he writes, "a long road running for three leagues through the mountains."

14. Sayo no nakayama appears in such verses as *Kokinshū* 12: 594, where it is rendered Saya no nakayama:

azumaji no	Like Between Mountain in the east,
saya no nakayama	Saya no nakayama,
nakanaka ni	how did I begin to drift
nani shi ka hito o	betwixt and between
omoisomekemu	into this affair?

See also *Kokinshū* 20: 1097 (*JS*: 268, n. 6). Both *Kokinshū* poems read Sa*ya* no nakayama rather than Sa*yo* no nakayama. Katagiri (1983: 183) believes that the name *saya* 狹谷 indicates a narrow valley. Verses from the Heian period use the word in connection with such homophones as *saya ni*. Both the *Sōchō michi no ki* and Saiokuji mss. clearly render the name Sa*yo*, which Katagiri asserts is a later corruption.

15. Saigyō's *Travels in the Eastland* (*Azuma michi no ki* 東路の記, given on Shimazu 1975: 80 as 東国道の記), is unknown.

16. This etymology was apparently a new discovery for Sōchō, as he rendered the name Sayo no nakayama earlier (*JS* no. 1).

17. Kasuya Nakatsukasa Matsutsuna 糟谷中務松綱 was an Imagawa retainer.

Notes to Book One (1526), Page 92

18. It is now the second month of 1526.
19. *Oi no mimi* no. 126. Cf. *Shūishū* 19: 1230:

hashitaka no	Even if the leaves
tokaeru yama no	of the sweet acorns on the hills
shiishiba no	where sparrow hawks return
hagae wa su to mo	fall as do hawk feathers,
kimi wa kaeseji	you, my dear, will never change.

Sweet acorns (*shii*) do not lose their leaves in the autumn; the poet asserts that even if that impossible event should occur, the feelings of the loved one would not change. Another verse employing the same imagery appears in *Gosenshū* 16: 1171:

wasuru to wa	Do not despise me,
uramizaranan	thinking I have forgotten you—
hashitaka no	the sweet acorns
tokaeru yama no	where the sparrow hawks molt
shii wa momijizu	do not change to fall colors.

Tokaeru (or *togaeru*) means either "to return" or "to change color (of feathers)," i.e., "to molt." Sweet acorn leaves appear white when blown by the wind, and they are therefore associated with the verbs "to change" and "to return" (*kaesu/kaeru*). The relationship between those various meanings may have given rise to the poetic conceit that sparrow hawks return to molt in mountains with sweet acorn trees. Sōchō observes that the mountains have both sweet acorns and cherries, and he wonders if the cherries may have been the trees for which the sparrow hawks returned, for just as the trees change their raiment in spring, so do the hawks. In spring the sparrow hawks change from winter to summer plumage, and the poem may include the overtone that the white feathers harmonize with the white undersides of the sweet acorns and with the cherry blossoms.

20. *Oi no mimi* no. 128.
21. Rokurō 六郎 is probably Horikoshi Ujinobu 堀川氏延 (c. 1491–1570), a member of a cadet branch of the Imagawa house (Ōshima 1964 [May]: 23). For more on the Horikoshi house, see Owada 1986. Fuchū 府中 refers here to Mitsuke 見付, capital of Tōtōmi. It is now Iwata 磐田 City, Mitsuke, in Shizuoka Prefecture.
22. *Oi no mimi* no. 127. The verse is deliberately auspicious to counter the unlucky nature of the day. The tree "said to bloom and ripen once in three thousand years" is the "three-thousand-year peach" (*michitose no momo*), the peach of immortality that according to Chinese legend Wu Di received from the Queen Mother of the West (Xiwangmu). The phrase thus became a metaphor for a rare and auspicious event. Cf. *Shūishū* 5: 288, by Ōshikōchi Mitsune (attributed to Sakanoue Korenori in Teijiin Poetry Contest):

Notes to Book Two (1526), Pages 95–96

  michitose ni   We have now greeted
 naru chō momo no   the spring of the year
   kotoshi yori   in which will bloom
  hana saku haru ni   the peach said to ripen
  ainikeru kana.   once every three thousand years!

The "three" in Sōchō's verse reflects the date of its composition, the third day of the third month.

BOOK TWO: *Sixth Year of Daiei (1526)*

1. See *JS* no. 327. Cf. *Shinkokinshū* 1: 33, by Jichin:

  ama no hara   The smoke from Mount Fuji
 fuji no keburi no   trails high in the field of heaven
   haru no iro no   and becomes the hue
  kasumi ni nabiku   of springtime haze —
  akebono no sora   the sky at dawn.

2. Izumigaya 泉谷 is the valley in which Mariko is located. In Book One, Sōchō wrote that he met with Lady Kitagawa on the night of the ninth, then arrived at Mariko on the tenth, where he spent one night before setting out for Kogawa on the eleventh. Sōchō may mean here that he was at Mariko for two days, the tenth and the early part of the eleventh.

3. Sōchō's verse is based on *Kokinshū* 19: 1051, by Lady Ise:

  naniwa naru   They have rebuilt it,
 nagara no hashi mo   the ancient Nagara Bridge
   tsukuru nari   in Naniwa.
  ima wa waga mi o   To what can I compare
  nani ni tatoemu   my aged self hereafter?

Some commentators suggest the third phrase, *tsukuru nari*, means "it no longer stands." In either case, however, the bridge Lady Ise used to know is gone, as she herself soon will be. The same is true for Sōchō, but he is also glad to have such a spot for his last years.

4. See *JS* no. 329.
5. Hamuro Mitsuchika 葉室光親 was executed in 1221 at Kikugawa river (Aster River) for his role in the Jōkyū uprising. *Taiheiki* (1: 69) credits him with this death poem in Chinese, actually composed by Fujiwara Muneyuki:

  In antiquity at Aster River in Nanyang Province,
 one dipped water from downstream and prolonged one's years;

267

Notes to Book Two (1526), Pages 96–97

> today at Aster River on the Tōkai Circuit,
> I stop on the west bank and end my life.

More than a century later, Hino Toshimoto 日野俊基 was executed at the same spot. He left a death poem in Japanese:

> inishie mo   One recalls hearing
> kakaru tameshi o   a similar tale in the past
> kikugawa no   of Aster River—
> onaji nagare ni   is it now to be my lot
> mi o ya shizumen   to sink into the same stream?

The rhetoric of the verse is based on a kakekotoba pivoting between *kiku* (to hear) and *kikugawa* (Aster River).

6. The verse makes reference to *Kokinshū* 20: 1097:

> kai ga ne o   Would I had a clear view
> saya ni mo mishi ga   of the Kai Mountains,
> kekerenaku   but lying between
> yokōri fuseba   with no thought for others
> saya no nakayama   is Saya no nakayama.

7. Nissaka 日坂, on the west slope of Sayo no nakayama, is now in Kakegawa City.
8. The verse appears in Sōchō's first personal poem anthology, *Kabekusa* no. 2548.
9. See *JS* no. 335.
10. Horikoshi Rokurō 堀越六郎 (Ujinobu 氏延). Mitsuke was the provincial capital of Tōtōmi.
11. Iyonokami Sadayo 伊予守貞世 (Ryōshun 今川了俊, 1326–1420) was a warrior literatus and the most poetically distinguished member of the Imagawa house. *Gyokuyō wakashū* (1313) and *Fūga wakashū* (1349) are the fourteenth and seventeenth imperial poetic anthologies, both of which reflect Kyōgoku-Reizei ideals. Ryōshun studied waka with Reizei Tamehide 冷泉為秀 (d. 1372).
12. See *JS* no. 337.
13. See *JS*: 9, 55.
14. *Oi no mimi* no. 129.
15. Hikuma 引馬, in Hamamatsu City, is mentioned in such poems as *Man'yōshū* 1: 57, by Naga no Imiki Okimaro:

> Composed in the second year of Taihō [702], when the Retired Empress Jitō traveled to Mikawa Province:

> hikumano ni   Fly pellmell
> niou haribara   into the stand of colored alders
> irimidare   on Hikuma Field;

| koromo niowase | go, let them dye your robes |
| tabi no shirushi ni | in memory of your journey! |

16. Hamana 浜名 Bridge, an utamakura, was destroyed when an earthquake opened Lake Hamana to the sea in 1498.

17. Because of the prophecy establishing his life expectancy at seventy-nine years (see JS: 125, 161), Sōchō expected this to be his final journey. He was seventy-nine (by the Japanese count) in this year, 1526.

18. The bridge no longer stands, of course; Sōchō is being ferried past the site.

19. See JS: 9.

20. See JS: 55.

21. Both Denzō and his father, Makino Shigekata 牧野成方, were killed fighting Matsudaira Kiyoyasu 松平清康 in 1529 (JS: 303, n. 81). Kiyoyasu was the grandfather of Tokugawa Ieyasu. Denzō's grandfather was Makino Kohaku Shigetoki 牧野古白成時, an old friend of Sōchō mentioned in *Utsunoyama no ki* (396). He too was killed in battle, in 1506. All three men were allies of the Imagawa. Shigetoki had one of his renga verses included in *Shinsen tsukubashū*, and Sōchō composed a solo memorial sequence for him on the first anniversary of his death, entitled Eishō 4 [1507]:11:3 *Makino Kohaku Zenmon uchijini isshūki* (First Anniversary of the Death in Battle of Makino Kohaku Zenmon). He was one of Sōchō's most devoted patrons.

22. Sōchō has reached the border between Tōtōmi and Mikawa Provinces.

23. See JS: 14.

24. Ina 猪名 or 井名, now written 伊名, is now Kozakaichō 小坂井町, Hoi 宝飯 District, Aichi Prefecture. Makino Heisaburō 牧野平三郎 was lord of Ina Castle (JS: 150).

25. Fukōzu 深溝 is in Kōtachō 幸田町, Nukata 額田 District, Aichi Prefecture. Sōchō's host was Matsudaira Ōinosuke Tadasada 松平大炊助忠定 (d. 1531). Sōboku was later to lodge with Tadasada's son Yoshikage 好景 (*Tōgoku kikō* [820]). On Sōchō's Matsudaira acquaintances in Mikawa, see Suzuki Mitsuyasu 1973.

26. Shimazu (1975: 82) suggests that Sōchō may be referring to Kira Tōjō Yoshiharu 吉良東条義春, vice constable of Mikawa. Tōjō Castle was in Yokosukachō 横須賀町, Nishio 西尾 City. The Kira house, which traced its roots to the same progenitor as the Imagawa, later split into the East (Tōjō) and West (Saijō) branches.

27. The verse includes felicitous overtones in *sakari* (bloom / prosper).

28. Cf. *JS* no. 544. The verse includes two kakekotoba pivoting between *nami ya yuku* (the waves go out) and *yuku haru* (late spring) and between *kazashi no wata* (floss garlands) and *watatsuumi* (the great ocean). *Kazashi no wata* were artificial flowers made of silk floss that garlanded the crowns worn by participants in the *otokotōka* 男踏歌, in which a troupe of male courtiers on the fifteenth day of the first month sang *saibara* at various temples and noble residences. The foundation poem is from *Ise monogatari* (83–84):

Notes to Book Two (1526), Page 99

watatsumi no	The God of the Sea
kazashi ni sasu to	did not begrudge giving
iwau mo mo	you, my lords,
kimi ga tame ni wa	this sea plant that he treasures
oshimazarikeri	as a garland for his hair.

29. See JS: 15.

30. Moriyama 守山 is now Moriyama Ward, Nagoya City. Matsudaira Yoichi Nobusada 松平与一信定 (d. 1532) was the third son of Matsudaira Nagachika 松平長親 and progenitor of the Sakurai Matsudaira 桜井松平 house. Nagachika hosted Sōchō during the poet's journey to Kyoto in 1518. At that time Sōchō, Nagachika, and others composed Eishō 15 [1518]:4:26 (an alternate ms. gives 1518:4:23) *Yamanani hyakuin* (A Hundred-Verse Sequence Entitled "A Kind of Mountain") at Myōgenji 明源寺 temple. The house head, Matsudaira Kiyoyasu (JS: 303, n. 81), Yoichi's nephew, moved his headquarters from Anjō 安城 to Okazaki 岡崎 on the twenty-ninth of the following month, the fourth. See Tsurusaki 1973 and 1987.

31. Oda Chikuzennokami Yoshiyori 織田筑前守良頼 was one of the three commissioners (*bugyō*) of Kiyosu 清須 (now Kiyosuchō 清洲町, Nishikasugai 西春日井 District, Aichi Prefecture). Shimazu (1975: 82) believes Iganokami 伊賀守 was Oda Kurō Hironobu 織田九郎広延, another of the three commissioners of Kiyosu. Sakai Settsunokami Muramori 坂井摂津守村盛, deputy vice constable of Owari, participated with Sōchō, Sōboku, and other local Owari lords in Daiei 7 [1527]:4:2 *Nanibito hyakuin* (A Hundred-Verse Sequence Entitled "A Kind of Person") at Atsuta Shrine (cited in *RSR* 2: 946). He also appears on JS: 124. On the Oda family before the time of Nobunaga, see Okuno Takahiro 1961.

32. Tsurusaki (1973: 32–33) believes the linked-verse sequence was held to pray for the prosperity of Nobusada's new land and to confirm his holding in the presence of the other lords at the session.

33. Atsuta 熱田 Shrine, located in Atsuta Ward, Nagoya City, is one of Japan's central Shintō institutions. Its major deity is Atsuta Daijin, whose attribute is the sword Kusanagi no tsurugi 草薙剣, one of the three sacred treasures. The Sun Goddess Amaterasu Ōmikami and her brother Susanoo no Mikoto are also worshipped there, as is Yamato Takeru no Mikoto (see following note).

34. This refers to Yamato Takeru no Mikoto 日本武尊. Tsurusaki (1973: 30–31) observes that Sōchō makes no mention of the fact that Atsuta Shrine's patron deity, Yamato Takeru no Mikoto, is identified in *Kojiki* (220) as the founder of the art of linked verse. Sōchō's disciple Sōboku does not neglect to make mention of that connection in his own travel diary *Tōgoku kikō* (814).

35. Narumi 鳴海 is an utamakura originally on the Pacific coast and now further inland in Midori 緑 Ward, Nagoya City. Hoshizaki 星崎 is an utamakura now in Minami 南 Ward, Nagoya City.

36. Takinobō 滝の坊, now Takinodera 滝乃寺, is a Tendai temple west of Atsuta Shrine.

37. *Oi no mimi* no. 131. There is a pun on *matsu* (wait / pine).

38. *Oi no mimi* no. 132. This verse again appears to employ kakekotoba pivoting between *matsu* (wait / pine) and between Atsuta and *tsuta no wakaba*, young ivy leaves. Another interpretation of the verse that ignores those likely kakekotoba reads simply: "The pale red of the young leaves amid the pines at Atsuta." The season is summer, and though some leaves begin to turn red in late spring and early summer, *usumomiji* (pale red leaves) is more normally an autumn word, which suggests in turn that *matsu* does indeed include the overtone "to wait" for autumn. The verse is also phonetically skillful, contrasting *usu* (thin) and *atsu* (thick) as well as *matsu* and *atsu*.

39. The sequence is also referred to as *Eikyū hyakushu* 永久百首, composed on Eikyū 4:12:20 (early 1117). Minamoto Shunrai and others participated.

40. Indeed, no such line is found in the sequence.

41. Shin'eki 心易. "Entertainer-priest" translates *zarebōzu*.

42. *Kokinshū* 20: 1104, by Ono no Komachi:

On Okinoi Miyakoshima:

okinoite	Sharper than the pain
mi o yaku yori mo	of flesh seared by fiery coals
kanashiki wa	is the grief I feel
miyakoshimabe no	on your leaving this island
wakare narikeri	to go to the capital.

(translation after McCullough 1985)

Sōchō plays on *atsu* (hot) in Atsuta, and introduces the kindred words *oki* (glowing coals) and *yaku* (burn), as in the foundation poem.

43. Sōchō may have taken the last part of the line from *Genji monogatari*, where it appears in several places, e.g., the "Yūgao" chapter (*Genji monogatari* 1: 114).

44. *Oi no mimi* no. 133.

45. The residence was actually that of the vice constable (*shugodai*).

46. *Travels in the Eastland* (*Tōgoku michi no ki* 東国道の記) is another name for *Nagusamegusa* なぐさめ草, by the waka poet Shōgetsu'an Shōtetsu 招月庵正徹 (1381–1459). The passage in question (588) reads "This is where the province is governed . . . it seems no different from Kyoto." It is curious that this work and the one attributed to Saigyō (*JS*: 92, 96) bear the same title.

47. Oda Yoshiyori (*JS*: 99).

48. Cf. *Man'yōshū* 11: 2754:

| asakashiwa | By Uruya River, |
| uruyakawae no | of dewy morning oaks, |

>   shinonome no   I slept in longing as secret
>   shinoite nureba   as if behind bamboo blinds
>   ime ni miekeri   and dreamt of you at dawn!

49. Oda Tōzaemon 織田藤左衛門 was the son of Oda Yoshiyori and the uncle of Oda Nobuhide 織田信秀 (1508–51), who appears below as Saburō. Nobuhide was the father of Nobunaga. His given name begins with the word "wisteria."

50. Cf. *JS* no. 526.

51. See *JS*: 99.

52. *Oi no mimi* no. 135, where it appears as *unohana wa kiyosu ka*. There is a kakekotoba pivoting between Kiyosu and *yosu* (to approach) (cf. *JS* no. 542).

53. Takahata (or Takabatake) Magozaemon 高畠孫左衛門 is unknown.

54. *Oi no mimi* no. 134.

55. Tsushima 津島 City, Aichi Prefecture.

56. Shōgakuin 正覚院, a Shingon sect temple in Tsushima, which is now called Seitaiji 清泰寺.

57. Oda Sōdai 織田霜台 was Oda Nobusada 織田信定, one of the three Kiyosu commissioners, who served the Shiba house. His son Saburō was Oda Nobuhide.

58. Three chō was about one third of a kilometer. The Long Bridge of Seta (Seta no nagahashi 勢田の長橋 or 瀬田の長橋, also known as Seta no karahashi 瀬田の唐橋), one of the most famous bridges in premodern Japan, crossed the mouth of Setagawa river at Lake Biwa. It is an utamakura and also one of the "Eight Views of Ōmi" (*Ōmi hakkei*).

59. Oyobigawa 及川 river flowed near Hashima 羽島 City, Gifu Prefecture and was a tributary of Kisogawa 木曽川 river; Sunomatagawa すの又河 (墨俣河) was the old name of Kisogawa river and Nagaragawa 長良川 river after they flowed together at Sunomata 墨俣. The present course of the river is not the same. The Sea of Ōmi (Ōmi no umi 近江の海) was another name for Lake Biwa.

60. Kuwana 桑名 is the present Kuwana City in Mie Prefecture. It was on the west bank at the mouth of the river. Sōchō quotes the same *Wakan rōeishū* line earlier (*JS*: 46).

61. I have emended *wasureji* in the Shōkōkan ms. (Shimazu 1975: 85) on the basis of the *SKGSRJ* ms. (677).

62. Tōun 等運, a resident of Kuwana, was a disciple of Sōseki. He took part in a linked-verse sequence in 1515 at Sanetaka's residence welcoming Sōchō back to the capital, Eishō 12 [1515]:11:11 *Yamanani hyakuin* (A Hundred-Verse Sequence Entitled "A Kind of Mountain"). He is not to be confused with Tōunken, vice constable of Yamashiro Province (*JS*: 47).

63. Sōchō refers to Kisogawa, Nagaragawa, and Ibigawa 揖斐川 rivers.

64. West Lake (Xihu 西湖), in China's Zhejiang Province, is famous for its beauty and is a favorite subject in Chinese and Japanese landscape painting.

Notes to Book Two (1526), Pages 102–3

65. *Ise monogatari* (83):

haruru yo no	Are they stars
hoshi ka kawabe no	on this clear night,
hotaru ka mo	or fireflies by the riverbank,
waga sumu kata no	or fires lit by fisherfolk
ama no taku hi ka	near my dwelling?

66. Eight Peaks Pass (Happūgoe 八峰越 or 八風越) was located on a route to Ise and Owari established by the Rokkaku, constables of Ōmi, to assure themselves access to commerce and to frustrate attempts by a rival house, the Gamō, to cut off the route through the Suzuka Mountains. Rokkaku Takayori 六角高頼 arranged for his son Takazane 高実 to be adopted by the lord of Umedo 梅戸 to guarantee the security of that pass and another, Chigusagoe 千種越, through which a flourishing trade was conducted. See Tsurusaki 1983.

67. Umedo is in Inabe 員弁 District, Mie Prefecture.

68. Sōchō employs a kakekotoba pivoting between *oi no koshi* (lit., aged back) and *koshikaki* (palanquin bearers) (cf. *JS* no. 369).

69. Yamakami 山上 is in Eigenjichō 永源寺町, Kanzaki 神崎 District, Shiga Prefecture; Takano たか野 (高野) is located in the same district. By *egedera* 会下寺, Sōchō means a Zen temple, possibly Eigenji.

70. Gotō Tajimanokami 後藤但馬守 was a retainer of the Rokkaku house and majordomo of their Kannonji 観音寺 Castle (for the latter, see *JS*: 32); Chōkōji 長光寺 temple is in Ōmi Hachiman 近江八幡 City, Shiga Prefecture. In Sōchō's day it stood at the junction of the Happū kaidō 八峰街道 and Nakasendō 中山道 highroads, and Shogun Ashikaga Yoshiharu 足利義晴 (1511–1550) and his ally Hosokawa Takakuni made it their temporary fortress the following year (1527, see *JS*: 142).

71. The Tani House, of which Tani Nakatsukasa 谷中務 was a member, was a cadet branch of the Sasaki. Nakae Tosanokami Kazutsugu 中江土佐守員継 was the host of the *Jikka senku* linked-verse session in 1516, in which Sōchō participated. See Tsurusaki 1976 and 1983.

72. Shōrin'an temple 小林庵 (or 少林庵, also Shōrinji), located in Yashima 矢島 or 矢嶋, Moriyama 守山 City, Shiga Prefecture, is a Rinzai Zen temple of the Daitokuji lineage. Shōrin'an is believed to have been founded by Ikkyū's disciple Tōgaku Jōhō, also fifth abbot of Shinjuan at Daitokuji and Shūon'an in Takigi (*JS*: 221, n. 44).

73. *Kokinshū* 17: 899 (popularly attributed to Ōtomo Kuronushi, according to a *Kokinshū* note):

kagamiyama	I think I will
iza tachiyorite	stop by and have a look
mi ni yukamu	at Mirror Mountain,

273

Notes to Book Two (1526), Pages 103–5

> toshi henuru mi wa to see whether after all these years
> oi ya shinuru to I have become an old man.

74. For Konohama Crossing, see *JS*: 48.

75. This haikai verse incorporates a complex kakekotoba pivoting between *shigeru ko no ha ma no watari* (crossing through flourishing leaves) and *Konohama no watari* (Konohama Crossing) (cf. *JS* no. 351).

76. Konrin'in 金輪院 lived in a temple by that name in what is now Shimosakamoto 下坂本 in Ōtsu City.

77. The verse describes a cuckoo on Mount Hiei in terms of *Ise monogatari* (22): "[Fuji] Mountain is like twenty Hiei Mountains piled one on top of another." But even so, the cry of the cuckoo on the Kyoto mountain sounds high. *Iza* in Shimazu 1975: 87 should read *isa*. There is a pun on *ne* (mountain/cry) (cf. *JS* no. 551).

78. See *JS*: 220. Jōkōin is a subtemple of Miidera. Its abbot requested the verse.

79. *Oi no mimi* no. 136. The conceit here is that the moon is so bright the waterrail thinks the dawn has come. Cf. *Genji monogatari* 3: 117:

> oshinabete If you respond
> tataku kuina ni to every waterrail that comes
> odorokaba tapping on your door
> uwa no sora naru heaven only knows what moonlight
> tsuki mo koto ire may find its way within!

80. For Sōkei, see *JS*: 48.

81. Cf. *JS* no. 2.

82. The Mountain of Meeting was the site of Ōsaka Gate. Awataguchi 粟田口, in Higashiyama Ward, was one of the main eastern entrances to the city.

83. The imperial palace burned in 1207. Rebuilding commenced the next year but the project was subsequently discontinued, and what was left on the site was lost in another fire in 1227. In Sōchō's day, the imperial residence was Tsuchimikado 土御門 Palace, located at the intersection of Higashinotōin 東洞院 and Tsuchimikado Avenues. After the destruction of the Ōnin War, the area around it reverted to fields.

84. Mushanokōji 武者小路 avenue was located in what is now Kamigyō Ward.

85. Sōchō puns on *koshi* (palanquin / back).

86. Sōchō uses fewer dates in the travel passages of his journal, marking his progress instead largely through the names of the places he passes. He is probably writing here at the end of the fourth month.

87. This note suggests Sōchō's pleasure at seeing his long labors on behalf of the Sanmon gate project come to fruition. See *JS*: 74, where he remarks on selling his own copy of *Genji monogatari* to raise funds for the project. His journeys to the Asakura domain in Echizen in 1519 and 1523 (for the latter, see *JS*: 31–33) involved fund-raising activities for Daitokuji as well. The gate that was eventually built was a single-story one. A two-story

Notes to Book Two (1526), Page 105

gate was completed in 1589, through the efforts of the great tea master Sen no Rikyū 千利休 (1522–91). But Rikyū had a portrait sculpture of himself installed inside and in so doing angered Hideyoshi. This is thought to have been one of the reasons Hideyoshi caused him to commit suicide (Kumakura 1989).

88. Emperor Gokashiwabara 後柏原 (1464–1526, r. 1500–26), son of Emperor Gotsuchimikado 後土御門 (1442–1500, r. 1464–1500), was a zealous poet and literatus. He was succeeded by his son Gonara 後奈良 (1497–1557, r. 1526–57). On linked verse and the imperial house during this period, see Kaneko 1993.

89. Sennyūji 泉涌寺 had been associated with the imperial house since the time of Emperor Shijō 四条 (1220–42) and was a place of study of Tendai, Shingon, Zen, and Ritsu doctrines.

90. Banjūzanmaiin 般舟三昧院 was a Tendai temple located at the time in Fushimi and later moved to what is now Kamigyō Ward. Buddhist belief holds that a spirit's next life is determined on the forty-ninth day after death.

91. "The Mountain" refers to Enryakuji 延暦寺, headquarters of the Sanmon 山門 (Mountain Gate) sect of Tendai Buddhism, located on Mt. Hiei; "the prefect of the Temple" refers to the head monk (*chōri* 長吏) of Onjōji 園城寺, also called Miidera 三井寺, headquarters of the Jimon 寺門 (Temple Gate) Tendai sect, located on the west coast of Lake Biwa; Nanzenji 南禅寺 is the main Rinzai Zen temple in Kyoto and oversees the Gozan 五山 (Five Mountains) organization of Zen temples in the capital: Tenryūji 天竜寺, Shōkokuji 相国寺, Kenninji 建仁寺, Tōfukuji 東福寺, and Manjuji 万寿寺; the Ritsu 律 establishment refers to one of the six Nara sects, headquartered at Tōshōdaiji 唐招提寺.

92. Gokashiwabara's remains were cremated at Sennyūji on the third of the fifth month (*Shiryō sōran* 9: 490) and they were interred the following day at Hokkedō 法華堂 in Fukakusa, Yamashiro Province. Gonara's accession actually took place on the twenty-ninth of the fourth month (*ibid.*). The enthronement ceremony, however, was postponed due to lack of funds. The Hōjō, Asakura, Imagawa, and Ōuchi all later made donations, and the ceremony finally took place on the twenty-sixth of the second month, 1536. Sōchō is writing some time after events he did not witness personally.

93. *Oi no mimi* no. 137. The verse is also recorded in *Hokku kikigaki* (37). Therein, the verse appears with Sōseki's waki and a third verse by Takamori 孝盛:

> yaegumo kakure   Off into the eightfold clouds
> yuku hototogisu   flies the cuckoo.
>   Sōseki

> shigeriau   It lingered
> yama no hatsuka ni   but a moment in the leafy trees
> yadori shite   of the mountain crest.
>   Takamori

94. *Oi no mimi* no. 138. Hollyhock is mentioned in reference to the Aoi Matsuri or Hollyhock Festival, held by the Kamigamo 上賀茂 and Shimogamo 下賀茂 Shrines in Kyoto. Traditionally observed in the fourth month on the second day of the cock, it now occurs on May 15. One of the most impressive religious events in Kyoto, it was often simply referred to as The Festival.

95. *Oi no mimi* no. 139. *Tokonatsu* (wild pinks) is a summer word appropriate for the season of composition, but *chigusa* (thousand grasses) is conventionally used in reference to autumn (*RJGPS* no. 895). The latter word is used here to reflect the solemnity of the mourning period.

96. It is now the sixth month, 1526.

97. Jōkōin 常光院 (with which Shōun 湘雲 Hall was affiliated), Ikkein 一華院 (or Ikkeken [cf. *JS*: 45], and Ryōsen'in 霊泉院 were all subtemples of Kenninji. The retired abbot of Ikkein was Gesshū Jukei (*JS*: 45). Jōan Ryōsū 常庵竜崇 (d. 1536) was the retired abbot of Ryōsen'in. He was a son of Tō no Tsuneyori 東常縁 (1401-c.84), the poet who had transmitted the secret traditions of *Kokinshū* to Sōgi. Ryōsū wrote the kanbun version of Shōhaku's "Three Loves" (*San'aiki*), see *Song in an Age of Discord*).

98. Sōchō later writes of a Kitamura Hyōgonosuke 北村兵庫助 who has the same surname as Jujōken. He may have been the Tsuda Bizen Lay Priest mentioned earlier (*JS*: 156).

99. "*Kure* bamboo" is a kindred word (*engo*) for Fushimi, *yo* (world), and *shigeki* (thick).

100. See *JS*: 46.

101. Yamashiro Province. Sōchō variously refers to Tōunken as "commissioner" (*bugyō*) and as "constable" (*shugo*); he was actually vice constable (*shugodai*). See *JS*: 47.

102. Sōchō puns on *tatsumi* (southeast / dragons and snakes) and on *shika* (thus/deer). His hut, of course, is in Takigi. The foundation poem is *Kokinshū* 18: 983, by Kisen:

waga io wa	My rustic hut
miyako no tatsumi	lies southeast of the capital,
shika zo sumu	where I live in peace,
yo o ujiyama to	though they say the Uji hills
hito wa iu nari	are for those who scorn the world.

Kojima and Arai (1989: 295) cite the *Analects* of Confucius to suggest that *tatsumi / shika zo sumu* means "where I live modestly."

103. This verse also appears in *Hokku kikigaki* (38), with this preface: "Seventh Month, third day, near Izumigawa." Amanogawa 天之河 (or 天野川) river (River of Heaven) is a tributary of Yodogawa river, which flows through Hirakata 枚方 City due west of Takigi. Izumigawa ("Izumi River" in *JS* no. 50) is another name for Kotsugawa (now Kizugawa) river, and it is also the name of the district between Kamochō 加茂町 and Kizuchō 木津町, just before Kotsugawa river turns north. Mikanohara 三日原, Third-Day Moor

(also written 瓶原) is now part of Kamochō. It was the site of Emperor Shōmu's Kuni 恭仁 capital in the eighth century. The foundation poem is *Kokinshū* 9: 408:

miyako idete	Here at Mika Moor,
kyō mikanohara	three days from the capital,
izumigawa	the wind blows cold
kaze samushi	off Izumi River.
koromo kaseyama	A robe, please, Lending Mountain!

Sōchō's hokku also ingeniously anticipates the arrival of the *Tanabata* festival on the seventh day of the seventh month by mentioning *Amanogawa*, River of Heaven, which the Herd Boy crosses on his annual visit to the Weaver Maiden. The poet thus includes the references both to the place and to the time the hokku was composed.

104. I have emended the last line of the Shōkōkan ms. (Shimazu 1975: 90), *omoi ni naremu*, to *omoihanaren* on the basis of *Sōchō michi no ki* (241).

105. "Borrowed robes" (*karigoromo*) relates to poems such as *Shūishū* 17: 1091, by Taira Sadafun:

For an imperial screen in the Ninna era (885–89) that depicted a woman bathing in the river on the seventh day of the seventh month:

mizu no aya o	Going down to the river,
oritachite kimu	she weaves a watery brocade
nugichirashi	to wear on the night
tanabatatsume ni	she removes her robe
koromo kasu yo wa	to lend to the Weaver Maid.

There is a kakekotoba pivoting between *oritatsu* (to weave) and *oritatsu* (to go down [to the river]).

106. This marks the twenty-fourth anniversary of Sōgi's death in 1502. It was also on this day that news of Imagawa Ujichika's death reached Sōchō at Shūon'an. He mentions nothing about it here, but the poem is reminiscent of the one he composed with Ujichika for Sōgi's death anniversary the year before (*JS* no. 219).

107. The abbot was Tōgaku Jōhō (*JS*: 221, n. 44).

108. Shinden'an was where Sōchō's son Jōha was raised for a time (*JS*: 28–29).

109. The verse appears in slightly different form (*asagao ya / tsuyu kusa hana no / hitosakari*) in *Hokku kikigaki* (38) with the preface, "For the anniversary of Sōgi's death." It also appears as *Oi no mimi* no. 143. It is the last hokku in that collection, which suggests that Sōchō expected to die at Takigi and therefore collected his verses to that point as a last personal anthology (cf. *JS* no. 574).

110. On his return to Takigi, Sōchō found that the abbot had not visited Ōmi because of warfare in the capital.

111. An entry for 1526:7:12 in *Sanetakakōki* (6a: 399) reads "Finished copying *Kokinshū* for Sōchō."

112. See *JS*: 28, 47.

113. See *JS*: 47.

114. The verse also appears in *Hokku kikigaki* (38), prefaced by "At Uji."

115. Tea was made on board the boat.

116. Makinoshima 槙の嶋 refers to a sandbar shallows in Ujigawa river (Uji River in the following poem, *JS* no. 380).

117. Insei 印政 was a renga poet who participated with Sōchō in *Higashiyama Senku*. Shūkei 周桂 (d. 1544) was a well-known linked-verse poet and disciple of Sōseki. He and Sōboku were the central figures in the linked-verse world after Sōseki's death.

118. The verse also appears in *Hokku kikigaki* (38), prefaced by "At Fushimi."

119. This passage is unclear. Fifty-nine verses survive from a linked-verse sequence entitled *Hyakuin* bearing the date Daiei 6 [1526]:8:15, composed by Sōchō, Sōseki, Sōboku, Shūkei, and others at Akino Dōjō 秋野道場 in the Lower Capital. Sōseki composed the hokku (found also in *Hokku kikigaki* [38]), which may be the reason Sōchō did not record it. Sōseki had taken over ownership of Sōgi's Shugyokuan hermitage in the Upper Capital after Sōgi's death; it stood next to the Irie Palace 入江御所, also called Sanjichionji 三時知恩寺, a nunnery located near the intersection of Nishinotōin and Ōgimachi avenues. Sanetaka's elder sister was mistress of that temple's Eastern Cottage (Tōan), and Sōgi and Sanetaka often met there (Kaneko 1993). In light of the above, it seems likely that Sōseki invited Sōchō to the Lower Capital, where the linked-verse session was held, then the group proceeded to the Upper Capital, where they called on Sanetaka, after which they retired to Sōseki's house.

120. The Lower Capital Tea Coterie (Shimogyō chanoyu) was formed in the early years of the sixteenth century after the death of Murata Jukō 村田珠光 (1422–1502), the founder of wabi tea and, like Sōchō, a disciple of Ikkyū. Jukō himself resided in the Lower Capital. It was supported in large part through the participation of wealthy townsmen (*machishū*) who resided in the southern part of the capital. The smaller rooms and rustic decor of the Lower Capital Tea Coterie represented a major change from the large, elegantly appointed spaces in which tea gatherings had theretofore been held. Sanetaka also possessed a small tea room, which he called Kadoya 角屋, on the grounds of his mansion, and Toyohara Muneaki also owned one, named Sanrian 山里庵. Both men were among Sōchō's closest colleagues in the capital, and they, plus Sanetaka's student and aspiring renga master Takeno Jōō 武野紹鴎 (1502–55), were in the vanguard of the new tea style. See Moriya 1984: 71–73.

121. Kidō Saizō believes the text is mispunctuated here and should be read, "Sōju came. Within the gate are great pines and cedars" (personal communication). Sōju 宗珠 was Jukō's successor.

122. See JS: 29.

123. This verse appears in *Hokku kikigaki* (26) together with a variant, *utsushi yo ya*.

124. It is now the ninth month. The aster is associated with the Double Yang Festival, observed on the ninth day of that month.

125. Ise Bitchūnokami 伊勢備中守 is believed to have been related to Hōjō Sōun and his younger sister, Lady Kitagawa, who was Ujichika's mother (Yonehara 1979: 832). Shimazu (1975: 92) suggests that this may be the Ise Hachirō who later appears in Sōchō's journal (*JS*: 111).

126. Dewdrops from asters were gathered on the ninth of the ninth month and applied to the face or consumed for longevity. The hokku, however, was composed on the tenth, and Sōchō suggests for celebratory reasons that some restorative dew has nevertheless appeared, though from where he does not know.

127. Shimazu (1975: 93) speculates that Isshiki Sōshū 一色総州 (Isshiki Kazusanokami 一色上総守) may have been Isshiki Shinkurō 一色新九郎, who appears on the next page (*JS*: 111).

128. This hundred-verse sequence, entitled Daiei 6 [1526]:9:13 *Nanibito hyakuin* (A Hundred-Verse Sequence Entitled "A Kind of Person"), is extant. Participating were Sōchō, Sōseki, and others, including Kendō 堅等 [or 賢等], who appears on *JS*: 121. Kendō, identified in the manuscript of another sequence as "A physician from Kyoto," and Shōzōbō (*JS*: 43) were two of those who accompanied Sōchō back to Suruga the following year. Kendō also participated in Daiei 7 [1527]:4:2 *Nanibito hyakuin* (A Hundred-Verse Sequence Entitled "A Kind of Person").

129. See *JS*: 29.

130. The poem relies for its effect on the wordplay between *utsutsu* (reality) and Utsunoyama in Suruga. In an entry for 1526:9:25 in his personal poetry collection *Saishōsō*, Sanetaka mentions sending the poem to Sōchō. The verse recalls *Ise monogatari* (22):

suruga naru	Neither in reality,
utsunoyamabe no	like Reality Mountain
utsutsu ni mo	here in Suruga,
yume ni mo hito ni	nor in dreams
awanu narikeri	have I had the chance to see you.

In the absence of personal pronouns, Sanetaka's poem also expresses Sōchō's thoughts, and Sōchō therefore subsequently sends the poem back to the courtier by way of a reply.

131. For Shinjuan, see *JS*: 205, n. 96; I retain the conventional "plum" for *ume*, more accurately translated "apricot."

132. Wet verandas (*nureen*) constitute the outermost perimeter of the building and are unprotected from the rain.

133. A reference to *Ise monogatari* (74):

Notes to Book Two (1526), Pages 111–13

akanedomo	Though it not suffice,
iwa ni zo kauru	I present this rock instead,
iro mienu	for I have no way
kokoro o misemu	to show you the colors
yoshi no nakereba	that are hidden in my heart.

The unknown verse Gokokuji sent probably recast the *Ise monogatari* foundation poem, substituting a plum tree for the rock in the honka. Sōchō pretends to take literally the phrase "though it not suffice." Note that Sōchō's good friend Rikijū lived at that temple and that Sōchō sent him joking verse before (*JS* no. 53). The translation assumes that a repetion mark has been deleted and that the text should read *ume no meisho shomō seshi* (. . . famous for its plums, and I asked that they send one).

134. Sōchō humorously requests *tsutsuji* (azaleas) too, as *tsutsuji* and *ume* (plum) are kindred words.

135. The five trees and eight herbs (*goboku hassō*) were used for medicinal purposes. Lists vary as to which plants are included. The "five trees" include Japanese pagoda tree (*enju*), Japanese bead tree (*ōchi*), paulownia (*kiri*), mulberry (*kuwa*), magnolia (*hōnoki*), peach (*momo*), paper mulberry (*kōzo*), and willow (*yanagi*). The "eight herbs" include mugwort (*yomogi*), sweet-flag (*sekishō* or *shōbu*), broad-leafed plantain (*shazensō* or *ōbako*), lotus (*hasu*), chickweed (*hakobe*), ambrosia (*onamomi*), honeysuckle (*nindō*), and verbena (*kumatsuzura*).

136. The three poems that follow are "morning-after" verses. *JS* no. 390 is based on the poetic convention that it is the first cold rain that brings color to the leaves. The "first cold rain" here signifies Shinkurō. The "young men" are wakashu.

137. "Dew" here also refers to tears of loneliness.

138. This verse is based on the notion that if one is thinking of a person, one's spirit will visit that person in dreams. Cf. *Ise monogatari* (22) (*JS*: 279, n. 130).

139. Sōchō is evidently writing at some remove, and he records his response to Ise Hachirō's poem here out of concern for thematic consistency rather than for strict chronological order.

140. This is a humorous reply. Sōchō pretends not to believe Hachirō's statement that he had been thinking of Sōchō, for had that been the case, he jokes, Hachirō would have appeared in Sōchō's dreams.

141. Jujōken 聚情軒 literally means "cottage of accumulated feeling."

142. Kitamura Hyōgonosuke 北村兵庫助 was also known by the surname Tsuda (Shimazu 1975: 95); Daigo 醍醐 is in Fushimi Ward, Kyoto City, and is the site of Daigoji temple, headquarters of the Daigoji branch of the Shingon sect.

143. The Kohata 木幡 area, an utamakura in Yamashiro Province and now in Uji City, was associated with horses because of poems such as *Shūishū* 19: 1243 (itself a version of *Man'yōshū* 11: 2425), by Hitomaro:

yamashina no	Though there are horses
kohata no sato ni	in the village of Kohata
uma wa aredo	in Yamashina,
kachi yori zo kuru	I come on foot,
kimi o omoeba	out of love for you.

Commentators variously suggest that this means the lovers would have been discovered by the sound of a horse's hooves or that the lover is showing his sincerity by thinking of his love each step of the way.

144. The accident occurred in 1524 (*JS*: 59–60).

145. This is Hino Yakushi 日野薬師, also known as Hōkaiji 法界寺; the village of Hino is two kilometers south of Daigoji.

146. The site of the hermitage described by Kamo no Chōmei 鴨長明 (c. 1155–1216) in his *Hōjōki* (1212) was located east of Hōkaiji on the way toward Uji. Taira Shigehira 平重衡 (1156–85), son of Taira Kiyomori, is a particularly tragic figure in *Heike monogatari*. He was captured after the Taira defeat at Ichinotani and later sent to Kamakura, only to be returned to Nara thereafter. He was executed on the bank of Kotsugawa (now Kizugawa) river, about half a kilometer north of Hōkaiji, where his wife later had services performed in his memory. A marker stands today in Daigo Sotoyama Kaidōchō 醍醐外山街道町 in Fushimi Ward.

147. Jōmi 上味, according to the *Sutra on the Great Extinction* (*Daihatsunehangyō* 大般涅槃経), was the last of the five stages in the processing of milk products and is used as a metaphor for the supreme teaching of the Buddha. Another word for it is *daigomi* 醍醐味, an expression meaning "the best," hence Sōchō's pun.

148. Bodaiin 菩提院 was founded by Kenshun 賢俊 (1299–1357), abbot of Sanbōin 三宝院 and himself a renga poet represented by a verse in *Tsukubashū*. Sanbōin is one of the five imperial temples (*monzeki*) of Daigoji. Mansai Jugō 満済准后 (1378–1435) was another abbot of Sanbōin at Daigoji and an advisor to Shōgun Ashikaga Yoshinori. His diary, *Mansai Jugō nikki*, which covers the years 1411 to 1435, is a prime source of information about the period. He administered the temple during its period of greatest prosperity. Much of the temple was later destroyed in the Ōnin War (1467–77). "Hall of private worship" translates *jibutsudō* 持仏堂, the building in which the statue of a tutelary deity is kept.

149. The rocks in the garden were named after the "Nine Mountains and Eight Seas," a synecdoche for the Buddhist universe.

150. The Suruga Counselor (Suruga no Saishō 駿河の宰相) may be the monk under whom Sōchō studied after taking Shingon holy orders at seventeen. Since the composition of the early biography of Sōchō by Kurokawa Dōyū, it has been generally assumed that Sōchō studied at Bodaiin subtemple at Daigoji. But as pointed out by Nakagawa Yoshio (1981: 1284–94), Sōchō's comment in his journal that he "had a look" at Bo-

daiin may imply that he had not seen it before, as do the lines, "They looked even more impressive than I had heard" and "it was just as he always used to tell me." Nakagawa further suggests that it was Mansai Jugō that the Suruga Counselor served. This would mean that Sōchō did not take his religious training at Daigoji, despite the Suruga Counselor's affiliation there, but instead probably in Suruga, where the Counselor perhaps had connections.

151. The name of the mountain (Kasatoriyama), embedded in Sōchō's hokku, is often associated in poetry with cold rain (*shigure*).

152. Toba 鳥羽 straddles Minami 南 Ward and Fushimi Ward in Kyoto City.

153. Sōchō links the gift to the dove cane (*hato no tsue*) (*JS*: 48).

154. The term "five tones" (*goin* 五音) in its widest sense is the aural equivalent of the five elements. It also refers in court music (*gakaku*) to the five modes of *ichikotsuchō* 壱越調, *hyōjō* 平調, *sōjō* 双調, *ōshikichō* 黄鐘調, and *banshikichō* 盤渉調, or more popularly to the tones of *kyū* 宮, *shō* 商, *kaku* 角, *chi* 徴, and *u* 羽. The term thence becomes a synecdoche for "music" in a general sense. "Five tones" is a particularly apt word for the music of the shakuhachi flute, as the instrument has five holes.

155. The instrument is doubly felicitous because of the thousand years traditionally associated with bamboo and Tōenbō's remarkable eighty-year life span.

156. Sōchō evidently returned to Daitokuji in the capital, then went to Sōseki's.

157. Nōyū 能祐; Sōchō would have been attending the monthly linked-verse session at Kitano, the shrine dedicated to the worship of Sugawara Michizane, patron deity of poetry.

158. Kamiya River (Kamiyagawa 紙屋川, Paper-Maker River) is a tributary of Katsuragawa river and flows between Kitano and Hirano Shrines. Kamiyain, the official paper-making establishment in the Heian period, was located there.

159. Linked verse in Japanese and Chinese (wakan renku) was an even more popular form of linked verse than Japanese renga in Zen monasteries. The even-numbered verses are rhymed.

160. This is based on a line from Du Fu's poem entitled *Qujiangshi* 曲江詩: "A life span of seventy through the ages has been rare." Here the line has been changed to match Sōchō's age. Du Fu's poem was famous; Shōhaku quotes it in his *San'aiki*.

161. The lines are from a *dengaku* song which appears in *Kanginshū* (no. 140) and also in Sōchō's *Utsunoyama no ki*. Dengaku originally were song and dance performances for the gods while work went on in the fields. Later they contributed to the development of the nō theater.

162. Cf. *Kokinshū* 17: 894:

oshiteru ya	Bitter as the salt
naniwa no mizu ni	that they boil from brine
yaku shio no	at Naniwa Harbor,

Notes to Book Two (1526), Pages 117–18

karaku mo ware wa   famous for its sunlit sea,
oinikeru kana   is having grown old!

163. The verse is loosely based on a poem alluded to in *Genji monogatari* and quoted in Fujiwara Teika's *Genji monogatari okuiri* (479):

aru toki wa   While she was alive
ari no susami ni   it was my habit
nikukariki   to fault her always,
nakute zo hito no   but now that she is no more,
koishikarikeru   I find myself missing her.

164. The verse is based on *Shinkokinshū* 11: 1035, by Princess Shokushi:

wasurete wa   At times I forget,
uchinagekaruru   only to repine once more
yūbe kana   when evening comes.
ware nomi shirite   Days have lengthened into months
suguru tsukihi o   with none but myself aware.

I have emended *nakakaranu oi o* in the Shōkōkan ms. (Shimazu 1975: 98) on the basis of *Sōchō michi no ki* (245).

165. The honka is *Kokinshū* 17: 895:

oiraku no   Had I but known
komu to shiriseba   that old age was coming for me,
kado sashite   I would have locked the door
nashi to kotaete   and refused to admit it,
awazaramashi o   feigning not to be at home.

166. The preface is written in kanbun.

167. In his poetic diary *Saishōsō*, Sanetaka writes in an entry for 1526:10:10 (13: 95) that Sōchō sent him three of the above poems (*JS* nos. 413, 414, and 416) and that he responded with three (*JS* nos. 423, 424, and 426). Then in an entry for 1526:10:15 (13: 96–97) he writes that he wrote responses for the rest. The entry for the latter date in *Sanetakakōki* (6a: 434) reads, "Sōchō came to call. Our talk ranged to events of long ago. I found it relaxing and enjoyable. I offered him sake and had him show me his ten waka poems, to which I wrote responses that night."

168. "Oil-tapers" (*shisoku* 脂燭) were twists of paper or cloth coated with wax and held in the fingers while lit. They might also be made of thin pieces of pine dipped in oil. An "oil-taper poem" was one written in the short time it took for one such light to burn down, or any quickly composed verse. Sanetaka uses the term as a modest disclaimer. "I beg your indulgence" translates *isshō isshō*.

169. The poem is a paronomastic masterpiece, playing on *ukime o mitsu* meaning both

"to experience (lit., see) pain" and, in conjunction with the following *yaku shio*, "salt from the brine they boil / at the harbor," which in turn invites a kakekotoba pivoting between the place name Naniwa and *nani wa no koto* (everything). Mitsu (lit. Fair Harbor), located at Naniwa, was so called because of its connection with official trade.

170. I have emended *nikukaramu / hito koso toga wa* in the Shōkōkan ms. (Shimazu 1975: 99) on the basis of *Sōchō michi no ki* (246).

171. Cf. *Shinkokinshū* 12: 1109, by Fujiwara Tadasada:

omoedomo	I love but do not tell,
iwade tsukihi wa	and the days and months pass
sugi no kado	behind my cedar gate—
sasuga ni ikaga	how will I ever endure
shinobihatsubeki	these hidden feelings?

172. "Frozen brush" (*tōhitsu* 凍筆) suggests rude, poorly written characters.

173. Iwayama Dōken 岩山道堅 (Hisamune 尚宗, d. 1532) was a member of the Sasaki house in Ōmi and a good friend of Sanetaka. He was a student of the poet Asukai Masachika (see *JS*: 290, n. 220). Sōchō also refers to him by the name Hōgaiken 方外軒 (*JS*: 126). The Saiokuji ms. of *The Journal of Sōchō* was based on a copy made by Dōken, who is referred to in a postscript therein as a disciple of Sōchō. On Dōken, see Yonehara 1979: 144–48 and 1979: 286–87, Inoue 1987: 279, and Itō Kei 1969. "Lines from *Kokinshū*" refers to one hundred well-known passages of five or seven syllables from that anthology that Dōken chose as the topics for Sanetaka's hundred-waka sequence (hyakushu).

174. *Sanetakakōki* 1526:10:22 (6a: 438) reads, "Sōchō came to visit. He thanked me for judging his hundred-waka sequence."

175. The poem also appears in Sanetaka's poetic diary, *Saishōsō*, in an entry for 1526: 10:20 (13: 97).

176. Sōchō is referring to the Yanagimoto Discord (Yanagimoto no ran 柳本の乱). Hosokawa Takakuni had been shogunal deputy since 1508, despite several major challenges to his ascendancy. Another occurred in the seventh month of 1526. Hosokawa Korekata 細川尹賢, constable of Tanba and a relative of Takakuni, fell out with Takakuni's vassal Kōzai Motomori 香西元盛. Korekata used a forged document to convince Takakuni that Motomori was plotting against him, and Motomori was subsequently killed or driven to suicide. Motomori's relatives Hatano Tanemichi 波多野植通 and Yanagimoto Kataharu 柳本賢治, the latter an erstwhile favorite of Takakuni, determined to have their revenge on Hosokawa Korekata, and they joined with Miyoshi Motonaga 三好元長 (grandson of Takakuni's old enemy Miyoshi Yukinaga), Hosokawa Harumoto 細川晴元 (the son of another of Takakuni's old enemies, Hosokawa Sumimoto), and Ashikaga Yoshitsuna 足利義維 (brother of Shōgun Ashikaga Yoshiharu) to effect that end. Takakuni sent Korekata to defeat the Hatano-Yanagimoto coalition in Tanba, but the expedition was beaten off, giving Yanagimoto Kataharu and his allies heart to counter-

attack. On 1527:2:13 Kataharu's army of local Tanba warriors and the forces of his allies attacked Takakuni and Korekata at Katsuragawa river and defeated them. Takakuni was forced to flee to Ōmi with the shōgun, Yoshiharu. They later made camp close to Sōchō. For Sōchō's account of the history leading up to this event, see *JS*: 141–42. Takakuni took shelter with various allies in other provinces for several years. Though he engineered the murder of Kataharu in 1530, he himself was defeated in 1531 by Miyoshi Motonaga. He was discovered hiding in an indigo vat, taken prisoner, and later forced to commit suicide.

177. Shimazu (1975: 101) suggests that this is the tenth month; Fukuda and Plutschow (1975: 170) assert that it is the eleventh. The latter seems less likely, since that would have the abbot of Shūon'an leaving Takigi for the Lower Capital after violence had erupted there on 1526:10:24–25.

178. The poem is based on *Kokinshū* 8: 369, by Ki no Toshisada:

> Composed on the night of a banquet at the residence of Prince Sadatoki, when Fujiwara Kiyoo was to take up his duties as vice governor of Ōmi:

kyō wa wakare	Though I know
asu wa ōmi to	we can meet in Ōmi
omoedomo	again tomorrow,
yo ya fukenuramu	is it because the night is late
sode no tsuyukeki	that dew lies upon my sleeves?

179. Shirutani Pass 潘谷越, now Shibutani 渋谷, runs from Higashiyama to Yamashina. Wakamatsu no ike 若松の池 lies south of Shirutani, on the northwest slope of Amida Peak. See Ishikawa 1976.

180. Kazan 花山, site of Bishop Henjō's temple Genkeiji 元慶寺, where Emperor Kazan 花山 (968–1008) took holy orders, is in Higashiyama Ward.

181. A *kaminabi no mori* (or *kannabi no mori* 神奈備の森) is a forest where a god is believed to have descended. But here, Kaminabi no mori refers to a specific place, written 神無の森, at the eastern border of Yamashiro, near the Ōsaka Gate. Also called Kanname or Kannami 神並, it figures in *Genpei seisuiki*. See Ishikawa 1976: 30–33. "The gatehouse" (*sekiya* 関屋) refers to the ancient Ōsaka Gate, the most famous entrance to the capital.

182. The name Kaminabi no mori and "cold rain" of the tenth month (*Kaminazuki* [Godless Month]) carry overtones of *Kokinshū* 5: 253:

kaminazuki	Although the cold rain
shigure mo imada	that falls in the Godless Month
furanaku ni	has yet to begin,
kanete utsurou	already the leaves are turning
kaminabi no mori	in the sacred forest.

Sōchō's description is based on the "Sekiya" chapter of *Genji monogatari*. Genji, on a pilgrimage to Ishiyamadera, meets the entourage of the vice governor of Hitachi and exchanges poems with the vice governor's consort, Utsusemi, "Cicada Shell." But the "Sekiya" chapter includes no mention of cold rain. Sōchō evidently conflated it with the "Aoi" chapter (*Genji monogatari* 2: 293), in which this passage appears after Lady Aoi has died of spirit possession:

> Prince Genji thought, "I cannot continue to mope about like this," and he resolved to visit the palace of [his father] the Retired Emperor. While his carriage was being brought out and his outriders were gathering, a cold rain began to fall, knowing that its time had come (*orishirigao naru shigure uchisosogite*), and the wind that entices the leaves began to scatter them in confusion. Gloom settled over the company, and sleeves that had just dried grew moist once again.

Sōgi uses the same phrase, again in reference to the tenth or "godless" month, in *Tsukushi michi no ki* (Account of a Kyushu Journey, 1480)(81).

183. Sōchō participated in renga sessions at Sōkei's residence on his way back to Suruga in 1524 (*JS*: 48) and en route to Kyoto in 1526 (*JS*: 104).

184. For Kendō, see *JS*: 279, n. 128.

185. For Shōzōbō, see *JS*: 47.

186. Uchidenohama 打出浜 is an utamakura near Ōtsu City, on the pilgrimage route to Ishiyamadera. Sakamoto 坂本 is at the eastern foot of Mount Hiei, about ten kilometers north of Ōtsu.

187. Hōsenji 法泉寺. Hieitsuji 比叡辻 is in Sakamoto, Ōtsu City. Einō 栄能 is unknown. Chōgetsuken 聴月軒.

188. Sōchō puns on Mount Hie(i) and *hie*, freezing.

189. Myōshōan 妙勝庵 in Yashima was named after Myōshōji, the temple Daiō Kokushi founded in Takigi (*JS*: 221, n. 45).

190. *Inetsukiuta* 稲舂歌 (rice-threshing songs) were sung while threshing the rice to be offered up during the Great Thanksgiving Service (Daijōe 大嘗会), a harvest ritual held in the first or second year of a new imperial reign. It was the most important Shinto ceremony at court and involved complex preparations, including the collection of rice from a Yuki 悠紀 district (one of two places in Ōmi Province) and a Suki 主基 district (in Tanba or Bitchū Provinces). Sakata was one of the two Yuki districts. Inetsukiuta often included references to the Yuki and Suki regions, e.g., *Shinkokinshū* 7: 753, by Fujiwara Shunzei:

> A rice-threshing song for the Great Thanksgiving Service in the first year of Nin'an [1166] (a Yuki song):
>
> ōmi no ya　　　　　　　Rice from Sakata
> sakata no ine o　　　　in Ōmi Province,

Notes to Book Two (1526), Pages 122–23

kaketsumite	rack-dried and then stacked,
michi aru miyo no	we thresh at the beginning
hajime ni zo tsuku	of our sovereign's righteous reign.

For more on the Great Thanksgiving Service, see McCullough and McCullough 1980, 1: 375–77.

191. Both Katada 堅田 and Sakamoto 坂本 are on the other side of Lake Biwa from Yashima.

192. The foundation poem is the first verse in the *Kokinshū* preface:

naniwazu ni	At Naniwa Port
saku ya ko no hana	the trees are now in blossom!
fuyugomori	Proclaiming the spring
ima o harube to	after winter seclusion,
saku ya ko no hana	the trees are now in blossom!

193. There is a kakekotoba pivoting between *yasushi* (safe) and Yasu River (Yasugawa 野洲川), which originates in the Suzuka range and empties into Lake Biwa near Yashima. The poem recalls *Shinchokusenshū* 19: 1308, by Gokyōgoku Yoshitsune:

haruka naru	Taking as my mark
mikami no take o	Mikami Mountain
me ni kakete	in the far distance,
ikuse watarinu	I cross the many shallows
yasu no kawanami	through the waves of Yasu River.

Mount Mikami is ten kilometers or so from Yashima.

194. The remark is in self-criticism of his powers as a poet.

195. For Nakae Kazutsugu, see *JS*: 103.

196. There is a kakekotoba pivoting between *kokochi sae shi* (to even have the feeling) and Shigaraki 信楽, a village east of Yashima famous for pottery and tea. Shigaraki was also the site of Emperor Shōmu's Shigaraki capital. Shimazu (1975: 167) suggests that Kazutsugu may have been living there, but Sōchō says Kazutsugu was only two or three leagues (c. 8 to 12 km.) away, and Shigaraki is more than eight leagues (c. 32 km) from Yashima. Perhaps Kazutsugu had the charcoal sent from there.

197. The verse is a parody of *Kokinshū* 19: 1030, by Ono no Komachi:

hito ni awamu	On a moonless night
tsuki no naki yo ni	with no chance for a meeting,
omoiokite	I wake with longing,
mune hashiribi ni	my heart burning in the fire
kokoro yakeori	that rages through my breast.

Sōchō's point is that if he were going to burn, it might at least have been with love, but he wakes burnt yet empty-handed. The garment in question was a *katasuso*, a narrow-sleeved *kimono* with different patterns on the top and bottom.

198. Shimazu (1975: 103) suggests Suke (no) Hyōgo 杉江（の）兵庫 may be the same person as Baba Hyōgonosuke 馬場兵庫助 who lived in Yashima (*JS*: 138).

199. See *JS*: 54–55.

200. Mikami Echigonokami Yoriyasu 三上越後守頼安 was a subordinate of the Rokkaku house, and he lived in Mikami, Yasu 野洲 District, Ōmi Province (see Tsurusaki 1983). His messenger, Tsubota Chūemonnojō 坪田中右衛門尉, is identified as Tsubouchi 坪内 in alternate manuscripts.

201. This was the forty-fifth anniversary of Ikkyū's death on that day in 1481.

202. *Tokaeri*, "ten repetitions" (here translated "centennial"), is a celebratory expression usually used in reference to the pine tree, said to bloom once in a hundred years, thus ten times in a thousand. Less commonly, it may also mean ten repetitions, once every thousand years, for a total of ten thousand.

203. Sōchō's verse may be based on *Kokinshū* 17: 874, by Fujiwara Toshiyuki:

> In the Kanpyō era [889–98], a number of the men serving in the palace had a flask of wine sent to the apartments of the empress, asking that whatever remained be returned to them. Laughing, the ladies-in-waiting accepted the flask but sent no reply. When the messenger returned and told what had happened, Toshiyuki sent them this poem:
>
> | | |
> |---|---|
> | tamadare no | Whither that jewelled flask? |
> | kogame ya izura | Like a turtle it went out |
> | koyorogi no | into the breakers |
> | iso no nami wake | off Koyorogi Strand |
> | oki ni idenikeri | and then far into the depths. |

Kogame means both "small flask" and "turtle," and *oki* (depths) relates to *oku*, the penetralia of the palace. Sōchō may also be alluding to this popular song related to the *Kokinshū* verse:

tamadare no	"A jewel-like flask
ogame o naka ni suete	you have put before us, but nothing else,
aruji wa mo	master, O master,
ya	Ya!"
sakana maki ni	"I'm off to find some fish,
sakana tori ni	I'm off to catch some fish,
koyurugi no	I'm going off
iso no wakame	to Koyurugi's rocky strand
kariage ni	to gather sea plant!"

The song, "Tamadare" 玉垂れ ("Fūzokuuta" no. 3, in Tsuchihashi and Konishi 1957: 433), is a dialogue between guests and a host.

204. Nothing is known of Genshū 玄周 other than that he participated with Sōchō in Daiei 7 [1527]:4:2 *Nanibito hyakuin*. He most likely accompanied Sōchō and the others back to Suruga the next year.

205. For Sakai Settsunokami, see *JS*: 99. *Myōhōjiki* (32) states that on 1527:7:30 Takeda Nobutora, perhaps thinking to take advantage of Ujichika's death, attacked Suruga and defeated Hōjō Ujitsuna in Suntō 駿東 District. He thereafter withdrew without pressing his advantage. This may be the reason that Sōchō was so pleased to hear that Suruga and Tōtōmi were at peace. Akaike 赤池 is in Nisshinchō 日進町, Aichi District, Aichi Prefecture.

206. The ice forms as if to freeze the sky itself, keeping it from growing light.

207. The poet wakes to the cock's crow and finds a light snow has fallen on his sleeve.

208. Sōchō refers to *Shinkokinshū* 16: 1504, by Fujiwara Norikane (*JS*: 236, n. 17).

209. "Long night" may also relate to "the long night of ignorance" (*mumyō jōya*) preceding enlightenment (cf. *JS* no. 244). Here Sōchō bemoans his inability to achieve satori.

210. Sōchō may have in mind here the "Yomogiu" chapter of *Genji monogatari* (3: 149): "[Koremitsu] approached and cleared his throat to announce his presence; after coughing (*mazu shiwabuki o saki ni tatete*), an ancient voice inquired, 'Who is it? Who's there?'" Translation after Seidensticker 1976, 1: 298.

211. Sōchō also refers to this prophecy, based on *yijing* divination, on *JS*: 132.

212. This poem too relates to Saigyō's famous Sayo no nakayama poem, *Shinkokinshū* 10: 987 (*JS*: 192, n. 2).

213. Amazake is a sweetened beverage made of rice and yeast that has not been allowed to ferment, or of sake lees. It is often served hot.

214. The constable was Hatakeyama Yoshifusa, a noted warrior literatus (*JS*: 209, n. 137). Dōken called on the Hatakeyama several times; the sojourn Sōchō speaks of here lasted from 1525:10 until 1527:3.

215. "Blind attendant" translates *zatō* 座頭, lowest of the official grades of blind *biwa* performers, or more generally blind musicians, guides, storytellers, masseurs, practitioners of acupuncture and moxibustion, and so forth.

216. The land of Koshi includes Noto Province.

217. For White Mountain (Shirayama), see *JS*: 223, n. 56.

218. There are a number of extant portraits of Ikkyū with a red sword, an image recalling New Year's Day of 1435, when Ikkyū paraded down the streets of Sakai carrying a bamboo sword to symbolize the empty knowledge of contemporary Zen priests. It is also a visual metaphor for his incisive intellect. Such portraits, called *chinzō* 頂相, were meant as nonverbal inspirations for disciples. For a list of extant red-sword portraits of Ikkyū, see Covell 1980: 315, and for an illustration of one such work in the collection of Shūon'an temple, see *Song in an Age of Discord*.

219. The sword image is used in the last poem in *Biyanlu* (The Blue Cliff Record), a

basic Zen text. Linji used the image of the "blown-hair sword," so sharp it would slice a hair blown by the wind, in his death poem as a metaphor for the Zen mind. Daitō 大燈 (1282–1337), the founder of Daitokuji, later adopted the same image in his death poem, where it is translated in Kraft (1992: 169) as "Mind-sword":

> I cut aside all buddhas and patriarchs,
> my Mind-sword honed to a razor edge.
> Activity's wheel begins to turn—
> emptiness gnashes its teeth.

The image of the mirror also has a long tradition in Buddhist texts. It is found, for example, in "the Merits of the Dharma-Preacher" chapter (*Hosshi kudoku hon*) of the *Lotus Sutra* (Hurvitz 1976: 275):

> Also, as in a pure, bright mirror
> One sees all physical images,
> The bodhisattva, in his pure body,
> Sees whatever is in the world.

The same imagery is employed in poems on enlightenment in *Liuzu tanjing* (The Platform Sutra of the Sixth Patriarch), another favorite Zen text probably read by Ikkyū and Sōchō. Among them is this (Yampolsky 1967: 132):

> The mind is the Bodhi tree,
> The body is the mirror stand.
> The mirror is originally clean and pure;
> Where can it be stained by dust?

220. Asukai Masachika 飛鳥井雅親 (1417–90) was a major court poet and Sōgi's waka teacher. He was directed by Emperor Gohanazono 後花園 (1419–71) to compile a twenty-second imperial poem anthology, but the project was never realized due to the Ōnin War.

221. Sōchō also wrote about the dream to Sanetaka, who in turn recorded the event in an entry after 1526:11:15 in *Saishōsō* (13: 101).

222. The poem, a kyōka, puns on Ibukioroshi, winds blowing down from the Ibuki Mountains north of Yashima, and *ibiki* (snore). *Susu hana* (flower-like cinders) also contains overtones of *susubana* (runny nose).

223. The eighth of the twelfth month was believed to be the date upon which Prince Gautama attained enlightenment. Of all the stars that are twinkling in the sky, Sōchō wonders which one it was that enlightened the Buddha.

224. "Those who knew" may refer to Ikkyū or to earlier sages in general.

225. The verse suggests that dawn has arrived but brought with it no enlightenment, for only Sōchō's eyes open and not his mind.

226. For Nakae Kazutsugu, see *JS*: 103.

227. In this kyōka Sōchō puns on *yoi* (evening/intoxication).

228. Sōchō is wintering at Yashima, near the east coast of Lake Biwa.

229. Hirai Uhyōenojō Takayoshi 平井右兵衛尉高好 was a retainer of the Rokkaku House. A linked-verse poet, he appears with Sōchō in Daiei 3 [1523]:9:2 *Yamanani hyakuin*.

230. For Kawai Matagorō, see *JS*: 241, n. 59.

231. Kawai Suruganokami (Sunshū) was a resident of Ōmi Province whom Sōchō last met in the summer of 1524 (*JS*: 49). Perhaps the manuscript should read "year before last" rather than "last year." Sōchō has just heard of his friend's death.

232. This is a felicitous verse (*shūgen*) for Ōsaka Gate; it suggests that despite the snow, there is a constant stream of travelers to and fro. It contains a kakekotoba pivoting on *au* (to meet) and Ōsaka, and it recalls *Gosenshū* 15: 1089, by Semimaru:

Composed after building a hermitage at Ōsaka Gate and watching people pass by:

kore ya kono	It is here
yuku mo kaeru mo	where those leaving and returning
wakaretsutsu	part company,
shiru mo shiranu mo	and where known and unknown meet,
ōsaka no seki	here at Ōsaka Gate.

The poem became famous as an expression of the principle that "all who meet must part" (*esha jōri* 会者定離).

233. The verse is orthodox; it is the remarks following it that Sōchō identifies as light-hearted. Shimazu (1975: 108) offers an alternate interpretation to the effect that Sōchō is comparing his hermitage to the Ōsaka Gate and taking pleasure in the visitors who come and go.

234. Shimazu (1975: 108) identifies Yatarō as Asahina Yatarō Yasumoto 朝比奈弥太郎泰元, otherwise unknown; the journal is out of chronological sequence here.

235. See *JS*: 289, n. 205.

236. One ryō 両 (sometimes translated "tael") of gold in the Tenbun era (1532–54) weighed about 16.5 g. (about half an ounce). The two ryō spoken of here may have been in a single lump or in two one-ryō pieces (perhaps flat *bankin* 板金). See Okuno Takahiro 1960: 228 for an account of the ryō and of Imagawa mining and minting activities. For Asahina Yasumochi, see *JS*: 10; for Asahina Tokishige, see *JS*: 11. Bōshū 房州 may have been Ihara Awanokami Tadatane 庵原安房守忠胤, a vassal of the Imagawa and lord of Ihara Castle in Ihara District (Yamamoto and Owada 1981: 331). Sōchō received the gift after Bōshū's death.

237. There are kakekotoba pivoting on *yuki* (snow) and *yukiau* (meet) and then on *yukiau* and Ōmi.

238. Sōtetsu 宗鉄 was Kajisai's cognomen. See also *JS*: 207, n. 102.

Notes to Book Two (1526), Pages 131–33

239. Sōchō and Kajisai did indeed meet again (*JS*: 144–45).

240. Wakatsuki Kunisada 若槻国定 was a vassal of Hosokawa Takakuni. The defeat mentioned here occurred at the beginning of the Yanagimoto Discord (*JS*: 120).

241. Kawarabayashi Masayori 河原林正頼 (or 政頼) was acquainted with Sōchō and is mentioned on *JS*: 29. An ally of Takakuni, he had been besieged in Koshimizu 越水 Castle in Settsu by Hosokawa Sumimoto and Miyoshi Yukinaga. Takakuni went to his rescue but was forced to retreat, unable to drive off the besieging army. Masayori surrendered on 1520:2:3, at which point the aged Wakatsuki Nagazumi 若槻若狭守長澄, one of Masayori's retainers, committed suicide. The event is recorded in *Hosokawa ryōkeki* (Account of the Two Hosokawa Houses)(588), where Nagazumi is referred to as Izunokami. Despite his prolonged defense of Koshimizu fortress, Kawarabayashi Masayori was forced to commit suicide by Takakuni later that year.

242. The poem is attributed to Sōchō in Sanetaka's poetry collection *Saishōsō* (13: 111). There is a kakekotoba pivoting on the name Wakatsuki and *tsukiyumi* (zelkova bow). There may be overtones in the verse of the word *shinau* (to bend), which creates internal cohesion through its relationship to the word *yumi* (bow).

243. Setsubun 節分 is the day before the start of a new season, especially spring. Here the beginning of spring by the solar calendar falls in the old lunar year. Sōchō is therefore eighty (by the Japanese count) in terms of seasons, while still seventy-nine in terms of years. A similar overlap is recorded in *Kokinshū* 1: 1. One of the observances of the day is still to throw beans while shouting "Good fortune in! Demons out!" (*Fuku wa uchi, oni wa soto*). Sōchō posits a humorous reason for the demons' exit.

244. Tenmyō 天明 is unknown.

245. Sōbai 宗梅 was a disciple of Sōgi. He took part with Sōchō in Daiei 7 [1527]:1:19 *Yamanani hyakuin*. See also Tsurusaki 1983: 288.

246. "Horse load" translates *ichida* 一駄, which equalled thirty-six *kan* 貫 or 133 kg (one *kan* equalled 3.7 kg.). For Tanemura Sadakazu (to whom Sōchō refers as Nakatsukasanojō earlier), see *JS*: 44.

247. The Miyaki Lay Priest Shinkan 宮木入道真観 had been a Rokkaku retainer before taking religious vows. He too participated in the linked-verse session with Sōbai, above.

248. The foundation poem is *Kokinshū* 1: 21, by Emperor Kōkō:

A poem sent to someone by the Ninna Emperor [Kōkō] when he was still a prince, together with some young greens:

kimi ga tame	For you, good sir,
haru no no ni idete	I ventured out on springtime fields
wakana tsumu	to gather young greens,
waga koromode ni	and upon my robe's sleeves
yuki wa furitsutsu	the snow never ceased to fall.

249. Sōchō's poem is based on the legend of Mengzong 孟宗, one of the twenty-four paragons of filial piety, who went out in the winter snow to find bamboo shoots for his mother and because of the depth of his filial piety was able to accomplish the seemingly impossible task.

250. Tani Sōboku 谷宗牧 (d. 1545) was a disciple of Sōchō and Sōseki, and he became the doyen of the renga world after their deaths.

251. Kurama and Ono, both in the Kyoto region, were famous for charcoal production. Sōboku employs a kakekotoba pivoting between *keshi* (mustard) and *keshikaranu* (lit., inconvenient), translated here as "unseasonable."

252. See *JS* no. 324.

253. The text referred to is *The Sutra on the Buddha's Repayment of his Indebtedness to his Parents by Great and Skillful Means* (*Daihōbenbutsuhōongyō* 大方便仏報恩経).

254. The verse is actually *Shinkokinshu* 16: 1586, by Fujiwara Shunzei (see *JS*: 258, n. 88).

BOOK TWO: *Seventh Year of Daiei (1527)*

1. *Azusayumi*, catalpa bow, is a makurakotoba to introduce *yasoji* (eightieth year), whose first syllable is a homophone for "arrow." *Haru* (spring) is a kindred word through its homonym "to bend back [a bow]." *Kokinshū* 1: 20, the foundation poem for *JS* no. 17, uses the same imagery.

2. The political situation in Ōmi was complex. The north was controlled by the Kyōgoku and later the Asai houses; the south, to which Sōchō refers here, by the Rokkaku house, specifically Rokkaku Sadayori (*JS*: 208, n. 113). The west was under the strong influence of Enryakuji and Miidera. Ōmi was of great commercial and strategic importance. The Rokkaku castle was at Kannonji (*JS*: 32), where Sōchō participated in Daiei 3 [1523]:9:2 *Yamanani hyakuin*.

3. The poem involves two kakekotoba, pivoting on *hito mochi* (people revere) and *mochiikagami* (mirror rice cakes, or as in the translation, New Year's rice cakes) and then on *mochiikagami* and *kagamiyama* (Mirror Mountain). Sōchō also refers to the following passage from the "Hatsune" chapter of *Genji monogatari* (4: 155) to justify his use of the word *michiikagami* in a poem of very lofty intent:

> They gathered here and there in groups, carrying out the Tooth-Hardening Ritual and even having rice cakes [mochiikagami] brought over. Someone joked, "We will all of course have 'a thousand years beneath its shade'; just grant us health and safety in the present one!"

That in turn refers to *Kokinshū* 7: 356, by Sosei:

Composed by Sosei on behalf of the daughter of Yoshimune Tsunenari in celebration of her father's fortieth birthday:

yorozuyo o	I celebrate
matsu ni zo kimi o	your longevity with this pine,
iwaitsuru	and like a crane
chitose no kage ni	I look forward to dwelling
sumamu to omoeba	a thousand years beneath its shade.

The poem was chanted at the Tooth-Hardening (*hagatame*) ceremony, held during the first three days of the New Year, at which time one also partook of rice cakes and other specified foods for longevity.

4. Sōchō is writing in 1527. Since Book One of the journal covers 1522 to 1526, and Book Two, 1526 to 1527, the phrase "for the last year or two" would seem to refer only to Book Two, which further suggests that the author conceived of Book One and Book Two of the diary as separate entities. This is corroborated by the fact that Sōchō repeats at the beginning of Book Two the events at the end of Book One.

5. Sanetaka in Kyoto looks out at the slopes of the Hira Mountains and thinks of Sōchō on the far side of those peaks in Yashima, blown by the Hira wind.

6. Sanetaka recorded his poem in an entry for 1527:1:9 in his *Saishōsō* (13: 107), then noted that he received Sōchō's reply from Shōrin'an on the twenty-fourth (13: 108).

7. This is Daiei 7 [1527]:1:18 *Yashima Shōrin'an naniki hyakuin*.

8. Sanetaka uses as his foundation poem *Kokinshū* 1: 7:

kokorozashi	Was it since my heart
fukaku someteshi	was so deeply tinged
orikereba	with the desire for them
kieaenu yuki no	that I mistook the lingering snow
hana to miyuran	for blossoms?

9. "Both places" perhaps refers to Ōmi and Sakai (Sakai 堺 City, Osaka Prefecture). Both have a view of water and mountains.

10. The master of Jizōin 地蔵院 is unknown.

11. Spring knows the gentle character of Sōchō's friend and presents a gentle natural scene in tribute.

12. See *JS*: 291, n. 229.

13. For Nakae Tosanokami, see *JS*: 103.

14. Cf. *JS* nos. 11 and 327 for similar conceptions.

15. Baba Hyōgonosuke 馬場兵庫助, a retainer of the Sasaki, may be the same person as Suke no Hyōgo (*JS*: 123). His given name was most likely Saneyuki 実行, as that is the person to whom the second verse, conventionally composed by the host, is attributed in the manuscript of the sequence (see the following note).

16. This is the hokku for Daiei 7 [1527]:1:19 *Yamanani hyakuin*.

17. The foundation poem is *Shikashū* 1: 1, by Ōe Masafusa:

> Composed on the topic "The Beginning of Spring" for a hundred-waka sequence in the reign of Emperor Horikawa:
>
> | kōriishi | The long-frozen ice |
> |---|---|
> | shiga no karasaki | off Karasaki in Shiga |
> | uchitokete | has melted away, |
> | sazanami yosuru | and the spring wind blows |
> | haru kaze zo fuku | the rippling waves toward the shore. |

18. Mabuchi Kunainoshō 馬淵宮内少輔 is identified in *Ōmi Gamōgunshi* 近江蒲生郡志 (2: 831) as Mabuchi Yamashironokami Munetsuna 馬淵山城守宗綱 (see Ōshima 1963–64, 32: 30). The Mabuchi were major vassals of the Rokkaku. They controlled the town of Mabuchi in Gamō 蒲生 District and later extended their influence into Yasu 野洲 District as well.

19. Fukuda Hachirō 福田八郎, also known as Sōkan 宗観, is unknown.

20. This is probably Sugawara Shrine, supported by the Mabuchi. *Hokku kikigaki*, which contains many verses by Sōchō, is in the collection of the shrine (see *JS*: 219, n. 33). An annual dedicatory sequence for Sugawara Michizane was held there until the Meiji period (Tsurusaki 1983: 272).

21. Both verses recall the Naniwazu poem in the *Kokinshū* preface (*JS*: 287, n. 192).

22. The foundation poem is *Gyokuyōshū* 11: 1550, by Izumi Shikibu:

> On hearing from someone that he could not come:
>
> | nakoso to wa | Whoever said, |
> |---|---|
> | tare ka wa iishi | "Stay away!" as if at Nakoso? |
> | iwanedomo | Although I did not, |
> | kokoro ni suuru | one would think I had put up |
> | seki to koso mire | a barrier in my heart. |

The name of Nakoso 勿来 Gate, located in the distant north in what is now Fukushima Prefecture, also means "stay away." In view of the religious nature of Sōchō's verse and the amorous subject of Izumi Shikibu's, *kokoro* in translation becomes "mind" in the former and "heart" in the latter. Sōchō's poem suggests that only the unenlightened mind constructs a distinction between life and death.

23. The foundation poem is *Kokinshū* 11: 473, by Ariwara Motokata:

> | otowayama | I hear news of you, |
> |---|---|
> | oto ni kikitsutsu | Tidings recalling Otowa Mountain's name, |
> | ōsaka no | but here on the near side |
> | seki no konata ni | of the Gate at the Moutain of Meeting |
> | toshi o furu kana | years go by without you! |

Notes to Book Two (1527), Pages 140–41

The "Otowa Mountain" (Otowayama mountain) to which this verse refers is located south of the "Gate at the Mountain of Meeting" (Ōsaka Gate). See *JS* no. 60.

24. For Matsudaira Ōinosuke, see *JS*: 98.
25. Cf. *Kokinshū* 14: 689:

samushiro ni	This evening too
koromo katashiki	does the Uji Bridge Princess
koyoi mo	lie alone on her robe
ware o matsuramu	on a cold, narrow mat,
uji no hashihime	waiting for me to visit?

26. The foundation poem is *Kokinshū* 20: 1092, an Azumauta:

mogamigawa	Unlike the rice boats
noboreba kudaru	that go up and turn down
inabune no	Mogami River,
ina ni wa arazu	I am not turning you down,
kono tsuki bakari	just asking for this one month.

27. The humor of the verse is based on the repetition of *mojikotoba* 文字詞, argot used by palace ladies-in-waiting, where the suffix *moji* is added to a syllable or two of a word. Here *numoji* stands for *nu*subito (thief) and *tomoji* stands for *to*ru (take, or here, steal).

28. Sōchō is again referring to the Yanagimoto Disturbance, the name of which is embedded in the poem: miyako wa *yanagi* / hito*moto* no haru. The foundation poem is *Kokinshū* 2: 56, by Sosei (*JS*: 228, n. 88).

29. Takeda Izunokami Motomitsu 武田伊豆守元光 was an ally of Hosokawa Takakuni and the shogun, Ashikaga Yoshiharu. He was also a friend of Sanetaka. Motomitsu left Wakasa Province (Fukui Prefecture) for Kyoto on the twenty-sixth of the twelfth month of Daiei 6 (early 1527). At the border of Wakasa and Ōmi Provinces he composed this poem:

miyako ni to	Today at the start
kyō tatsu haru ni	of springtime I set out
ware mo mata	for the capital—
nodoka narubeki	all must be peaceful
tabi no yukusue	at my journey's destination.

He sent the poem to Sanetaka when he arrived in the capital, and Sanetaka recorded it in his poetic diary, *Saishōsō* (13: 106). On the morning of the thirteenth of the second month, he and his allies were defeated at the battle of Senshōji 専勝寺 at Shichijō avenue near Katsuragawa river.

30. Kataharu had raised troops in Tanba Province, then had returned and occupied Kyoto.

Notes to Book Two (1527), Pages 141–42

31. Sōchō here begins a chronicle of the conflicts in the capital in the last century and a half. The account demonstrates a Hosokawa bias, which reflects Sōchō's longstanding acquaintance with Hosokawa Takakuni. The battle described here is the Discord of the Meitoku Era (Meitoku no ran 明徳乱) of 1391, which began as a succession dispute. Yamana Mitsuyuki 山名満幸 (d. 1395), referred to here by Sōchō as Yamana Mutsunokami 山名陸奥守, appealed to Ashikaga Yoshimitsu when Yamana Tokihiro 山名時熙, was chosen head of the family. Yoshimitsu, seeking to exploit the conflict for his own purposes, ordered Mitsuyuki and an ally, Yamana Mutsunokami Ujikiyo 山名陸奥守氏清 (1344–91), to attack Tokihiro and his ally, Yamana Ujiyuki 山名氏幸. Hosokawa Yoriyuki 細川頼之 was part of the striking force. The attackers won and were granted lands belonging to the losers. The following year Yoshimitsu adroitly reversed his position and drove Mitsuyuki from Kyoto and made amends to Tokihiro and Ujiyuki, which caused Mitsuyuki and Ujikiyo to rise in the rebellion subsequently known as the Discord of the Meitoku Era. Yoshimitsu was victorious in battle on New Year's Eve in the second year of Meitoku (early 1393) at Uchino. He thus succeeded in splitting the Yamana and diminishing their power, which had posed a threat to Ashikaga hegemony. The conflict is recounted in *Meitokuki*.

32. Sōchō refers here, of course, to the Ōnin War, the largest civil upheaval since the Genpei War (1180–85). The conflict lasted from 1467 to 1477 and resulted in the destruction of much of the capital. The conflict had its origins in succession disputes within two warrior houses, the Hatakeyama and the Shiba, which were complicated in 1464 by a similar dispute within the shogunal government itself. All three disputes were manipulated for personal gain by two other rivals, Hosokawa Katsumoto 細川勝元 (1430–1473) and Yamana Sōzen 山名宗全 (1404–1473). Though sporadic violence accompanied those controversies for years, the Ōnin War itself began when forces of Hatakeyama Yoshinari 畠山義就 (d. 1490) and Yamana Sōzen clashed with those of Yoshinari's rival Hatakeyama Masanaga 畠山政長 (1442–1493) and Hosokawa Katsumoto. Sōzen also opposed Katsumoto in the matter of shogunal succession. Hostilities spread to the provinces soon thereafter. Katsumoto's forces became known as the Eastern Army and Sōzen's, the Western. George Sansom (1984: 226) writes that "the records say that the central trench between the two parties was ten feet deep and twenty feet wide." In 1469 Yoshimi had switched sides, and Yoshimasa accordingly named his son Yoshihisa his heir. By 1472 the conflict was exhausting both parties, and the principals, Katsumoto and Sōzen, both died in 1473. Ōuchi Masahiro left the capital in 1477, which effectively brought the war there to an end. Fighting escalated in the provinces, however, and peace would not be restored for a more than a century. The conflict is described in *Ōninki*. See Varley 1967 and Berry 1994.

33. Ōuchi Masahiro, referred to by Sōchō as Ōuchi Sakyōnodaibu 大内左京大夫, had left Kyushu with 20,000 men in support of Sōzen. Sansom (1984: 223) relates that one

297

Notes to Book Two (1527), Page 142

version of *Ōninki* states that when Masahiro and his reinforcements arrived, Sōzen "felt like a dragon refreshed by water or a tiger sniffing the breeze." By the end of 1467 Katsumoto's position was grave; his forces were bottled into a small space around Shōkokuji temple (where Sōgi and Sesshū had once studied), the bakufu buildings, and his own mansion. The temple was then razed by Sōzen's troops. By the end of 1467 the capital had been so destroyed as to be described in *Ōninki* as "a lair of wolves and foxes" (Sansom 1984: 226). But the war thereafter resulted in a stalemate. Hosokawa Katsumoto, however, was successful in fomenting uprisings in other parts of the country against Yamana allies, forcing those allies to divide their forces and diminish their strength. The order to Sōchō's patron Imagawa Yoshitada to rise against Shiba partisans in the east (*JS*: 13) was part of this strategy.

34. Sōchō is again writing as a Hosokawa partisan; Masahiro was not in actuality defeated. Sōchō knew him personally, having traveled to his domains in the company of Sōgi in 1488, part of which journey Sōgi recorded in *Tsukushi michi no ki*.

35. Again, Sōchō's account requires background information. Hosokawa Katsumoto's son Masamoto engineered a coup d'état in 1493, which resulted in the deposal of Shogun Ashikaga Yoshitane 足利義植 (then called Yoshiki 義材, 1466–1523), and the appointment of Ashikaga Yoshizumi 足利義澄 (then called Yoshitaka 義高, 1481–1511) to the post. Yoshitane was the son of Yoshimi and had been made shogun in 1490 after the death of Yoshihisa.

But Masamoto had no sons, and he accordingly named Hosokawa Sumiyuki 澄之 (1489–1507) as his heir, but he then appointed Hosokawa Sumimoto in Awa as his heir instead. Each candidate was supported by various warrior houses. Sumimoto entered Kyoto in 1506 and war ensued. He was backed by the real holder of power in Awa, Miyoshi Yukinaga (referred to here by Sōchō as Miyoshi Chikuzennokami 三好筑前守), who was intent on toppling Masamoto. This conflict is described in *Hosokawa ryōkeki*.

Sumiyuki's supporters assassinated Masamoto in 1507, whereupon Sumimoto fled to Ōmi, leaving Sumiyuki in power. But some weeks later Sumimoto and Yukinaga returned and destroyed him. At this point Shogun Yoshizumi was manipulated by Sumimoto, who was in turn controlled by Miyoshi Yukinaga. The rapidly changing power structure now encouraged the ex-shogun Ashikaga Yoshitane (now called Yoshitada 義尹), living under the protection of Ōuchi Yoshioki in Suō, to return to Kyoto with Yoshioki's support in 1508 and attempt to recover his lost position. Hosokawa Takakuni, yet another of Masamoto's adopted sons, took this as an opportunity to seize power for himself, and he went to meet Yoshitane at Sakai. He subsequently attacked Sumimoto and Yukinaga and drove them back to Ōmi, where Ashikaga Yoshizumi joined them. He then restored Yoshitane to power and was in turn appointed shogunal deputy. Ōuchi Yoshioki was made his assistant (*kanreidai*).

Sumimoto made several later attempts to wrest power from Takakuni, and in 1520, with the help of Miyoshi Yukinaga, he succeeded in momentarily driving Takakuni from Kyoto. Sumimoto thereupon made peace with Yoshitane. But Takakuni returned soon after and defeated Sumimoto and Yukinaga yet again on the fifth of the fifth month. These are the events that Sōchō is discussing here. Yukinaga and his two sons committed suicide, and Sumimoto was forced to retire to Awa, where he died later that year. Yoshitane in turn again fled the city in 1521, this time to Sakai and finally Awa, coming to be known as the "Island Shogun" (Shima Kubō) in consequence. Takakuni made Ashikaga Yoshizumi's son Yoshiharu 義晴 (1511–50) shogun, and Yoshitane died in exile in 1523. Takakuni adopted the name Dōei 道永, by which Sōchō refers to him here, on taking holy orders in 1525. For his subsequent career, see *JS*: 284–85, n. 176.

36. Yamanoue 山上 is north of Miidera in Ōtsu.

37. Yoshiharu moved to Honkokuji 本圀寺 on the twelfth of the second month.

38. Sōchō, as a Takakuni partisan, is making the best of a bad job here, as Takakuni and the shogun actually lost the battle.

39. Shiga 志賀; Konohama 木浜; Yamada 山田; Yabase 矢橋, and Moruyama 守山.

40. Sōchō bases his celebratory poem on the auspicious nature of the temple's name, "Long Light" (Chōkō 長光). Chōkōji is also mentioned on *JS*: 103.

41. The Tōkaidō 東海道 included fifteen provinces east of Kyoto along Japan's east coast; the Hokuriku 北陸, seven eastern provinces along the Japan Sea; the Saikoku 西国, provinces west of Kyoto; and the Chūgoku 中国, either the sixteen provinces of western Honshū or the "central provinces," i.e, the Kyoto region itself.

42. *Shinkokinshū* 17: 1689, by Emperor Tenji:

asakura ya	While I sojourn here,
ki no marodono ni	in the palace of rough-hewn logs
ware oreba	at Asakura,
nanori o shitsutsu	who is he that takes his leave
yuku wa taga ko zo	after announcing his name?

Asakura 朝倉, in Chikuzen Province (Fukuoka Prefecture), was the site of a temporary palace during a campaign to Paekche by Empress Saimei, when Emperor Tenji was Crown Prince. Kamo no Chōmei refers to it in *Hōjōki*, and it is the setting of the nō play *Aya no tsuzumi* (The Damask Drum). The poem also appears in slightly different form as *kagurauta* no. 75 (Usuda and Shinma 1976: 97). Though commentators speculate that the verse refers to a courtier taking leave of the palace in the morning, they also suggest that it may originally have been a love song.

43. Evidence from *Sanetakakōki* and *Tōgoku kikō* indicates that Sōchō was accompanied by several others on this trip, most notably his disciple Sōboku. His departure may have been motivated by the presence of the troops of Hosokawa Takakuni and Ashikaga Yoshiharu so close to his hermitage in Yashima.

Notes to Book Two (1527), Pages 143–44

44. Minakuchi 水口, in Kōga 甲賀 District, Shiga Prefecture. The palace in question was located in Tongū 頓宮, Tsuchiyamachō (*JS*: 242, n. 62).

45. There are puns on *minakuchi*, the town's name and "where one pours in the water," and on *seki* (toll gate / stop [up]). The poem is based on *Ise monogatari* (38–39):

> Once upon a time a man spent one night with a woman and then did not return. Thereafter, at her wash basin, the woman removed the bamboo lid and saw herself reflected in the water therein, whereupon she composed:

ware bakari	Although I thought
mono omou hito wa	there could be no one else whose heart
mata mo araji to	was as heavy as mine,
omoeba mizu no	I now behold another
shita ni mo arikeri	beneath the water's surface.

> The man, who had only then returned, stood by and listened, then replied:

minakuchi ni	I must have appeared
ware ya miyuramu	at the water's mouth,
kawazu sae	for even frogs
mizu no shita ni te	beneath the surface
morogoe ni naku	cry together.

Ishida (*Ise monogatari* 1984: 124–25) believes the woman sees the man's reflection in the basin the entire time but pretends in her poem to mean her own reflection. The response metaphorically relates the wash basin to the place where water is directed into a paddy field, where frogs are often found. The man suggests that the woman is not alone in her grief, for just as the frogs cry together in the paddy water, so does the man's weeping reflection appear in the basin together with the woman's.

46. Saji Nagamasa 佐治長政, whose sobriquet was Shōunken 少雲軒 or San'unken 三雲軒, resided in Ōno 大野, about ten kilometers east of Minakuchi.

47. Kōga 甲賀 Valley, through which runs Yokotagawa 横田川 river.

48. The poem makes reference to the Buddhist proverb "Taking shelter in the shade of the same tree, or drinking from the stream—even these are bonds from a former life" (*ichiju no kage, ichiga no nagare mo, tashō no en*).

49. For Kawai Matagorō, see *JS*: 251. A "sequence on the Holy Name" (*myōgō* 名号) starts each verse with a syllable from Namu Amida Butsu (see also *JS*: 69–71).

50. Iguchi Saburōzaemon 井口三郎左衛門 was related to the Sasaki family. Konohama 木浜 is located in Moriyama 守山 City, about two kilometers south of the Biwa Ōhashi bridge on Lake Biwa's east side. It was an important commercial center.

51. According to Chinese legend, the prints of a bird inspired Cang Xie 蒼頡, who served the Yellow Emperor, to invent writing.

52. The foundation poem is *Kokinshū* 1: 68, by Lady Ise:

Notes to Book Two (1527), Pages 144–46

Composed for the Teijiin Poetry Contest:

miru hito mo	Cherries blossoming
naki yamazato no	in mountain villages
sakurabana	but seen by no one—
hoka no chirinamu	far better if they blossomed
nochi zo sakamashi	after the others scattered!

53. For "waka sequence," see *JS*: 52.
54. Cf. *Man'yōshū* 19: 4291, by Ōtomo Yakamochi:

waga yado no	The wind blows
isasamuratake	in the sparse stands of bamboo
fuku kaze no	about my dwelling
oto no kasokeki	and sets them softly soughing
kono yūbe ka mo	at the close of day.

55. Cf. *Man'yōshū* 5: 897, by Yamanoue Okura:

tamakiharu	Until the time
uchi no kagiri wa	that the spirit leaves the body,
tairakeku	let there be peace
yasuku mo aramu o	and tranquillity,
koto mo naku	no calamities
mo naku aramu o . . .	and no causes for mourning . . .

Sōchō's verse is an auspicious prayer on a Shintō topic for his host's welfare.

56. For Amidaji temple, see *JS*: 54.
57. It was believed that teeth could grow again in old age in place of others that had fallen out. This is one suggested etymology for the word *mizuhagumu* (a great age) (cf. *JS* no. 570). The word is usually employed in praise of longevity.
58. Kanbe 神戸 is in Suzuka 鈴鹿 City, Mie Prefecture. Satō Nagatonokami 佐藤長門守 was connected with the Seki House.
59. *RJGPS* no. 888 states that *fuji* (wisteria) and *yamabuki* (kerria) are associated with late spring.
60. "Ise no umi" is the title of *saibara* no. 10:

ise no umi no	On the brilliant beach
kiyoki naagisa ni	by the Bay of Ise
shiogai ni	in the ebbing tide,
nanoriso ya tsumamu	let us go pick sea lentils!
kai ya hirowamu ya	Let us gather sea shells!
tama ya hirowamu ya	Let us gather pearls!

61. I have emended *kaikakarekere* in the Shōkōkan ms. (Shimazu 1975: 122) on the basis of the *SKGSRJ* text (692). The Saiokuji ms. gives *oirasu* instead of *oishisu*.

62. Waka Pine Strand (Waka [no] matsubara 若[の]松原) is a famous place on the coast of Suzuka City. It is possibly the same place as Aga no matsubara 吾の松原, mentioned in *Man'yōshū* 6: 1030, by Emperor Shōmu.

63. Sōchō is concerned about using two words referring to morning, and he justifies his composition on the basis of *Man'yōshū* 8: 1513, by Prince Hozumi:

kesa no asake	At daybreak this morning
karigane kikitsu	I heard the calls of the geese.
kasugayama	On Mount Kasuga
momichinikerashi	the trees seem to have turned to yellow.
aga kokoro itashi	My heart is overflowing.

64. Hinaga 日永, today's Yokkaichi 四日市 City, was the place where the Sangū Kaidō 参宮街道 road to Ise diverged from the Tōkaidō. The name literally means "long day," and Sōchō's remark that he passed by at daybreak gives the sentence a droll effect. For Tōunken, see *JS*: 47.

65. See *JS*: 101–2.

66. For Shōgakuin, see *JS*: 101. The scribe was a *wakashu*.

67. See *JS*: 100–101.

68. For Sakai Settsunokami Muramori, see *JS*: 99.

69. There is a kakekotoba pivoting between *iwakaki* (stone palisade) and *kakitsubata* (irises).

70. Oda Tanbanokami 織田丹波守 is unidentified.

71. Cf. *Ise monogatari* (34):

aki no yo no	If I were to count
chiyo o hitoyo ni	a thousand autumn nights
nazuraete	as but one,
yachiyo shi nebaya	I would lie here for eight thousand,
aku toki no aranu	never having my fill.

The reply:

aki no yo no	Even if you made
chiyo o hitoyo ni	this one night as long
naseri tomo	as all the nights of autumn,
kotoba nokorite	we would still have more to say
tori ya nakinamu	at cock's crow.

Genji monogatari (5: 125) later refers to this poem in part two of the "Wakana" chapter: "It was all so delightful they felt they would not tire of it even if the night were long as a thousand."

72. This is the hokku for Daiei 7 [1527]:4:2 *Nanibito hyakuin*. Sōboku, Shōzōbō, and Kendō were among the participants.

73. For Narumi, see *JS*: 99.

74. Rain Hat Temple (Kasadera 笠寺, more formally Ryūfukuji 笠履寺) is in Nagoya City, Minami Ward.

75. The statue is mentioned in *Kasadera engi*.

76. For Mizuno Izumonokami Chikamori, see *JS*: 15.

77. Anjō 安城 City, in Aichi Prefecture, was the site of the castle of Matsudaira Nagachika 松平長親. Sōchō composed linked verse with Nagachika in 1518 (see Tsurusaki 1987: 401). The sequence, Eishō 15 [1518]:4:23/26 *Yamanani hyakuin* (A Hundred-Verse Sequence Entitled "A Kind of Mountain"), is extant.

78. Matsudaira Yoichi 松平与一 (Nobusada 信定) was lord of Moriyama 守山 Castle (*JS*: 99).

79. Sōchō crossed Yahagigawa river at Yahagi (Okazaki 岡崎 City). The course of the river was changed to its present one in 1605 to prevent the flooding that had theretofore been endemic. Myōdaiji 妙大寺, in Okazaki, is not extant, but it survives as a place name in the city.

80. Lady Jōruri (Jōruri Gozen 浄瑠璃御前) is the heroine of *Jōruri Gozen monogatari*, a medieval tale of tragic love. Yoshitsune meets her at her father's mansion in Yahagi, but they spend only one night together before he must leave. She later travels to where he lies ill and nurses him back to health before returning home. On his way back to the capital three years later, he calls at Yahagi, only to find she has died. He subsequently builds a temple in her memory before setting out on his campaign against the Heike. One version of the story was presented with a chanter and puppets and met with great success, the puppet theater coming to be known as *jōruri* in consequence. Sōchō in *Sōchō nikki* (*SN*: 164) mentions hearing the story chanted in 1531.

81. A note in the *Shōkōkan* ms. identifies Matsudaira Jirōzaburō as Nobutada 松平信忠, heir of Nagachika and brother of Yoichi, and Shimazu (1975: 125) follows this. But Suzuki Mitsuyasu (1973: 323) shows that Nobutada was forced to retire in 1523 in favor of his son Kiyoyasu 清康 when he lost the support of his housemen. On 1526:4:29 Kiyoyasu moved his headquarters from Anjō to Okazaki. The Jirōzaburō Sōchō mentions must therefore be Kiyoyasu, who killed Sōchō's warrior patron Makino Denzō (*JS*: 55) in battle two years later.

82. See *JS*: 98.

83. Suzuki Mitsuyasu (1973: 318) believes Udono Saburo 鵜殿三郎 was probably Nagamochi 長持 (d. 1557). Sōboku, as one of Sōchō's companions, also met Udono Saburō on this trip, and he later called on him again in the journey he recorded in *Tōgoku kikō*. See Yogo 1983.

84. See *JS*: 98.

85. Cf. *JS* nos. 357 and 544. I have altered *moteyuzuru* in the Shōkōkan ms. (Shimazu

1975: 125) to *moteyueru* on the basis of the the *SKGSRJ* (693) and Saiokuji mss., as that is the version in the foundation poem, *Kokinshū* 17: 911 (anon.): *watatsumi no / kazashi ni saseru / shirotae no / nami moteyueru / awajishimayama*.

86. Makino Kohaku was Makino Denzō's grandfather (*JS*: 55).

87. The verse refers to *Kokinshū* 3: 139 (see *JS* no. 66).

88. Deutzia, *unohana* 卯の花, is associated with the fourth month, *uzuki* 卯月, in which it blooms.

89. Utsuyama 鵜津山 (now 宇津山) Castle, in Iride 入出, Kosai 湖西 City, Shizuoka Prefecture, stood on a peninsula on the west coast of Lake Hamana, near the border of Mikawa and Tōtōmi Provinces. It is not to be confused with Utsunoyama near Sōchō's cottage in Mariko. It was probably begun in 1506 when Ujichika was advancing into Mikawa. The castle was enlarged between 1521 and 1527, and the remains of two compounds may still be seen. For the history of this castle, see Matsumoto 1980.

90. Horie 堀江 Castle was located in Kanzanjichō 館山寺町, Hamamatsu City. Hamana 浜名 Castle was located in Mikkabichō 三ヶ日町, Inasa 引佐 District. Osakabe 刑部 Castle was located in Kanasashi 金指, Inasachō 引佐町, Inasa District.

91. Nagaike Kurōzaemonnojō Chikayoshi 長池九郎左衛門尉親能 was an Imagawa vassal.

92. The wording suggests that a hundred verses were composed but that Sōchō stayed only for the first round.

93. *Ise monogatari* (83–84):

watatsumi no	The God of the Sea
kazashi ni sasu to	did not begrudge giving
iwau mo mo	you, my good lords,
kimi ga tame ni wa	this sea plant that he treasures
oshimazarikeri	as a garland for his hair.

94. Floating seaweed (*ukimiru*, lit., floating sea pine) that washed up on the shore ornaments the pines, celebratory symbols of longevity, in a manner complementary to the way the breakers garland the ocean in the hokku. *Ukimiru* responds particularly closely to the *iwau mo* (seaweed he treasures) of the foundation poem. Moreover, the word *ukimiru* is used earlier in the *Ise monogatari* episode from which the foundation poem is taken: "The next day the girls of the house went out and gathered floating seaweed carried in by the waves, and they brought it back inside."

95. See *JS*: 97, where Sōchō writes Hikuma.

96. Lord Rokurō was Horikoshi Ujinobu (*JS*: 97), who resided in the Mitsuke, capital of Tōtōmi. The nature of Sōchō's request is unknown.

97. See *JS*: 7.

98. For Sayo no [naka]yama, see *JS*: 7; for Sugihara Iganokami (Takamori), see *JS*: 54.

Notes to Book Two (1527), Pages 152–53

99. For Kanaya, see *JS*: 91.
100. The foundation poem is *Gosenshū* 9: 507, by Minamoto Muneyuki:

Sent when he had finally become intimate with someone and then was forced to conceal the affair and could not see her:

azumaji no	Like Between Mountain in the east,
saya no nakayama	Saya no nakayama,
nakanaka ni	after meeting then being left
aimite nochi zo	betwixt and between,
wabishikarikeru	my pain is all the greater.

This is in turn based on *Kokinshu* 12: 594 (*JS*: 265, n. 14). Sōchō reverts here to Sayo no nakayama (cf. *JS* no. 1) despite his conclusion that Sayo no nagayama is etymologically correct and his use of that reading in *JS* no. 334. He avoids the question entirely in the preface to the poem, where he calls it simply Sayonoyama.

101. This too is based on *Shinkokinshū* 10: 987, by Saigyō (*JS*: 192, n. 2).
102. Ōigawa river formed the boundary between Tōtōmi and Suruga Provinces; Fujieda 藤枝 is the modern city of the same name in Shizuoka Prefecture.
103. Sōchō is referring to Ariwara Narihira's journey to the east in *Ise monogatari* (21–23) (*JS*: 262, n. 132).
104. Bōshū 房州 refers to Ihara Awanokami (*JS*: 130). The identity of Zushū is unclear; Shimazu (1975: 117) identifies him as Takeda Motomitsu, who was defeated in battle at Katsuragawa river on 1527:2:12–13. Motomitsu was not killed in that encounter, however, and lived until 1551.
105. For Kiyomi Gate, see *JS*: 215, n. 4.
106. For Okitsu Hikokurō, see *JS*: 77.
107. Sōchō assumes that his letter of introduction was ineffective, and he directs his pique in the verse toward Seikenji.
108. This was sent to Shōzōbō (*JS*: 43).
109. Cf. *JS* no. 365. The poem plays on an alternate name for the cuckoo, *fujoki* 不如帰 (lit., nothing like returning home), taken from onomatopoeia for its call. Moreover, the old *kana* orthography for the name, ふじよき, begins with "fu-ji." *Ne* (mount) is a homonym for the cuckoo's call. The cuckoo may signify Shōzōbō, who returned home to Miidera after accompanying Sōchō at least as far as Atsuta Shrine and who may or may not have seen Mount Fuji in Suruga. But it may also signify Sōchō, for whom Suruga is home.
110. For Matsudaira Ōinosuke (Tadasada), see *JS*: 98. "Blind master" translates *kōtō* 勾当, an official rank for those in vocations for the blind; it was below *kengyō* 検校 (blind expert) and above *zatō* 座当 (blind attendant) (see *JS*: 126). The men Sōchō assisted may have been traveling chanters of *Heike monogatari* (*Heikyoku*).

111. Sonjō Kōtōbō 存城匂当坊 was a biwa musician of the Yasakagata 八坂方 School, founded by Jōgen 城玄. He was probably the blind master mentioned earlier.

112. The poet is establishing a contrast between the high reputation of Mount Fuji (or according to Shimazu 1975: 128–29, of Sōchō himself) and the poverty-stricken reality of the poet's actual straitened circumstances.

113. The verse is a reference to *Kokinshū* 18: 982 (see *JS* no. 125).

114. Iwaki Minbunotaifu Yoshitaka 岩城民部大輔由隆 (d. 1542) was lord of Iwaki-daira Castle in what is now Fukushima Prefecture. Michinoku 陸奥, which corresponds to the area of Fukushima, Miyagi, Iwate, and Aomori Prefectures, began at the Shirakawa and Nakoso Gates; Sōchō's unsuccessful attempt to visit the Shirakawa Gate is documented in his earlier travel diary, *Azumaji no tsuto*.

115. Taishō 泰昭, son of Taijin (*JS*: 81), was affiliated with the Shōren'in imperial temple (*monzeki*). He journeyed to the northern provinces in 1525 and composed an extant hundred-verse sequence (Daiei 5 [1525]:9:21 *Nanibito hyakuin*) with Sōchō, Asahina Yasumochi, Asahina Tokishige, and others in Suruga. He reached Shirakawa in 1526, passed the New Year with Iwaki Yoshitaka, and returned to Suruga.

116. Iwaki, site of the Shirakawa Gate and Yoshitaka's residence, is homophonous with "rocks and trees." Sōchō mentions corresponding with Yoshitaka in *Sōchō nikki* (*SN*: 153) as well:

> I have corresponded with Iwaki Minbunotaifu of Michinoku these ten years and more. Three letters this spring alone. I had long been planning to visit him during the summer but was not able to do so. In my response to his request for a hokku, I composed this in the conviction that I would visit in the autumn:

seki koen	I plan to pass
aramashi ya kono	through the gate this year
aki no kaze	with the autumn wind.

> He wrote back that he would send an escort if I went.

The foundation poem for the *Sōchō nikki* poem is *Goshūishū* 9: 518, by Nōin:

miyako o ba	Though I set out
kasumi to tomo ni	from the Imperial City
tachishikado	in the springtime haze,
akikaze zo fuku	the wind of autumn now blows
shirakawa no seki	at Shirakawa Gate.

117. Sōchō may have had in mind here *Shinkokinshū* 1: 38, by Fujiwara Teika:

haru no yo no	A night in springtime
yume no ukihashi	when the floating bridge of dreams
todae shite	has come asunder,

mine ni wakaruru and the trailing clouds in the sky
yokogumo no sora part from the mountain peak.

118. Sōchō implies *suzumushi* (bell crickets) by *suzu* in line two and *mushi* in line five (cf. *JS* nos. 69 and 256).

119. I have emended "Chōkanji" 長閑寺 in the Shōkōkan ms. (Shimazu 1975: 130), which is unknown, to the orthographically similar Chōrakuji (*JS*: 82) on the basis of the Saiokuji ms.

120. Sōchō responds to the two lines of Chinese verse with one waka here, not two (cf. *JS*: nos. 490–93).

121. The benevolence and love referred to here are those of the late Ujichika. The fifth character in the verse is problematic; there are several manuscript variants, and there is a lacuna in place of the character in the *GSRJ* ms. (320). The version here follows the Shōkōkan ms. (Shimazu 1975: 130), though it seems to be incorrect, as it is the only character having the wrong rhyme for regulated verse (it is an oblique tone, whereas it should be a level one).

122. The verse relates to Su Dongpo's line, "Willows are green, blossoms red; this is their true appearance." A well-known expression in the medieval period, it was used in a Zen context to mean that all things reveal their true nature of themselves. The verse is used here to suggest that the character of Ujichika was manifest naturally. Sōchō responds to the allusion in his verse. See Okami 1951: 21.

123. Nakamikado Nobuhide 中御門宣秀 (1469–1531) was the son of the courtier literatus Nakamikado Nobutane and the elder brother of Ujichika's wife Jukei, mother of Imagawa Ujiteru. He resided in Sunpu from 1527:4:23 to 1529:4:26. To commemorate the anniversary of the death of his brother-in-law Ujichika, Nobuhide sponsored a waka sequence involving a group of poets, each of whose verses was to begin with a different character in the *iroha* syllabary. "Mountain Dwelling" applies to both of Sōchō's poems.

124. For Ujichika, the Pure Land too will be a kind of rebirth, but an estimable one. Sōchō alludes to *Kokinshū* 8: 404 (*JS*: 240, n. 42).

125. Crossing the mountain guarded by the dragon god, one reaches the Pure Land.

126. The foundation poem is *Kokinshū* 11: 489 (*JS*: 237, n. 24).

127. I have emended *nami yori* in the Shōkōkan ms. (Shimazu 1975: 131) on the basis of *Sōchō michi no ki* (265). The way of Shikishima is the way of poetry; pines and cranes are standard symbols of longevity.

128. No note survives.

129. The poem borrows phraseology from *Man'yōshū* 5: 813, by Yamanoe Okura: *kakemaku mo / aya ni kashikoshi* (so awesome / to put it into words).

130. The poem is only slightly unorthodox in its use of *aihate*, a colloquial expression for death, which pivots with *ai* (to meet).

131. The foundation poem is *Kokinshū* 14: 694:

> miyagino no
> motoara no kohagi
> tsuyu o omomi
> kaze o matsu goto
> kimi o koso mate
>
> Like sparse branches
> of bush clover on Miyagi Plain
> that await the wind
> because of their burden of dewdrops,
> just so do I wait for you.

Note also *Kokinshū* 19: 1014, by Fujiwara Kanesuke (a haikai verse):

Composed on the sixth of the seventh month, awaiting the Festival of the Weaver Maid:

> itsushika to
> matagu kokoro o
> hagi ni agete
> ama no kawara o
> kyō ya wataranu
>
> Unable to wait
> in his anticipation,
> has he rolled his robe
> above his shins and crossed
> the River of Heaven today?

132. The foundation poem is *Kokinshū* 15: 771, by Bishop Henjō:

> ima kon to
> iite wakareshi
> ashita yori
> omoikurashi no
> ne o nomi zo naki
>
> Since morning,
> when he parted from me,
> saying he would soon be back,
> I have spent the day in longing,
> crying with the cicalas.

"Cicala" translates *higurashi*, a type of cicada.

133. *Nadeshiko* (baby's breath or wild pink, *Dianthus superbus*) is written with the characters for "caressed child," 撫子.

134. Sōchō is referring to his journey to Echizen in 1523 (*JS*: 31–33).

135. Sōchō returned to Suruga in the sixth month of 1524 (*JS*: 55), but he did not take up residence in his cottage in Mariko until early 1526 (the twenty-sixth of the twelfth month of Daiei 5) (*JS*: 86–88). He mentions work done on the house at that time and on his next visit there on the ninth and tenth of the second month, 1526 (*JS*: 90, 95–96).

136. Sōchō employs a kakekotoba pivoting between *mizu wa kumu* (ladle water) and *mizuwakumu made* (more normally *mizuhagumu made*, lit., to a great age). Cf. *Yamato monogatari* (362):

> mubatama no
> waga kurokami wa
> shirakawa no
> mizu wa kumu made
> narinikeru kana
>
> My hair,
> once black as leopard-flower seeds,
> has turned white
> as White River, where I ladle water
> now in my great age.

Cf. also *Goshūishū* 19: 1116, by Minamoto Shigeyuki 源重之:

> toshi o hete
> sumeru izumi ni
> kage mireba
> mizu wa kumu made
> oi zo shinikeru

> Looking at myself
> in the water I ladle
> from the clear spring
> by which I have lived over the years,
> I find I have grown old.

137. Sōchō refers to the spirits of the dead who departed after the Festival of the Dead, Urabon (see *JS*: 250, n. 18).

138. *Mabikina* are the greens plucked to thin a vegetable patch. They are used for food as well. The poem includes a kakekotoba pivoting between *oi no nochi* (old age) and *nochimaki no tane* (seeds sown late in the year).

139. Tsurusaki (1978) notes that incorporating a dry field into a garden was a specific gardening technique related to the late Muromachi aesthetic ideal of wabi.

140. There is a pun on *oi* (listen [lit., follow] / old).

141. The foundation poem is *Shinkokinshū* 16: 1562, by Saigyō:

> kumo kakaru
> tōyamabata no
> aki sareba
> omoiyaru dani
> kanashiki mono o

> The coming of autumn
> to distant fields in mountains
> cloaked with clouds—
> simply the thought of it
> fills me with melancholy!

142. The poem refers to the theme of evanescence. All the spring flowers have fallen, and now the autumn morning glory is the last to blossom, but it too lasts only the morning. Sōgi's life too was just as dream-like as those of the flowers (cf. *JS* no. 378).

143. This verse too relates to *Shinkokinshū* 16: 1562 (*JS*: 309, n. 141).

144. This is a rare example of an isolated fourteen-syllable verse (*shimo no ku*). It involves a pun on *mame* (bean) and *mamemameshi* (hard at work or energetic ["full of beans"]).

145. Sōchō puns on *asana* (morning greens) and *asana asana* (each morning).

146. *Ishibushi* 石伏 is the name of a fish of the *Gobiidae* genus and is related to the *ukigori* 浮吾里 (gobi), a very common fresh-water fish. It is also sometimes known as *kajika* 鰍, though the name *kajika* is more properly used in reference to the bullhead, of the *Cottidae* genus. But *kajika* 河鹿 is also the name of a singing frog, *Polypedates buergeri*. That is obviously what Sōchō means here. *Ishibushi* would thus seem also to be a type of frog, and Harada (1979: 375–76) thinks *ishibushi kajika* is simply a compound noun for a single type of frog. *Korokoro to* applies both to the sound of the water at the beginning of the poem and the sound of the frogs at the end.

147. There is a kakekotoba pivoting between *te o nomi utsu* (just clap) and *Utsunoyama*.

148. Cf. *JS* no. 65.

149. This refers to a *hongyō waka* 品経和歌, in which poets compose verses on topics taken from the twenty-eight chapters of the *Lotus Sutra*. For Imagawa Noritada, see *JS*: 12, 174.

150. This is the same poem as *JS* no. 575; Sōchō is writing long after the fact and seems disorganized here.

151. There is a kakekotoba pivoting between *harau mo oshi* (a pity they brush it off) and *oshi no uwage* (mandarin duck feathers).

152. Sōchō is writing more than a year later. Rinsen'an 臨川庵 may be the same "residence by the river" mentioned on *JS*: 62. This passage is in epistolary style (*sōrōbun*) and would seem to be a letter, but possibly to someone other than Yasumochi, the recipient of the letter that immediately follows this section. Note that Sōchō is being very careful about dates here, perhaps in self-exoneration. Nakagawa (1981: 1326) thinks that the courier from Sunpu carrying the news of Ujichika's death to Sōchō did not even leave Suruga until after the funeral was over. If Nakagawa is correct, then the Imagawa would not have blamed Sōchō for not having attended the funeral ceremony.

153. Asahina Yasumochi and Asahina Tokishige probably had the same wet nurse or nurses (*menoto*) as Imagawa Ujichika and thus shared lifelong ties to him.

154. Cf. the similar project for the thirty-third death anniversary of Imagawa Ryōshun (*JS*: 160–61, 173). Sōgi had requested the same favor from Sanetaka on the death of Uesugi Sadamasa 上杉定昌 in 1488 (Sanetaka recorded the request in an entry for 1488:4:11 in *Sanetakakōki* [2: 57]).

155. The son of Nakamikado Nobuhide (*JS*: 156) was Nakamikado Nobutsuna 中御門宣綱 (1511–c. 1568); he married Ujichika's daughter (see Owada 1981a: 1219–20).

156. See *JS*: 108.

157. Cf. *JS*: 81, where Sōchō says that he presented Ujiteru with five books of lecture notes and eight sheets of oral teachings. This may be different material, a misrecollection, or a copyist's error.

158. This may be the interview that occurs at the end of Book One of the journal (*JS*: 90).

159. *Utsunoyama no ki* relates that Sōchō was sent by Ujichika to Takeda Nobutora in Kai Province to parley for the release of a besieged Imagawa army in 1517. He also was an intermediary between the Imagawa and people in the capital.

160. This letter and the passage preceding it may have been written separately as indicated here, but there is a chance that they originally formed a single letter, with poem *JS* no. 587 and its one-sentence preface inserted incorrectly later. The poem and its preface appear alone in *Sōchō michi no ki*, and the poem, without the preface, is also recorded in *Sōchō nikki* as having been sent to a certain Kiinokami, otherwise unidentified. If the poem and its preface were written in *The Journal of Sōchō* as they now appear, it seems likely from the context that the poem was affixed to the head of the letter after it was finished, as a postscript (*ottegaki*), and that the preface was added in explanation when

the letter was copied into the journal. If the poem and preface were later incorrectly inserted into what was originally a single letter, it is then unclear who the letter's recipient was, since Yasumochi is referred to in the body of the document with his full office title Sakyōnosuke, making it unlikely it was addressed to him directly.

161. This waka appears in different forms in *Sōchō shuki* (the *Shōkōkan* ms., Shimazu 1975: 136), *Sōchō nikki* (the *Kunaichō Shoryōbu* ms., entitled *Saiokuken Sōchō nikki*, Shimazu 1975: 154), the *Gunsho ruijū* text of *Sōchō shuki* (323), and the *Zoku gunsho ruijū* text of *Sōchō nikki* (1259). The last is the clearest and most regular metrically, and I have accordingly substituted it for the garbled and irregular version in the Shōkōkan base text.

162. I have emended *kako* (past) in the Shōkōkan ms. (Shimazu 1975: 136) to the orthographically similar *kagen* (falsehood) on the basis of the *GSRJ* ms. (323).

163. This is only one interpretation of a document fraught with ambiguity; Sōchō may be pleading his own case here.

164. This may refer to a medicinal treatment in which Sōchō was covered with a heated mixture of brine and sand. Okitsu Saemonnojō Moritsuna 興津左衛門尉盛綱 died the following year, and Sōchō composed a solo hundred-verse sequence in his memory, *Sōchō dokugin Daiei 8 [1528]:4:12 myōgō hyakuin* (A Hundred-Verse Solo Sequence by Sōchō on the Holy Name, Composed on the Twelfth Day of the Fourth Month of the Eighth Year of Daiei). Each of the hundred verses begins with a syllable of the Holy Name.

165. Sōchō's visit to Atami may mean that in view of the changing political climate in Suruga, he was ingratiating himself with the Hōjō of Sagami Province, where Atami is located.

166. The old friend probably was Iwaki Yoshitaka (*JS*: 154–55).

167. The Hall of No Renunciation (Fushain 不捨院) appears to have been close to Okitsu Moritsuna's residence.

168. I have emended *meguru* in the Shōkōkan ms. (Shimazu 1975: 137) to *mezuru* on the basis of the *SKGSRJ* ms. (699). This is a Zen poem referring to re-renunciation, *saishukke*. Sōchō is already a monk, but here he is considering cutting his last secular ties.

169. I have emended *kikiarashitsuru* in the Shōkōkan ms. (Shimazu 1975: 138) to *kikikashitsuru* on the basis on the *SKGSRJ* ms. (699). The foundation poem is *Goshūishū* 6: 399, by Ōe Kin'yori:

sugi no ita o	Upon the rough-laid
mabara ni fukeru	cedar shakes of the roof
neya no ue ni	of my bed chamber,
odoroku bakari	hail enough to have woken me
arare fururashi	seems to be falling.

170. Sōchō seems to have forgotten that he already introduced Nakamikado Nobuhide in an entry several months earlier in connection with a memorial poem sequence for Ujichika in Suruga (*JS*: 156).

171. Socho puns on the location of his lodgings (Okitsu) and *okiitsutsu* (sitting).

172. I have emended *te no uchi wa* in the Shōkōkan ms. (Shimazu 1975: 138) to the orthographically similar *toshi no uchi wa* on the basis of the *SKGSRJ* ms. (699).

173. The verse is based on *Shinkokinshū* 3: 259, by Gondainagon [Minamoto] Michiteru:

On a screen painting at Saishō Shitennōin of the Kiyomi Gate:

kiyomigata	At Kiyomi Strand
tsuki wa tsurenaki	the moon lingers
ama no to o	in the heavens,
matade mo shiramu	while without waiting for it to set
nami no ue kana	the sky grows light above the waves.

The translation of the *Shinkokinshū* poem follows the interpretation of Tanaka and Akase (1992: 90) and Ishida (1960: 128). Kubota Jun (1979, 2: 101) believes that the waves grow white without waiting for the sky to grow light. Kubota Utsubo (1964, 1: 244) and Minemura (1974: 106–7) hold that the scene depicts a short summer night in which the sky begins to grow light without waiting for the late moon to appear.

174. The chief assistant priest (*ichi no negi* 一彌宜, cf. suffragan) was in charge of ten assistants who served under the head priest (*daigūji* 大宮司) and the assistant head priest (*shōgūji* 小宮司). The chief assistant priest at the time was Arakida Morikane 荒木田守兼 (d. 1541). He was preceded at that post by Arakida Moritoki 荒木田守晨 (d. 1516), elder brother of Arakida Moritake, author of the famous early haikai sequence *Moritake senku*. Morikane, Moritoki, and Moritake all joined with Sōchō, Sōboku, and others in composing Eishō 13 [1516]:7:8 *Nanibito hyakuin* (A Hundred-Verse Sequence Entitled "A Kind of Person").

175. See *JS*: 19–20.

176. The foundation poem is *Sankashū* no. 77, by Saigyō (*JS*: 214–25, n. 157).

177. Sōchō refers both to the length of a wakeful night and also to the wait before death and rebirth.

178. Chōzenji 長善寺 is a Ji-sect temple in Shizuoka City.

179. Yoshikawa Jirōzaemon Yorishige 吉川次郎左衛門頼茂 is otherwise unknown. This is another example of a tragic anecdote of a person with no source of support. Stories of stepmother abuse (*mamako ijime*) figure prominently in the medieval period, e.g., *Shintokumaru* and *Hachikazuki*.

180. This refers to an Imagawa foray into Kai in 1521, the reason for which is unknown. Mizaki (1983: 128) suspects it may have been undertaken in support of other movements by Hōjō Sōun's son, Ujitsuna. Ujichika may also have been attempting to exploit local warriors (kokujin) in Kai, who were opposing the daimyō of that province, Takeda Nobutora. The invasion was led by Fukushima (read Kushima in Yamamoto and Owada 1984) Masanari 福島正成, and after fighting in the area of Iidagawara 飯田河原

(near Kōfu 甲府) the Imagawa forces were defeated by Nobutora on 1521:11:22–23 at Kamijōgawara 上条河原 (in Shikishimachō 敷島町, Nakakoma 中巨摩 District) with a loss of six hundred men. On the Kamijōgawara battle, see Sakamoto 1988. Yorishige was "neither with master nor without" perhaps because his affiliations in Awa (Tokushima Prefecture) were ineffectual but not broken, and he was not a formal retainer of the Imagawa.

181. Tōgorō 藤五郎 is identified in the Shōkōkan ms. (Shimazu 1975: 140) as having later become the adopted son of Ohara Hyōgonokami Takachika 小原兵庫頭高親.

182. Shionoyama (cf. *JS* no. 210) and Sashiidenoiso 差出の磯 (also Sashidenoiso) are utamakura in Kai Province. Cf. *Kokinshū* 7: 345:

shionoyama	The plovers that dwell
sashidenoiso ni	on Sashide Strand
sumu chidori	by Mount Shio
kimi ga miyo o ba	cry "May His Majesty's reign
yachiyo to zo naku	endure eight thousand ages!"

The poem is based on the fact that *chiyo* (thousand ages) is a homonym for the sound of the plover's cry.

183. For Taishō, see *JS*: 154.

184. Mount Tsukuba, the legendary site of the birth of the linked-verse art, is located in Ibaraki Prefecture.

185. Shimazu (1975: 140) suspects that Taiken 泰賢 may have been Taishō's younger brother.

186. Shimazu (1975: 140) suggests that Ohara Hyōgonokami Takachika 小原兵庫守 嵩親 (written both 高親 and 嵩親 in the *SKGSRJ* ms.) may be the same person as Ohara Chikataka 小原親高 (*JS*: 56), but Matsumoto Masako (1980: 105) identifies the latter as Ohara *Bizennokami* 備前守 Chikataka in a list of Asahina retainers, making it less likely that they are the same individual.

187. This is an auspicious verse in which Sōchō looks forward to another meeting next spring, when his visitors now about to leave will tell him of the cherry blossoms at Shirakawa in the capital.

188. The implication of the waki verse is that Taishō and Sōchō have enjoyed a long acquaintance.

189. The verse is *Shinkokinshū* 16: 1456, by Fujiwara Masatsune 藤原雅経. It bears this preface:

> A cherry tree had long stood by the kickball [*kemari*] field at Saishōji. Masatsune heard that it had been blown over in a storm, so old had it grown, and he ordered his men to plant another in its place. On going to see the spot, he was struck by how long the old tree had stood there, until the end of that spring, and he composed the following verse.

Saishōji 最勝寺 temple is located in Shirakawa, Higashiyama Ward, Kyoto. An alternate translation, interpreting the kakekotoba on Shirakawa as the negative *shirazu* rather than the conjectural *shiramu*, would read "Long a friend it was—how could I not have known that this would be the last spring I would see it, the shade beneath its Shirakawa blossoms?"

190. The foundation poem is *Sankashū* no. 77, by Saigyō (*JS*: 214-15, n. 157).

191. The text is vague here; possibly the émigré courtier Nobuhide is expressing his desire to return to the capital, his home, as Taishō is doing. The geese fly in that direction in winter.

192. The poem refers to an episode in the Former Han dynasty, when Su Wu 蘇武, captured by the Xiongnu, sent a letter back to the capital attached to the leg of a goose. Sōchō used a related phrase in a link included in *Shinsen tsukubashū* (16: 3090):

kari no tsute ni mo	I found consolation
nagusaminikeri	in even a goose-borne missive.
hitasura ni	Could one live so far
miyako tōku wa	from the capital
sumareme ya	without having second thoughts?
	Sōchō

193. Bōjō Toshina 坊城俊名 (d. 1540), a Provisional Middle Counselor of the Senior Second Rank, was related to the Nakamikado family. He was apparently in Suruga at this time.

194. Sōchō's remarks are evidently in part self-deprecating, as he nevertheless presented the branch as a gift.

195. The foregoing passage on misunderstandings between people is itself extremely elliptical and ambiguous. It may refer to the events surrounding Jukei's regency for Ujiteru after the death of Ujichika.

"Katsu! Katsu!" is a formulaic Zen expression shouted to indicate feelings unexpressible in words. Sōchō may have conducted a ritual in which he sat in front of a paper on which he had written his grievances and then mentally consigned each grievance to the flames, thus ridding himself of them. The *GSRJ* ms. gives *yoso ni shiru chō* (one . . . knows the other's thoughts). The poem is not included in *Sōchō michi no ki*, the version of the journal that contains only the waka poetry in the journal, perhaps because of the verse's intrinsic difficulties.

196. This too is a vague poem. Kaneko believes Shimazu's *mukomuko* should instead be read *mugomugo*, in the sense of "endlessly" (personal communication).

197. *Kokinshū* 1: 7 (*JS*: 294, n. 8).

198. I have emended *kikiaenu yuki mo* in the Shōkōkan ms. (Shimazu 1975: 143) on the basis of the *GSRJ* ms. (327).

Note to Book Two (1527), Page 70

199. The poem relates to *Goshūishū* 20: 1163, by Saishu Sukechika:

In response to an oracle from Ise:

ōji chichi	For three generations,
mumago sukechika	from grandfather to father
miyo made ni	to grandson Sukechika,
itadakimatsuru	we have received the blessings
suberaōnkami	of the Great Sun Goddess.

Cf. *JS* no. 333.

Bibliography

Abbreviations are listed on p. xi. Unless otherwise noted, all publishers are located in Tokyo. Multiple works by modern authors are listed chronologically, but multiple works by premodern authors appear alphabetically. Renga sequences are listed alphabetically, but chronologically within each era name. For the reader's convenience, alternate published manuscripts of select titles are provided in addition to the specific versions used in this text (the latter are in each case cited first). Rare, unprinted manuscripts are cited together with the published work that makes reference to them.

Abe Takeshi 阿部猛, and Nishimura Keiko 西村圭子. 1990. *Sengoku jinmei jiten* 戦国人名事典. Shin Jinbutsu Ōraisha.

Akimoto Taiji 秋本太二. 1984. "Imagawa Ujichika to Tōtōmi no keiryaku" 今川氏親の遠江の経略. In Arimitsu 1984: 113–35.

Anrakuan Sakuden 安楽庵策伝. 1986. *Seisuishō* 醒睡笑. Ed. Suzuki Tōzō 鈴木棠三. 2 vols. Iwanami Bunko.

Arai Eizō 新井英蔵. 1976. "Sakuramachi Jōkō chokufū Manjuinzō *Kokin denju* hitohako" 桜町上皇勅封曼殊院蔵古今伝授一箱. *Kokugo kokubun* 45.7: 43–56.

Araki Yoshio 荒木良雄. 1947. *Chūsei Nihon no shomin bungaku* 中世日本の庶民文学. Osaka: Shin Nihon Tosho.

Arakida Morihira 荒木田守平, comp. *Nikonshū* 二根集. Ed. Okuno Jun'ichi 奥野純一. Vols. 335 and 343 of *KB*.

Arakida Moritake 荒木田守武. *Moritake senku* 守武千句. See Iida 1977.

Arimitsu Yūgaku 有光有学, ed. 1984. *Imagawashi no kenkyū* 今川氏の研究. Vol. 11 of Nagahara 1983–85.

Arntzen, Sonja, trans. 1986. *Ikkyū and the Crazy Cloud Anthology*. University of Tokyo Press.

Asakura Norikage 朝倉教景. 1972. *Asakura Sōteki waki* 朝倉宗滴話記. In Yoshida Yutaka 吉田豊, ed., *Buke no kakun* 武家の家訓, pp. 107–40. Tokuma Shoten.

Asukai Masayasu 飛鳥井雅康. *Fuji rekiranki* 富士歴覧記. In *GSRJ* 18: 621–26.

Aya no tsuzumi 綾鼓. In Vol. 2 of Koyama, Satō, and Satō 1973–75: 200–9.

Bibliography

Berry, Mary Elizabeth. 1994. *The Culture of Civil War in Kyoto*. Berkeley: University of California Press.

Biyanlu 碧巖録. See Cleary and Cleary 1992.

Blue Cliff Record, The. See Cleary and Cleary 1992.

Bokusai 墨斎 (Motsurin Jōtō 没倫紹等). *The Chronicle of Ikkyū*. In Sanford 1981: 69–117.

Bontō 梵燈. *Bontōanshu hentōsho* 梵燈庵主返答書. In *ZGSRJ* 17b: 1041–55.

Botanka Shōhaku 牡丹花肖柏. See Shōhaku.

Brownlee, John. 1974. "*Jikkinshō*: A Miscellany of Ten Maxims." *Monumenta Nipponica* 29.2 (Summer): 121–61.

Carter, Steven D. 1983. *Three Poets at Yuyama*. Japan Research Monograph 4. Berkeley: Institute of East Asian Studies / Center for Japanese Studies, University of California.

———, trans. 1991. *Traditional Japanese Poetry: An Anthology*. Stanford: Stanford University Press.

———, ed. 1993. *Literary Patronage in Late Medieval Japan*. Michigan Papers in Japanese Studies. Ann Arbor: Center for Japanese Studies, The University of Michigan.

Cleary, Thomas, and J. C. Cleary, trans. 1992. *The Blue Cliff Record*. Boston: Shambala Publications.

Covell, Jon Carter, in collaboration with Abbot Sobin Yamada. 1980. *Unraveling Zen's Red Thread: Ikkyū's Controversial Way*. Elizabeth, N.J. and Seoul: Hollym International.

Dai Nihon shoga meika taikan 大日本書画名家大鑑. 1934. Ed. Araki Tadashi 荒木矩. 4 vols. Dai Nihon Shoga Meika Taikan Kankōkai.

Dokushi biyō 読史備要. 1978. Ed. Tōkyō Daigaku Shiryō Hensanjo. Kōdansha.

Eikyū hyakushū 永久百首. In *KT* 4: 248–63.

Etō Yasusada 江藤保定. 1967. *Sōgi no kenkyū* 宗祇の研究. Kazama Shobō.

Fūga wakashū 風雅和歌集. In *KT* 1: 554–99.

Fujiwara Teika 藤原定家. *Genji monogatari okuiri* 源氏物語奥入. In *GSRJ* 17: 479–512.

Fukuda Hideichi 福田秀一, and Herbert Plutschow. 1975. *Nihon kikō bungaku benran* 日本紀行文学便覧. Musashino Shoin.

Fukuda Hideichi et al., eds. 1990. *Chūsei nikki kikōshū* 中世日記紀行集. Vol. 51 of *SNKBT*.

Fukui Kyūzō 福井久蔵, ed. 1938. *Minase sangin hyōshaku* 水無瀬三吟評釈. Mizuho Shoin.

Furokuki. See *Imagawaki*.

Fusō shūyōshū 扶桑拾葉集. 1898. Ed. Tokugawa Mitsukuni 徳川光圀. 4 vols. Osaka: Shiyūkan.

Genji monogatari. 1964–75. Murasaki Shikibu. Ed. Tamagami Takuya 玉上琢彌. 10 vols. Kadokawa Shoten. See also Seidensticker 1976.

Genpei seisuiki 源平盛衰記. 1991. Eds. Ichiko Teiji 市古貞次 et al. Miyai Shoten, 1991.

Gessonsai Sōseki 月村斎宗碩. See Sōseki.

Gorai Shigeru 五来重. 1965. *Kōya hijiri* 高野聖. Kadokawa Shoten.

Gosen wakashū 後撰和歌集. In Kubota and Kawamura 1986: 55–122.

Goshūi wakashū 後拾遺和歌集. 1983. Ed. Fujimoto Kazue 藤本一恵. 4 vols. Kōdansha.

Gunsho ruijū 群書類従. 1959-60. Ed. Hanawa Hokiichi 塙保己一. 30 vols. Zoku Gunsho Ruijū Kanseikai.

Gyokuyō wakashū 玉葉和歌集. In *KT* 1: 421-81.

Hachikazuki 鉢かづき. 1974. In Ōshima Tatehiko 大島建彦, ed., *Otogizōshishū* 御伽草子集, pp. 76-109. Vol. 36 of *NKBZ*.

Haga Kōshirō 芳賀幸四郎. 1960. *Sanjōnishi Sanetaka* 三条西実隆. Yoshikawa Kōbunkan.

Hall, John Whitney, and Toyoda Takeshi, eds. 1977. *Japan in the Muromachi Age*. Berkeley: University of California Press.

Hara Katsurō 原勝郎. 1978. *Higashiyama jidai ni okeru ichishinshin no seikatsu* 東山時代に於ける一縉紳の生活. Kōdansha.

Harada Yoshioki 原田芳起. 1979. *Tankyū Nihon bungaku: chūko, chūsei hen* 探求日本文学——中古・中世編. Kazama Shobō.

Harrington, Lorraine F. 1985. "Regional Outposts of Muromachi Bakufu Rule: The Kantō and Kyushu." In Jeffrey P. Mass and William B. Hauser, eds., *The Bakufu in Japanese History*, pp. 66-98. Stanford: Stanford University Press.

Hashimoto Fumio 橋本不美男, and Takizawa Sadao 滝沢貞夫, eds. 1977. *Horikawain ontoki hyakushu waka to sono kenkyū: kochū, sakuin hen* 堀河院御時百首和歌とその研究——古注，索引編. Collated ed. (*kōhon* 校本). Kasama Shoin.

Heike monogatari. Eds. Takagi Ichinosuke 高木市之助 et al. Vols. 33-34 of *NKBT*. See also McCullough 1988.

Hoff, Frank, trans. 1982. *Like a Boat in a Storm: A Century of Song in Japan*. Hiroshima: Bunka Hyoron Publishing Co.

Hokekyō 法華経. 1976. Eds. Sakamoto Yukio 坂本幸雄 and Iwamoto Yutaka 岩本裕. 3 vols. Iwanami Shoten.

Hokku kikigaki 発句聞書. Comp. Senchō 仙澄. See Kaneko 1977a.

Horikawa hyakushu 堀川百首. In *KT* 4: 217-48.

Horton, H. Mack. 1993. "Saiokuken Sōchō and Imagawa Daimyō Patronage." In Carter 1993: 105-61.

Hosokawa ryōkeki 細川両家記. In *GSRJ* 20: 580-639.

Hurvitz, Leon, trans. 1976. *Scripture of the Lotus Blossom of the Fine Dharma (The Lotus Sutra)*. New York: Columbia University Press.

Hyakunin isshu 百人一首. Comp. Fujiwara Teika 藤原定家. In *KT* 5: 933-34. See also "One Hundred Poems by One Hundred Poets," in Carter 1991: 203-38.

Ichijō Kaneyoshi (or Kanera) 一条兼良. *Renju gappekishū* 連珠合璧集. In Kidō 1972-, 1: 25-202. See also *Renju gappekishū*, in *ZGSRJ* 17b: 1134-204.

Iida Shōichi 飯田正一, ed. 1977. *Moritake senkuchū* 守武千句注. Furukawa Shobō.

Iio (or Inō) Sōgi 飯尾宗祇. See Sōgi.

Ijichi Tetsuo 伊地知鉄男. 1952. "Sōchō no kushū *Kabekusa* sono ta ni tsuite no oboegaki" 宗長の句集『壁草』その他についての覚書. *Kokubungaku kenkyū* 7 (Oct.): 70-83.

———, ed. 1975. *Renga hyakuinshū*. Facsimiles of sequences in *Renga shūsho* 連歌集書 (Seikadō Bunko 靜嘉堂文庫). Kyūko Shoin.

Bibliography

———, ed. 1985. *Rengaronshū*. 2 vols. Iwanami Shoten.

Ijichi Tetsuo, Omote Akira 表章, and Kuriyama Riichi 栗山理一, eds. 1973. *Rengaronshū, nōgakuronshū, haironshū*. Vol. 51 of *NKBZ*.

Ikkyū Sōjun 一休宗純. 1976. *Kyōunshū, Kyōunshū shishū, Jikaishū* 狂雲集・狂雲詩集・自戒集. Ed. Nakamoto Tamaki 中本環. Vol. 5 of *Shinsen Nihon koten bunko*. Gendai Shichōsha. See also Arntzen 1986.

Ikkyūbanashi 一休咄. 1976. In vol. 3 of Mutō Sadao 武藤禎夫 and Oka Masahiko 岡雅彦, eds., *Hanashibon taikei* 噺本体系, pp. 3–62. Tōkyōdō.

Imagawa kafu 今川家譜. In *ZGSRJ* 21a: 141–60.

Imagawa Norimasa 今川範政, attrib. *Fuji goran nikki* 富士御覧日記. In Shirai 1976: 162–68.

———. *Genji monogatari teiyō* 源氏物語提要. 1978. Ed. Inaga Keiji 稲賀敬二. Vol. 2 of *Genji monogatari kochū shūsei*. 15 vols. Ōfūsha, 1978–84.

Imagawa Ryōshun 今川了俊. *Imagawajō* 今川状. In Ozawa 1985: 238–42.

Imagawaki 今川記. In *ZGSRJ* 21a: 216–51.

Imagawaki (*Furokuki* 富麓記). In *ZGSRJ* 21a: 161–215.

Inazawa Yoshiaki 稲沢好章. 1973. "*Sōchō shuki* ni miru renga sakusha no haikai shikō ni tsuite" 『宗長手記』にみる連歌作者の俳諧嗜好について. *Kokugo to kokubungaku* 50.12 (Dec.): 50–65.

Inō (or Iio) Sōgi 飯尾宗祇. See Sōgi.

Inoue Muneo 井上宗雄. 1987. *Chūsei kadanshi no kenkyū: Muromachi kōki* 中世歌壇史の研究・室町後期. Rev. ed. Meiji Shoin.

Inu tsukubashū. See *Shinsen inu tsukubashū*.

Ise monogatari. 1984. Ed. Ishida Jōji 石田穣二. Kadokawa Shoten. See also McCullough 1968.

Ishida Yoshisada 石田吉貞. 1960. *Shinkokin wakashū zenchūkai*. Yūseidō.

Ishii Susumu 石井進. 1974. "Uzumorete ita Sengoku no jōkamachi" 埋もれていた戦国の城下町. In Ishii, *Chūsei bushidan* 中世武士団, pp. 334–75. Vol. 12 of Kodama, Inoue, and Nagahara 1972–77.

Ishikawa Hiroshi 石川広. 1976. "*Sōchō shuki* no ni chimei oboegaki: Wakamatsu no ike, Kannabi no mori" 『宗長手記』の二地名覚書——若松の池・神無の森. *Renga haikai kenkyū* 51 (July): 28–33.

Itō Kei 伊藤敬. 1969. "Muromachi kōki uta shoshi: Sanetaka, Mototsuna, Naritsugu, Muneaki, Sōgi, Dōken" 室町後期歌書誌——実隆・基綱・済継・統秋・宗祇・道堅. *Tomakomai Kōgyō Kōkō Senmon Gakkō kiyō* 4 (March): 116–34.

Iwashita Noriyuki 岩下紀之. 1985. "*Oi no mimi* ni kansuru oboegaki" 『老耳』に関する覚え書. In Kaneko Kinjirō, ed., *Renga kenkyū no tenkai* 連歌研究の展開, pp. 303–28. Benseisha.

Iwashita Noriyuki, and Kishida Yoriko 岸田依子. 1978. "Honkoku Sōseki kaishō to Sōchō shōkushū shūsei" 翻刻宗碩回章と宗長小句集集成. In Ijichi Tetsuō, ed., *Chūsei bungaku: shiryō to ronkō* 中世文学——資料と論考, pp. 435–505. Kasama Shobō.

Jikkinshō: honbun to sakuin 十訓抄——本文と索引. 1982. Ed. Izumi Motohiro 泉基博. Kasama Shoin. See also Brownlee 1974.

Kamo no Chōmei. *Hōjōki* 方丈記. In Miki Sumitō 三木紀人, ed., *Hōjōki, Hosshinshū*, pp. 13-39. Vol. 5 of *SNKS*. See also "An Account of My Hut," in McCullough 1990: 379-92.

Kana mokuroku かな目録. In *Imagawaki (Furokuki)*, pp. 204-13. See also Matsudaira 1982 and Ozawa 1977.

Kanaoka Shūyū 金岡秀友. 1970. *Koji meisatsu jiten* 古寺名刹辞典. Tōkyōdō Shuppan.

Kaneko Kinjirō 金子金治郎. 1969. *Shinsen tsukubashū no kenkyū* 新撰菟玖波集の研究. Kazama Shobō.

——. 1971. "Renga sōshō no yukue" 連歌宗匠の行くえ. *Kokugakuin zasshi* 72.11 (Nov.): 104-16.

——. 1974. *Renga kochūshaku no kenkyū* 連歌古注釈の研究. Kadokawa Shoten.

——. 1976. *Sōgi tabi no ki shichū* 宗祇旅の記私注. Ōfūsha.

——. 1977a. "Hokku kikigaki" 発句聞書. In Kaneko 1977c: 10-46.

——. 1977b. *Rengashi Kensai den kō* 連歌師兼載伝考. Rev. ed. Ōfūsha.

——, ed. 1977c. *Renga to chūsei bungei*. Kadokawa Shoten.

——, ed. 1978-83. *Renga kichō bunken shūsei* 連歌貴重文献集成. 16 vols. Benseisha, 1978-83.

——, ed. 1979. *Renga kochūshakushū* 連歌古注釈集. Kadokawa Shoten.

——. 1985. *Sōgi meisaku hyakuin chūshaku* 宗祇名作百韻注釈. Ōfūsha.

——. 1993. "Sōgi and the Imperial House: One Model of Medieval Literary Patronage." Trans. H. Mack Horton. In Carter 1993: 63-93.

Kanginshū 閑吟集. In Usuda and Shinma 1976: 353-472. See also *The Kanginshu*, in Hoff 1982: 29-131.

Kansei chōshū shokafu 寛政重修諸家譜. 1964. Eds. Hayashi Jussai 林述斎 et al. Newly revised (*shintei* 新訂). Zoku Gunsho Ruijū Kanseikai.

Katagiri Yōichi 片桐洋一. 1983. *Utamakura utakotoba jiten* 歌枕歌ことば辞典. Kadokawa Shoten.

Katō, Eileen, trans. 1979. "Pilgrimage to Dazaifu: Sōgi's *Tsukushi no michi no ki*." *Monumenta Nipponica* 34.3 (autumn): 333-67.

Katsuranomiyabon sōsho 桂宮本叢書. 1949-62. Eds. Shiba Katsumori 芝葛盛 and Yamagishi Tokuhei 山岸徳平. 21 vols. Yōtokusha.

Kawai Masaharu 河合正治. 1985. *Chūsei buke shakai no kenkyū* 中世武家社会の研究. Yoshikawa Kōbunkan.

Keene, Donald, comp. and ed. 1955. *Anthology of Japanese Literature: From the Earliest Era to the Mid-Nineteenth Century*. 2 vols. New York: Grove Press.

——, trans. 1967. *Essays in Idleness: The Tsurezuregusa of Kenkō*. New York: Columbia University Press.

Bibliography

———. 1977. "The Comic Tradition in Renga." In Hall and Toyoda 1977: 241–77.
Kensai 兼載. *Kensai zōdan*. 兼載雑談. In *NKT* 5: 390–425.
Kidō Saizō 木藤才蔵. 1971–73. *Rengashi ronkō* 連歌史論考. 2 vols. Meiji Shoin.
———. 1972–. *Rengaronshū*. 4 vols. to date (vol. 1 co-edited with Shigematsu Hiromi 重松裕巳). Miyai Shoten.
———. 1984. *Chūsei bungaku shiron* 中世文学試論. Meiji Shoin.
Kimura Miyogo 木村三四五, and Iguchi Hisashi 井口壽, eds. 1988. *Chikuba kyōginshū, Shinsen inu tsukubashū* 竹馬狂吟集・新撰犬筑波集. Vol. 77 of *SNKS*.
Kin'yō wakashū 金葉和歌集. In Kubota and Kawamura 1986: 253–352.
Kishida Yoriko 岸田依子 et al., eds. 1985. Vol. 6 of *Senku rengashū* 千句連歌集. Vol. 467 of *KB*.
Kodama Kōta 児玉幸多, Inoue Mitsusada 井上光貞, and Nagahara Keiji, eds. 1972–77. *Nihon no rekishi*. Shōgakukan.
Kojiki 古事記. 1973. Ed. Ogihara Asao 荻原浅男. In Ogihara and Kōnosu Hayao 鴻巣隼雄, eds., *Kojiki, jōdai kayō* 古事記・上代歌謡, vol. 1 of *NKBZ*, pp. 1–367. See also Philippi 1969.
Koi no omoni 恋重荷. In vol. 1 of Yokomichi and Omote 1972: 324–30.
Kojima Noriyuki 小島憲之, and Arai Eizō, eds. 1989. *Kokin wakashū* 古今和歌集. Vol. 5 of *SNKBT*.
Kokin waka rokujō 古今和歌六帖. In *KT* 2: 193–255.
Kokin wakashū 古今和歌集. In Kubota and Kawamura 1986: 3–54. See also Kojima and Arai 1989 and McCullough 1985.
Kokka taikan 国歌大観. 1983–92. New ed. (*shinpen* 新編). Ed. Shinpen Kokka Taikan Henshū Iinkai. 10 vols. Kadokawa Shoten.
Kokusho sōmokuroku 国書総目録. 1963–76. Eds. Ichiko Teiji 市古貞次 et al. 9 vols. Iwanami Shoten.
Konparu Zenpō 金春禅鳳. 1986. *Zenpō zōdan* 禅鳳雑談. Ed. Kitagawa Tadahiko 北川忠彦. In Hayashiya Tatsusaburō 林屋辰三郎, ed., *Kodai chūsei geijutsuron*, pp. 479–509. Vol. 23 of *Nihon shisō taikei*.
Koten bunko 古典文庫. 1946–. 517 vols. to date.
Koyama Hiroshi 小山弘志, Satō Kikuo 佐藤喜久雄, and Satō Ken'ichirō 佐藤健一郎, eds. 1973–75. *Yōkyokushū* 謡曲集. Vols. 33–34 of *NKBZ*.
Kraft, Kenneth Lewis. 1992. *Eloquent Zen: Daitō and Early Japanese Zen*. Honolulu: University of Hawaii Press.
Kubo Tenzui 久保天随, Shaku Seitan 釈清潭, and Iwatare Noriyoshi 岩垂憲徳, eds. 1978. *So Tōba zenshishū* 蘇東坡全詩集. 6 vols. Seishinsha.
Kubota Jun 久保田淳, ed. 1976–77. *Shinkokin wakashū zenhyōshaku*. Kōdansha.
———, ed. 1979. *Shinkokin wakashū*. Vols. 24 and 30 of *SNKS*.
Kubota Jun, and Kawamura Teruo 川村晃生, eds. 1986. *Gappon Hachidaishū* 合本八代集. Miyai Shoten.

Kubota Utsubo 久保田空穂, ed. 1964. *Kanpon Shinkokin wakashū hyōshaku*. 3 vols. Tōkyōdō Shuppan.

Kumakura Isao. 1989. "Sen no Rikyū: Inquiries into His Life and Tea." Trans. Paul Varley. In Paul Varley and Kumakura Isao, eds., *Tea in Japan: Essays on the History of Chanoyu*, pp. 33–69. Honolulu: University of Hawaii Press.

Kurokawa Dōyū 黒川道祐. *Sōchō Kojiden* 宗長居士伝. In *ZZGSRJ* 3: 392–94.

Kurosawa Osamu 黒澤脩. 1977. "Zōzenjidono Kyōzan Jōki Daizenjōmon Imagawa Ujichika nenpyō" 増善寺殿喬山紹僖大禅定門今川氏親年表. In *SI* 2: 159–79.

Kyōka taikan 狂歌大観. 1983–85. Ed. Kyōka Taikan Kankōkai. 3 vols. Meiji Shoin.

Legge, James, trans. 1871. *The She King*. London: Trubner and Co.

Liuzu tanjing 六祖檀経. See Yampolsky 1967.

Lotus Sutra. See Hurvitz 1976 and *Hokekyō*.

Man'yōshū. 1974–75. Ed. Sakurai Mitsuru 桜井満. 3 vols. Ōbunsha.

Matsudaira Norimichi 松平乗道. 1982. *Imagawa kana mokuroku* 今川仮名目録. In *SI* 1: 36–48.

Matsumoto Masako 松本真子. 1980. "Utsunoyamajō no Asahinashi ni tsuite" 宇津山城の朝比奈氏について. In *SI* 5: 103–33.

Matsushita Shōkō 松下正広. See Shōkō.

McCullough, Helen C., trans. 1959. *The Taiheiki: A Chronicle of Medieval Japan*. New York: Columbia University Press.

———, trans. 1968. *Tales of Ise: Lyrical Episodes from Tenth-Century Japan*. Stanford: Stanford University Press.

———, trans. 1985. *Kokin Wakashū*. Stanford: Stanford University Press.

———, trans. 1988. *The Tale of the Heike*. Stanford: Stanford University Press.

McCullough, William H., and Helen Craig McCullough, trans. 1980. *A Tale of Flowering Fortunes*. 2 vols. Stanford: Stanford University Press.

Meidai waka zenshū 明題和歌全集. 1976. Ed. Mimura Terunori 三村晃功. Okayama: Fukutake Shoten.

Meikōawase 名香合. In *GSRJ* 19: 536–600.

Meitokuki 明徳記. 1985. In Koten Isan no Kai 古典遺産の会, ed., *Muromachi gunki sōran* 室町軍記総覧, pp. 250–66. Meiji Shoin.

Minegishi Sumio 峰岸純夫, ed. 1977. *Chihō bunka no shintenkai* 地方文化の新展開. Vol. 5 of *Chihō bunka no Nihonshi*. Bun'ichi Sōgō Shuppan.

Minemura Fumito 峰村文人, ed. 1974. *Shinkokin wakashū*. Vol. 26 of *NKBZ*.

Miner, Earl. 1979. *Japanese Linked Poetry*. Princeton: Princeton University Press.

Moriya Takeshi 守屋毅. 1984. *Nihon chūsei e no shiza* 日本中世への視座. Nihon Hōsō Shuppankai.

Morris, Ivan, trans. 1967. *The Pillow Book of Sei Shōnagon*. 2 vols. London: Oxford University Press.

Motsurin Jōtō. See Bokusai.

Bibliography

Murasaki Shikibu. *Genji monogatari*. See *Genji monogatari*.

Myōhōjiki 妙法寺記. 1967. In Shimizu Shigeo 清水茂夫 and Hattori Harunori 服部治則, eds., *Takeda shiryōshū* 武田史料集, pp. 5–63. Vol. 13 of *Sengoku shiryō sōsho*, second series (*dai ni ki* 第二期). Jinbutsu Ōraisha.

Nagahara Keiji 永原慶二. 1975. *Sengoku no dōran* 戦国の動乱. Vol. 14 of Kodama, Inoue, and Nagahara 1972–77.

―――, ed. 1983–85. *Sengoku daimyō ronshū*. 18 vols. Yoshikawa Kōbunkan.

Nagakura Chieo 長倉智恵雄. 1978. "Imagawa Yoshitada Fujin Kitagawadono ni tsuite" 今川義忠夫人北川殿について. In *SI* 3: 59–93.

Nagasaki Ken 長崎健 et al., eds. 1994. *Chūsei nikki kikōshū* 中世日記紀行集. Vol. 48 of *Shinpen Nihon koten bungaku zenshū*. Shōgakukan.

Nagoya kassenki 名古屋合戦記. In *ZGSRJ* 21a: 104–07.

Nakagawa Yoshio 中川芳雄. 1981. "Rengashi Sōchō. In Owada et al. 1981: 1269–1370.

Nakamoto Tamaki 中本環. 1967. "Ikkyū Sōjun to Saiokuken Sōchō." In *Renga to sono shūhen: Kaneko Kinjirō Hakase kanreki kinen ronbunshū* 連歌とその周辺―金子金治郎博士還暦記念論文集, pp. 254–71. Hiroshima: Hiroshima Chūsei Bungei Kenkyūkai.

Nihon kagaku taikei 日本歌学大系. 1956–63; *Bekkan*, 1958–86. Ed. Sasaki Nobutsuna 佐々木信綱. 9 vols. Plus *Bekkan*. Ed. Kyūsojin Hitaku 久曽神昇 (vol. 1 co-edited with Higuchi Yoshimaro 樋口芳麻呂). 8 vols. Kazama Shobō.

Nihon koten bungaku taikei. 1957–68. 102 vols. Iwanami Shoten.

Nihon koten bungaku zenshū. 1971–76. 51 vols. Shōgakukan.

Nihon koten zensho. 1953–. Asahi Shinbunsha.

Nihon shisō taikei 日本思想大系. 1970–82. 67 vols. Iwanami Shoten.

Ogi Sanae 小木早苗. "Imagawashi no Tōtōmi shihai" 今川氏の遠江支配. In *SI* 4: 119–45.

Okami Masao 岡見正雄. 1951. "Muromachigokoro" 室町ごころ. *Kokugo kokubun* (Nov.): 7–26.

Ōkubo Toshiaki 大久保俊昭. 1987. "Mikawa kokujin Saigōshi ni tsuite no kōsatsu: Imagawashi, Matsudairashi to no kanren ni oite" 三河国人西郷氏についての考察―今川氏・松平氏との関連において. In *SI* 10: 153–66.

Okuno Jun'ichi 奥野純一. 1975. *Ise Jingūkan renga no kenkyū* 伊勢神宮官連歌の研究. Nihon Gakujutsu Shinkōkai.

Okuno Takahiro 奥野高広. 1960. *Sengoku daimyō*. Hanawa Shoten.

―――. 1961. "Shoki no Odashi" 初期の織田氏. *Kokugakuin zasshi* 62.9 (Sept.): 149–62.

Ōshima Toshiko 大島俊子. 1962. "Sōchō nenpu" 宗長年譜. *Joshidai bungaku* 24 (Feb.): 38–54.

―――. 1963–64. "Sōchō no shūhen" 宗長の周辺. *Joshidai bungaku* 28 (Feb., 1963): 28–40; 32 (Feb., 1964): 29–33; 33 (May, 1964): 20–28; and 35 (Oct., 1964): 76–85.

Owada Tetsuo 小和田哲男. 1981a. *Sengoku bushō* 戦国武将. Chūōkōronsha.

―――. 1981b. "Shugo daimyō Imagawashi no hatten" 守護大名今川氏の発展. In Owada et al. 1981: 949–1057.

———. 1983. *Suruga Imagawa ichizoku* 駿河今川一族. Shin Jinbutsu Ōraisha.
———. 1984a. "Imagawa Ujichika to sono monjo" 今川氏親とその文書. In Arimitsu 1984: 94-112.
———. 1984b. *Sengoku kassen jiten* 戦国合戦事典. Sanseidō.
———. 1986. "Sengokuki no Tōtōmi Imagawashi (Horikoshishi)" 戦国期の遠江今川氏（堀越氏）. In *SI* 9: 79-98.
Owada Tetsuo et al. 1981. *Shizuokashi shi: genshi, kodai, chūsei* 静岡市史 — 原始・古代・中世. Shizuoka: Shizoka Shiyakusho.
Ozawa Seiichi 小沢誠一. 1977. "Imagawa kana mokuroku no kaidoku" 今川仮名目録の解読. In *SI* 1: 29-35.
Philippi, Donald L., trans. 1969. *Kojiki*. University of Tokyo Press.
Platform Sutra of the Sixth Patriarch, The. See Yampolsky 1967.
Plutschow, Herbert, and Fukuda Hideichi, trans. 1981. *Four Japanese Travel Diaries of the Middle Ages*. Cornell University East Asia Papers 25. Ithaca, New York: China-Japan Program, Cornell University.
Ramirez-Christensen, Esperanza. 1981. "The Essential Parameters of Linked Poetry." *Harvard Journal of Asiatic Studies* 41:2 (Dec.): 555-95.
———. 1983. "Shinkei: Poet-Priest of Medieval Japan." Diss. Harvard University.
———. 1994. *Heart's Flower: The Life and Poetry of Shinkei*. Stanford: Stanford University Press.
Reizei Tamemori 冷泉為守, attrib. *Kyōka sake hyakushu* 狂歌酒百首. In *Kyōka taikan* 1: 13-16.
Resshi 列子 (C: *Liezi*). 1976. Ed. Kobayashi Shinmei 小林信明. Vol. 22 of *Shinshaku kanbun taikei*.
Saigyō 西行. *Saigyō Shōninshū* 西行上人集. 1983. In Kubota Jun 久保田淳, ed., *Saigyō zenshū*, pp. 353-421. Nihon Koten Bungakkai.
———. *Sankashū* 山家集. 1982. Ed. Gotō Shigeo 後藤重郎. Vol. 49 of *SNKS*.
Saiokuken Sōchō 柴屋軒宗長. See Sōchō.
Sakamoto Tokuichi 坂本徳一. 1988. "Kamijōgawara no kassen" 上条河原の合戦. *Nihon kassen sōran* 日本合戦総覧. *Rekishi to tabi* 15.2: 202.
Saku Misao 佐久節, ed. 1978. *Haku Rakuten zenshishū* 白楽天全詩集. 4 vols. Seishinsha.
Sanetaka. See Sanjōnishi Sanetaka.
Sanford, James H. 1981. *Zen-Man Ikkyū*. Vol. 2 of Studies in World Religions. Chico, California: Scholars Press.
Sanjōnishi Sanetaka 三条西実隆. *Saishōsō* 再昌草. 1949-54. Vols. 11-13 of *KNS*.
———. *Sanetakakōki* 実隆公記. 1957-67. Ed. Shiba Katsumori 芝葛盛, Sanjōnishi Kin'masa 三条西公正, and Korezawa Kyōzō 是沢恭三 (vols. 1-6); Takahashi Ryūzō 高橋隆三 (vols. 7-13). 13 vols. Zoku Gunsho Ruijū Kanseikai.
Sansom, George. 1984. *A History of Japan, 1334-1615*. Rutland, Vt. and Tokyo: Tuttle.
Sato, Hiroaki, and Burton Watson. 1981. *From the Country of Eight Islands: An Anthology*

of Japanese Poetry. Introduction by Thomas Rimer. Garden City, NY: Anchor Press/Doubleday.

Satomura Jōha 里村紹巴. See Jōha.

Sawa Ryūken 佐和隆研 et al., eds. 1984. *Kyōto daijiten*. Kyōto: Tankōsha.

Seidensticker, Edward, trans. 1976. *The Tale of Genji*. 2 vols. Charles E. Tuttle Co.

Sei Shōnagon. 1974. *Makura no sōshi*. Eds. Matsuo Satoshi 松尾聰 and Nagai Kazuko 永井和子. Vol. 11 of *NKBZ*. See also Morris 1967.

Seishū shikeki 勢州四家記. In *GSRJ* 20: 640–55.

Seisuishō. See Anrakuan Sakuden 1986.

Seki Shichirō 関七郎. 1981. "Kakegawajō" 掛川城. In Seki et al., *Tōkai no shiro* 東海の城, pp. 216–26. Shōgakukan.

Semoto Hisao 瀬本久雄. 1983. "Reizei Tamekazu to Imagawa Ujiteru, Yoshimoto" 冷泉為和と今川氏輝・義元. In *SI* 7: 137–67.

Senda Ken 千田憲. 1964–69. "Sōchō, Sōseki ryōgin no *Daijingū hōraku onsenku ni tsuite*" 宗長・宗碩両吟の大神宮法楽御千句について. *Mizukaki* 62–84 (except numbers 68, 72, 79, and 81).

Senzai wakashū 千載和歌集. 1986. Ed. Kubota Jun. Iwanami Shoten.

Shichijūichiban shokunin utaawase 七十一番職人歌合. 1993. Ed. Iwasaki Kae 岩崎佳枝. In Iwasaki et al., eds., *Shichijūichiban shokunin utaawase, Shinsen kyōkashū, Kokon ikyokushū* 七十一番職人歌合・新撰狂歌集・古今夷曲集, pp. 3–146. Vol. 61 of *SNKBT*.

Shigematsu Hiromi 重松裕巳. 1973. "*Sōchō renga jichū*: shohon oyobi seiritsu o chūshin ni" 『宗長連歌自注』—諸本および成立を中心に. *Kumamoto Joshi Daigaku kokubun kenkyū* 19: 27–43.

———. 1978. "*Sōchō nikki* kōchū oboegaki" 『宗長手記』校注覚書. *Kumamoto Joshi Daigaku gakujutsu kiyō* 30 (March): 9–17.

———. 1979. "Saiokuken ketsuan nenji shiron" 柴屋軒結庵年次試論. *Renga haikai kenkyū* 56 (Jan.): 9–19.

———. 1982. "Yūtokubon *Sōchō michi no ki* o megutte" 祐徳本『宗長道之記』をめぐって. In *Imai Gen'e Kyōju taikan kinen ronbunshū* 今井源衛教授退官記念論文集, pp. 117–39. Kyūshū Daigaku.

———, ed. 1983. *Sōchō sakuhinshū: nikki, kikō*. Vol. 443 of *KB*.

———, ed. 1990. *Sōchō sakuhinshū: renga gakusho hen*. Vol. 517 of *KB*.

Shikashū taisei 私家集大成. 1973–76. Eds. Hashimoto Fumio et al. 7 vols. Meiji Shoin, 1973–76.

Shika wakashū 詞花和歌集. 1988. Ed. Matsuno Yōichi 松野陽一. Izumi Shoin.

Shikyō 詩経 (C: *Shijing*) 1964. Ed. Takada Shinji 高田真治. Vol. 2 of *Kanshi taikei* 漢詩大系. Shūeisha. See also Legge 1871.

Shima Takeshi 島武史. 1980. *Odawara rekishi sanpo* 小田原歴史散歩. Sōgensha.

Shimazu Tadao 島津忠夫. 1969. *Renga shi no kenkyū* 連歌史の研究. Kadokawa Shoten.

———. 1970. *Ōsaka Tenmangū Bunko rengasho mokuroku* 大阪天満宮文庫連歌書目録. Osaka: Ōsaka Tenmangū Shamusho.

———. 1975. *Sōchō nikki*. Iwanami Shoten.

Shin Nihon koten bungaku taikei. 1989-. Iwanami Shoten.

Shinchokusen wakashū 新勅撰和歌集. In *KT* 1: 259-88.

Shinchō Nihon koten shūsei. 1976-89. 82 vols. Shinchōsha.

Shingyō Norikazu 新行紀一. 1977. "Mikawa bushi" 三河武士. In Minegishi 1977: 157-81.

Shinkei 心敬. *Sasamegoto* ささめごと (Sonkeikaku Bunko 尊敬閣文庫 ms.). In Kidō and Imoto 1964: 119-204. See also *Sasamegoto*, in *GSRJ* 17: 31-67; *Sasamegoto* (Shoryōbu ms.), ed. Ijichi Tetsuo, in Ijichi, Omote, and Kuriyama 1973: 63-160; and *Sasamegoto* (Shoryōbu ms.), in Kidō 1972-, 3: 177-257.

Shinkei et al. *Shinkei Sōzu hyakku ta* 心敬僧都百句他. Ms. in Fukui Bunko, Hiroshima Daigaku.

Shinkō gunsho ruijū 新校群書類従. 1928-38. Eds. Hanawa Hokiichi et al. 24 vols. Naigai Shoseki.

Shinkokin wakashū 新古今和歌集. Kubota and Kawamura 440-531. See also Ishida Yoshisada 1960, Kubota Jun 1976-77, id. 1979, Kubota Utsubo 1964, Minemura 1974, and Tanaka and Akase 1992.

Shinsen inu tsukubashū 新撰犬筑波集 (also called *Inu tsukubashū*). Attributed to Yamazaki Sōkan 山崎宗鑑. See Kimura and Iguchi 1988 and Suzuki 1965.

Shinsen tsukubashū 新撰菟玖波集 (Meiō 明応 ms.). 1958. Ed. Yokoyama Shigeru 横山重 and Noguchi Eiichi 野口英一. Kazama Shobō.

Shinshaku kanbun taikei 新釈漢文大系. 1976-85. 96 vols. Meiji Shoin.

Shinshoku kokin wakashū 新続古今和歌集. In *KT* 1: 722-69.

Shintokumaru しんとく丸. 1977. In Muroki Yatarō 室木弥太郎, ed., *Sekkyōshū* 説経集, pp. 153-207. Vol. 8 of *SNKS*.

Shirai Chūkō 白井忠功. 1976. *Chūsei no kikō bungaku*. Bunka Shobō Hakubunsha.

Shiryō sōran 資料総覧. 1936. Ed. Tōkyō Daigaku Shiryō Hensanjo. Naikaku Insatsukyoku Chōyōkai.

Shōhaku 肖柏. *San'aiki* 三愛記. In *GSRJ* 17: 394-95. See also *San'aiki*, in *SKGSRJ* 21: 188 (the *GSRJ* ms. collated with an unnamed ms.); and *San'aiki*, in *Fusō shūyōshū* 3: 89-90.

Shōkō 正広. *Shōkō eiga* 正広詠歌. In *ST* 6: 247-53.

———. *Shōkō nikki* 正広日記. In *GSRJ* 18: 643-47.

———. *Shōkashū* 松下集. In *ST* 6: 254-352.

Shokusenzai wakashū 続千載和歌集. In *KT* 1: 481-525.

Shōtetsu 正徹. *Nagusamegusa* なぐさめ草. In *GSRJ* 18: 583-95. See also *Nagusamegusa* (Waseda Daigaku Toshokan ms.), ed. Inada Toshinori 稲田利徳, in Nagasaki et al. 1994: 427-53.

Shūi wakashū 拾遺和歌集. In Kubota and Kawamura 1986: 123-84.

Bibliography

Sōboku 宗牧. *Tōgoku kikō* 東国紀行. In *GSRJ* 18: 802–42.

Sōchō 宗長. *Azumaji no tsuto* 東路の津登. In *GSRJ* 18: 770–82. See also *Azumaji no tsuto*, in *SKGSRJ* 15:246–54 (the *GSRJ* ms. collated with the Fujino 藤野 ms.); *Azumaji no tsuto*, in Shigematsu 1983 (Ōta Takeo 太田武夫 ms. 25–40; Shōkōkan 彰考館 ms. 41–63; Ijichi Tetsuo ms. 65–87; Dazaifu Tenmangū 太宰府天満宮 ms. 89–113; and Yūtoku Inari Jinja 祐徳稲荷神社 ms. 115–48); and *Azumaji no tsuto* (Yūtoku Inari Jinja ms.), ed. Itō Kei, in Nagasaki et al. 1994: 483–512.

———. Eishō 4 [1507] *Makino Kohaku Zenmon uchijini isshūki* 牧野古白禅門討死一周忌. Cited in Shimazu 1970: 22 and in *RSR* 2: 931–32.

———. *Jukkai hyakuin dokugin* (*Renga shūsho* ms.). Ijichi 1975: 244–48.

———. *Kabekusa* 壁草. In *Kabekusachū* 壁草注 (Shoryōbu ms.). In Kaneko 1979: 371–512. See also *Kabekusa* (Mite Bunko 三手文庫 ms.), ed. Shigematsu Hiromi, vol. 424 of *KB*; *Kabekusa*, in *ZGSRJ* 17b: 945–1011; *Kabekusa* (Masamune Bunko 正宗文庫 ms.), in Okamoto Noriko 岡本史子, 1969, "Honkoku Masamune Bunko-zō *Kabekusa*," *Nōtoru Damu Seishin Joshi Daigaku kokubungakka kiyō* 3: 91–135; and *Kabekusa* (Ōsaka Tenmangū ms.), ed. Shigematsu Hiromi, vol. 398 of *KB*.

———. *Nachigomori* 那智籠 (Hiroshima Daigaku ms.). Ed. Shigematsu Hiromi. Vol. 379 of *KB*. See also *Nachigomori* (Kitano Tenmangū 北野天満宮 ms.), Shigematsu Hiromi, vol. 376 of *KB*.

———. *Nagabumi* (or *Nagafumi*) 永文. In Ijichi 1985, 2: 188–93.

———. *Oi no higagoto* 老のひがごと (Yūtoku Inari Jinja 祐徳稲荷神社 ms. of *Utsunoyama no ki*). In Shigematsu 1983: 149–74.

———. *Oi no mimi* 老の耳. Ed. Shigematsu Hiromi. Vol. 362 of *KB*.

———. *Renga tsukeyō* 連歌付用. In Iwashita and Kishida, 1978: 464–79.

———. *Rengashū* 連歌集. In Iwashita and Kishida 1978: 480–87.

———. *Shutsujin senku* 出陣千句. In *ZGSRJ* 17a: 1359–67.

———. *Sōchō dokugin Daiei* 8 [1528]:4:12 *myōgō hyakuin*. In *ZGSRJ* 17a: 614–16.

———. *Sōchō kawa* 宗長歌話. In Kidō and Shigematsu 1979: 7–48.

———. *Sōchō michi no ki* 宗長道之記 (an abridged version of the *Sōchō shuki*, Yūtoku Inari Jinja ms.). In Shigematsu 1983: 201–273.

———. *Sōchō nikki* (Shoryōbu 書陵部 ms.). In Shimazu 1975: 145–164. See also *Sōchō nikki*, in *ZGSRJ* 18b: 1252–266.

———. *Sōchō renga jichū* 宗長連歌自註. In *KNS* 18: 95–183.

———. *Sōchō shuki* 宗長手記 (Shōkōkan 彰考館 ms.). In Shimazu 1975: 7–143. See also *Sōchō shuki*, in *GSRJ* 18: 256–327; *Sōchō shuki*, in *SKGSRJ* 14: 645–701 (the *GSRJ* ms. collated with a ms. in the Naikaku Bunko 内閣文庫); *Sōchō michi no ki*; and *Sōchō Suruga nikki*.

———. *Sōchō Suruga nikki* 宗長駿河日記 and *Sōchō Suruga zoku nikki* 宗長駿河続日記 (Nakaku Bunko ms.). Ed. Uzawa Satoru. Vol. 344 of *KB*.

———. *Sōgi shūenki* 宗祇終焉記 (the *GSRJ* ms. collated with Naikaku Bunko ms.).

In Kaneko 1976: 101–25. See also *Sōgi shūenki*, in *GSRJ* 29: 442–48; *Sōgi shūenki*, in *SKGSRJ* 22: 673–77 (the *GSRJ* ms. collated with the Naikaku Bunko ms.); *Sōgi shūenki* (Ōta Takeo ms.), in Shigematsu 1983: 7–23; and *Sōgi shūenki* (Naikaku Bunko ms.), ed. Tsurusaki Hiroo and Fukuda Hideichi, in Fukuda et al. 1990: 449–61.

———. *Utsunoyama no ki* 宇津山記. In *GSRJ* 17: 395–405. See also *Utsunoyama no ki*, in *SKGSRJ* 21: 189–95 (collated with the Naikaku Bunko ms.); *Utsunoyama no ki* (Matsudaira Bunko 松平文庫 ms.), in Shigematsu 1983: 174–200; and *Oi no higagoto*.

Sōchō, Asahina Yasumochi 朝比奈泰以, and Imagawa Ujichika 今川氏親. Eishō 15 [1518]: 1:3 *Yamanani hyakuin*. In Shinkei et al., *Shinkei Sōzu hyakku ta*.

Sōchō, Imagawa Ujichika, and Saitō Yasumoto 斉藤安元. Eishō 15 [1518]:1:1 *Nanimichi hyakuin*. In Shinkei et al., *Shinkei Sōzu hyakku ta*.

Sōchō, and Imagawa Ujiteru 今川氏輝. Daiei 5 [1525]:1:25 *Naniki* (or *Nanibito*) *hyakuin* (*Renga shūsho* ms.). In Ijichi 1975: 212–16.

Sōchō, Sanjōnishi Sanetaka, and Shōhaku. *Sōchō hyakuban rengaawase*. In *KNS* 18: 21–93.

Sōchō, Sanjōnishi Sanetaka, and Sōseki. *Gessonsai senku* 月村斎千句. See id., *Iba senku*.

———. *Iba senku* 伊庭千句 (Matsui Akiyuki 松井明之 ms.). Ed. Tsurusaki Hiroo. In Tsurusaki et al., eds., vol. 7 of *Senku rengashū*, pp. 7–112. Vol. 471 of *KB*.

Sōchō, and Sōboku. Daiei 7 [1527]:1:8 *Yashima Shōrin'an naniki hyakuin* 矢嶋少林庵何木百韻. In *KNS* 18: 201–30.

Sōchō, and Sōgi. *Guku wakuraba* 愚句萱草. In Kaneko 1979: 7–153.

Sōchō, Sōgi, and Shōhaku. *Minase sangin* 水無瀬三吟 (*Renga shūsho* ms.). In Kaneko Kinjirō, ed., *Minase sangin hyakuin chūshaku*, in id. 1985: 83–187. See also *Chōkyō ni nen Minase sangin hyakuin* 長享二年水無瀬三吟百韻, in *ZGSRJ* 17a: 576–78; Fukui 1938; *Three Poets at Minase*, in Keene 1955: 1, 314–21 (partial translation); Yasuda 1956; *Minase Sangin nanibito hyakuinchū* (Konishi Jin'ichi ms.), in Ijichi 1968: 343–66; *Minase sangin* (Tsurumai Toshokan 鶴舞図書館 ms.), in Shimazu 1979: 211–46; *Three Poets at Minase*, in Miner 1979: 171–225; and *Three Poets at Minase*, in Carter 1991: 303–26.

———. *Yuyama sangin* 湯山三吟 (Tenmangū ms.). In Kaneko Kinjirō, ed., *Yuyama sangin hyakuin chūshaku*, in id. 1985: 189–288. See also *Yuyama sangin hyōshaku*, in Fukui 1938: 69–115; *Yuyama sangin* (Daitōkyū Kinen Bunko 大東急記念文庫 ms.), in Shimazu 1979: 247–79; *Three Poets at Yuyama*, in Sato and Watson 1981: 254–61; and Carter 1983.

Sōchō, and Sōseki. Bunki 2 [1502]:8:6 *Sōgi tsuitō nanibito hyakuin* 宗祇追悼何人百韻 (Shoryōbu ms.). Cited in *RSR* 2: 929.

———. *Ise senku* 伊勢千句 (Naikaku Bunko ms.). In Kaneko 1974: 340–421. See also *Ise senku* (Jingū Bunko 神宮文庫 ms.), in Senda 1964–69.

———. *Sōseki Sōchō ryōgin nanimichi hyakuin* (n.d.) (Shoryōbu ms.). Cited in *RSR* 2: 950.

Sōchō et al. Chōkyō 2 [1488]:4:5 (or 25) *Nanimichi hyakuin* (Ōsaka Tenmangū ms.). Cited in *RSR* 2: 916.

———. Daiei 3 [1523]:4:4 *Nanibito hyakuin* (Kokkai Toshokan ms.). Cited in *RSR* 2: 943.

———. Daiei 3:9:2 *Yamanani hyakuin* (Ōsaka Tenmangū ms.). In Tsurusaki 1983: 274–79.

Bibliography

———. Daiei 5 [1525]:9:21 *Nanibito hyakuin* (Ōsaka Tenmangū ms.). In Yonehara 1979: 881–87.

———. Daiei 6 [1526]:8:15 *Hyakuin*. In Kaneko 1978–83, 9: 502–4.

———. Daiei 6:9:13 *Nanibito hyakuin* (Ōsaka Tenmangū ms.). Cited in *RSR* 2: 946.

———. Daiei 7 [1527]:1:19 *Yamanani hyakuin* (Ōsaka Tenmangū ms.). In Tsurusaki 1983: 282–87.

———. Daiei 7:4:2 *Nanibito hyakuin* (Jingū Bunko ms.). Cited in *RSR* 2: 946.

———. Eishō 1 [1504] (Eishō 3? [1506?]) *Nanibito hyakuin*. In Shigematsu 1982: 133–39.

———. Eishō 2 [1505]:8:22 *Tamanani hyakuin* (*Renga shūsho* ms.). In Ijichi 1975: 64–68.

———. Eishō 12 [1515]:11:11 *Yamanani hyakuin* (*Renga shūsho* ms.). In Ijichi 1975: 110–14.

———. Eishō 13 [1516]:7:8 *Nanibito hyakuin* (*Renga shūsho* ms.). In Ijichi 1975: 83–87.

———. Eishō 15 [1518]:4:23/26 *Yamanani hyakuin* (Myōgenji 妙源寺 ms.). In Suzuki Mitsuyasu 1973: 325–32.

———. *Hamori senku* 葉守千句 (Kitano Tenmangū ms.). Ed. Hamachiyo Kiyoshi 浜千代清. In Kishida et al. 1985: 9–116.

———. *Higashiyama senku* 東山千句 (Naikaku Bunko ms.). Ed. Kishida Yoriko. In Kishida et al. 1985: 227–332.

———. *Jikka senku* 十花千句 (Ōta Takeo ms.). In Kaneko 1974: 308–39.

———. Meiō 8 [1499]:2:19 *Nanibito hyakuin* (Ōsaka Tenmangū ms.). In Etō 1967: 325–28.

———. *Settsu senku* 摂津千句. The first three verses of each of the ten hundred-verse sequences are preserved in the Ōsaka Tenmangū ms., reproduced in Tsurusaki 1971b: 4–5.

———. *Shin Sumiyoshi senku* 新住吉千句. The first three verses of each of the ten hundred-verse sequences are preserved in the Ōsaka Tenmangū ms., reproduced in Tsurusaki 1971b: 2–4.

Sōgi 宗祇. *Oi no susami* 老のすさみ. In Kidō 1972–, 2: 139–86.

———. *Shitakusa* 下草. In *ZGSRJ* 17b: 697–735. See also *Shitakusa*, ed. Morozumi Sōichi 両角倉一, vol. 387 of *KB*.

———. *Sōgi rengashū wakuraba* 宗祇連歌集老葉. Ed. Konishi Jin'ichi and Mizukami Kashizō 水上甲子三. Vol. 74 of *KB*. See also *Wakuraba*, in *ZGSRJ* 17b: 627–74.

———. *Sōgi rengashū wasuregusa* 宗祇連歌集萱草. Ed. Konishi Jin'ichi. Vol. 40 of *KB*. See also *Wasuregusa*, in *ZGSRJ* 17b: 675–96.

———. *Tsukushi michi no ki* 筑紫道記. In Kaneko 1976: 27–100. See also *Tsukushi michi no ki*, in *GSRJ* 18: 651–69; *Tsukushi michi no ki*, in *SKGSRJ* 15: 167–77 (the *GSRJ* ms. collated with the *Zoku Fusō shūyōshū* and Ban Kōjun 伴光淳 mss.); *Tsukushi michi no ki* (*GSRJ* ms.), eds. Kawazoe Shōji 川添昭二 and Fukuda Hideichi, in Fukuda et al. 1990: 405–32; and Eileen Katō 1979.

———. *Wakuraba*. See *Sōgi rengashū wakuraba*.

———. *Wasuregusa*. See *Sōgi rengashū wasuregusa*.

Sōkyū 宗久. *Miyako no tsuto* 都のつと (Fusō shūyōshū ms.). Ed. Fukuda Hideichi. In Fukuda et al. 1990: 345–61. See also *Miyako no tsuto*, in *GSRJ* 18: 529–40, and *Miyako no tsuto (Souvenir for the Capital)*, in Plutschow and Fukuda 1981: 61–75; 105–12.

Sōseki 宗碩. *Sano no watari* 佐乃々和太利. In *ZGSRJ* 186: 1282–87. See also *Sano no watari* 佐野のわたり (Bunsei shichinen ms.), eds. Tsurusaki Hiroo and Fukuda Hideichi, in Fukuda et al. 1990: 463–72.

Stevens, John. 1993. *Three Zen Masters: Ikkyū, Hakuin, Ryōkan*. Kodansha International.

Sugimoto Kōjirō 杉本幸次郎. 1970. *Kameyama chihō kyōdoshi* 亀山地方郷土史. Mie Prefecture: Mieken Kyōdo Shiryō Kankōkai.

Sugiyama Hiroshi 杉山博. 1974. *Sengoku daimyō*. Vol. 11 of *Nihon no rekishi*. Chūōkōronsha.

Suitō Makoto 水藤真. 1981. *Asakura Yoshikage* 朝倉義景. Vol. 182 of *Jinbutsu sōsho* 人物叢書. Yoshikawa Kōbunkan.

———. 1983. "Fukugen sareta jōkamachi" 復原された城下町. In *Chūbu daimyō no kenkyū* 中部大名の研究. Ed. Katsumata Shizuo 勝俣鎮夫. Vol. 4 of Nagahara 1983–85.

Suruga no Imagawashi 駿河の今川氏. 1975–87. Ed. Imagawashi Kenkyūkai. 10 vols. Shizuoka: Yajimaya.

Suzuki Mitsuyasu 鈴木光保. 1973. "Mikawa ni okeru Sōchō oboegaki" 三河における宗長覚え書き. In *Matsumura Hiroshi Kyōju taikan kinen kokugo kokubungaku ronshū* 松村博司教授退官記念国語国文学論集, pp. 311–32. Nagoya: Nagoya Daigaku.

Suzuki Tōzō 鈴木棠三, ed. 1965. *Inu tsukubashū* 犬つくば集. Comp. Yamazaki Sōkan. Kadokawa Shoten.

Tahara, Mildred, trans. 1980. *Tales of Yamato: A Tenth-Century Poem-Tale*. Honolulu: University of Hawaii Press.

Taiheiki 太平記. 1960–62. Eds. Gotō Tanji 後藤丹治 and Kamada Kisaburo 釜田喜三郎. Vols. 34–36 of *NKBT*. See also McCullough 1959.

Takahashi Yasuo 高橋康夫. 1983. *Kyōto chūsei toshishi kenkyū* 京都中世都市史研究. Shibunkaku Shuppan.

Takeuchi Gengen'ichi 竹内玄玄一. 1987. *Haika kijinden, Zoku haika kijinden* 俳家奇人伝・続俳家奇人伝. Ed. Kira Sueo 雲英末雄. Iwanami Bunko.

Tamai Kōsuke 玉井幸助, ed. 1960. *Tōnomine Shōshō monogatari: honbun hihan to kaishaku* 多武峰小将物語—本文批判と解釈. Hanawa Shobō.

Tanaka Yutaka 田中裕, and Akase Shingo 赤瀬信吾, eds. 1992. *Shinkokin wakashū*. Vol. 11 of *SNKBT*.

Tani Hiroshi 谷宏. 1952. "Haikai no renga." *Bungaku* 20.11: 61–72.

Tani Sōboku 谷宗牧. See Sōboku.

Tatoezukushi たとへづくし. 1979. Ed. Shōyōken Tōsei 松葉軒東井. Dōbōsha.

Tōnomine Shōshō monogatari. See Tamai 1960.

Toyohara Muneaki 豊原統秋 (also read Toyohara Sumiaki). *Shōkashō* 松下抄. *ST* 6: 660–91.

Bibliography

———. *Taigenshō* 体源抄. 1512. 22 vols. Ms. in the East Asian Library, University of California, Berkeley.

———. *Toyohara Muneaki senshu* 豊原統秋千首 (Tenri Toshokan ms.). Cited in Shimazu 1975: 56. Given as *Toyohara Sumiaki senshu* in *KSSMR*.

Tsuchihashi Yutaka 土橋寛 and Konishi Jin'ichi. 1957. *Kodai kayōshū* 古代歌謡集. Vol. 3 of *NKBT*.

Tsuge Kiyoshi 柘植清 et al. 1931. *Shizuokashi shi* 静岡史市. 5 vols. Shizuoka: Shizuoka Shiyakusho.

Tsukubashū 菟玖波集. 1948–51. Ed. Fukui Kyūzō. 2 vols. *NKZ*.

Tsurusaki, Hiroo 鶴崎裕雄. 1969a. "Sengoku bushi bungei no ichikōsatsu: *Sōchō shuki* o chūshin to shite" 戦国武士文芸の一考察—『宗長手記』を中心として. In *Senriyama bungaku ronshū* 2: 39–51.

———. 1969b. "Sōchō to Echizen Asakurashi: Sengoku bunka ni kansuru ichikōsatsu" 宗長と越前朝倉氏—戦国文化に関する一考察. *Tezukayama Gakuin Kōtōbu kenkyū ronshū teoria* 17 (Nov.): 1–18.

———. 1971a. "Chūseishi kenkyū ni okeru bunkazai hogo no mondai: rengashi Sōchō to Ise Sekishi no kōshō o chūshin to shite" 中世史研究における文化財保護の問題—連歌師宗長と伊勢・関氏の交渉を中心として. *Tezukayama Gakuin Chūgakubu, Kōtōbu kenkyū ronshū teoria* 20 (July): 1–18.

———. 1971b. "Sengoku shoki no Settsu kokujinsō no dōkō: Akutagawajōshu Noseshi to sono bungei, toku ni renga o chūshin to shite" 戦国初期の摂津国人層の動向, 芥川城主能勢氏とその文芸，特に連歌を中心として. *Shisen* 43 (Sept.): 1–36.

———. 1973. "Owari Atsutagū ni okeru rengashi Sōchō" 尾張熱田宮における連歌師宗長. *Tezukayama Gakuin Tanki Daigaku kenkyū kiyō* 21: 13–34.

———. 1976. "Ōmi kokujinshū no senku renga kōgyō" 近江国人衆の千句連歌興行. In *Nihon bunkashi ronsō*, pp. 586–99. Shibata Minoru Sensei Koki Kinenkai.

———. 1977. "Suruga ni okeru Saiokuken Sōchō" 駿河における柴屋軒宗長. In *Nihon bungaku kenkyū* (March): 25–39.

———. 1978. "Araara muge no niwazuki sōrō kana: rengashi Sōchō no bannen" あらあら無下の庭数寄候哉—連歌師宗長の晩年. *Tezukayama Gakuin Tanki Daigaku kenkyū nenpō* 26: 1–22.

———. 1979. "Seki Kajisai to rengashi Sōchō" 関何似斎と連歌師宗長. In "Shōhōjiato hakkutsu chōsa hōkoku, dainiji" 正法寺跡発掘調査報告第二次, pp. 8–16. Sekichō Kyōiku Iinkai.

———. 1983. "Rengashi Sōchō to Ōmi Kokujinshū" 連歌師宗長と近江国人衆. In Katsumata Shizuo 勝俣鎮夫, ed., *Chūbu daimyō no kenkyū* 中部大名の研究, pp. 265–91. Vol. 4 of Nagahara 1983–85.

———. 1987. "Oi no kurigoto." *Kokubungaku kaishaku to kyōzai no kenkyū* 32.4 (March): 144–45.

———. 1997. "Ise Yamada ni okeru rengashi Sōchō: hitotsu no chihō bunka shiron"

伊勢山田における連歌師宗長——一つの地方文化史論. In *Nihon bungaku shiron: Shimazu Tadao Sensei koki kinen ronshū* 日本文学史論——島津忠夫先生古希記念論集, pp. 214–29. Sekai Shisōsha.

Tsurusaki Hiroo et al., eds. 1985. Vol. 7 of *Senku rengashū* 千句連歌集. Vol. 471 of *KB*.

Usuda Jingorō 臼田甚五郎, and Shinma Shin'ichi 新間進一, eds. 1976. *Kagurauta, Saibara, Ryōjin hishō, Kanginshū* 神楽歌・催馬楽・梁塵秘抄・閑吟集. Vol. 25 of *NKBZ*.

Uzawa Satoru 鵜沢覚. 1956. "Sōchō shuki oboegaki." *Chiba Daigaku Bunrigakubu kiyō (Bunka kagaku)* 2.1 (Feb.): 1–10.

Varley, H. Paul. 1967. *The Ōnin War: History of its Origins and Background with a Selective Translation of The Chronicle of Ōnin*. New York: Columbia University Press.

Wakabayashi Atsushi 若林淳之. 1970. *Shizuokaken no rekishi*. Yamakawa Shuppansha.

Wakan rōeishū 和漢朗詠集. 1985. Comp. Fujiwara Kintō 藤原公任. Ed. Kawaguchi Hisao 川口久雄. Kōdansha.

Yamada Yoshio 山田孝雄. 1980. *Renga gaisetsu* 連歌概説. Iwanami Shoten.

Yamamoto Takeshi 山本大, and Owada Tetsuo. 1984. *Sengoku daimyō kashindan jiten: tōgoku hen* 戦国大名家臣団事典——東国編. Shin Jinbutsu Ōraisha.

Yamato monogatari. 1972. Ed. Takahashi Shōji 高橋正治. In Takahashi et al., eds., *Taketori monogatari, Ise monogatari, Yamato monogatari, Heichū monogatari*, pp. 267–438. Vol. 8 of *NKBZ*. See also Tahara 1980.

Yamazaki Sōkan. See *Shinsen inu tsukubashū*.

Yampolsky, Philip, trans. 1967. *The Platform Sutra of the Sixth Patriarch*. New York: Columbia University Press.

Yasuda, Kenneth, trans. 1956. *Minase sangin hyakuin: A Poem of One Hundred Links Composed by Three Poets at Minase*. The Tosho Insatsu Printing Company.

Yogo Toshio 余語敏男. 1983. "Nishinokōri Udonoshi no senku renga kōgyō" 西郡鵜殿氏の千句連歌興行. *Nishinokōri* 8 (Sept.): 10–16.

Yokota Ken'ichi 横田健一. 1957. "Daitokuji Shinjuan to Asakurashi" 大徳寺真珠庵と朝倉氏. *Shiseki to bijutsu* 27.6 (July): 202–9.

Yokomichi Mario 横道萬里雄, and Omote Akira 表章, eds. 1972. *Yōkyokushū* 謡曲集. Vols. 40–41 of *NKBT*.

Yokoyama Haruo 横山晴夫. 1978. "Chūbu no gun'yū" 中部の群雄. In vol. 3 of Kuwata Tadachika 桑田忠親, ed., *Nihon no kassen*, pp. 323–94. Jinbutsu Ōraisha.

Yonehara Masayoshi 米原正義. 1979. *Sengoku bushi to bungei no kenkyū* 戦国武士と文芸の研究. Ōfūsha.

Yoshida Kenkō 吉田兼好. 1971. *Tsurezuregusa* 徒然草. Ed. Yasuraoka Kōsaku 安良岡康作. Ōbunsha. See also Keene 1967.

Yoshida Yutaka 吉田豊, ed. 1983. *Buke no kakun* 武家の家訓. Tokkan Shoten.

Yoshii Kōji 吉井功兒. 1985. "Tōtōmi no kuni shugo enkaku shōkō: Kenmu seiken no kokushu, shugo oyobi Muomachi, Sengokuki no shugo" 遠江国守護沿革小稿——健武政権の国守・守護および室町・戦国期の守護. In *SI* 8: 1–88.

Bibliography

Yoshikawa Ichirō 吉川一郎. 1955. *Yamazaki Sōkanden* 山崎宗鑑伝. Yōtokusha.

Yōyōki 養鷹記. In *GSRJ* 19: 483–85.

Zōho shiryō taisei 増補史料大成. 1965–75. Ed. Zōho Shiryō Taisei Kankōkai. 48 vols. Rinsen Shoin.

Zoku gunsho ruijū. 1957–72. Eds. Hanawa Hokiichi et al. Rev. ed. (*teisei* 訂正). 37 vols., with three supplements (*hoi* 補遺). Zoku Gunsho Ruijū Kanseikai.

Zoku Gunsho Ruijū Kanseikai, ed. 1962–66. *Gunsho kaidai* 群書解題. 22 vols. Zoku Gunsho Ruiju Kanseikai.

Zoku zoku gunsho ruijū. 1978. Ed. Kokusho Kankōkai. 17 vols. (vol. 17 ed. Kosho Hozonkai 古書保存会). Zoku Gunsho Ruijū Kanseikai.

Index of First Lines

ai ni ainu / sono kisaragi no (*JS* no. 596), 165
ai ni ainu / urū no yayoi (*JS* no. 62), 30
ajikinaya (*JS* no. 616), 170
akanedomo / iwa ni shi kaeba (*JS* no. 389), 111
akanedomo / iwa ni zo kauru (*Ise monogatari* 74), 279–80
akanu yo no (*JS* no. 398), 113
akatsuki no / arashi ni musebu (*JS* no. 288), 79
akatsuki no / tomo o zo etaru (*JS* no. 183), 54
akatsuki o / ika ni chigirite (*JS* no. 286), 78
akatsuki o / takano no yama ni (*Senzaishū* 19: 1236), 257
akatsuki wa (*JS* no. 592), 164
aken toshi no (*JS* no. 324), 88
akenu to ya (*JS* no. 366), 104
aki fukashi (*JS* no. 24), 20
akihagi no (*Kokinshū* 4: 218), 223
aki kaze no (*JS* no. 269), 75
akikaze no / fukiage niou (*JS* no. 103), 36
akikaze no / fukiage ni tateru (*Kokinshū* 5: 272), 228
aki kaze wa (*JS* no. 270), 75
aki no kaze (*JS* no. 306), 83–84
aki no tsuki (*JS* no. 386), 110
aki no umi (*JS* no. 76), 33
aki no yo no / chiyo o hitoyo ni / nazuraete (*Ise monogatari* 34), 302
aki no yo no / chiyo o hitoyo ni / naseri to mo (*Ise monogatari* 34), 302
aki no yo no / nagaki yamiji mo (*JS* no. 238), 68
Also, as in a pure, bright mirror (*Lotus Sutra*), 290
ama ga shita (*JS* no. 579), 160
ama ga shita ya (*JS* no. 370), 105

ama no hara / fuji no keburi no (*Shinkokinshū* 1: 33), 267
ama no hara / fuji ya kasumi no (*JS* no. 338), 95
ama obune (*JS* no. 209), 61
ame kaoru (*JS* no. 66), 31
anbai kiezu (*JS* no. 443), 124
aoyagi o (*Kokinshū* 20: 1081), 237
aoyagi ya (*JS* no. 5), 10
aratama no / hatsumotoi kiri (*JS* no. 138), 41
aratama no / toshi no iku haru (*JS* no. 208), 61
ariake ya (*JS* no. 80), 33
aru ga naka ni (*JS* no. 284), 78
aruji mo zusa mo (*JS* no. 96), 35
aru toki wa (*Genji monogatari okuiri* 479), 283
asagao ni sake (*JS* no. 219), 65
asagao no (*JS* no. 259), 73
asagao ya / hana to iu hana no (*JS* no. 574), 159
asagao ya / yume tsuyu hana no (*JS* no. 378), 108
asagasumi / minami o yomo no (*JS* no. 497), 138
asagasumi / sumizumi made wa (*JS* no. 137), 39
asagiri no (*JS* no. 73), 32
asahikage / nioeru yama no (*Shinkokinshū* 1: 98), 206
asahikage / yomo ni nioeru (*JS* no. 11), 15
asa kashiwa (*JS* no. 355), 100
asakashiwa (*Man'yōshū* 11: 2754), 271–72
asakeredo (*JS* no. 295), 81
asakura ya (*Shinkokinshū* 17: 1689), 299
asamidori / somekaketari to (*Man'yōshū* 10: 1847), 216
asamidori / yanagi ni mume no (*JS* no. 55), 28
asatoake no (*JS* no. 381), 109

Index of First Lines

asatsuyu ni (*JS* no. 371), 106
asayū no (*JS* no. 47), 26–27
asukagawa (*Kokinshū* 18: 990), 213
asukai ni (*Saibara* no. 8), 250
asu no shiru (*JS* no. 82), 34
asu wa komu (*JS* no. 217), 64
ato tareshi (*JS* no. 293), 80
atsurae no (*JS* no. 302), 82
au tabi ni (*JS* no. 226), 66
awajishima (*JS* no. 600), 166
aware koso (*JS* no. 255), 72
aware naru / kari no koe kana (*JS* no. 462), 129
aware naru / waga kotozute ya (*JS* no. 204), 60
azumaji no / saya no nakayama / nakanaka ni / nani shi ka hito o (*Kokinshū* 12: 594), 265
azumaji no / tego no yobisaka (*Man'yōshū* 14: 3442), 262
azusayumi / hana ni torisoe (*JS* no. 350), 99
azusayumi / oshinabete haru no (*JS* no. 148), 43
azusayumi / oshite harusame / kyō furinu (*Kokinshū* 1: 20), 209
azusayumi / oshite harusame / kyō mo furu (*JS* no. 16), 17
azusayumi / yashima no sato no (*JS* no. 436), 122
azusayumi / yasoji no haru o (*JS* no. 483), 135

bōen ya nari to iedomo (*JS* no. 495), 138

chigiri are ya (*JS* no. 517), 143
chigirishi mo (*JS* no. 189), 56
chigo ka onna ka (*JS* no. 94), 35
chigo kosode (*JS* no. 101), 35
chihayaburu / kami no shimenawa (*JS* no. 565), 157
chihayaburu / miwayamamoto no (*JS* no. 125), 37
chiin metsugo (*JS* no. 458), 128
chiru a miyo (*JS* no. 534), 147
chitose hemu (*JS* no. 277), 76

eshinazu wa (*JS* no. 449), 126
Even if someone whose thoughts are malicious (*Lotus Sutra*), 259

Four or five mountain peaks painted in rainy colors (*Wakan rōeishū* no. 319), 243
fudō mo koi ni (*JS* no. 123), 37

fujinami ya (*JS* no. 347), 98
fuji no yuki (*JS* no. 40), 25
fujiwara uji ka (*JS* no. 84), 34
fuji ya kore (*JS* no. 327), 89
fukaku irite (*Senzaishū* 20: 1278), 211
fukiaezu (*JS* no. 382), 109
fuku wa uchi e (*JS* no. 473), 132
funabito mo (*JS* no. 528), 146
fureba kaku (*JS* no. 262), 73
furu ga uchi no (*JS* no. 468), 131
furusato ni (*JS* no. 609), 168
fushitsu korobitsu (*JS* no. 126), 38
fuyu ya itsu (*JS* no. 29), 21
fuzei mo tsukite (*JS* no. 92), 35

goban no ue ni (*JS* no. 135), 38–39
gojō atari ni (*JS* no. 110), 36
gojō watari ni (*Shinsen inu tsukabashū* no. 51), 229

hagi ga hana (*JS* no. 266), 74
hagi susuki (*JS* no. 70), 32
hakanasa wa (*JS* no. 590), 164
hakanashi ya (*JS* no. 230), 66
hana ni chō (*JS* no. 63), 30
hana sakite (*JS* nos. 337, 343), 92, 97
hannyaji no (*Shinsen inu tsukubashū* no. 161), 227
hannyajizaka no (*JS* no. 90), 34
hansō tsuki ochi (*JS* no. 492), 137
haru goto ni (*Kokinshū* 2: 97), 192
haru ikue (*JS* no. 535), 148
haruka naru (*Shinchokusenshū* 19: 1308), 287
haruka ni te (*JS* no. 314), 87
haru no ame no (*JS* no. 336), 92
haru no kiru (*Kokinshū* 1: 23), 229
haru no kumo no (*JS* no. 212), 62
haru no iro no (*Kokinshū* 2: 93), 264
haru no yo no (*Shinkokinshū* 1: 38), 306–7
harusame no (*JS* no. 54), 28
haru wa kurenu (*JS* no. 540), 149
haru ya hana (*JS* no. 58), 29
haru ya kono (*JS* no. 526), 146
haru ya toki (*JS* no. 502), 139
haru yo tada (*JS* no. 537), 148
hashitaka no / tokaeru hana ka (*JS* nos. 335, 342), 92, 96
hashitaka no / tokaeru yama no (*Shūishū* 19: 1230)

Index of First Lines

hatsuboku ni (*JS* no. 461), 128
hatsune no hi to ya (*JS* no. 207), 61
hatsuseyama / iriai no kane o / kikumade ni (*JS* no. 27), 20
hatsuseyama / iriai no kane o / kikutabi ni (*Senzaishū* 17: 1154), 211
hatsushigure (*JS* no. 400), 114
hayashisomete (*JS* no. 200), 59
hesokata no (*Man'yōshū* 1: 19), 248
hidari migi (*JS* no. 446), 125
higashi naru (*JS* no. 303), 83
hikidemono (*JS* no. 107), 36
hikitsuretsutsu mo (*JS* no. 86), 34
hikkunde (*JS* no. 121), 37
hikumano ni (*Man'yōshū* 1: 57), 268–69
hitasura ni (*Shinsen tsukubashū* 16: 3090), 314
hitofude no (*JS* no. 507), 140
hito gogatsu no (*JS* no. 176), 52
hito ni awamu (*Kokinshū* 19: 1030), 287
hito ni tsuki (*JS* no. 93), 35
hito no nasake ya / ana ni aruran (*JS* no. 118, *Shinsen inu tsukubashū* no. 141), 37, 231
hito no tame (*JS* no. 425), 118–19
hito no ue ni / ii wa kawasedo (*JS* no. 241), 68
hito no ue ni / nashite wa ika ni (*JS* no. 423), 118
hito no ue ni / tsune wa kikedomo (*JS* no. 413), 117
hitori futari (*JS* no. 510), 141
hitori shite (*JS* no. 220), 65
hitori to saka o (*Shinsen inu tsukabashū* 61), 227
hito shirezu (*JS* no. 390), 111
hito yori mo (*JS* no. 181), 53
hoka hoka no (*JS* no. 552), 154
hokekyō ni / chigiri musuberu (*JS* no. 244), 70
hokekyō ni / waga eshi koto wa (*Shuishū* 20: 1346), 215
honobono to / akashi no ura no (*Kokinshū* 9: 409), 233
honobono to / akashi no ura wa (*Shinsen inu tsukubashū* no. 81), 233
honobono to / ariake no tsuki no (*Shinkokinshū* 6: 591), 233
hototogisu / akatsukigata no (*Gosenshū* 4: 197), 257
hototogisu / hatsune zo hana no (*JS* no. 538), 148
hototogisu / makoto o kyō wa (*JS* no. 213), 62
hototogisu / matsu no hagoshi ka (*JS* no. 351), 99
hototogisu / naku naku koso wa (*Sankashū* no. 751), 251
hototogisu / shigeru konohama no (*JS* no. 364), 103
hototogisu / tsuki ya ariake no (*JS* no. 159), 47
hototogisu / yama no i no akanu (*JS* no. 160), 47

I cut aside all buddhas and patriarchs, 290
ichijō nijō (*JS* no. 106), 36
ika de kimi (*JS* no. 17), 17
ika ni seba (*JS* no. 391), 111
ika ni sen (*JS* no. 203), 60
ika ni shite / nakoso to towaba (*JS* no. 505), 140
ika ni shite / shigure furinishi (*JS* no. 429), 119
ika ni to mo (*JS* no. 393), 112
ike no omo ya (*JS* no. 3), 8
iku iwane (*JS* no. 60), 30
iku tabi ka (*JS* no. 547), 152
iku tabi mo (*JS* no. 334), 91
iku tose no (*JS* no. 279), 77
iku yo ware (*JS* no. 396), 112
ima iku ka (*JS* no. 376), 107
ima kon to (*Kokinshū* 15: 771), 308
ima mo yo wa (*JS* no. 185), 54
ima yori wa (*JS* no. 312), 312
ima wa tada (*JS* no. 232), 67
ima wa ware (*JS* no. 415), 117
ima zo omou (*JS* no. 488), 136
In antiquity at Aster river in Nanyang Province (*Taiheiki*), 267
inishie mo (*Taiheiki*), 268
inishie no (*Ise monogatari* 41), 256
ise no umi no (*saibara* no. 10), 301
isogarenu (*Shinkokinshū* 6: 701), 236
isogu to mo (*Shinchokusenshū* 8: 517), 242
iso no ue no (*JS* no. 77), 33
itodoshiku (*Ise monogatari* 20), 245
ito haya mo (*JS* no. 39), 25
itsu idete (*JS* no. 163), 48
itsu ka mimu (*JS* no. 222), 65
itsushika to (*Kokinshū* 19: 1014), 308
iwao mo shiroshi (*JS* no. 161), 48
iza saraba (*JS* no. 549), 153
izuko o ka (*JS* no. 45), 26
izuko yori (*JS* no. 145), 43

Index of First Lines

izuku mo ka (*JS* no. 216), 64
izuku moru (*JS* no. 385), 110

kaeru ni wa (*JS* no. 551), 153
kaeruyama / ari to wa kikedo (*Kokinshū* 8: 370), 191–92
kaeruyama / nani zo wa arite (*Kokinshū* 8: 382), 210
kaeru yo o (*JS* no. 19), 18
kagamiyama / iza tachiyorite / mi ni yukamu (*Kokinshū* 17: 899), 273–74
kagamiyama / iza tachiyorite / mite yukaji (*JS* no. 363), 103
kage mo te mo (*JS* no. 569), 158
kai ga ne o (*Kokinshū* 20: 1097), 268
kai ga ne wa (*JS* no. 341), 96
kakitsukeshi (*JS* no. 197), 58
kaku omou to wa (*JS* no. 264), 74
kami matsuru (*Shokusenzaishū* 3: 214), 243
kaminazuki / momiji o fukeru (*JS* no. 26), 20
kaminazuki / shigure mo imada (*Kokinshū* 5: 253), 285
kaminazuki / shigure no ame no (*Kin'yōshū* 4: 262), 209
kami no yo yori no (*JS* no. 124), 37
kanete yori (*JS* no. 359), 101
kaoru ka wa (*JS* no. 178), 52
kao wa shiwasu no (*JS* no. 83), 34
karakoromo (*Ise monogatari* 21), 253
karigane mo (*Horikawa hyakushū* no. 696), 203
kari nakite (*JS* no. 387), 110
kari ni shi mo (*JS* no. 180), 53
kari no tsute ni mo (*Shinsen tsukubashū* 16: 3090), 314
karisome mo (*JS* no. 227), 66
kasaneage (*JS* no. 365), 104
kasumikeri (*JS* no. 210), 62
kasumi komaka ni (*JS* no. 128), 38
kasumi no koromo / suso wa nurekeri (*JS* no. 108, *Shinsen inu tsukubashū* no. 1), 36, 229
kasumi tachi (*JS* no. 321), 88
kasumumeri (*JS* no. 522), 144–45
katae sakite (*JS* no. 298), 82
kawabune no (*Shinkokinshū* 18: 1775), 239
kawabune o (*Eguchi*), 210
kaze wa nao (*JS* no. 554), 154
kaze ya haru / furutoshi ni tokuru (*JS* no. 296), 81
kaze ya haru / iso no hana saku (*JS* no. 349), 99

kaze ya haru / sazanami yosuru (*JS* no. 499), 139
kazoureba / hitotsu otori mo (*JS* no. 229), 66
kazoureha / nanatsu mo mutsu mo (*JS* no. 53), 28
kazoureba / ware hachijū no (*JS* no. 474), 132
kazoureba / ware taga tame mo (*JS* no. 548), 153
kazukazu ni (*JS* no. 285), 78
kesa chiru ya (*JS* no. 30), 21
kesa no asake (*Man'yōshū* 8: 1513), 302
kesa te ni mo (*JS* no. 406), 115
kesa wa katsu (*JS* no. 475), 132
kesa wa tare (*JS* no. 532), 147
kesa ya yo no (*JS* no. 383), 109
kiehatsuru (*Kokinshū* 9: 414), 223
kikazu to mo (*Shinkokinshū* 3: 217), 220
kikishi yori (*JS* no. 23), 19
kiku hito no (*JS* no. 612), 169, 314
kiku tabi ni (*JS* no. 202), 59
kimi ga nasu (*JS* no. 404), 115
kimi ga tame / fuyu no no ni idete (*JS* no. 478), 133
kimi ga tame / haru no no ni idete (*Kokinshū* 1: 21), 292
kimi inaba (*JS* no. 607), 168
kimi kozuba (*Kokinshū* 14: 693), 258
kimi mo ware mo (*JS* no. 151), 44
kimi ni to te (*Genji monogatari* 9: 20), 218
kimi ni tsutae (*JS* no. 249), 70
kimi ni yori (*JS* no. 154), 45
kimi o inoru (*Goshūishū* 7: 429), 192
kimi sumaba / towamashi mono o / tsu no kuni no (*Shikashū* 3: 83), 214
kimi sumaba / towamashi mono o / yamashiro no (*JS* no. 36), 23
kiri no asake (*JS* no. 379),
kiri no ha mo (*Shinkokinshū* 5: 534), 222
kiyomigata / akemaku oshiki (*JS* no. 272), 75
kiyomigata / sekimoru tsuki no (*JS* no. 273), 76
kiyomigata / seki no aragaki (*JS* no. 198), 58
kiyomigata / tsuki wa tsurenaki (*Shinkokinshū* 3: 259), 312
koe zo seki (*JS* no. 64), 30
koishi no mukashi ya (*JS* no. 408), 116
koishisa mo (*JS* no. 224), 65–66
kokimaze no (*JS* no. 512), 141
koko mo koko mo (*JS* no. 434), 122

Index of First Lines

kokomoto no (*JS* no. 511), 141
kokoro are ya (*JS* no. 614), 170
kokoro kara (*JS* no. 253), 71
kokoro mina (*JS* no. 91), 34
kokoro ni mo (*JS* no. 182), 53
kokoro nomi (*JS* no. 447), 125
kokorozashi / fukaku someteshi (*Kokinshū* 1: 7), 294
kokorozashi / kieaenu yuki mo (*JS* no. 615), 170
kokorazashi / miyama no shigeki (*JS* no. 184), 54
koko wa mata (*Miyako no tsuto*), 264–65
kono tabi no (*JS* no. 571), 158
kono tabi wa (*JS* no. 1), 7
kono toki to (*JS* no. 513), 142
kono tsue wa (*JS* no. 402), 114
kono yo ni te (*Sankashū* no. 750), 251
kono yūbe (*JS* no. 20), 18
kon to shirite (*JS* no. 417), 117
kore mo mata (*JS* no. 414), 117
kore ya kono / tōku motomeshi (*JS* no. 152), 44
kore ya kono / yuku mo kaeru mo (*Gosenshū* 15: 1089), 291
kore ya yo ni (*JS* no. 6), 11
kōriishi (*Shikashū* 1: 1), 295
koshiji ni zo (*JS* no. 22), 19
koshōdō mina (*JS* no. 100), 35
koto ni fure (*JS* no. 516), 143
kōya hijiri no / ato no yarimochi (*JS* no. 133), 38
kōya hijiri no / saki no himegoze (*JS* no. 134), 38
kōya hijiri no / yado o karu koe (*Shinsen inu tsukabashū* no. 35), 227
kōya hijiri no / yado o kau koe (*JS* no. 88), 34
koyoi kore (*JS* no. 457), 127
koyoi yori (*JS* no. 392), 111
kozo kotoshi (*JS* no. 589), 164
kozo no kyō (*JS* no. 221), 65
kozo no yume o (*JS* no. 509), 140
kuina naku / ashihara kuraki (*JS* no. 358), 101
kuina naku / muranae hakobu (*JS* no. 165), 49
kumo kakaru (*Shinkokinshū* 16: 1562), 309
kumori naki (*JS* no. 454), 127
kuramazumi (*JS* no. 480), 133–34
kuretake no / natsu fuyu izure (*JS* no. 157), 46

kuretake no / shigeki fushimi no (*JS* no. 373), 106
kurete nao (*JS* no. 81), 33
kurikaeshi / onaji koto nomi (*JS* no. 418), 117
kurikaeshi / shizu no okamaki (*JS* no. 275), 76
kuru to iu (*JS* no. 325), 89
kyōgoto no (*JS* no. 274), 76
kyō ika ni (*JS* no. 568), 157
kyō ni kurete (*JS* no. 282), 77
kyō sara ni (*JS* no. 543), 151
kyō wa wakare (*Kokinshū* 8: 369), 285
kyō yori wa / ikite itsu made (*JS* no. 476), 133
kyō yori wa / nani ni kawaramu (*JS* no. 267), 74
kyō wakare (*JS* no. 248), 70
kyō wataru (*JS* no. 170), 50

mabikina wa (*JS* no. 572), 158
mae ushiro (*JS* no. 95), 35
majire chire (*JS* no. 31), 21
maki no ha wa (*JS* no. 271), 75
makoto ni ya (*JS* no. 485), 136
makuzuhara (*Man'yōshū* 10: 2096), 230–31
mamemameshiku mo (*JS* no. 576), 159
maotoko (*JS* no. 113), 36
mata kikazu (*JS* no. 155), 145
mataru na yo (*JS* no. 491), 137
matsumushi ya (*JS* no. 69), 32
matsu ni nokoreru (*JS* no. 545), 152
matsu no ha wa (*JS* nos. 329, 340), 90, 96
matsu no ue ni (*Shūishū* 1: 22), 249
matsuran to (*JS* no. 188), 56
matsu tateru (*JS* no. 61), 30
me no mae ni (*JS* no. 242), 69
michitose ni (*Shūishū* 5: 288), 267
mikagirite (*JS* no. 141), 42
mimi yasuki (*JS* no. 435), 122
minakuchi ni / ware ya miyuramu / kadogoto ni (*JS* no. 514), 143
minakuchi ni / ware ya miyuramu / kawazu sae (*Ise monogatari* 39), 300
minazuki no (*JS* no. 215), 62–64
minazuki wa (*JS* no. 7), 11
The mind is the Bodhi tree (*Liuzu tanjing*), 290
mi ni amaru (*JS* no. 610), 168–69
mi o tsumeba (*JS* no. 460), 128
mireba ge ni (*Sōchō renga jichū* 156–57), 225
mireba nao (*JS* no. 305), 83
miru hito mo (*Kokinshū* 1: 68), 300

339

Index of First Lines

miru tabi ni (*JS* no. 205), 60
miru tabi no (*JS* no. 268), 74–75
mishi hito no (*JS* no. 192), 57
mishi ya mina (*JS* no. 74), 32
mite mo mite mo (*JS* no. 194), 57
mite nageki (*JS* no. 308), 84
mitsusegawa / wataru mizao mo / nakarikeri (*Shūishū* 9: 542), 255
mitsusegawa / wataru mizao ni / kake yukan (*JS* no. 260), 73
miwataseba / hana mo momiji mo (*Shinkokinshū* 4: 363), 210
miwataseba / yanagi sakura o (*Kokinshū* 2: 56), 228
miyagino no (*Kokinshū* 14: 694), 308
miyakobito ni (*JS* no. 550), 153
miyako idete (*Kokinshū* 9: 408), 277
miyako ni to (*Saishōsō* 13: 106), 296
miyako ni wa (*JS* no. 305), 83
miyako o ba (*Goshūishū* 9: 518), 306
mizu harete (*JS* no. 8), 14
mizu ni kage sou (*JS* no. 536), 148
mizu no aya o (*Shūishū* 17: 1091), 277
mogamigawa (*Kokinshū* 20: 1092), 296
mono wa mina (*JS* no. 611), 169
morotomo ni / kokorobosoku mo (*JS* no. 320), 88
morotomo ni / koshiore uta o (*JS* no. 97), 35
morotomo ni / oi a zo chigiru (*JS* no. 280), 77
morotomo ni / oizu shinazu no (*JS* no. 228), 66
motenashi no (*JS* no. 105), 36
motoara no (*JS* no. 567), 157
The mountains are like a painted screen *Wakan rōeishū* no. 503), 239
mubatama no (*Yamato monogatari* no. 362), 308
mube mo koso (*JS* no. 258), 73
mujōshin (*JS no.* 33), 22
mukashi kimi (*JS* no. 452), 126
mukashi omou (*Shinkokinshū* 6: 697), 263
mukashi ware (*JS* no. 399), 113
mune wa fuji (*Shikashū* 7: 213), 215
murasaki no (*Kokinshū* 17: 867), 260
musubi oku (*JS* no. 195), 57
musubite wa (*JS* no. 397), 112
musubu te no (*Kokinshū* 8: 404), 240
mutsumaji to (*JS* no. 247), 70

nabete haru (*JS* no. 328), 90
nabete yo ya (*JS* no. 525), 145
nabiku yo wa (*JS* no. 149), 44
nagakaraji (*JS* no. 426), 119
nagameyaru (*JS* no. 487), 136
nagaraeba / kyō no kokoro mo (*JS* no. 530), 146
nagaraeba / mata mo noboran (*JS* no. 156), 46
nagare mo kiri no (*JS* no. 15), 17
nagori naku (*JS* no. 257), 73
naki ni shi mo (*JS* no. 518), 144
nakoso to wa (*Gyokuyōshū* 11: 1550), 295
nakute zo to (*JS* no. 422), 118
namida nomi (*JS* no. 583), 161
nami no oto (*JS* no. 187), 56
nami no ue (*JS* no. 463), 129
nami no ue no (*JS* no. 496), 138
nami ya kore (*JS* no. 544), 151
nami ya yuku (*JS* no. 348), 98
nanasoji ni (*JS* no. 139), 41
nanatose no (*JS* no. 601), 166–67
nanbō gozareta (*JS* no. 98), 35
nani ka sore (*JS* no. 503), 139
nani mo ka mo (*JS* no. 326), 89
naninani ni (*JS* no. 289), 79
naniwa naru (*Kokinshū* 19: 1051), 267
naniwazu ni (*Kokinshū* preface), 287
nao jin'ai o todome (*JS* no. 559), 155
nao zo omou (*JS* no. 451), 126
narekoshi wa (*JS* no. 394), 112
narenareshi (*JS* no. 608), 168
narenarete (*JS* no. 605), 167
nareshi yo o (*JS* no. 508), 140
natsu no ame (*JS* no. 367), 104
natsu no yo no (*JS* no. 89), 34
natsu to wa shirushi (*JS* no. 539), 149
natsu ya toki (*JS* no. 356), 101
nawashiro o (*JS* no. 109), 36
negaikinu (*JS* no. 566), 157
negawaku wa / hana no moto ni te (*Sankashū* no. 77), 214
negawaku wa / kotoshi no kure no (*JS* no. 37), 23
negawaku wa / kyō gannichi no (*JS* no. 606), 168
nikukaranu (*JS* no. 424), 118
nio no umi ya (*Shinkokinshū* 4: 389), 224
niwa no matsu (*JS* no. 440), 123–24

Index of First Lines

nochi mo oshi (*JS* no. 307), 84
nochiseyama (*JS* no. 240), 68
nodoka naru (*JS* no. 143), 42
nodoka ni te (*JS* no. 38), 25
noki no matsu (*JS* no. 599), 166
nokoshitsuru (*JS* no. 218), 65
nori ni au (*JS* no. 377), 107
no wa aki no (*JS* no. 581), 160
nowaki seshi hi no (*Yuyama sangin* no. 32), 223
nyake no atari wa (*JS* no. 102), 35

ocha no mizu (*JS* no. 99), 35
ōchi saku (*JS* no. 9), 14
odorokasu (*JS* no. 44), 26
oguruma no (*JS* no. 231), 67
oi no koshi (*JS* no. 369), 105
oi no nami (*JS* no. 419), 118
oi no nochi / onaji kokoro to te (*JS* no. 428), 119
oi no nochi / sute sutezu to mo (*JS* no. 588), 163
oi no tomo (*JS* no. 153), 45
oinureba / asu wa ōmi to (*JS* no. 430), 120
oinureba / negaimono zo yo (*JS* no. 450), 126
oinu to mo (*Shinkokinshū* 16: 1586), 258
oiraku no / kaku chō yado wa (*JS* no. 276), 76
oiraku no / komu to shiriseba (*Kokinshū* 17: 895), 283
oiraku no / nao yukusue mo (*JS* no. 281), 77
oitsukan (*JS* no. 132), 38
oitsutsu mo (*JS* no. 48), 27
oi wa tada (*JS* no. 421), 118
ōji chichi / kimi made oi ga (*JS* no. 333), 91
ōji chichi / mumago no toshi no (*JS* no. 617), 170
ōji chichi / mumago sukechika (*Goshūishū* 20: 1163), 315
ōji wazuka ni (*JS* no. 300), 82
ōkata no (*JS* no. 481), 134
ōki naru (*Shinsen inu tsukubashū* no. 80), 227
okinoite / mi o yaku yori mo / kanashiki wa (*Kokinshū* 20: 1104), 271
okinoite / mi o yaku yori mo/ oboyuru wa (*JS* no. 353), 100
ōki no semi no (*Shinsen inu tsukubashū* no. 104), 232
okitsunami (*JS* no. 524), 145
okiwakare (*JS* no. 598), 166

ōmi no ya (*Shinkokinshū* 7: 753), 286–87
omoedomo / iwade tsukihi wa (*Shinkokinshū* 12: 1109), 284
omoedomo / kaeranu nami ya (*JS* no. 455), 127
omoiaezu (*JS* no. 304), 83
omoi dani (*JS* no. 225), 66
omoigawa (*Gosenshū* 9: 515), 254
omoiizuru (*JS* no. 190), 56
omoitatsu (*JS* no. 13), 16
omoiyare / waga yamabata no (*JS* no. 573), 159
omoiyare / yanagi no ito no (*JS* no. 147), 43
omokage wa / fumiwakegataki (*JS* no. 68), 32
omokage wa / mazu tachikiete (*JS* no. 235), 68
omokage wa / sanagara akashi (*JS* no. 560), 155–56
omoki kata ni wa (*JS* no. 116), 37
omoshiroge ni mo (*JS* no. 114), 37
omoshirosō ni (*Shinsen inu tsukubashū*), 230
omowazu mo (*JS* no. 292), 80
omawazu no (*JS* no. 21), 18
onaji toshi koso (*JS* no. 112), 36
onna fumi (*JS* no. 119), 37
onozukara (*JS* no. 43), 26
ori ni au (*JS* no. 34), 22–23
ori ni fure (*JS* no. 486), 136
oriori wa (*JS* no. 234), 67–68
oshikaeshi (*JS* no. 420), 118
oshinabete (*Genji monogatari* 3: 117), 274
oshiteru ya (*Kokinshū* 17: 894), 282–83
osozakura (*JS* no. 521), 144
otomera ga (*Man'yōshū* 4: 501), 254
oto ni nomi (*JS* no. 283), 78
otowayama / kikite mo ika de (*JS* no. 506), 140
otowayama / oto ni kikitsutsu (*Kokinshū* 11: 473), 295

reijin no (*JS* no. 246), 70
rin'e seba (*JS* no. 561), 156
ryōchi kōzan (*JS* no. 490), 137
ryū no sumu (*JS* no. 562), 156

sabishi to yo (*JS* no. 553), 154
saioku no (*JS* no. 339), 95
sakaki toru (*Goshūishū* 3: 169), 243
saki sakazu / ki wa natsu kodachi (*JS* no. 354), 100

Index of First Lines

saki sakazu / matsu to shirakawa (*JS* no. 602), 167
saku hagi no (*JS* no. 233), 67
sakuraba nokoru (*JS* no. 527), 146
samidare ni (*JS* no. 177), 52
samidare wa / kumoi no kishi no (*JS* no. 2), 8
samidare wa / kumo no konata no (*JS* no. 368), 104
sa mo araba (*JS* no. 587), 163
samukaranu (*JS* no. 142), 42
samuki yo wa (*JS* no. 591), 164
samushiro ni (*Kokinshū* 14: 689), 296
saohime no (*Shinsen inu tsukubashū* no. 1), 229
sarade dani (*JS* no. 555), 154
sara ni hen (*JS* no. 278), 77
saranu dani (*Shinkokinshū* 20: 1963), 231
sasowareba (*JS* no. 201), 59
sasowaruru (*JS* no. 531), 147
sato tsuzuki (*JS* no. 519), 144
satsuki matsu (*Kokinshū* 3: 139), 222
sawa no ue no (*JS* no. 346), 98
sekiiruru (*JS* no. 578), 160
seki koen (*SN* no. 153), 306
shichijūkyūnen (*JS* no. 407), 116
shigeriau / kozue no natsu no (*JS* no. 541), 150
shigeriau / yama no hatsuka ni (*Hokku kikigaki* 37), 275
shigure sae (*JS* no. 585), 161
shiite mina (*JS* no. 494), 138
shika no ne o (*Yuyama sangin* no. 31), 222
shika no ne ya / onoe no arashi (*JS* no. 75), 32
shika no ne ya / tōyamabata no (*JS* nos. 575, 584), 159, 161
shimeokite (*Shinkokinshū* 16: 1560), 222
shimo ni tatsu (*JS* no. 131), 38
shimo o aya (*JS* no. 28), 21
shimo tōshi (*JS* no. 294), 80
shimo wa kesa (*JS* no. 586), 161
shinagadori / inano o yukeba (*Shinkokinshū* 10: 910), 224
shinagadori / inano o yuki no (*JS* no. 79), 33
shinau to mo (*JS* no. 477), 133
shionoyama (*Kokinshū* 7: 345), 313
shirayuki no (*Kokinshū* 6: 324), 240–41
shirazu sate (*JS* no. 395), 112
shitau zo yo (*JS* no. 252), 71
shizuka naru (*JS* no. 186), 55
sode hichite (*Kokinshū* 1: 2), 259
somakata no (*Man'yōshū* 1: 19), 248
somekakuru (*JS* no. 51), 27
somo koi yo (*JS* no. 117), 37
sono kami wa (*JS* no. 427), 119
sono sato ni (*JS* no. 438), 123
sora midare (*JS* no. 582), 160
sora wa tsuki (*JS* no. 444), 125
The sound of the bell of Changle Palace (*Wakan rōeishū* no. 81), 239
sue no tsuyu (*Shinkokinshū* 8: 757), 252
sue ya mina (*JS* no. 211), 62
sugi no ita o (*Goshūishū* 6: 399), 311
sumi fude mo (*JS* no. 520), 144
sumire saku (*JS* no. 344), 97
sumiutsuru (*JS* no. 570), 158
suruga naru / tago no uranami (*Kokinshū* 11: 489), 237
suruga naru / utsunoyamabe no (*Ise monogatari* 22), 279
suruga yori (*JS* no. 375), 107
susameoke (*JS* no. 403), 114
susu hana wa (*JS* no. 456), 127
suzukayama / furisutenu mi no (*JS* no. 169), 50
suzukayama / furiuzumoruru (*JS* no. 467), 130
suzukayama / iroiro ni naru (*JS* no. 18), 17
suzukayama / sazo na furitsumu (*JS* no. 466), 130
suzukayama / shino ni nakikeru (*JS* no. 167), 50
suzukayama / ukiyo o yoso ni (*JS* no. 168, *Shinkokinshū* 17: 1613), 50, 208
suzukayama / yasose watarite (*Man'yōshū* 12: 3156), 208

tabi goto ni (*JS* no. 580), 160
tabine wasururu (*JS* no. 469), 131
tabitabi no (*JS* no. 345), 97
tachikaeri (*JS* no. 501), 139
tachikawari (*JS* no. 256), 72
tachiwakare (*JS* no. 332), 91
tachiwasure (*JS* no. 432), 121
taga goke no (*JS* no. 111), 36
taga sato no (*JS* no. 401), 114
taga uki mo (*JS* no. 265), 74
tago no ura ya (*JS* no. 563), 156
take no yo no (*JS* no. 405), 115
tamadare no / kogame wa mirume (*JS* no. 442), 124

Index of First Lines

tamadare no / ogame o naka ni suete (*Fūzokuuta* no. 3), 288
tamakiharu (*Man'yōshū* 5: 897), 301
tama no o yo (*Shinkokinshū* 11: 1034), 263
tamayura mo (*JS* no. 223), 65
tamazusa o (*Shinsen inu tsukubashū* no. 141), 231
tanabata no / iohata oreru (*Shinsen inu tsukubashū*), 230
tanabata no / iohata tatete (*Man'yōshū* 10: 2034), 230
tanabikare (*JS* no. 533), 147
tanabiku ya (*JS* no. 4), 10
tani fukami (*JS* no. 158), 47
tanomanedo (*JS* no. 470), 131
tanomikoshi (*JS* no. 32), 21–22
tanomu wakazō (*JS* no. 120), 37
tarachine no (*JS* no. 261), 73
tare o ka mo / shiru hito ni semu (*Kokinshū* 17: 909), 244
tare o ka mo / tomo to wa iwan (*JS* no. 179), 53
tare to naki (*JS* no. 263), 74
tare zo kono (*JS* no. 309), 85
tare zo kono (*JS* no. 448), 125
tatenarabe (*JS* no. 115), 37
tateueshi (*JS* no. 315), 87
tazunetsu to (*JS* no. 199), 58
teru tsuki mo (*JS* no. 254), 71
The mind is the Bodhi tree (*Liuzu tanjing*), 290
The mountains are like a painted screen (*Wakan rōeishū* no. 503), 239
The sound of the bell of Changle Palace (*Wakan rōeishū* no. 81), 193
tobu hotaru (*JS* no. 362), 102
tokaeri no (*JS* no. 441), 124
tokonatsu no (*JS* no. 372), 106
tomo ni min (*Sōgi shūenki*), 251
tori no ne ni (*JS* no. 459), 128
torinukashitaru (*JS* no. 104), 36
toritsutae (*JS* no. 472), 132
toru tabi ni (*JS* no. 172), 51
toru tokoro (*JS* no. 439), 123
toshidoshi ni / kyō no namida no (*JS* no. 291), 80
toshidoshi no / haru ya tachikaeru (*JS* no. 144), 43
toshi ni narenuru (*JS* no. 603), 167
toshi no kure no (*JS* no. 311), 86
toshi no uchi ni (*Kokinshū* 1: 1), 235
toshi no uchi wa (*JS* no. 594), 165
toshi o hete (*Goshūishū* 19: 1116), 309
toshi takete (*Shinkokinshū* 10: 987), 192
towataru ya (*JS* no. 595), 165
toyakaku to (*JS* no. 127), 38
tsubame tobu (*JS* no. 330), 90
tsukihi nomi (*JS* no. 380), 109
tsuki izuru (*JS* no. 557), 155
tsuki nagara / iku yo no nami o (*JS* no. 196), 58
tsuki nagara / yukiore no take no (*JS* no. 433), 121
tsuki ni awaba (*JS* no. 57), 29
tsuki o nado / matare nomi su to / omoikemu / ge ni yama no ha wa / ideukarikeri (*Shinkokinshū* 16: 1504), 236
tsuki o nado / matare nomi su to / omoiken / ge ni yama no ha wa / ideukarikeri (*JS* no. 164), 48–49
tsuki wa shiru ya (*JS* no. 193), 57
tsuki wa yūbe no (*JS* no. 25), 20
tsuki yo ika ni (*JS* no. 71), 32
tsuki zo yuku (*JS* no. 191), 56
tsumade koso (*JS* no. 577), 159
tsunadenawa (*JS* no. 361), 102
tsu no kuni no (*JS* no. 87), 34
tsurezure to (*JS* no. 35), 23
tsuta kaede (*JS* no. 318), 87
tsutsumi yuku (*JS* no. 360), 101
tsuyu fukami (*JS* no. 236), 68
tsuyukesa wa (*JS* no. 56), 28–29

uchiharau (*JS* no. 453), 126–27
uchimawasu (*Shinsen inu tsukubashū*), 230
uchinasu ni (*JS* no. 245), 70
ueshi yo ya (*JS* no. 384), 110
uete konata (*JS* no. 174), 51
ugoki naki (*JS* no. 484), 135
uguisu no / ito ni yoraruru (*JS* no. 52), 27
uguisu no / ito ni yoru chō (*Gosenshū* 3: 131), 217
uguisu no / sugomori to iu (*JS* no. 136), 39
uguisu ya (*JS* no. 150), 44
uji no kawase no (*Kanginshū* no. 64), 239
umakura wa (*JS* no. 85), 34
uma ni noritaru / hitomaro o miyo (*JS* no. 130, *Shinsen inu tsukubashū* no. 81), 38, 233

Index of First Lines

ume ga ka o (*JS* no. 489), 137
ume no hana (*JS* no. 146), 43
ume sakite / arashi mo nabiku (*JS* no. 12), 15
ume sakite / nioteru nami no (*JS* no. 500), 139
ume yanagi (*JS* no. 498), 138
unohana ya / miru miru fureru (*JS* no. 166), 49
unohana ya / nami moteyueru (*JS* no. 542), 150
unohana wa (*JS* no. 357), 101
urami are ya (*JS* no. 388), 110
usu kine no (*JS* no. 471), 131
usumomiji (*JS* no. 352), 100
utsukushi na (*JS* no. 129), 38
utsusemi no / usuhanazakura (*JS* no. 59), 29
utsusemi no / usuki maroya no (*JS* no. 431), 120
utsusemi no / yo ni mo nitaru ka (*Kokinshū* 2: 73), 219
utsusemi no / yo no uki fushi ya (*JS* no. 243), 69
utsutsu aru (*JS* no. 251), 70–71
uzumibi no (*JS* no. 297), 81

wabibito no (*JS* no. 310), 85
waga io wa / kayaya komogaki (*JS* no. 313), 87
waga io wa / miwa no yamamoto (*Kokinshū* 18: 982), 232
waga io wa / miyako no tatsumi / shika mo sume (*JS* no. 374), 107
waga io wa / miyako no tatsumi / shika zo sumu (*Kokinshū* 18: 983), 276
waga kado ni (*Ise monogatari* 74), 238
waga tame ni / motomuru shinone (*JS* no. 479), 133
waga tame ni / omoiokikemu (*JS* no. 465), 130
waga yado no (*Man'yōshū* 19: 4291), 301
waga yowai (*JS* no. 49), 27
wakarubeki (*JS* no. 493), 137
wakite tare (*JS* no. 504), 140
ware bakari (*Ise monogatari* 39), 300
ware mo ima (*JS* no. 42), 26
ware yori mo (*JS* no. 122, *Shinsen inu tsukabashū* no. 104), 37, 232
ware zo kono (*JS* no. 482), 134
washi no sumu (*JS* no. 175), 52
wasurete wa / nagakaranu oi o (*JS* no. 416), 117
wasurete wa / uchinagekaruru (*Shinkokinshū* 11: 1035), 283

wasuru to wa (*Gosenshū* 16: 1171), 266
wataru se ya (*JS* no. 437), 122
watatsumi no (*Ise monogatari* 83–84), 270
We warm wine in the woods, burning fallen leaves (*Wakan rōeishū* no. 221), 213

yaegumo kakure (*Hokku kikigaki* 37), 275
yakumo tatsu (*Kokin waka rokujō* no. 1026), 260
yaku shio to (*JS* no. 411), 116
yama kasumu / tani no to hiroki (*JS* no. 515), 143
yama kasumu / yukige no mizu ka (*JS* no. 50), 27
yamabatake no (*JS* no. 597), 166
yamabito no (*JS* no. 41), 26
yamadera no (*Shūishū* 20: 1329), 219
yamashina no (*Man'yōshū* 11: 2425), 281
yamazato no (*JS* no. 316), 87
yasoji made (*JS* no. 322), 88
yasoji zo yo (*JS* no. 556), 155
yaso no se no (*JS* nos. 14, 171), 16, 51
yasugenami (*JS* no. 409), 116
yasumu beki (*JS* no. 46), 26
yayoya mate (*JS* no. 250), 70
yo fukaki tori ni (*JS* no. 445), 125
yoki ni tsuke (*JS* no. 613), 169
yo o fukaku (*JS* no. 319), 87
yo to tomo ni (*JS* no. 564), 156
yorozuyo o (*Kokinshū* 7: 356), 294
yoru nami ya (*JS* no. 162), 48
yoru wa shigure (*JS* no. 78), 33
yosekaeru / izuko mo waga mi (*JS* no. 410), 116
yosekaeru / shiohi no kata no (*JS* no. 529), 146
yoshi ya ima (*JS* no. 237), 68
yoshi ya oi (*JS* no. 412), 116–17
yosoge ni mo (*JS* no. 593), 165
yoso ni dani (*JS* no. 287), 79
yūdachi ya (*JS* no. 67), 31
yūgao no (*Shinsen inu tsukubashū* no. 51), 230
yū kakete nake (*JS* no. 173), 51
yūkaze ni (*JS* no. 558), 155
yuki fureba (*JS* no. 317), 87
yuki kaeri (*JS* no. 604), 167
yuki kiete (*JS* no. 299), 82
yuki ni hito (*JS* no. 464), 129
yuki no uchi (*JS* no. 323), 88
yuki no uchi no (*JS* no. 206), 61

Index of First Lines

yuki okite (*JS* no. 72), 32
yuki tozoru (*JS* no. 523), 145
yuki wa nokoreru (*Oi no mimi* no. 151), 206
yuki wa tada (*JS* no. 290), 79
yuku sode o (*JS* no. 10), 14
yukusue mo (*JS* no. 140), 42

yuku to ku to / izuko mo kari no (*JS* no. 331), 91
yuku to ku to / kozue ya ōchi (*JS* no. 65), 31
yume narade (*JS* no. 239), 68
yume nare ya (*JS* no. 546), 152
yūsuzumi (*JS* no. 214), 62

General Index

Page numbers in boldface type indicate the most important entry.

Abekawa river, 200, 249
Abeyama, 12, 200
Aburanokōji, 27, 111, 217
Ago no matsubara, 302
Ajiro Hirosada (Tarōzaemonnojō), 205
Akaike, 289
Akashi Bay (Akashi no ura), 233, 241
Akino Dōjō, 278
Aki Province (now part of Hiroshima Prefecture), 182
Akogi Bay (Akogi no ura), 61, 249
Akutagawa Castle, 217
Akutagawa river, 225
Amako Tsunehisa, 182
Amanogawa. *See* River of Heaven
Ama no hashidate, 219
Ama no kawa. *See* River of Heaven
Amaterasu Ōmikami (Sun Goddess), 270, 315
Amida, 73, 119, 140, 300. *See also* Holy Name
Amidaji, 54, 145, 245, 301
Analects of Confucius, 276
Anjō, 149–50, 195, 270, 303
Anonotsu, 16–19, 181–82, 207, 224, 249
An'yōin, 20, 212
An'yōji, 28, 218
Aoi, Lady, 286
Aoi matsuri. *See* Hollyhock Festival
Appendix A: The Imagawa House, 173–76
Appendix B: The Historical Context of the "Asahina Battle Chronicle," 177–80
Appendix C: Chronology of *The Journal of Sōchō*, 181–88
Arakida Morihira, 209, 256

Arakida Morikane, 165, 312
Arakida Moritake, 207, 312
Arakida Moritoki, 165, 312
Arima (Mountain), 33, 183, 224
Ariwara Motokata, 235, 295
Ariwara Narihira, 181, 245, 305
Ariwara Yukihira, 229
"Asahina Battle Chronicle," 8–14, 194, 203
Asahina house, 181, 185, **191–92**
Asahina Tokishige (Shimotsukenokami), 11, 82, 84, 130, 161, 170, 185, **199**, 256, 259–60, 291, 306, 310
Asahina Yasuhiro (Bitchūnokami), 8–10, 178, **193–94**, 198
Asahina Yasumochi (Sakyōnosuke), 10–11, 14, 90–91, 96, 161–62, 185, **198–99**, 256, 264, 291, 306, 310–11
Asahina Yasumori (Higonokami), 13, 202
Asahina Yasumoto (Yatarō?), 291
Asahina Yasutomo, 193
Asahina Yasutsugu (Jūrō), 264
Asahina Yasuyoshi, 7, 14, 92, 130, 193, 198
Asahiyama. *See* Sunrise Mountain
Asai house, 293
Asakura, 299
Asakura house 178–79, 181–82, **191**, 207, 209, 220–21, 238, 274–75, 299
Asakura Norikage (Tarōzaemon, Sōteki), 19, 30–31, 45, 183, 188, **191**, 220, 222, 238, 262
Asakura Sōteki waki (Asakura Sōteki's Anecdotes), 191, 262
Asakura Takakage, 237
Asakura Toshikage, 221

General Index

Asakura Ujikage, 191, 221
Ashikaga house, 173–74, 177, 297
Ashikaga Masatomo (Horikoshi Kubō), 175
Ashikaga Mochiuji, 174–75
Ashikaga Shigeuji (Koga Kubō), 175, 201
Ashikaga Takauji (Tōjiin), 58, 173, 177, 247
Ashikaga Yoshiharu, 142, 183, 188, 273, 284–85, 296, 299
Ashikaga Yoshihisa, 298
Ashikaga Yoshiki. *See* Ashikaga Yoshitane
Ashikaga Yoshimasa, 13, 142, 175, 200–201
Ashikaga Yoshimi, 298
Ashikaga Yoshimitsu, 142, 297
Ashikaga Yoshinori, 174–75, 201, 281
Ashikaga Yoshitada. *See* Ashikaga Yoshitane
Ashikaga Yoshitaka. *See* Ashikaga Yoshizumi
Ashikaga Yoshitane (Yoshiki, Yoshitada), 298–99
Ashikaga Yoshitsuna, 284
Ashikaga Yoshizumi (Yoshitaka), 298
Assistant head priest (*shōgūji*), 312
Aster River (Kikugawa river), 267–68
Asukai Masachika (Kashiwagi Zenmon Eiga), 127, 207, 284, 290
Asukai Masayasu, 207
Asukai Masayo, 207
Atami, 10, 163, 197, 311
Atsuta Shrine, 99–100, 148, 186, 188, **270–71**, 305
Awa, Deputy Constable of, 166
Awaji, 150, 166
Awa Province (now Tokushima Prefecture), 142, 298–99, 313
Awataguchi, 104, 274
Ayanokōji, 82, 260
Aya no tsuzumi (The Damask Drum), 231, 299
Azumaji no tsuto (Souvenir of the Eastland), 196, 256, 306

Baba Hyōgonosuke (Suke Hyōgo?, Saneyuki?), 138, 288, 294
Banjūzanmaiin, 105, 275
Bishamondō, 153
Bitchū Province (now part of Okayama Prefecture), 286
Biwa, Lake (Nio Sea, Sea of Ōmi), 102, 139, 184, 187, 206, 224, 272, 275, 287, 291, 300
Biyanlu (The Blue Cliff Record), 289
Blind attendant (*zatō*), 126, 153–54, 289, 305

Blind expert (*kengyō*), 305
Blind master (*kōtō*), 153–54, 305
Bo Ya, 253
Bodaiin, 113, 281–82. *See also* Daigoji
Bōjō Toshina, 168, 314
Bo Juyi, 213, 262
Bon. *See* Festival of the Dead
Bōnotsu, 33, 224
Bōshū (Ihara Awanokami Tadatane?), 130, 153, 291, 305
Botanka Shōhaku. *See* Shōhaku
Bo Ya, 235
Brushwood Cottage (Saioku, shiba no io, sanka no sōan), **86–87**, **95–96**, 119, 154, 157, 161, 163, 165, 185, 188, **192**, 215, 249, **262**, 304, 308
Buddha, Buddhahood, 71, 84, 113, 145, 214–15, 218, 229, 244, 256–57, 281, 290, 293. *See also* Amida, Gautama
Bunki 2 [1502]:8:6 *Sōgi tuitō nanibito hyakuin* (A Hundred-Verse Sequence Entitled "A Kind of Person" in Memory of Sōgi), 252

Cang Xie, 300
Capital. *See* Kyoto
Castle town (*jōkamachi*), 191
Central Tōtōmi Uprising (Chūen ikki), 177
Chief assistant priest (*ichi no negi*), 312
Chigusagoe, 273
Chikayoshi. *See* Nagaike Chikayoshi
Chikurinshō, 245
Chikuzennokami. *See* Oda Chikuzennokami
Chikuzen Province (now part of Fukuoka Prefecture), 299
Chinzō, 289
Chita, 15, 55
Chō (unit of measure) 196, **199**
Chōei (Hōgen), 21, 212
Chōfukuji, 54, 245
Chōgetsuken, 121, 286
Chōkanji, 307
Chōkōji, 103, 142, 273, 299
Chōkyō 2 [1488]:4 *Nanimichi hyakuin* (A Hundred-Verse Sequence Entitled "A Kind of Path"), 218
Chōrakuji, 82, 155, 259, 307
Chōzenji, 166, 312
Chūgoku, 142, 299
Chūnagon Moronaka, 265

General Index

Daibosatsu Mountain, 11, 198
Daiei 3 [1523]:9:2 *Yamanani hyakuin* (A Hundred-Verse Sequence Entitled "A Kind of Mountain"), 223, 291, 293
Daiei 5 [1525]:1:25 *Naniki* (or *Nanibito*) *hyakuin* (A Hundred-Verse Sequence Entitled "A Kind of Tree," or "A Kind of Person"), 248
Daiei 5 [1525]:9:21 *Nanibito hyakuin* (A Hundred-Verse Sequence Entitled "A Kind of Person"), 199, 246, 256, 306
Daiei 6 [1526]:8:15 *Hyakuin*, 278
Daiei 6 [1526]:9:13 *Nanibito hyakuin* (a Hundred-Verse Sequence Entitled "A Kind of Person"), 279
Daiei 7 [1527]:1:18 *Yashima Shōrin'an naniki hyakuin*. See *Yashima Shōrin'an naniki hyakuin*
Daiei 7 [1527]:1:19 *Yamanani hyakuin* (A Hundred-Verse Sequence Entitled "A Kind of Mountain"), 236, 292, 294
Daiei 7 [1527]:4:2 *Nanibito hyakuin* (A Hundred-Verse Sequence Entitled "A Kind of Person"), 236, 270, 279, 289, 303
Daigo, Emperor, 249
Daigoji, 113, 187, 209, 280–81
Daihatsunehangyō (Sutra on the Great Extinction), 281
Daihōbenbutsuhōongyō (Sutra on the Repayment of His Indebtedness to His Parents by Great and Skillful Means), 293
Daijōe. See Great Thanksgiving Service
Dainichi Nyorai, 211
Daiō Kokushi, 213, 286
Dairyōji, 51, 243
Daisen'in, 22, 106. See also Daitokuji
Daitokuji, 15, 22, 30–31, 46, 50, 74, 105–6, 115, 161–62, 181–83, 185–87, 205–6, 213, 220–21, 238, 242, 255, 274, 282, 290. See also Daisen'in; Shinjuan
Daitō Kokushi, 261, 290
Dengaku, 282
Deputy, the. See Hosokawa Takakuni
Diamond Sutra (Kongōkyō), 218
Discord of the Eikyō Era (Eikyō no ran), 176
Dora Ikkōdō, 55, 246
Double Yang Festival, 279
Dove-Tipped Staff (hato no tsue, Eighty-Year Staff), 48, 241
Du Fu, 282
Du Xunhe, 242

Echizen Province (now part of Fukui Prefecture), 7, 18, 30–31, 158, 178, 181–83, 188, 191, 201, 207, 210, 237, 261, 308
Edo, 9
Edo Castle, 175, 196
Egedera, 273
Eguchi, 210
Eigenji, 273
Eight Bridges (Yatsuhashi), 15, 181, 203
Eight Peaks Pass (Happūgoe), 102, 186, 273
Eight views of Ōmi (Ōmi hakkei), 272
Eikyū hyakushu. See *Latter Hundred-Waka Sequence at the Palace of the Retired Emperor Horikawa*
Einō, 121, 286
Eishō 1 [1504] (Eishō 3? [1506?]) *Nanibito hyakuin* (A Hundred-Verse Sequence Entitled "A Kind of Person"), 195
Eishō 2 [1505]:8:22 *Tamanani hyakuin* (A Hundred Verse Sequence Entitled "A Kind of Gem"), 256
Eishō 4 [1507]:11:3 *Makino Kohaku Zenmon uchijini isshūki* (First Anniversary of the Death in Battle of Makino Kohaku Zenmon), 269
Eishō 12 [1515]:11:11 *Yamanani hyakuin* (A Hundred-Verse Sequence entitled "A Kind of Mountain"), 272
Eishō 13 [1516]:7:8 *Nanibito hyakuin* (A Hundred-Verse Sequence Entitled "A Kind of Person"), 312
Eishō 15 [1518]:1:3 *Yamanani hyakuin* (A Hundred-Verse Sequence Entitled "A Kind of Mountain"), 198
Eishō 15 [1518]:4:26 [1518:4:23?] *Yamanani hyakuin* (A Hundred-Verse Sequence entitled "A Kind of Mountain"), 270
Enryakuji (Mountain Gate [Sanmon], the Mountain), 105, 184, 209, 216, 275, 293. See also Hiei, Mount
Entoku 3 [1491]:10:20 *Nanibito hyakuin* (A Hundred-Verse Sequence Entitled "A Kind of Person"). See *Yuyama sangin*
Equinoxes (Higan), 86, 261

Festival, the. See Hollyhock Festival
Festival of the Dead (Bon, Urabon), 63, 86, 158, 250, 261, 309

General Index

Festival of the Weaver Maid (Tanabata), 156–57, 186, 188, 230, 277, 308
Fifth Ward (Gojō), 36, 229
Five Mountains (Gozan), 105, 238, 240, 259, 275; in Kamakura, 259. *See also* Zen
Five trees and eight herbs (*goboku hassō*), 111, 280
Former Han, 314
Fuchū (Suruga). *See* Sunpu
Fuchū (Tōtōmi), 92
Fudō (Fudō Myōō, Acala), 37, 232
Fūgashū (*Fūga wakashū*), 97, 173
Fuji, Mount, 25, 28, 59, 63, 89, 95, 104, 126, 147, 153, 167, 215, 217, 248, 257–58, 264, 267, 274, 305–6
Fujieda, 55, 152, 305
Fuji goran nikki, 174
Fujimasu, 59, 247
Fuji rekiranki, 207
Fujiwara Ariie, 206, 211
Fujiwara house, 34, 226
Fujiwara Ietaka, 224
Fujiwara Kamatari, 212
Fujiwara Kanesuke, 308
Fujiwara Kiyoo, 285
Fujiwara Masatsune, 167, 247, 313
Fujiwara Michitoshi, 242
Fujiwara Muneyuki, 267
Fujiwara Norikane, 236, 289
Fujiwara Okikaze, 244
Fujiwara Sanefusa, 236
Fujiwara Shunzei, 48, 222, 258, 286, 293
Fujiwara Tadahira, 238
Fujiwara Tadasada, 284
Fujiwara Teika, 210, 255, 283, 306
Fujiwara Toshiyuki, 223, 288
Fujiwara Yorisuke, 239
Fukakusa, 46, 238
Fukiage, 228
Fukōin, 12, 201
Fukōzu, 98, 150, 269
Fukuda Hachirō (Sōkan), 139, 294
Fukushima Masanari, 312
Fukushima Saemonnojō (Sukeharu?), 9, 196
Funakata (Mountain), 13, 202
Furu, 254
Furu, Mount (Furuyama), 254
Fusaiji, 12, 200

Fushimi, 46, 105–6, 108, 111–14, 183, 186–87, 238, 276, 278
Fushinomiya Sadaatsu, 183
Futamata Castle, 8, 195
Futami Bay, 22, 211, 213, 275

Gamō Hidenori, 182
Gamō house, 17, 273
Gautama, Prince, 290
Genji monogatari (The Tale of Genji), 29, 74, 136, 183, 210, 215–16, 218–19, 229–30, 241, 246, 250, 255, 271, 274, 283, 286, 289, 295, 302
Genji monogatari okuiri, 283
Genji monogatari teiyō, 174
Genpei seisuiki, 285
Genpei War, 297
Genshū, 124, 289
Gesshū Jukei. *See* Ikkeken
Gessonsai senku. *See Iba senku*
Gessonsai Sōseki. *See* Sōseki
Go, 234
Gohanazono, Emperor, 290
Gohōjō house, 195. *See also* Hōjō house
Gojō. *See* Fifth Ward
Gojō Yoshisuke, 258
Gokashiwabara, Emperor (Gokashiwabarain), 105, 186, 275
Gokokuji, 27, 111, 217, 280
Gokyōgoku Yoshitsune, 287
Gonara, Emperor, 186, 275
Gondainagon [Minamoto] Michiteru, 312
Goose-skin paper (ganpi no kami, ganpishi), 253
Gorō Ujiteru. *See* Imagawa Ujiteru
Goseibai shikimoku, 184
Gosenshū (*Gosen wakashū*), 216–17, 254, 257, 266, 291, 305
Goshūishū (*Goshūi wakashū*), 192, 306, 309, 311, 315
Gotō Tajimanokami, 103, 273
Gotsuchimikado, Emperor, 275
Gozan. *See* Five Mountains
Great Buddha, 21, 182, 212
Great Thanksgiving Service (Daijōe), 122, 286–87
Guku Wakuraba (My Ignorant Blighted Leaves), 204

Gyōki, 214, 224
Gyokuyōshū (*Gyokuyō wakashū*), 97, 268, 295

Hachigata, 9, 196–97
Hachikazuki, 312
Hachiman, 11, 199, 235
Hachirō. *See* Ise Hachirō
Hahakabe Hyōgonosuke (Morikuni), 29, 110, 218, 279
Haikai, 17, 34, 46–47, 50, 57, 103, 120–21, 124, 136, 155, 157, 207, 209, 225–28, 230, 239, 242, 250, 274, 308, 312
Haikai renga, 232
Haikai rengashō, 227, 232
Hakatanotsu, 224
Hakone Bettō (Hōjō Gen'an), 47, 240
Hakone Yumoto, 204
Hakusan. *See* White Mountain
Hakusan Shrine, 217
Hall of No Renunciation (Fushain), 163–65, 311
Hamamatsu Estate, 9–10, 14, 97, 186, 195, 203
Hamana, Lake (Bridge), 9, 13, 97, 151, 186, 195–96, 202, 269, 304
Hamana Bitchūnokami, 14, 203
Hamana Castle, 151, 304
Hamori senku, 259
Hamuro Mitsuchika, 267
Hannyaji, 21, 212
Hannyaji Hill (Hannyajizaka), 21, 34, 182, 227
Happū kaidō, 273
Hasedera, 20, 81, 182, 211
Hasedō, 81, 259
Hasegawa Masanobu, 264
Hasegawa Motonaga, 90, 264
Hashimura Kiyomasa (Shinjirō), 205
Hatakeyama house, 297
Hatakeyama Masanaga, 297
Hatakeyama Yoshifusa, 247, 289
Hatakeyama Yoshinari, 297
Hatano Tanemichi, 284
Hatsuse, Mount (Hatsuseyama), 20, 182, 211
Head priest (*daigūji*), 312
Heike house. *See* Taira house
Heike monogatari, 187, 216, 238, 281, 305
Heikyoku, 305
Heisenji, 32, 223
Henjō, Bishop, 285, 308

Hesokata, 248
Hida Province (now part of Gifu Prefecture), 131
Hiei, Mount (Hieizan), 26, 121, 209, 216, 248, 274–75, 286
Hieitsuji, 121, 286
Hie Shrine, 241
Higan. *See* Equinoxes
Higashinotōin, 274
Higashiyama, 22, 29, 105, 167, 213, 219, 230
Higashiyama senku, 29, 182, 218, 279
Higonokami Yasumori. *See* Asahina Yasumori
Higuchi, 27, 111, 217
Hikima. *See* Hikuma
Hikuma (Hikima), 97, 152, 179, 195, 268, 304
Hikuma Castle, 10, 13, 55, 179, **195**, 198–201, 203
Hinaga, 147, 302
Hindrance Gate (Tema no seki), 82, 260
Hino, 113, 281
Hino Toshimoto, 268
Hino Yakushi, 281
Hirai Takayoshi (Hirai Uhyōenojō). *See* Uhyōenojō Takayoshi
Hira Mountains (Hira no ne), 128, 136, 164, 294
Hirano Shrine, 282
Hirao, 16, 19
Hitomaro. *See* Kakinomoto Hitomaro
Hitotsugi, 244
Hōgaiken Dōken. *See* Iwayama Dōken
Hōgen Chōei. *See* Chōei
Hōjō Gen'an. *See* Hakone Bettō
Hōjō house, 193, 275, 311
Hōjōji, 281, 299
Hōjō Sōun (Ise Nagauji), 9, **176**, 179, 183, 195–97, 201, 245, 262, 279, 312
Hōjō Ujitsuna, 183–84, 187, 289, 312
Hōkaiji, 281
Hokekyō. *See Lotus Sutra*
Hokkedō, 275
Hokku kikigaki, 219–20, 275–76, 278–79, 294
Hokuriku, 142, 191, 299
Hollyhock Festival (Aoi matsuri), 243, 276
Holy Name, 73, 144, 261, 300, 311. *See also* Amida
Honganji, 246
Hongyō waka, 310

General Index

Honji suijaku (manifestation from the original state), 258
Honkokuji, 299
Honnogahara, 14, 203
Honsaka, 14, 203
Honshū, 299
Horie Castle, 151, 304
Horie Shimotsukenokami, 9, 195
Horikawa hyakushu, 203
Horikawain godo hyakushu. See *Latter Hundred-Waka Sequence at the Palace of the Retired Emperor Horikawa*
Horikawa no Tsubone, 251
Horikoshi Castle, 177
Horikoshi house, 177, 225, 266
Horikoshi Kubō. See Ashikaga Masatomo
Horikoshi Mutsunokami (Sadanobu, Sena Sadanobu), 13, 178, 202
Horikoshi Norimasa, 177–78
Horikoshi Rokurō (Ujinobu), 92, 97, 186, 266, 268, 304
Horikoshi Sadamoto, 178
Hōsenji, 121, 286
Hoshizaki, 99, 270
Hōshōji, 46, 238
Hosoe Inlet, 151
Hosokawa Harumoto, 284
Hosokawa house, 218, 297–98
Hosokawa Katsumoto, **193**, 201, 297–98
Hosokawa Korekata, 284–85
Hosokawa Masamoto, 205, 298
Hosokawa ryōkeki (Account of the Two Hosokawa Houses), 292, 298
Hosokawa Sanukinokami (Shigeyuki? Yoshiyuki?), 13, 201
Hosokawa Sumimoto, 205, 284, 292, 298–99
Hosokawa Sumiyuki, 298
Hosokawa Takakuni (the Deputy, Dōei), 15, 44, 131, 142, 181, 183, 188, **205–6**, 217, 236, 273, 284–85, 292, 296–99
Hosokawa Yoriyuki, 297
House laws (*kakun*), 261
Hozumi, Prince, 302
Hyakunin isshu, 245
Hyōbukyō, 47–48, 240–41

Iba Sadakazu. See Tanemura Sadakazu
Iba senku (*Gessonsai senku*), 44, 183, 236–37

Ibigawa river, 272
Ibuki Mountains, 128, 164, 290
Ichida Castle, 203
Ichijōdani, 30, 191, 220
Ichijō Kaneyoshi (Kanera), 220, 241
Ichikawa, 59, 248
Ichinotani, 281
Iganokami. See Oda Iganokami
Iganokami Takamori. See Sugihara Iganokami
Iguchi Saburōzaemon, 144, 300
Ihara Castle, 291
Ihara Tadatane (Awanokami). See Bōshū
Ihara Tangonokami, 199
Iidagawara, 312
Ii house, 179
Ii Jirō (Nobutsuna), 11, 198
Iio house, 195–96
Iio Sōgi. See Sōgi
Iio Zenrokurō Tamekiyo, 9, 97, 195, 269
Iio Zenshirō Katatsura (Iio Zenzaemon Katatsura?), 9, 195, 200
Iio Zenshirō Noritsura, 9, 14, 55, 97, 186, 195, 246, 268
Iio Zenzaemon Katatsura (Iio Zenshirō Katatsura?), 9, 195
Iio Zenzaemonnojō Nagatsura, 9, 195
Ikkein. See Ikkeken
Ikkeken (or Ikkein, Gesshū Jukei), 45, 106, 238, 276
Ikkō ikki, 191, 221
Ikkyū (Ikkyū Sōjun), 45, 47, 107, 123, 181, 183, 186–87, **205–6**, 213, 217–18, 220–21, 238, 261, 278, 288–90; with sword, 126–27, 289–90
Ikuta, 23, 214
Imagawa house, 173–77, 181, 184, 195–96, 200–203, 245, 264, 266, 269, 275, 291, 304, 310, 312–13
Imagawajō, 174
Imagawa kafu (Lineage of the Imagawa House), 194
Imagawaki (Imagawa Chronicle), **194**, 196, 198, 202
Imagawaki (Imagawa Chronicle) (*Furokuki* [Chronicle Beneath Mount Fuji]), 177, 179, **194**
Imagawa Norikuni (Jōkōjidono), 12, 173, 177
Imagawa Norimasa, 12, 174–75, 247

Imagawa Noritada, 12, 160, 174–75, 310
Imagawa Noriuji, 12, 173
Imagawa Residence, 170
Imagawa Ryōshun (Iyonokami Sadayo), 97, 160, 173–74, 177, 186, **247**, **268**, 310
Imagawa Ujichika (Honjosama, Jōki, Kyōzan, Shōsaku, Shurinodaibu), 9–13, 55, 69, 76, 78, 90, 153–55, 161–63, **176**, 179, 181, 184–85, 187–88, 193, 196–99, 245, 251–52, 256, 260, 264, 277, 279, 289, 304, 307, 310–12, 314
Imagawa Ujiteru (Ryūōmaro [Tatsuomaro], Gorō), Honjo, 55, 80–82, 89, 155–56, 162–64, 174, **176**, 185, 187, 246, 258, 310, 314
Imagawa Ujizane, 176, 193
Imagawa Yasunori, 12, 174, 200
Imagawa Yoshimoto, 176
Imagawa Yoshitada (Chōhōjidono), 9, 12–13, 58, 162, **174–76**, 178–79, 193, 195, 200–203, 247, 264, 298
Imahashi, 55, 98, 150, 179, 186, 195, 246
Imperial Palace, 104, 274
Ina, 98, 150, 269
Inagawa river, 224
Inano, 33, 224
Inasa Inlet, 14
Inasa Mountain, 151
Inetsukiuta (rice-threshing songs), 286
Inner Shrine. *See* Ise Shrine
Inohana, 49, 241
Inō Sōgi. *See* Sōgi
Insei, 109
Inu Tsukubashū. *See Shinsen inu tsukubashū*
Irie Palace (Irie Goshọ, Sanjichionji), 278
Ise, Lady, 213, 250, 254, 267, 300
Ise Bay, 99, 145, 181
Ise Bitchūnokami (Ise Hachirō?), 110, 279
Ise Hachirō (Ise Bitchūnokami?), 111–12, 279–80
Ise monogatari, 181, 192, 204, 210, 217, 238, 245, 256, 262, 269, 273–74, 279–80, 300, 302, 30405
Ise Morisada, 202
Isenokami. *See* Ise Sadachika
Ise Province (now part of Mie Prefecture), 15, 18, 49, 55, 133, 144, 181, 207, 210, 245, 273, 302
Ise Sadachika (Isenokami), 13, 201–2
Ise senku, 15, 181, 204–5

Ise Shinkurō. *See* Hōjō Sōun
Ise Shrine (Inner Shrine, Outer Shrine), 19, 22, 143, 165, 181–82, 204–5, 207, 209, **211**, 249, 315
Ishiyamadera, 286
Isonokami Shrine, 54, 245, 254
Isshiki Shinkurō (Sōshū?), 111–13, 279
Isshiki Sōshū (Kazusanokami, Shinkurō?), 110, 279
Isuzu Mimosusogawa river, 19, 211
Iwakidaira Castle, 306
Iwaki Yoshitaka (Minbunotaifu), 154–55, 306, 311
Iwashimizu Hachiman Shrine, 199, 235, 239. *See also* Hachiman
Iwata, 23, 214
Iwayama Dōken (Hisamune, Hōgaiken), 119, 126, 284, 289
Iyonokami Sadayo. *See* Imagawa Ryōshun
Izu Kanō house, 177
Izumi Province (now part of Ōsaka Prefecture), 22, 137
Izumi River. *See* Izumigawa river
Izumi Shikibu, 295
Izumigawa river (Izumi River), 107, 216, 276–77
Izumigaya valley, 95, 267
Izumo Province (now part of Shimane Prefecture), 260
Izu Province (now part of Shizuoka Prefecture), 179, 195, 262

Jakuren, 257
Jibukyō Hōgan Taijin. *See* Taijin
Jichin (Jien), 85, 261, 267
Jien. *See* Jichin
Jikka senku, 273
Jikō, 28–29, 182, 217–18
Jimon. *See* Miidera
Jingoji, 51, 243
Jionji, 52, 54, 244–45
Ji sect, 22, 28, 217
Jison'in, 21, 212
Jitō, Empress, 268
Jizōin, 138, 294
Jōan Ryōsū, 276
Jōdo sect. *See* Pure Land sect
Jōei Code. *See Goseibai shikimoku*

General Index

Jōetsu. *See* Soshin Jōetsu
Jōfukuji, 22, 213
Jōgen, 306
Jōha, 28–29, 182, 218, 277
Jōjuin, 16
Jōkamachi. See Castle town
Jōkōin, 47, 104, 106, 240, 274, 276
Jōkyū uprising, 267
Jōruri, 303
Jōruri, Lady (Jōruri Gozen), 150, 188, 303
Jōruri Gozen monogatari, 303
Jōsū, 22, 182, 213
Jugō. *See* Mansai Jugō
Jujōken. *See* Tsuda Jujōken
Jukei, 176, 260, 264, 307, 314
Jukkai hyakuin dokugin (A Solo Hundred-Verse Sequence in Lamentation), 194

Kabekusa, 268
Kachiyama, 14, 203
Kadoya, 278
Kaeruyama mountain. *See* Mountain of Returning
Kagamiyama. *See* Mirror Mountain
Kaga Province (now part of Ishikawa Prefecture), 221
Kagurauta, 299
Kai house, 178, 198, 201
Kai Minonokami, 11
Kai Nobuhisa, 178
Kai Province (now Yamanashi Prefecture), 11, 13, 62, 96, 166, 179, 249, 310, 312–13
Kajisai. *See* Seki Kajisai
Kakegawa (Castle), 7–8, 11, 14, 92, 96, 152, 177–78, 181, **192-93**, 199, 304
Kakegawa Estate, 12, 178, 200–201
Kakinomoto Hitomaro, 38, 233, 254, 280
Kakun. See House laws
Kamakura, 9–10, 194, 225, 259, 281
Kamakura Bakufu. *See* Kamakura Shogunate
Kamakura Shogunate (Kamakura Bakufu), 204
Kameyama, 16–17, 49–50, 53–55, 102, 130, 144, 181, 184–85, 188, 207, 242
Kamigamo Shrine, 276
Kamigyō. *See* Upper Capital, Kyoto
Kamiji, Mount, 20, 211
Kamijōgawara, 313
Kaminabi, 120, 285
Kamiyama, 243

Kamiya River (Kamiyagawa, Paper-Maker River), 282
Kamo no Chōmei, 113, 187, 281, 299
Kamo Shrines, 243
Kana mokuroku, 176, 187
Kanaya, 91, 152, 305
Kanbe, 145, 301
Kanbe Morinaga (Ukyōnoshin), 54, 245
Kanginshū, 239, 252, 282
Kanjin hijiri, 211
Kankoku (Kanchi? Kanshō?), 58, 247
Kannon, 17, 72, 81, 149, 209
Kannonji, 32, 103, 133, 138, 223, 241–42, 273, 293
Kanō house, 177, 179, 202
Kanō Jirō, 13, 201
Kanō Kaganokami, 13, 178
Kanō Kunainoshō, 12–13, 201
Kanō Shichirōemonnojō (Shichirōzaemonnojō, Hisachika), 177–78
Kanō Suke (of Abe), 13, 201
Kanō Suke (of Izu), 13, 201
Kanō Suke Nyūdō, 177–78
Kansai, 181, 184–86, 199, 205
Kansei chōshū shokafu (Kansei Continued Lineage of the Various Houses), 202
Kantō, 174
Kantō league (*bandōri*) (unit of measure), 196
Kantō Shogun (Kantō Kubō). *See* Ashikaga Mochiuji
Karasaki, 295
Karasuma, 260
Kariya, 15, 55, 99, 149, 188, 204
Kasadera. *See* Rain Hat Temple
Kasadera engi, 303
Kasai Estate, 10, 198
Kasatoriyama mountain, 114
Kashiwagi Zenmon Eiga. *See* Asukai Masachika
Kasshiki. See Novice
Kasuga Mountain (Kasugayama), 113, 212, 302
Kasuya Matsutsuna (Nakatsukasa), 92, 265
Katada, 122, 287
Katariyama, 212
Katsumata house, 178, 195, 202
Katsumata Motonaga, 178
Katsuragawa river, 142, 282, 285, 296
Katsuyama Castle, 199
Kawagoe Castle, 9, 196

General Index

Kawai Gorō (Kawai Matagorō?), 49, 129, 241
Kawai Matagorō (Kawai Gorō?), 49, 129, 144, 291, 300
Kawai Suruganokami (Sunshū), 49, 129, 241, 291, 300
Kawarabayashi Tsushimanokami (Masayori), 29, 132, 218, 292
Kawawa Estate, 12, 200
Kazan, 120, 285
Kazan, Emperor, 285
Ken (unit of measure), 193
Kenchōji, 82, 259
Kendai, 244
Kendō, 121, 279, 286, 303
Kengyō. See Blind expert
Kenkokoji, 19–20, 211
Kenmu Restoration, 173
Kenninji, 45, 106, 238, 275–76
Kensai, 238, 250
Kensai zōdan, 250
Kenshun, 281
Kibi, 55, 246
Kiganji, 55
Kiinokami, 310
Kikugawa river, 96
Ki no Akimune, 240
Ki no Toshisada, 285
Ki no Tsurayuki, 240
Kin'yōshū (*Kin'yō wakashū*), 209
Kira house, 9–10, 12, **195**
Kira Tōjō house, 98, 186, 201
Kira Tōjō Yoshiharu, 269
Kisogawa river, 272
Kitabatake house, 207
Kitagawa, Lady (Kitagawadono), 90, 162, **176**, 185, 195, 201–2, 245, 264–65, 267, 278
Kitamuki, 246
Kitamura Hyōgonosuke (Tsuda Bizen Lay Priest?), 113, 238, 280
Kitano Shrine, 115, 182, 187, 282
Kiyomi (Gate, Strand, Seikenji), 25, 55–58, 62, 75, 127, 153, 165, 184, 215, 247, 256, 305, 312
Kiyomizu Temple, 219
Kiyomizuyama, 219
Kiyosu, 99–101, 148, 270, 272
Kōbō Daishi, 257
Kōfukuji, 256
Kōga, 143, 300
Koga Kubō. See Ashikaga Shigeuji

Kogawa, 90–91, 96, 185, 264, 267
Kohaku. See Makino Shigetoki
Kohata, 113, 280–81
Koi no omoni (The Heavy Burden of Love), 231
Kojiki, 270
Kokin denju. See Secret Traditions of *Kokinshū*
Kokinshū (*Kokin wakashū*), 81, 85, 108–9, 119, 162, 185–86, 191, 192, 210, 213, 215–16, 219, 223–24, 228, 232–33, 235–37, 240, 244, 250, 255, 259–62, 264–65, 267–68, 271, 273, 276–78, 282–85, 287–88, 292–96, 300, 304–8, 310, 313, 315
Kokin waka rokujō, 260
Kōkō, Emperor (Ninna Emperor), 292
Kokujin, 175, 178
Kongara (Kinkara), 232
Konjikidō, 226
Konoe Hisamichi, 81, 183, 258
Konoe Masaie, 81, 258
Konohama, 48, 103, 121, 128, 142, 144, 241, 274, 299–300
Konparu Shichirō, 21, 182, 212
Konparu Zenpō, 245
Konrin'an, 103, 274
Koremitsu, 289
Koshi, 126, 289
Koshimizu Castle, 292
Kōtō. See blind master
Kotsugawa river, 46, 216, 239, 276, 281
Kōya, Mount (Kōyasan, Takano no yama), 34, 38, 78, 211, 226, 256–57
Koyadera, 224
Kōya hijiri, 226–27
Koyorogi (Koyurugi) Strand, 288
Koyurugi Strand. See Koyorogi Strand
Kōzai Motomori, 284
Kōzanji, 243
Kōzenji, 52, 244
Kozu, 27, 216
Kubota, 16–17, 207
Kumagai (Urikumagai) house, 203
Kumagai Echigonokami, 14, 98, 269
Kumozugawa river, 16, 19, 207
Kunai of the Palace of the Dowager, 249
Kuni, 277
Kurama, 133, 293
Kurokawa Dōyu, 194, 281
Kuroyama Castle, 9
Kusanagi no tsurugi, 270

355

Kushima. *See* Fukushima
Kuwana, 102, 147, 186, 272
Kyōgoku house, 293
Kyoto, 20, 29–30, 32, 42–46, 56–57, 59, 62–63, 66–67, 84, 90, 101, 103–5, 108–10, 112, 119–22, 124–25, 127, 130, 133, 141–42, 149, 153, 160, 162, 168, 181, 183–84, 186–88, 193, 195, 199, 201–2, 204–6, 213–14, 216, 219, 228, 230, 238, 248–49, 252, 259–60, 270, 274, 276, 286, 293, 296, 298–99; history of violence in, 120, 122, 141–42, 284–85, 296–99, 310, 314. *See also* Lower Capital (Shimogyō); Upper Capital (Kamigyō)
Kyōunshū, 261
Kyūsei, 174
Kyushu, 173, 297

Latter Hundred-Waka Sequence at the Palace of the Retired Emperor Horikawa (*Horikawain godo hyakushu, Eikyū hyakushu*), 100, 271
Lending Mountain (Kaseyama), 277
Liezi, 237, 253
Linji, 261, 290
Li Qiao, 193
Liu Yuxi, 239
Liuzu tanjing (The Platform Sutra of the Sixth Patriarch), 290
Long Bridge of Seta (Seta no nagahashi, Seta no karahashi), 101, 272
Lotus Sutra (*Hokekyō, Myōhō rengekyō*), 69–70, 160, 162, 214–15, 253–54, 253, 259, 290, 310
Lower Capital (Shimogyō), 46, 106, 109, 111, 119–20, 186–87, 217, 224, 238, 278, 285. *See also* Kyoto
Lower Capital Tea Coterie (Shimogyō chanoyu), 109, 187, 278

Mabuchi house, 294
Mabuchi Kunainoshō (Yamashironokami Munetsuna), 139, 294
Machishū (townsmen), 278
Maiden-Calling Slope (Tego no yobisaka), 87, 262
Maitreya, 257
Makino Denzō (Nobushige), 55, 98, 150, 186, **246**, 269, 303
Makino Heisaburō, 98, 150, 269, 303
Makino house, 188
Makino Kohaku. *See* Makino Shigetoki

Makinoo, 243
Makino Shigekata, 98, 269
Makino Shigetoki (Kohaku), 98, 269, 304
Makinoshima, 108
Makino Shirōzaemonnojō, 14, 203
Mamako ijime, 312
Manjuji, 275
Mansai Jugō, 113, 281–82
Mansai Jugō nikki, 281
Man'yōshū, 59, 206, 214, 216, 230–31, 242, 248, 254, 262, 268, 280, 301–2, 307
Mariko, 90, 119, 152, 157, 162–63, 165, 176, 185, 188, **192**, 195, 249, 255, 262, 267, 304, 308. *See also* Brushwood Cottage; Utsunoyama Mountain
Martial Defender (Buei, Shiba Yoshitatsu), 11–12, 179, **198–200**
Masatsune. *See* Fujiwara Masatsune
Masukata, 9, 196
Matsudaira house, 186, 188, 269
Matsudaira Jirōzaburō (Kiyoyasu), 150, 269–70, 303
Matsudaira Kiyoyasu. *See* Matsudaira Jirōzaburō
Matsudaira Nagachika, 270, 303
Matsudaira Ōinosuke (Tadasada), 98, 140, 150, 153, 269, 303, 305
Matsudaira Yoichi (Nobusada), 99, 149, 270, 303
Matsudaira Yoshikage, 269
Matsushita Shōkō. *See* Shōkō
Meet-Again Mountain (Nochiseyama), 68, 253
Meidaishū (*Meidai waka zenshū?*), 52
Meikōawase, 218
Meiō 8 [1499]:2:19 *Nanibito hyakuin* (A Hundred-Verse Sequence Entitled "A Kind of Person"), 237
Meitoku Era, Discord of the (Meitoku no ran), 141–42, 297
Mengzong, 293
Menoto, 310
Michinoku, 154, 306
Mihogasaki, 57, 247
Miidera (Jimon, Onjōji, the Temple), 30, 43, 47, 104–5, 114, 120–21, 124–25, 138, 153, 183–84, 186–87, **220**, 236, 240, 274–75, 293, 299, 305
Mikanohara. *See* Third-Day Moor
Mikami Mountain, 287

Mikawa Echigonokami (Yoriyasu), 123, 288
Mikawa kudari (Down to Mikawa). See *Sōchō kawa*
Mikawa Province (now part of Aichi Prefecture), 9–10, 13, 55, 98, 124, 149, 151, 153, 179, 186, 195, 201, 203, 268–69, 304
Mimosusogawa utaawase, 211
Minakuchi, 54, 143, 300
Minamoto Michiteru. See Gondainagon (Minamoto) Michiteru
Minamoto Muneyuki, 305
Minamoto Saneakira, 233
Minamoto Shigeyuki, 309
Minamoto Shunrai, 203, 271
Minamoto Yorimasa, 195, 265
Minamoto Yoritomo, 204
Minamoto Yoshitomo, 15, 204, 225
Minamoto Yoshitsune (Genkurō), 34, 150, 188, 225, 303
Ming, 183, 213, 224
Mino Province (now part of Gifu Prefecture), 102
Mirror Mountain (Kagamiyama), 49, 103, 135, 241, 273, 293
Mishima, 10, 197
Mishima senku. See *Shutsujin senku*
Mitake (Castle, Mountain), 11, 179, 198
Mitsuke, 92, 97, 152, 185, 266, 304
Mitsuke Castle, 177–79, 195
Mitsusada, 205
Mitsuse River (Mitsusegawa, Sanzunokawa), 73, 255
Miura Yatarō, 79, 257
Miwa, Mount (Miwayama), 37, 232
Miyagi Plain, 308
Miyahara Moritaka (Shichirōbyōenojō), 16, 18–19, 207
Miyaki Nyūdō Shinkan, 133, 292
Miyako no tsuto, 264
Miyoshi Chikuzennokami (Yukinaga), 142, 205, 284, 292, 298–99
Miyoshi house, 195
Miyoshi Motonaga, 284–85
Miyoshi Yukinaga. See Miyoshi Chikuzennokami
Mizuno Izuminokami (Chikamori, Tōkurō), 15, 99, 149, 188, **204**, 246, 270, 303
Mizuno Kisaburō, 15, 204
Mizu no mimaki, 46

Mogami River, 296
Mon'ami, 54, 245
Monju (Manjusri), 227
Monjuin, 34
Monzenmachi. See Castle town
Mori Hayatonosuke, 55
Moritake senku, 207, 312
Moriyama, 99, 270, 303
Moruyama, 49, 142, 241, 299
Motosu Yamatonokami, 48, 241
Mountain, the. See Enryakuji
Mountain Gate [Sanmon]. See Enryakuji
Mountain of Meeting (Gate at the) (Ōsaka [no seki], Sekiyama), 104, 120, 129, 140, 186, 220, 274, 285, 291, 296
Mountain of Returning (Kaeruyama), 7, 19, 49, **191–92**, 210
Mountain of the Dead (Shide no yama), 64, 242
Mukogawa, 224
Muneaki. See Toyohara Muneaki
Murakushi, 9, 179, 195
Muramori. See Sakai Settsunokami
Murasakino 30, 205, 238. See also Daitokuji
Murata Jukō, 278
Murata Sōju, 109, 187, 278
Muromachi, 82, 260
Musashi Province (now Tokyo Metropolitan Prefecture, Saitama Prefecture, and part of Kanagawa Prefecture), 9, 179, 184
Mushanokōji, 105, 274
Myōdaiji, 150, 303
Myōgenji, 270
Myōhōjiki, 289
Myōhō rengekyō. See *Lotus Sutra*
Myōshōan, 122, 164, 286
Myōshōji, 213, 221, 286
Myōson, 192

Nachigomori (Beneath Nachi Falls), **191**, 199, 204, 207, 217–18, 221, 235
Nagaike Chikayoshi (Kurōzaemonnojō), 151, 304
Nagara Bridge (Nagara no hashi), 267
Nagaragawa river, 272
Nagatonokami. See Satō Nagatonokami
Nagoya kassenki (Nagoya Battle Chronicle), 200
Nagusamegusa, 271

General Index

Nakae Tosanokami (Kazutsugu), 103, 123, 128, 138, 273, 287, 291, 294
Nakamikado Nobuhide, 156, 162, 164, 168, 188, 260, **307**, 310–11, 314
Nakamikado Nobutane, 42, 45, 83–84, 156, 183, 185, **235**, 237, 264, 307
Nakamikado Nobutsuna, 162, 310
Nakasendō, 273
Nakoso Gate, 140, 295, 306
Naniwa, 282, 284, 287
Nanto (Southern Capital). *See* Nara
Nanzenji, 105, 275
Nara (Southern Capital, Nanto), 21–22, 27, 42, 84, 124, 182, 227, 256, 275
Narumi, 99, 149, 270, 303
Nasu house, 241, 256
Nasu Suketarō, 78, 256–57
Nichiren sect, 184
Nihachi meidaishū, 244
Nijō Yoshimoto, 174
Nikonshū, 209, 256
"Nine Mountains and Eight Seas" (Kusen hakkai), 114, 281
Ningbo, 183
Ninna Emperor. *See* Kōkō, Emperor
Nio Sea. *See* Biwa, Lake
Nirayama, 10, 197–98
Nishinokōri, 150
Nishinotōin, 278
Nissaka, 96, 268
Nō (*sarugaku*), 21, 182, 212, 231, 245, 282
Nobutane. *See* Nakamikado Nobutane
Nobutora. *See* Takeda Nobutora
Nochiseyama. *See* Meet-Again Mountain
Nōin, 306
Noma, 15, 204
Nomura Ōinosuke, 50, 53, 242
Norikage (Sōteki) senku, 191
Nose Gengorō (Kuniyori), 33, 225
Nose Yorinori (Inabanokami), 29–30, 182, 217, 220, 225
Nose Yorinori, widow of. *See* Jikō
Noto Province (now part of Ishikawa Prefecture), 126, 247, 289
Novice (*kasshiki*), 28, 217
Nōyū, 115, 282
Nukada, Princess, 248
Nunobiki Falls (Nunobiki no taki), 219

Oda Chikuzennokami (Yoshiyori), 99, 270–72
Oda house, 238
Oda Iganokami (Kurō Hironobu?), 99, 101, 270, 272
Oda Nobunaga, 176, 186, 270, 272
Oda Saburō (Nobuhide), 101, 186, 272
Oda Sōdai (Nobusada), 101, 272
Oda Tanbanokami, 148, 302
Oda Tōzaemon, 101, 272
Ōe Kin'yori, 311
Ōe Masafusa, 295
Ōgigayatsu (Uesugi) Tomoyoshi, 179, **196**
Ōgigayatsu Uesugi, 9, 175, 196
Ōgimachi, 278
Ōgimachisanjō Kin'e (Onkata), 62, 76, 90, 249, 256, 264
Ōgimachisanjō Sanemochi (Jōkū, Jikōin), 56, 62, 67, 76, 83, 165, 170, 184–85, 188, **246**, 249, 252–53, 256
Ogura Pond (Ogura no ike), 239
Ohara Chikataka (Bizennokami), 76, **246**, 256, 313
Ohara Takachika (Hyōgonokami), 167, 313
Ōigawa river, 152, 200, 305
Ōi Nobutatsu, 199
Oi no mimi (Aged Ears), **193**, 203–4, 206, 208–9, 212, 219–20, 222–25, 235–37, 240–41, 243–44, 246–52, 258–59, 263–64, 266, 271–72, 274–77
Oi no susami (Aged Consolation), 191
Okabe Saemonnojō, 13, 202
Okazaki, 150, 195, 270, 303
Okehazama, 176
Okinoi Miyakoshima, 271
Okitsu, 55, 60, 62, 161, 163–65, 184, 188, 215, 246, 312
Okitsu Chikataka, 56
Okitsu Hikokurō (Chikahisa), 75, 77, 153, 161, **256**, 305
Okitsu Masanobu (Tōbyōenojō), 55, 246, 249, 255
Okitsu Saemon (Saemonnojō Moritsuna), 163, 311
Ōkōchi Bitchūnokami (Sadatsuna), 9–12, 179, **195**, 198–99, 203
Ōkōchi house, 11, 179, 195, 200
Okunoin, 219
Okunoyama Castle, 11–12, 198

Ōmi, Sea of. *See* Biwa, Lake
Ōmi Gamōgunshi, 295
Ōmi house, 12–13, 200
Ōminato, 15, 204
Ōmi Province (now Shiga Prefecture), 15–17, 32, 48, 103, 108, 120, 126, 130, 135, 138, 142, 144, 182, 188, 205–6, 237, 241, 273, 277, 285, 288, 293–94, 296, 298
Ōmi sarugaku, 212
Ōmi Shinzaemonnojō (Michitsuna), 12, 200–201
Ōmiwa Shrine, 232
Ōmiya, 142
Omoigawa river. *See* River of Longing
Ōninki, 297–98
Ōnin War (Ōnin no ran), 142, 178, 193, 213, 220, 238, 274, 281, 290, 297–98
Onjōji. *See* Miidera
Ono, 133, 293
Ōno (Ōmi Province), 300
Ōno (Owari Province), 55, 246
Onogawa, 242
Ono no Komachi, 271, 87
Osada Chikashige (Shirōtarō), 72–74, 184, 255, 261
Ōsaka (Gate [Ōsaka no seki]). *See* Mountain of Meeting
Osakabe Castle, 151, 304
Ōshikōchi Mitsune, 223, 266
Ōta Dōkan, 175
Otokotōka, 269
Ōtomo Kuronushi, 215, 273
Ōtomo Yakamochi, 301
Otowa (Falls, Mountain), 30, 140, 219, 295–96
Ōtsu, 47–48, 104, 120–21, 184, 186, 220, 286, 299
Ōuchi house, 275
Ōuchi Masahiro (Sakyōnotaifu), 142, 297–98
Ōuchi Yoshioki, 182–83, 298
Outer Shrine (Gekū, Toyouke Daijingū, Toyuke Daijingū). *See* Ise Shrine
Owari Province (now part of Aichi Prefecture), 10–12, 15, 18, 45, 54–55, 99, 102, 124, 148–49, 151, 178, 201, 205, 210, 245, 270, 273
Oyobigawa river, 102, 272

Paekche, 299
Paperers (*hyōhoishi*), 259

Plum Cottage, 111, 187, 279
Prostitute, 210, 226, 229, 234
Pure Land (Jōdo) sect, 105, 261, 307

Qin, 253
Queen Mother of the West (Xiwangmu), 266
Qujiangshi, 282

Rain Hat Mountain (Kasatoriyama), 114, 282
Rain Hat Temple (Kasadera), 149, 188, 303
Reality Mountain. *See* Utsunoyama
Reizei house, 174, 247
Reizei Tamehide, 268
Renga tsukeyō, 255
Rengein, 21, 212
Renju gappekishū (Collection of Linked Pearls and Joined Jewels), 241, 301
Residence by the river, 62, 310. *See also* Rinsen'an
Ri (unit of measure), 207
Rikijū, 27, 217, 280
Rinsen'an, 161, 310. *See also* Residence by the river
Rinzai. *See* Linji
Rinzaiji, 259
Ritsu sect, 105, 275
River of Heaven (Amanogawa, Ama no kawa), 107, 156–57, 276–77, 308
River of Longing (Omoigawa), 70–71, 254
Rokkaku house, 223, 273, 288, 291, 293–94
Rokkaku Sadayori (the constable), 17, 182, 208, 237, 241, 293
Rokkaku Takayori, 273
Rokkaku Takazane, 273
Rokudaiin, 17
Rokujō, 142
Rokurō. *See* Horikoshi Rokurō
Ryō (unit of currency), 291
Ryōgonji temple, 10, 198
Ryōjusen, 244
Ryōsen'in, 106, 276
Ryōshun. *See* Imagawa Ryōshun
Ryōsū. *See* Jōan Ryōsū
Ryōzen, 22
Ryūhōzan Daitokuji. *See* Daitokuji

Saburō. *See* Oda Saburō
Saburōgorō, 82, 259

General Index

Sadatoki, Prince, 285
Saemonnosuke (Futamata Masanaga? Kanbara? Shiba Saemonnosuke Yoshio?), 8, 194–95
Saga, 142
Sagami Province (now part of Kanagawa Prefecture), 47, 195, 311
Saibara, 250, 269, 301
Saigō house, 14, 203
Saigyō (reverend priest), 19–20, 50, 91, 96, 159, 181–82, 192, 210–11, 214, 220, 225, 242, 251, 263–65, 305, 309, 312
Saigyō Valley, 19, 165, **211**, 312, 314
Saikoku, 142, 299
Saimei, Empress, 299
Saioku. *See* Brushwood Cottage
Saiokuken senku. *See Shutsujin senku*
Saiokuken Sōchō. *See* Sōchō
Saishō Shitennōin, 312
Saishōji, 167, 313–14
Saishōsō (Grasses of Recrudescence), 215, 279, 283–84, 290, 292, 294, 296
Saishu Suechika, 315
Saitō Shirō, 79, 257
Saitō Yasumoto (Kaganokami), 73, 185, 218, **255**, 262
Saji Nagamasa (Shōunken, San'unken), 143, 300
Sakai, 22, 84, 137, 213, 258–59, 289, 294, 298–99
Sakai Settsunokami (Muramori), 99–100, 124, 148–49, 188, 270, 289, 302
Sakamoto, 18, 48, 84, 103, 121–22, 142, 187–88, 209, 224, 241, 286
Sakanoshita, 49, 54, 241
Sakata, 122
Saku Castle, 203
Sakurai Matsudaira, 270
Sakuuken, 222
San'aiki (Three Loves), 282
Sanbi, 243
Sanbōin, 281. *See also* Daigoji
Sanemochi. *See* Ōgimachisanjō Sanemochi
Sanetaka. *See* Sanjōnishi Sanetaka
Sanetakakōki, 252, 278, 283–84, 299, 310
Sangū Kaidō, 302
Sanjichionji. *See* Irie Palace
Sanjōnishi Kin'eda, 183
Sanjōnishi Sanetaka (Gyōkū, Shōyōin), 22, 25, 29, 44, 67, 69, 71, 81, 105, 108–10, 116–19, 131, 136–37, 162, 182–84, 186–87, 205, **213–14**, 215–16, 218, 220, 237, 247, 253–54, 258, 272, 278–79, 284, 290, 292, 296, 299, 310
Sankashū, 214, 251, 312, 314
Sanmon. *See* Enryakuji
Sano no watari (Sano Crossing), 204–5, 211
Sanrian, 278
Sanuki, Lady, 243
Sanzunokawa river. *See* Mitsuse River
Sao, 216
Saohime, 216, 229
Sarugaku. *See Nō*
Sasaki house, 273, 284, 294, 300
Sashiide Strand (Sashide Strand, Sashiidenoiso, Sashidenoiso), 166, 313
Satō Nagatonokami, 145–46, 301
Satsuma Province (now part of Kagoshima Prefecture), 33
Sayo no nakayama mountain (Sayo no nagayama, Nagayama, Sayonoyama, Saya no nakayama, Sayo Long Mountain), 7, 13, 66, 91–92, 96, 152, 178, 181, 185, **192**, 264–65, 268, 304–5
Secret Traditions of *Kokinshū* (*Kokin denju*), 81, 162, 258–59, 276
Seiin Sōzu, 23
Seikenji. *See* Kiyomi
Sei Kunaikyō Hōin, 54, 123, 184, 245, 288
Seisuishō, 228–29
Seitaka (Cetaka), 37, 232
Sekiguchi Ujikane, 76, 256
Seki house, 242, 245, 301
Seki Kajisai (Minbunotaifu, Ikkan, Sōtetsu, Kohō, Lord Shōhōji), 16–18, 50–55, 102, 130–31, 181, 184, 186–88, **207–8**, 242, 245, 291–92
Seki Moriyoshi (or Masayoshi, Jirō), 52–53, 244
Seki Tanemori (Shirō), 52, 244
Semimaru, 291
Senchō, 219
Sengen Shrine, 258
Senjuin, 21, 212
Sen no Rikyū, 275
Sennyūji, 105, 275
Senshōji, 296
Senzaishū (*Senzai wakashū*), 49, 211, 256
Sessai, 176
Sesshōke no Mikawa, 209

Sesshū, 298
Setagawa river, 272
Setsubun, 132, 292
Settsunokami. *See* Sakai Settsunokami
Settsu Province (now part of Ōsaka and Hyōgo Prefectures), 23, 34, 142, 214, 217, 292
Settsu senku, 217–18
Seven Sages (*Shichiken*), 245
Seven Yakushi Buddhas, 113
Shaku (unit of measure), 194
Shakuhachi 22, 46, 48, 54, 113–15, 121, 124, 182, 186, 213, 236, 240, 245
Shiba house, 175, 177–79, 193, 195, 272, 297–98
Shiba Saemonnosuke Yoshio. *See* Saemonnosuke
Shiba Yoshikado, 201
Shiba Yoshinori (Yoshishige), 200
Shiba Yoshitatsu. *See* Martial Defender
Shiba Yoshitō (Yoshisuke), 179, 201
Shichijō, 141–42
Shichijūichiban shokunin utaawase (Poetry Competition in Seventy-One Rounds on the Professions and Trades), 229, 260
Shide no yama. *See* Mountain of the Dead
Shiga, 33, 142, 224, 240–41, 295, 299
Shigaraki, 123, 287
Shigehira. *See* Taira Shigehira
Shijing, 237
Shijō, 260
Shijō, Emperor, 275
Shijō Bōmon, 224
Shikashū (*Shika wakashū*), 134, 214–15, 294
Shiki senku, 197
Shikishima, way of, 156, 307
Shiki Yasumune (Suruganokami, Kunainoshō), 80, 258
Shima Kubō (Island Shogun), 299
Shimogamo Shrine, 276
Shimogyō. *See* Lower Capital, Kyoto
Shimogyō chanoyū. *See* Lower Capital Tea Coterie
Shimōsa Province (now part of Chiba and Ibaraki Prefectures), 175
Shimotsuke Province (now Tochigi Prefecture), 78
Shina, 128
Shinano Province (now Nagano Prefecture), 8, 10, 151

Shinchokusenshū (Shinchokusen wakashū), 242
Shinden'an, 28, 108, 182, 217–18, 277
Shin'eki, 100, 271
Shingakuji, 220–21
Shingon sect, 209, 226, 256, 272, 275, 281
Shinjuan, 15, 31, 111, 115, **205**, 211, 220–21, 279. *See also* Daitokuji
Shinkokinshū (Shinkokin wakashū), 57, 192, 206, 210, 220, 222, 224, 231, 233, 236, 239, 241–42, 247, 252, 258, 260, 263–64, 267, 283–84, 286–87, 289, 293, 299, 305–6, 309, 312–13
Shinkurō. *See* Isshiki Shinkurō
Shin Mishima senku. *See* Shutsujin senku
Shinpukuji, 16, 52, 54, 245
Shinsen inu tsukubashū, 183, 229–34
Shinsen tsukubashū, 217–18, 225, 227, 259, 269, 314
Shin Sumiyoshi senku, 217
Shintō, 243, 270, 301, 312
Shintokumaru, 312
Shio, Mount (Shionoyama), 62, 166, 241, 249, 313
Shiokaizaka, 178, **195**
Shionoyama. *See* Shio, Mount
Shirakawa (Gate) (Shirakawa [no seki]), 154, 306
Shirakawa (White River, in Higo Province), 308
Shirakawa (White River, in Kyoto), 167–68, 313–14
Shirakawa (White River, in Uji), 28–29, 47, 108, 167–68, 182, 217–18. *See also* Uji
Shiratsuchi, 21, 212
Shirayama. *See* White Mountain
Shiroyama, 33, 225
Shirutani, 120, 285
Shizuhatayama, 80
Shōgakuin, 101–2, 147, 272, 302
Shōgetsuan Shōtetsu. *See* Shōtetsu
Shogunal Deputy (Kanrei). *See* Hosokawa Takakuni
"Shogunal Deputy's Thousand Verses in One Day" (*Kanrei ichinichi senku*), 236
Shōhaku (Botanka Shōhaku), 29, 182, 188, **213**, 217–18, 224, 258–59, 282
Shōhōji (Ise Province), 50–52, 242
Shōhōji (Kyoto), 213
Shōkaian, 57
Shōkashō, 237

Shōkashū, 247
Shōkō, 57–58, **174**, 184, 247
Shōkō eiga, 247
Shōkokuji, 275, 298
Shōkō nikki, 247
Shokusenzaishū, 243
Shokushi, Princess, 222, 263, 283
Shōmu, Emperor, 277, 287, 302
Shōren'in, 81, 103, 259, 306
Shōrin'an (Shōrinji), 103, 108, 120–26, 135, 138–39, 164, 186–88, **206**, 273, 294
Shōtetsu, 100, **174**, 184, 247, 271
Shōtoku, Prince, 212
Shōun, 106, 276
Shōzōbō (Shōjun), 43, 47–48, 120–21, 124–25, 183–84, 187, **236**, 279, 286, 303, 305
Shueki, 76, 256
Shugyokuan, 204, 278
Shūgyokushū, 261
Shūishū (*Shūi wakashū*), 214, 219, 249, 255, 266, 277, 280
Shūkei, 109, 115, 278
Shukudai, 244
Shun Kinkei, 259
Shunzei. *See* Fujiwara Shunzei
Shūon'an, 22–23, 38, 47, 60, 103, 108, 120, 161, 182, **206**, 214, 218, 220–21, 285. *See also* Takigi
Shuten Dōji ekotoba, 183
Shutsujin senku (A Thousand-Verse Sequence for the Campaign), 10, **196–97**
Shuyiji, 243
"Since I" hymn, 254
Sōami, 185
Sōbai, 133, 292
Sōboku (Tani Sōboku), 133, 137, 187, **203**, 247, 269–70, 278, 293, 299, 303
Sōchō (Saiokuken Sōchō); Asahina, 7, 10–11, 82, 84–86, 90–92, 96, 130, 161–62, 185, 193–94, 198–99, 256, 259–60, 291, 306, 310–11, 313; Asakura, 19, 30–31, 45, 181–83, 188, 191, 222, 238, 262, 274; Brushwood Cottage, 86, 95–96, 119, 154, 157–59, 161–63, 165, 185, 188, 192, 195–96, 215, 249, 255, 262, 304; Buddhist training, 114, 281 (*see also* Ikkyū); Daitokuji, 15, 30–31, 46, 50, 74, 105–6, 111, 115, 161–62, 185–87, 205–6, 220–21, 238, 255, 274, 282; daughter, 217; death prophecy, 125, 161, 248, 269; desire to die in Takigi, 23, 60, 161, 277; dreams, 29, 42, 110, 112, 125, 127, 136, 139–40, 142, 144, 152–53, 164, 210, 220, 280, 290; Echizen journey, 31–33, 182–83; family, 217; father (Gojō Yoshisuke), 80, 185, 258; first journey from Kansai to Suruga, 45–55; first journey from Suruga to Kansai, 7–22; gardens, 21, 31, 45, 51, 53, 60–61, 63, 71–72, 74–75, 78, 86–88, 100, 106, 113–14, 123–24, 147–48, 157–61, 165; *Genji monogatari*, 29, 74, 136, 183, 185, 210, 215, 218–19, 241, 250, 255, 271, 286, 289; Hosokawa Takakuni, 14, 44, 181, 183, 205–6, 236; *Iba senku* (*Gessonsai senku*), 44, 183, 236–37; Ikkyū, 45, 47, 107, 123, 126–27, 181, 183, 186–87, 205–6, 217, 220, 238, 261–62, 288, 290; Imagawa Ujichika, 10–11, 55, 69, 76, 78, 90, 153–55, 161–63, 176, 179, 181, 184–85, 187–88, 193, 197–99, 251, 256, 260, 277, 307, 310–11, 314; Imagawa Ujiteru, 55, 80–82, 89, 155–56, 162–63, 174, 176, 185, 187, 246, 258, 310, 314; Imagawa Yoshitada, 58, 162, 175, 178, 202, 298; *Ise senku*, 15, 181, 204–5; Ise Shrine (*see* Yamada); Kameyama, 16–17, 49–50, 53–55, 102, 130, 144, 181, 184–85, 188, 207; Lady Kitagawa, 90, 162, 176, 185, 195, 267; longevity celebration 76–77, 185; Nakamikado house, 42, 45, 83–84, 156, 162, 164, 168, 183, 185, 188, 235, 237, 260, 307, 310–11, 314; Ōgimachisanjō house, 56, 62, 67, 76, 83, 90, 165, 170, 184–85, 188, 246, 249, 252–53, 256; residence by the river, 62, 161, 249; Saigyō, 19–20, 50, 91, 96, 159, 181–82, 192, 210, 214, 220, 225, 262, 264–65, 309; sake, 19, 21, 28, 47–49, 51–53, 55, 63–64, 75, 84, 102, 107–9, 111, 113, 115, 121, 123–26, 128–30, 146–48, 162, 209, 217, 261, 283; Sanjōnishi Sanetaka, 22, 25, 29, 44, 67, 69, 71, 81, 105, 108–10, 116–19, 131, 136–37, 162, 182–84, 186–87, 205, 213–16, 218, 253–54, 278, 283–84, 290, 292, 294, 299; *sarugaku*, 21, 182; second journey from Kansai to Suruga, 143–53; second journey from Suruga to Kansai, 90–104; Secret Traditions of *Kokinshū* (Kokin denju), 81, 162, 258–59; Seki Kajisai, 16–18, 50–55, 102, 130–31, 181, 184, 186–88, 207–8, 243–45, 291–92; *shakuhachi*, 22, 46, 48, 54, 113–15, 121, 124, 182, 186, 213; Shinden'an, 28, 108, 182, 217–18; *Shutsujin senku*, 10, 196–97; self-exoneration, 161–63;

Shōhaku, 29, 182, 217-18, 224; Shōrin'an (in Yashima), 103, 108, 120-26, 135, 138-39, 164, 186-88, 206, 294; Shūon'an (in Takigi), 22-23, 38, 47, 60, 103, 108, 120, 161, 182, 206, 214, 276-77; Sōboku, 133, 137, 187, 223, 247, 293, 299, 303, 312; son (Jōha) 28-29, 277; Sōgi 32, 56-57, 64, 81, 108, 127, 139, 159, 162, 175, 184-87, 191, 203-4, 224, 246-47, 251-52, 258-59, 277, 298, 309; Sōseki, 15, 23, 44, 48, 65, 82, 105, 109, 115, 126, 181-84, 186-87, 204, 214, 218, 236, 252, 282; tea, 35, 55, 63-64, 83, 108-10, 121, 124, 133-34, 161, 187, 218, 228, 232, 274-75, 278, 287, 289; Takigi, 21-23, 26, 28-29, 34, 42, 45-47, 60, 86, 103, 107, 120, 161-62, 181-84, 186, 206, 214-15, 217, 235, 262; Toyohara Muneaki, 44, 65-71, 183-84, 237, 252; waterfowl, 128-29; Yamada (and Ise Shrine), 15-17, 19-20, 22, 128, 142-43, 165, 181-82, 204-5, 207; *Yashima Shōrin'an naniki hyakuin*, 187; Yashima sojourn, 121-42; year's end conversation with Asahina Tokishige, 84-86; young men (*wakashu*), 18, 100, 102, 111, 115, 120, 124-25, 146-49, 181, 210, 302; Zen, 26, 28, 30, 82, 85-86, 103, 155-56, 163, 169, 185, 205, 215-16, 247, 259, 261, 273, 289, 307, 311, 314-15. *See also* Daisen'in; Daitokuji; Ikkyū; Shinden'an; Shōrin'an; Shūon'an; Takigi

Sōchō dokugin Daiei 8 [1528]:4:12 *myōgō hyakuin* (A Hundred-Verse Solo Sequence by Sōchō on the Holy Name, Composed on the Twelfth Day of the Fourth Month of the Eighth Year of Daiei), 311

Sōchōji, 249

Sōchō kawa (Sōchō's Talks on Waka), 207

Sōchō kojiden (Biography of the Lay Priest Sōchō), 194

Sōchō nikki, 247

Sōchō renga jichū (Personal Commentary on Sōchō's Linked Verse), 207, 225, 246, 255

Soga, 212

Sōgi (Iio Sōgi, Inō Sōgi), 32, 56-57, 64, 81, 108, 126, 139, 159, 162, 175, 184-87, 191, 203-4, 217, 224, 237, 245-46, 251-52, 258-59, 276-78, 286, 298, 290, 310

Sōgi shūenki (The Death of Sōgi), 196, 204, 246, 251-52, 292

Sōjō Henjō, 252, 261

Sōju. *See* Murata Sōju

Sōkan. *See* Fukuda Hachirō

Sōkan (Yamazaki Sōkan), 183, 225, 234

Sōkei. *See* Tsuda Sōkei

Sokudai, 244

Sōkyū, 264

Song That Opens the Blossoms (*kaika no shirabe*), 254

Sonjō Kōtōbō, 154, 305

Sōsei, 137

Sosei, 228, 293, 296

Sōseki (Gessonsai Sōseki), 15, 23, 44, 48, 65, 82, 105, 109, 115, 127, 181-84, 186-87, **204**, 211, 214, 218, 236-37, 247, 252, 272, 275, 278, 282

Sōseki Sōchō ryōgin nanimichi hyakuin (A Hundred-Verse Sequence Entitled "A Kind of Path," by Sōseki and Sōchō), 204

Soshin. *See* Soshin Jōetsu

Soshin Jōetsu, 30, 220-21

Soto no Shirakawa, 49, 242

Sōun. *See* Hōjō Sōun

Southern Capital (Nanto). *See* Nara

Sōzu Seiin, 214

Succession Conflict of the Bunmei Era (Bunmei no naikō), 176, 264

Succession Conflict of the Eikyō Era (Eikyō no naikō), 174

Su Dongpo, 307

Sugawara Michizane, 228, 282, 294

Sugawara Michizane, daughter of, 255

Sugawara Shrine, 219, 294

Sugihara Iganokami (Takamori), 54, 152, 304

Sugihara Sōi (Iga Lay Priest, Katamori), 54, 245

Sugihara Takamori. *See* Sugihara Iganokami

Suiharagami, 229

Suke Hyōgo (Baba Hyōgonosuke? Saneyuki?), 123, 288, 294

Suki, 109

Suki, 286

Sumeru, Mount (Suminoyama), 89, 263-64

Suminoe (Sumiyoshi), 8, 194

Suminoyama. *See* Sumeru, Mount

Sumiyoshi. *See* Suminoe

Sun Goddess. *See* Amaterasu Ōmikami, Ise Shrine

Sunomatagawa river, 102, 272

Sunpu (Fuchū), 55, 59, 71, 75, 82, 95, 155, 181,

General Index

184–85, 188, 191, 248–49, 258–59, 307, 310.
  See also Suruga Province
Sunrise Mountain (Asahiyama), 239
Suō Province (now part of Yamaguchi Prefecture), 298
Suruga Counselor (Suruga no Saishō), 114, 126, 173, 187, 281
Suruga Province (now part of Shizuoka Prefecture), 9–10, 30, 55, 57, 63, 82–83, 107, 119, 123–24, 127, 129, 147, 158, 161–63, 166, 168, 175, 177, 181, 183–84, 187–88, 193, 195, 200–202, 205, 215–16, 236–37, 246–47, 249, 251, 256–58, 264, 279, 286, 289, 291, 305–7, 310–11
Susanoo, 270
Suwa Shinanonokami, 13, 202
Su Wu, 314
Suzuka Mountains (Suzukayama), 16–17, 19, 49–50, 54, 130, 144–45, 184, 241–42, 273, 287
Suzuka River (Suzukagawa river), 50

Tachibanadera, 21, 182, 212
Tachikawa, 10, 196–97
Tago, 45, 156, 237
Tahara Danjōnochū (Toda Munemitsu), 13, 202
Taigenshō, 237
Taiheiki, 267
Taijin (Jibukyō Hōgan), 81, 167, **259**, 306
Taiken (Jibunokyō Hokkyō), 167, 313
Taikenmon'in, 251
Taira (Heike) house, 197, 281, 303
Taira Sadafun, 277
Taira Shigehira, 113, 187, 281
Taira Suketaka, 215
Taishō, 154, 167–68, 306, 313–14
Taka, 229
Takahashi (house), 12, 200
Takahashi Masasada (Saburōbyōenojō), 12, 200
Takahata Magozaemon, 101, 272
Takakuni. See Hosokawa Takakuni
Takamori, 275
Takamuku Jirōdayū, 205
Takano, 103, 273
Takao, Mount, 51, 243
Takaodera, 146
Takasago, 53, 223, 245
Takatenjin Castle, 196
Take, 16, 20, 182, 207

Takeda house, 179
Takeda Izuminokami (Motomitsu), 141, 296
Takeda Jirō (Nobutsuna), 11, 198–99
Takeda Nobutora, 179, 187, 198–99, 289, 310, 312–13
Takeda Shingen, 176, 193
Takeno Jōō, 278
Takigi, 21–23, 26, 28–29, 34, 42, 45–47, 60, 86, 103, 107, 120, 161–62, 181–84, 186, **206**, 214–15, 217, 235, 238, 262, 276, 285–86
Takinobō, 99, 271
Takinodera, 271
Tale of Genji. See *Genji monogatari*
Tamadare, 288
Tame Matazaburō, 14, 202
Tanabata, 37, 107
Tanba Mountains, 141
Tanba Province (now part of Kyoto and Hyōgo Prefectures), 131, 142, 284–86, 296
Tanemura Nakatsukasanojō (Sadakazu, Iba Sadakazu), 44, 49, 133, **236–37**, 241, 292
Tango Province (now part of Kyoto Prefecture), 30, 185, 219
Tani house, 273
Tani Nakatsukasa, 103, 273
Tani Sōboku. See Sōboku
Tego no yobisaka. See Maiden-Calling Slope
Tegoshi, 163
Teijiin Poetry Contest, 266, 301
Teika. See Fujiwara Teika
Tema no seki. See Hindrance Gate
Temple, the (Jimon). See Miidera
Temple town (*monzenmachi*), 209
Tendai sect, 209, 247, 275
Ten dumplings (tōdango), 246
Tenji, Emperor, 212, 299
Tenjingū, 139
Tenmyō, 133, 292
Tennōzan, 193
Tenryūgawa river, 9, 11, 198
Tenryūji, 82, 259, 275
Teraki Shirōzaemon, 31
Teramachi Saburōzaemon, 29, 110, 218, 279
Third-Day Moor (Pot Moor, Mikanohara), 107, 276–77
Three Crossings (Miwatari), 16, 207
Three Loves. See *San'aiki*
Time sect. See Ji sect
Toba, 114, 187, 282

General Index

Toda Munemitsu. *See* Tahara Danjōnochū
Tōdaiji, 182
Tōenbō, 48, 104, 114, 241, 282
Tōfukuji, 52, 238, 275
Tōgaku Jōhō, 41, 108, 121–22, 124, 127–28, **221**, 235, 273, 277, 285. *See also* Shinjuan, Shōrin'an, Shūon'an
Toganoo, 51, 243
Tōgoku kikō (Journey to the Eastern Provinces), 203, 269–70, 299, 303
Tōgorō, 166, 313
Tōji, 142
Tōjiin. *See* Ashikaga Takauji
Tōjō. *See* Kira Tōjō Yoshiharu
Tōjō Castle, 269
Tōjō Kuniuji (Ōminokami), 13, 201
Tōkaidō (Tōkai Circuit), 142, 150, 268, 299, 302
Tokishige. *See* Asahina Tokishige
Tokoname, 15, 204
Tokugawa house, 193
Tokugawa Ieyasu, 269
Tokusei, 187
Tomorrow River (Asukagawa river), 22, 64, 74
Tōnomine Shōshō monogatari, 212
Tōnomine, 20, 182, 212
Tō no Tsuneyori, 276
Tooth-Hardening Ritual, 293–94
Tosa Mitsunobu, 185
Tōshōdaiji, 275
Tōtōmi Province (now part of Shizuoka Prefecture), 8, 11–12, 55, 96, 124, 129, 151, 173, 175, 177–79, 181, 193, 196, 198, 200–203, 269, 289, 291, 304–5
Tōun, 272
Tōunken, 47, 107–9, 147, 186, 239, 272, 276, 302
Toyohara Muneaki (Sumiaki, Tōshū, Utanokami), 44, 65–71, 183–84, **237**, 252–53, 278
Toyohara Muneaki senshu (*Toyohara Sumiaki Senshu*), 67, 252
Toyotomi Hideyoshi, 275
Tōza, 244
Tōzaemon. *See* Oda Tōzaemon
Travels in the Eastland (*Azuma michi no ki* [*Tōgoku michi no ki*?], by Saigyō), 92, 96, 265

Travels in the Eastland (*Tōgoku michi no ki* [*Azuma michi no ki*?], by Shōtetsu), 100, 271
Tsubota (Tsubouchi?) Chūemonnojō, 123, 288
Tsuchi ikki, 187
Tsuchimikado, 274
Tsuchimikado Palace, 274
Tsuchiyama, 49
Tsuda Bizen Lay Priest (Kitamura Hyōgonosuke?), 46, 238, 280
Tsuda Jujōken, 106–7, 109, 111, 113–14, 186–87, 276
Tsuda Sōkei, 48, 104, 121, 241, 274, 286
Tsugiuta, 244
Tsujinobō, 28, 47, 108, 217
Tsukuba, Mount (Tsukubayama), 167, 313
Tsukubashū, 281
Tsukushi michi no ki (Account of a Kyushu Journey), 286, 298
Tsu Province. *See* Settsu Province
Tsurezuregusa, 229, 250, 260, 263
Tsushima, 101, 147, 186, 188

Uchide Strand (Uchidenohama), 121, 187, 286
Uchino, 141
Uchi no Shirakawa, 49, 242
Udono Saburō (Nagamochi?), 150, 303
Uesugi Asaoki, 184
Uesugi house, 9, 174–75. *See also* Ōgigayatsu Uesugi and Yamanouchi Uesugi
Uesugi Sadamasa, 310
Uhyōenojō Takayoshi (Hirai Uhyōenojō, Hirai Takayoshi), 129, 138, 291, 294
Uji, 26, 28–29, 46, 108, 113, 165, 182, 183, 186, 216, 218, 238, 276, 281, 296
Ujichika. *See* Imagawa Ujichika
Ujigawa river, 46, 107, 109, 183, 239
Umedo, 103, 273
Umenobō, 43, 235
Undiggable Well (Horikane no i), 8
Unpa, 57, 247
Upper Capital (Kamigyō), 109, 187, 238, 278. *See also* Kyoto
Urabon. *See* Festival of the Dead
Urikumagai. *See* Kumagai
Urin'an, 261
Uruya River (Uruyakawa river), 272
Utsunoyama mountain (Reality Mountain), 7–8, 55, 65, 67, 86, 90, 95, 110, 119, 152, 158, 160, **192**, 246, 253, 262, 279, 304, 309

General Index

Utsunoyama no ki (Account of Utsunoyama), **191**, 194, 196, 199, 204, 207, 235, 256, 262, 269, 282, 310
Utsuyama, 151, 188, 304
Uwado, 9, 196

Verse in Japanese and Chinese, 52, 82, 115–16, 137–38, 155–56, 199, 282

Wabi (tea), 278, 309
Wachigaya Castle, 203
Wakakusa Mountain (Wakakusayama), 21, 212
Wakamatsu Pond (Wakamatsu no ike), 120, 285
Wakan renku. *See* Verse in Japanese and Chinese
Wakan rōeishū, 193, 213, 239, 242, 272
Waka Pine Strand (Waka no matsubara), 147, 301
Wakasa Province (now part of Fukui Prefecture), 296
Wakashu. *See* Young men
Wakatsuki Jirō (Kunisada), 131, 292
Wakatsuki Wakasanokami (Nagazumi, Izuminokami?), 131, 292
Wakuraba (Blighted Leaves), 204, 247
Washinosuyama, 52, 184, 243–44
Washiyama, 50, 242
Wasuregusa, 175, 247
West Lake (Xihu), 102, 272
White Mountain (Hakusan, Shirayama), 32, 126, 217, 223, 289
White River. *See* Shirakawa
Wu Di, 266

Xingqing Palace, 193
Xiongnu, 314
Xuanzong, Emperor, 193

Yabase, 142, 299
Yabe Saemonnojō, 13, 202
Yagi, 21, 212
Yahagi, 303
Yahagigawa river, 15, 150, 203, 303
Yamada, 15–17, 19–20, 22, 128, 142, 165, 181–82, 204, 207, 299
Yamada senku. *See* Ise senku
Yamakami, 103, 273
Yamana house, 298

Yamana Mutsunokami (Mitsuyuki), 141, 297
Yamana Sōzen, 297–98
Yamana Tokihiro, 297
Yamana Ujikiyo, 297
Yamana Ujiyuki, 297
Yamanouchi (Uesugi) Akisada, 179, **196**
Yamanouchi Uesugi, 9, 175, **196**
Yamanoue, 142, 299
Yamanoue Okura, 301, 307
Yamashina, 30, 120, 219
Yamashiro Province (now part of Kyoto Prefecture), 21–23, 60, 86, 107, 187, 206, 213, 239, 276, 280, 285
Yamato monogatari, 308
Yamato Province (now Nara Prefecture), 21
Yamato Takeru no Mikoto, 99, 270
Yamazaki, 14, 203
Yamazaki Sōkan. *See* Sōkan
Yanagimoto Discord (Yanagimoto no ran), 284, 292, 296
Yanagimoto Kataharu, 141, 187–88, 191, 284–85, 296
Yasakagata School, 306
Yashima, 103, 108, 120–22, 126, 128, 130, 137–38, 143, 162, 164, 186, 188, 221, 286–88, 291, 294, 299
Yashima Shōrin'an naniki hyakuin (A Hundred-Verse Sequence Entitled "A Kind of Tree," Composed at Shōrin'an in Yashima), 187, 247, 294
Yashiroyama Castle, 8, 12, 179, 195
Yasuhiro. *See* Asahina Yasuhiro
Yasumochi. *See* Asahina Yasumochi
Yasu River (Yasugawa river), 122, 287
Yasuyoshi. *See* Asahina Yasuyoshi
Yatarō (Asahina Yasumoto?), 129, 291
Yatsuhashi. *See* Eight Bridges
Yawata (in Ise Province), 16, 207
Yawata (in Mikawa Province), 14, 203
Yawata (in Yamashiro Province), 43, 113, 183, 235, 239
Yawata Mountain, 46
Yellow Emperor, 300
Yijing, 289
Yodogawa river, 276
Yokawa Peak (Yokawa no mine), 121
Yokochi Hidekuni, 178
Yokochi house, 178, 195, 202
Yokotagawa river, 300

General Index

Yokoyama Castle, 62, 249, 255
Yoritomo. *See* Minamoto Yoritomo
Yosa, Sea of (Yosa no umi), 30, 219
Yoshida Kenkō, 229, 260
Yoshikawa Yorishige (Jirōzaemon), 166, 312–13
Yoshimune Tsunenari, daughter of, 294
Yoshitada. *See* Imagawa Yoshitada
Yoshitsune. *See* Minamoto Yoshitsune
Yōtokuji, 82, 259
Young men (*wakashu*), 18, 100, 102, 111, 115, 120, 124–25, 146–49, 181, 210, 302
Yōyōki (An Account of Raising Hawks), 45, 183, 237–38
Yui Hōgo (Mimasakanokami), 76, 79, 256, 258
Yuki, 286
Yunoyama (Yuyama), 34, 224
Yuyama sangin (Three Poets at Yuyama; Entoku 3 [1491]:10:20 *Nanibito hyakuin* [A Hundred-Verse Sequence Entitled "A Kind of Person"]), 222–24

Zatō. See Blind attendant
Zeami, 231
Zen sect (Rinzai, Sōtō), 26, 28, 30, 52, 82, 85–86, 103, 105, 155–56, 163, 169, 185, 200, 205, 215–17, 221, 244, 247, 259, 261, 273, 275, 282, 289–90, 275, 289–90, 307, 311, 314–15. *See also* Daisen'in; Daitokuji; Ikkyū; Shinden'an; Shōrin'an; Shūon'an
Zenpō zōdan, 245
Zentokuin, 259
Zhong Ziqi, 253
Zhuangzi, 220
Zuiun'an, 57, 247
Zushū, 153, 305

367

The authorized representative in the EU for product safety and compliance is:
Mare Nostrum Group
B.V Doelen 72
4831 GR Breda
The Netherlands

www.ingramcontent.com/pod-product-compliance
Lightning Source LLC
Chambersburg PA
CBHW060241240426
43673CB00048B/1937